[redacted]

INTRODUCTION TO STATISTICAL PATTERN RECOGNITION

ELECTRICAL SCIENCE
A Series of Monographs and Texts

Editors: Henry G. Booker and Nicholas DeClaris
A complete list of titles in this series appears at the end of this volume.

INTRODUCTION TO STATISTICAL PATTERN RECOGNITION

Keinosuke Fukunaga

SCHOOL OF ELECTRICAL ENGINEERING
PURDUE UNIVERSITY
LAFAYETTE, INDIANA

ACADEMIC PRESS New York and London 1972

ACADEMIC PRESS, INC.
111 Fifth Avenue, New York, New York 10003

United Kingdom Edition published by
ACADEMIC PRESS, INC. (LONDON) LTD.
24/28 Oval Road, London NW1 7DD

LIBRARY OF CONGRESS CATALOG CARD NUMBER: 72-75627

PRINTED IN THE UNITED STATES OF AMERICA

To Reiko, Gen, and Nina

CONTENTS

Chapter 8 Feature Selection and Linear Mapping for One Distribution

Chapter 9 Feature Selection and Linear Mapping for Multidistributions

Chapter 10 Nonlinear Mapping

Chapter 11 Clustering

PREFACE

This book presents an introduction to statistical pattern recognition. Pattern recognition in general covers a wide range of problems, and it is hard to find a unified view or approach. It is applied to engineering problems, such as character readers and waveform analysis, as well as to brain modeling in biology and psychology. However, statistical decision and estimation, which are the subjects of this book, are regarded as fundamental to the study of pattern recognition. Statistical decision and estimation is covered in various texts on mathematical statistics, statistical communication, control theory, and so on. But obviously each field has a different need and view. So that workers in pattern recognition need not look from one book to another, this book is organized to provide the basics of these statistical concepts from the viewpoint of pattern recognition.

The material of this book has been taught in a first-level graduate course at Purdue University and also in a special summer course at IBM, Rochester, Minnesota. Therefore, it is the author's hope that this book will serve as a text for the introductory courses of pattern recognition as well as a reference book for the workers in the field.

One difficulty in pattern recognition is that we have to handle a large number of correlated random variables. This leads us to rely heavily on linear algebra. In Chapter 2, a survey of linear algebra is included with a review of the properties of random variables and vectors. Throughout the book, particular emphasis is placed on viewing the problems in terms of the eigenvalues and eigenvectors.

In Chapters 3–7, classifier design is discussed. In addition to the standard material of hypothesis testing (Chapter 3) and parameter estimation (Chapter 5), the estimation of the error probability is emphasized in these chapters. The probability of error is the key parameter in pattern recognition. Chapter 4 is devoted to linear and piecewise linear classifiers because they often are the only classifiers that can be practically implemented. Another difficulty in pattern recognition is that the normal (Gaussian) assumption does not hold for most applications. Because of this fact, a nonparametric approach to the problem is unavoidable in practice (Chapter 6). Chapter 7 discusses successive approaches where the classifier is adaptively adjusted each time one sample is observed.

In Chapters 8–10, feature selection is discussed from the viewpoint of mapping the original measurement space into a lower-dimensional feature space, without losing the information of our interest. Linear mappings are applied to select a set of features which minimizes the error of representing samples from one distribution (Chapter 8) or maximizes the class separability for multidistributions (Chapter 9). The discussion is then extended to include nonlinear mappings (Chapter 10).

Chapter 11 is devoted to clustering or unsupervised classification where samples are classified with a minimum of *a priori* knowledge about their distribution.

ACKNOWLEDGMENTS

The author would like to express his gratitude to Dr. J. C. Hancock and his colleagues at Purdue University for their encouragement. Also, it is the author's pleasure to acknowledge the support of the National Science Foundation for research in pattern recognition. Much of the material in this book was contributed by the author's past and present co-workers, Mr. D. L. Kessell, Dr. W. L. G. Koontz, Dr. T. F. Krile, and Dr. D. R. Olsen. The author is particularly grateful to Dr. Koontz for his thoughtful and detailed criticism of the entire manuscript as well as his significant contribution to the content. In addition, the author wishes to thank his wife Reiko for her typing of the manuscript.

The author acknowledges the Institute of Electrical and Electronics Engineers, Inc., The Institute of Mathematical Statistics, and the American Telephone and Telegraph Co. for their authorization to use material from their journals.

Chapter 1

INTRODUCTION

This book presents and discusses the fundamental mathematical tools for statistical decision-making processes in pattern recognition. It is felt that the decision-making processes of a human being are somewhat related to the recognition of patterns; for example, the next move in a chess game is made based on the present pattern on the board, and the buying or selling of stocks is decided by a complex pattern of information. Therefore, the goal of pattern recognition is to clarify these complicated mechanisms of decision-making processes and to automate these functions using computers. However, because of the complex nature of the problem, most pattern recognition research has been concentrated on more realistic problems, such as the recognition of Latin characters and the classification of waveforms. The purpose of this book is to cover the mathematical models of these practical problems and to provide the fundamental mathematical tools necessary for solving them. Although many approches have been proposed to formulate more complex decision-making processes, these are outside of the scope of this book.

1.1 Formulation of Pattern Recognition Problems

Many important applications of pattern recognition can be characterized as either waveform classification or classification of geometric figures. For example, consider the problem of testing a machine for normal or abnormal operation by observing the output voltage of a microphone over a period of time. This problem reduces to discrimination of waveforms from good and bad machines. On the other hand, recognition of printed English characters corresponds to classification of geometric figures. In order to perform this type of classification, we must first measure some observable characteristics of the sample. The most primitive way to do this is to measure the time-samples values for a waveform, $x(t_1), \ldots, x(t_n)$, and the grey levels of meshes for a figure, $x(1), \ldots, x(n)$, as shown in Fig. 1-1. These n measurements form a vector, X. Even under the normal machine condition, the observed waveforms are different each time the observation is made. Therefore, $x(t_i)$ is a random variable and will be expressed, using

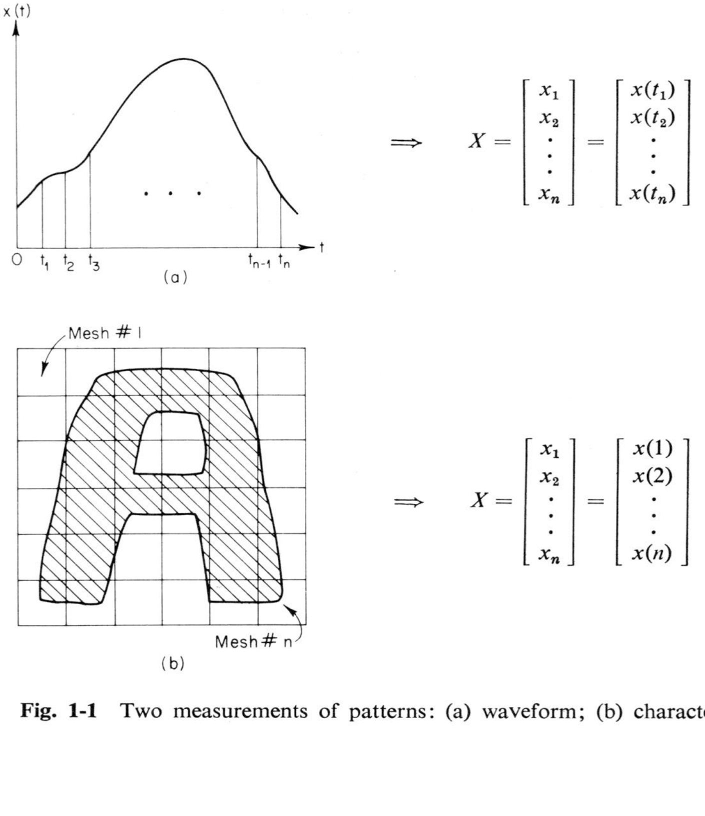

Fig. 1-1 Two measurements of patterns: (a) waveform; (b) character.

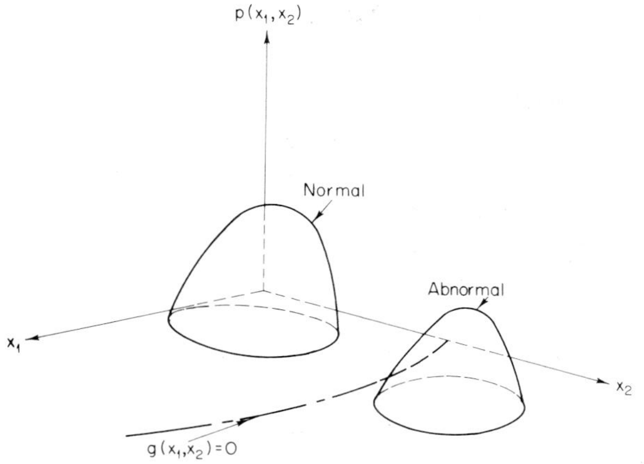

Fig. 1-2 Distributions of **X** for normal and abnormal conditions.

boldface, as $\mathbf{x}(t_i)$. Likewise, X is called a random vector if its components are random variables and is expressed as **X**. Similar arguments hold for characters: the observation, $x(i)$, varies from one A to another and therefore $\mathbf{x}(i)$ is a random variable, and **X** is a random vector.

Thus each waveform or character is expressed by a vector in an n-dimensional space, and many waveforms or characters form a distribution of **X** in the n-dimensional space. Figure 1-2 shows a simple two-dimensional example of two distributions corresponding to normal and abnormal machine conditions. If we know these two distributions of **X** from past experience, we can set up a boundary between these two distributions, $g(x_1, x_2) = 0$, which divides the two-dimensional space into two regions. Thus, when an unknown waveform is observed, we can decide whether the waveform comes from a normal or abnormal machine, depending on $g(x_1, x_2) < 0$ or $g(x_1, x_2) > 0$. We call $g(x_1, x_2)$ a discriminant function, and a network which detects the sign of $g(x_1, x_2)$ is called a pattern recognition network, a categorizer, or a classifier. Figure 1-3 shows a block diagram of a classifier in a general n-dimensional space. Thus, in order to design a classifier, we must study the characteristics of the distribution of **X** for each category and find a proper discriminant function.

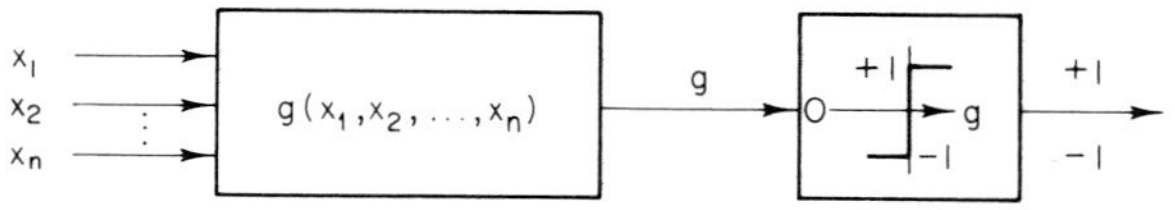

Fig. 1-3 Block diagram of a classifier.

In the above discussion we assumed a very primitive way of choosing measurements. Since each of these primitive measurements carries a very small amount of information about the sample, the number of measurements n usually becomes high, perhaps in the hundreds. This high dimensionality makes many pattern recognition problems difficult. On the other hand, classification by a human being is usually based on a small number of features, such as the peak value, fundamental frequency, etc. Each of these measurements carries significant information for classification purposes and is selected according to the physical meaning of the problem. Obviously, as the number of inputs to a classifier becomes smaller, the design of the classifier becomes simpler. In order to enjoy this advantage, we have to find some way to select or extract important features from the observed samples. This problem is called feature selection or extraction and is another important subject of pattern recognition. Feature selection can be considered as a mapping from the primitive n-dimensional space to a lower dimensional space. The class separability of the distributions of the primitive measurements is the same as that of the samples. Therefore, the mapping should be carried out without severely reducing this class separability.

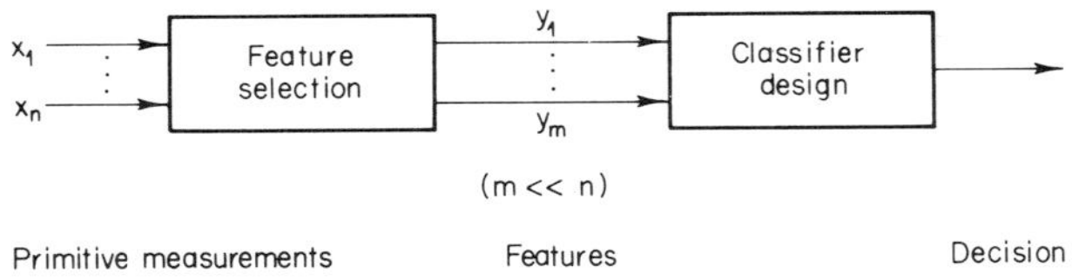

Fig. 1-4 Block diagram of pattern recognition.

Thus, as shown in Fig. 1-4, pattern recognition consists of two parts: feature selection and classifier design. In practice, there are no clear ways to separate these two operations. In fact, the classifier can be viewed as a feature selector which maps m features to one feature (the discriminant function). However, it is convenient to separate the problem into two parts and to study them independently.

1.2 Chapter Outlines

In order that pattern recognition be studied within the scope mentioned above, this book has been divided into ten chapters (2–11).

In *Chapter 2*, the various properties of random vectors and the methodology of linear algebra are surveyed. The knowledge of this material is required for a complete understanding of this book. However, it is assumed that the reader is familiar with the properties of a random variable and a random vector, so only a quick survey is presented here. Also, since vectors and matrices are used extensively throughout the book, linear algebra is surveyed, particularly from the viewpoint of eigenvalues and eigenvectors.

Chapter 3 through 7 are related to classifier design.

In *Chapter 3*, we seek the best theoretical way to design a classifier, assuming that the distributions of the random vectors to be classified are given. In this case, the problem becomes simple statistical hypothesis testing. The Bayes classifier is derived as optimum in that it minimizes the probability of error of classification or the risk under preassigned costs for various decisions. The Neyman–Pearson test and the minimax test are also introduced.

The probability of error is the key parameter in pattern recognition. It is the measure of the class separability of given distributions, if we assume the use of the Bayes classifier. Also, it is the measure of the performance of a classifier in comparison with the Bayes classifier for given distributions. Because of its importance, in Chapter 3, we discuss how to calculate the probability of error for given distributions. We also consider the simpler problem of finding an upper bound of the error probability.

In an alternate formulation of the pattern recognition problem, a sequence of samples from the same class is observed. It is well known that the class can be determined with considerably greater assurance by observing a sequence of samples rather than a single sample. Therefore, the sequential hypothesis test is also included.

In *Chapter 4*, linear classifiers are explored. Although the Bayes classifier is optimal, its implementation is often difficult in practice because of its complexity, particularly when the dimension is high. Therefore, we are often led to consider a simpler classifier. Linear or piecewise linear classifiers are the simplest and most common choices. Various design procedures for linear classifiers are discussed in Chapter 4. These include the Bayes classifier for certain distributions, the optimum linear classifier in the sense of the minimum probability of error or in the sense of the minimum mean-squared error, and so on. The case where the input measurements are binary is also considered.

In *Chapter 5*, parameter estimation is discussed. In the earlier chapters, we assume that the distributions to be classified are given. However, in practice, only a finite number of samples is available, and we have to estimate the distributions from these samples. When the functional form of a distribution is known, the density function can be estimated by replacing unknown parameters with suitable estimates. For example, a normal distribution can be estimated by using estimates of the mean vector and of the covariance matrix. This manner of estimating densities is called the parametric approach. The parameters to be estimated may be random variables or unknown constants; both cases are considered in Chapter 5.

Since the estimation of a parameter depends on the set of samples and can vary from set to set, we would like to set up a confidence interval for the estimation. This type of problem is called interval estimation and is discussed in Chapter 5.

As we mentioned before, the probability of error is the important parameter in pattern recognition, and we often have to estimate this parameter from available samples. However, the estimation of error is somewhat different from conventional parameter estimation, mainly because we have to use the available samples for both the design of a classifier and the test of the classifier. The parametric case in error estimation is discussed in Chapter 5.

In *Chapter 6*, we consider the estimation of a distribution without assuming any functional form. This approach is called a nonparametric approach. First, the Parzen estimate of a density function is introduced, which is used to generate kernel functions around each sample and sum these to form a continuous density function. After the mathematical properties of this estimate are studied, various variations follow with different kinds of kernel functions.

One of the important techniques in nonparametric classification is the k-nearest-neighbor decision rule, where an unknown sample is classified according to the class distribution of the k-nearest-neighbor samples.

Also, in Chapter 6 we discuss a more primitive histogram approach to the estimate of a density function, where the number of samples within a preassigned region is counted.

All of the techniques in Chapter 6 can be applied regardless of the distributions. However, we have to pay for that advantage with more complex computation because the techniques are based on the samples rather than a small number of parameters.

In *Chapter 7*, successive parameter estimation is discussed. In Chapter 5, estimates of parameters are determined from all of the observable samples. However, it is sometimes more practical to use a procedure based on a sequence of samples. In this case, the parameters are first approximated by an initial guess. Then each observation sample is used in turn to update the estimate. The problem is whether or not the estimate converges in some sense to the true parameters and how fast it converges.

First, successive parameter estimation for a linear discriminant function is discussed. The convergence can be proved, provided that the two distributions are linearly separable.

In order to prove convergence for overlapped distributions, we introduce stochastic approximation. Stochastic approximation has been developed as an iterative process for finding the roots or the optimum points of a regression function in a stochastic environment.

The estimate of a parameter is a random variable and has a density function. This density function can be updated successively by using the Bayes theorem. This problem, which is called the successive Bayes estimation, is briefly touched upon in Chapter 7.

The discussion in Chapters 8 through 10 is related to feature selection.

In *Chapter 8*, feature selection for one distribution is discussed. When one distribution is studied there are no classification problems—only representation problems. It is assumed that features which represent individual distributions should lead us to good features for classifying these distributions. Feature selection for one distribution is a mapping from the original n-dimensional space to an m-dimensional space ($m \ll n$) which does not distort the representation of a given distribution. Since the classification problem is not explicitly considered, we have no way to determine what kind of properties of a given distribution should be preserved. Therefore, the mappings to be used are limited to orthonormal linear transformations which preserve the whole structure of the distribution.

The basic approach is to adopt some kind of criterion and choose the linear transformation which optimizes the criterion. When the criterion is the mean-square representation error, the best transformation is the Karhunen–Loève expansion, which uses the eigenvectors of the covariance matrix as features. Scatter and entropy criteria also lead to features which involve eigenvector calculation.

Since eigenvalues and eigenvectors play an important role in feature selection, their estimation is discussed in Chapter 8. The problems are the effects of the number of samples and the sampling rate upon the estimation. Also, the estimation of dominant eigenvalues and eigenvectors is studied, since the number of dominant eigenvalues is usually far less than the dimension of the distribution.

In *Chapter 9*, feature selection for two distributions is discussed. When we have two distributions and our concern is to classify these two distributions, feature selection becomes a problem of choosing a small number of important features by a proper mapping, while preserving the class separability as much as possible. Since the class separability should be invariant under any one-to-one mapping, we can consider all kinds of mappings, including nonlinear mapping. In Chapter 9, only linear mapping is studied.

As a measure of class separability the probability of error is the optimum one. However, since the probability of error lacks an explicit mathematical expression in most cases, alternatives are sought.

Many measures can be formulated by combining between-class and within-class scatters in various ways which have been developed in discriminant analysis. These measures are simple and can be easily extended to multiclass problems.

The Bhattacharyya distance and the divergence are somewhat more complicated measures of the class separability, but they are more closely related to the probability of error.

In Chapter 9, various properties of these measures of class separability are studied. Also, the optimum linear mapping from the original space to a lower dimensional space is sought so as to minimize the reduction of the measure.

In *Chapter 10*, three problems of nonlinear mapping are discussed. The first problem concerns the intrinsic dimensionality of a given distribution. The intrinsic dimensionality is the number of dominant random parameters, characterizing a distribution and cannot be detected by linear mappings when observed measurements are nonlinear functions of these parameters. The intrinsic dimensionality gives the smallest number of features to represent a distribution.

The second problem is to find a nonlinear mapping for classification purposes such that the discriminant function in the mapped space could be a simpler function, such as a linear one, as well as a lower-dimensional function.

The third problem is display. The display of multivariate samples on a CRT screen is a powerful aid in understanding the properties of distributions. The display is a mapping from the original n-dimensional space to a two-dimensional space. Nonlinear mappings are discussed in Chapter 10 for both representation and classification purposes.

In *Chapter 11*, clustering, or unsupervised classification, is discussed. For example, the distribution of waveforms from abnormal machine conditions may consist of several modes. Separating individual modes without any outside supervision helps the detection of abnormal waveforms as well as the understanding of the nature of defects.

Clustering consists of criteria and search algorithms. Various parametric and nonparametric criteria are discussed. These are measures of class separability, cohesiveness of clusters, and so on. These criteria are very subjective and, when a criterion is selected, the characteristics of the clusters are determined.

Search algorithms are also discussed in order to find a class assignment so as to optimize a chosen criterion.

Finally, in each chapter, *problems* are given to help the reader understand the given material. Also, *computer projects* are provided. It has been found by experience that a proper assignment of these computer projects stimulates the students' interest. However, computer projects are more oriented toward helping those researchers in pattern recognition who would like to build up a basic program system as their research tool. The more sophisticated variations of programs could be extended on the user's specific data.

Chapter 2

RANDOM VECTORS AND THEIR PROPERTIES

In succeeding chapters, we often make use of the properties of random vectors. We also freely employ standard results from linear algebra. This chapter is a review of the basic properties of a random vector and the related techniques of linear algebra. The reader who is familiar with these topics may omit this chapter, except for a quick reading to become familiar with the notation.

2.1 Random Vectors and Their Distributions

Distribution and Density Functions

As we discussed in Chapter 1, the input to a pattern recognition network is a random vector as

$$\mathbf{X} = [\mathbf{x}_1 \mathbf{x}_2 \cdots \mathbf{x}_n]^T \tag{2-1}$$

where T shows the transpose of the vector.

Random vectors may be characterized by probability distribution functions, which are defined as follows:

Definition The *joint distribution function* of **X** is defined by

$$P(x_1, x_2, \ldots, x_n) = \Pr\{\mathbf{x}_1 \le x_1, \mathbf{x}_2 \le x_2, \ldots, \mathbf{x}_n \le x_n\} \tag{2-2}$$

where $\Pr\{A\}$ is the probability of the event A. For convenience, we often write (2-2) as

$$P(X) = \Pr\{\mathbf{X} \le X\} \tag{2-3}$$

The joint distribution function is monotonically nondecreasing in each of its arguments. Also, from basic considerations, we have

$$P(-\infty, -\infty, \ldots, -\infty) = 0 \tag{2-4}$$

and

$$P(+\infty, +\infty, \ldots, +\infty) = 1 \tag{2-5}$$

EXAMPLE 2-1 Suppose two random variables $\mathbf{x}_1$ and $\mathbf{x}_2$ are the height and weight of college students throughout the United States. Then P(5.5 ft, 160 lb) is the ratio of the number of students, whose heights and weights are less than or equal to 5.5 ft and 160 lb, respectively, to the total number of students (see Fig. 2-1).

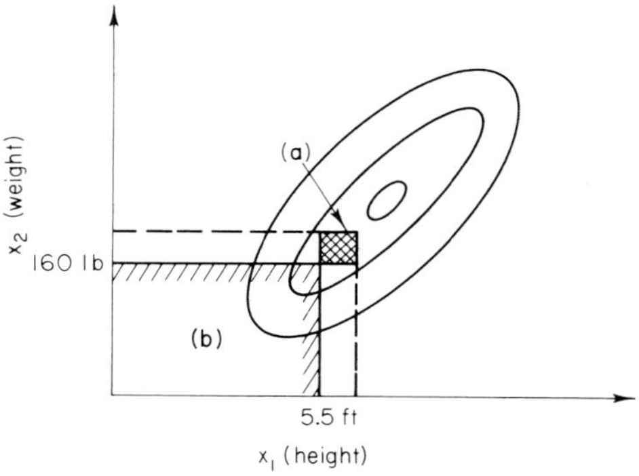

Fig. 2-1 Distribution and density functions:

(a) $p(5.5, 160)\,\Delta x_1\,\Delta x_2 = \dfrac{\text{no. of students in this region}}{\text{total no. of students}}$

(b) $P(5.5, 160) = \dfrac{\text{no. of students in this region}}{\text{total no. of students}}$

Definition The *joint density function* of **X** is defined by

$$p(X) = \lim_{\substack{\Delta x_1 \to 0 \\ \vdots \\ \Delta x_n \to 0}} \frac{\Pr\{x_1 < \mathbf{x}_1 \leq x_1 + \Delta x_1, \ldots, x_n < \mathbf{x}_n \leq x_n + \Delta x_n\}}{\Delta x_1 \, \Delta x_2 \cdots \Delta x_n}$$

$$= \partial^n P(X)/\partial x_1 \cdots \partial x_n \tag{2-6}$$

The definition is the straightforward generalization of the one-dimensional case where

$$\begin{aligned} p(x) &= \lim_{\Delta x \to 0} \Pr\{x < \mathbf{x} \leq x + \Delta x\}/\Delta x \\ &= \lim_{\Delta x \to 0} [\Pr\{\mathbf{x} \leq x + \Delta x\} - \Pr\{x \leq x\}]/\Delta x \\ &= \lim_{\Delta x \to 0} [P(x + \Delta x) - P(x)]/\Delta x = dP(x)/dx \end{aligned} \tag{2-7}$$

Inversely, the distribution function can be expressed in terms of the density function as follows:

$$P(X) = \int_{-\infty}^{X} p(X) \, dX = \int_{-\infty}^{x_1} \cdots \int_{-\infty}^{x_n} p(X) \, dx_1 \, dx_2 \cdots dx_n \tag{2-8}$$

where $\int_{-\infty}^{X} \{\cdot\} \, dX$ is a shorthand notation for an n-dimensional integral, as shown. The joint density function, $p(X)$, is not a probability but must be multiplied by a certain region $\Delta x_1 \, \Delta x_2 \cdots \Delta x_n$ (or ΔX) to obtain probability (see Fig. 2-1 and the related Example 2-1).

Conditional Density Functions

Two kinds of conditional density functions occur frequently in the study of pattern recognition. We distinguish them by the type of event upon which a random vector may be dependent.

Conditional Density Given a Random Event

Definition The *conditional distribution function* of **X**, given the *event* ω, is defined as

$$P(X/\omega) = \Pr\{\mathbf{X} \leq X/\omega\} \tag{2-9}$$

where $\Pr\{A/B\}$ is the conditional probability of event A, given that event B has occurred, and is given by

$$\Pr\{A/B\} = \Pr\{A \cdot B\}/\Pr\{B\}. \tag{2-10}$$

where $A \cdot B$ is the conjunction event of A and B.

Definition The *conditional density function* of $\mathbf{X}$, given the *event* ω, is defined by

$$p(X/\omega) = \partial^n P(X/\omega)/\partial x_1 \, \partial x_2 \cdots \partial x_n \tag{2-11}$$

Theorem Suppose that the union of m disjoint events, $\omega_1, \omega_2, \ldots, \omega_m$ is the certain event $\mathscr{S}$. Then the unconditional density function of $\mathbf{X}$ is given by

$$p(X) = \sum_{i=1}^{m} p(X/\omega_i)P(\omega_i) \tag{2-12}$$

where $P(\omega_i)$ is used for $\Pr\{\omega_i\}$.

The proof is left as an exercise.

EXAMPLE 2-2 Let ω_i be the event that a sample belongs to the ith class, $i = 1, 2, \ldots, m$. Let the random vector $\mathbf{X}$ be a set of n measurements made on this sample. The conditional density $p(X/\omega_i)$ plays a vital role in statistical hypothesis testing. If the *a priori* probabilities of each class, $P(\omega_i)$, are given, then

$$p(X) = \sum_{i=1}^{m} p(X/\omega_i)P(\omega_i) \tag{2-13}$$

In this context, $p(X)$ is sometimes called the *mixture density* function. An example is shown in Fig. 2-2.

Conditional Density Given a Random Variable

Definition The *conditional density function* of $\mathbf{X}$, given that the *random vector* $\mathbf{Y}$ has a specified value Y, is defined by

$$p(X/Y) = \lim_{\Delta Y \to 0} p(X/Y < \mathbf{Y} \leq Y + \Delta Y) \tag{2-14}$$

This is clearly a special case of the conditional density defined above. Here, the event ω is replaced by the event $\{Y < \mathbf{Y} \leq Y + \Delta Y\}$, and ΔY

approaches zero. It is easily shown that $p(X/Y)$ can be expressed in the more convenient form

$$p(X/Y) = p(X, Y)/p(Y) \tag{2-15}$$

where $p(X, Y)$, the joint density of all of the components of $\mathbf{X}$ and $\mathbf{Y}$, can also be written

$$p(X, Y) = p(x_1, x_2, \ldots, x_n, y_1, y_2, \ldots, y_k) \tag{2-16}$$

The term $p(Y)$ is the marginal density of $\mathbf{Y}$ and is obtained from the joint density by the integration

$$p(Y) = \int_{\mathscr{S}} p(X, Y)\, dX \tag{2-17}$$

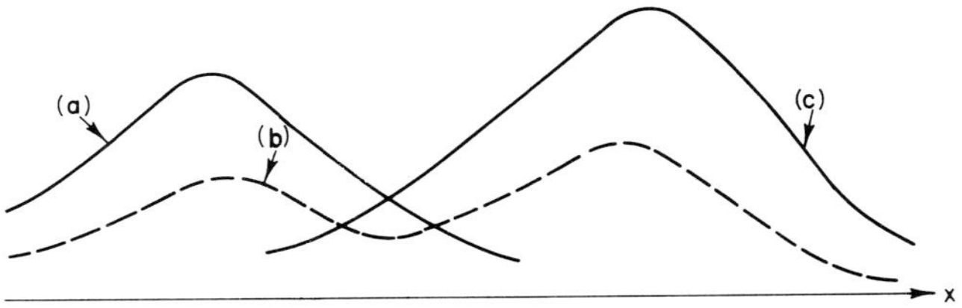

Fig. 2-2 A mixture density:
(a) $p(x/\omega_2)$, (b) $p(x) = P(\omega_1)p(x/\omega_1) + P(\omega_2)p(x/\omega_2)$, (c) $p(x/\omega_1)$.

EXAMPLE 2-3 When the previous observations $X_1, \ldots, X_N$ are the only information which is available to estimate the distribution of $\mathbf{X}$, then the conditional density of $\mathbf{X}$ is given by

$$p(X/X_1, X_2, \ldots, X_N) \tag{2-18}$$

Since each X_i has n components, k in (2-16) becomes $N \times n$.

Theorem The conditional densities $p(X/Y)$ and $p(Y/X)$ are related by

$$p(X/Y) = \frac{p(Y/X)p(X)}{p(Y)} \tag{2-19}$$

This result, which is *Bayes' theorem*, is easily shown by reversing the roles of X and Y in (2-15). Bayes' theorem plays an important role in estimation theory. Bayes' theorem can be extended, replacing Y by an event ω_i to give

$$p(X/\omega_i) = \frac{p(\omega_i/X)p(X)}{P(\omega_i)} \tag{2-20}$$

This relation is a basic tool in hypothesis testing.

EXAMPLE 2-4 Suppose **x** and **m** are two random variables and suppose the conditional density of **x**, given m, is

$$p(x/m) = (2\pi)^{-1/2}\sigma^{-1}\exp[-\tfrac{1}{2}(x - m)^2/\sigma^2] \tag{2-21}$$

Suppose, further, that the marginal distribution of **m** is normal, with expected value m_0 and variance $\sigma_m{}^2$. The conditional density of **m**, given x, can be calculated using Bayes' theorem as follows.

$$p(m/x) = \frac{p(x/m)p(m)}{p(x)} = \frac{p(x/m)p(m)}{\int_{-\infty}^{+\infty} p(x/m)p(m)\,dm}$$

$$= \frac{(2\pi)^{-1}\sigma^{-1}\sigma_m^{-1}\exp[-\tfrac{1}{2}\{(x-m)^2/\sigma^2 + (m-m_0)^2/\sigma_m{}^2\}]}{\int_{-\infty}^{+\infty}(2\pi)^{-1}\sigma^{-1}\sigma_m^{-1}\exp[-\tfrac{1}{2}\{(x-m)^2/\sigma^2 + (m-m_0)^2/\sigma_m{}^2\}]\,dm}$$

$$= \frac{(\sigma^2 + \sigma_m{}^2)^{1/2}}{(2\pi)^{1/2}\sigma\sigma_m}\exp\left[-\frac{1}{2}\,\frac{\sigma^2+\sigma_m{}^2}{\sigma^2\sigma_m{}^2}\left(m - \frac{x\sigma_m{}^2 + m_0\sigma^2}{\sigma^2 + \sigma_m{}^2}\right)^2\right] \tag{2-22}$$

The conditional density $p(m/x)$ is called the *a posteriori* density of **m** in some contexts and is used in estimating **m** from the observation **x**.

Densities Dependent on Nonrandom Parameters

Sometimes the dependence of the density function of a random vector **X** on a nonrandom parameter vector Θ is expressed explicitly. We will denote such a dependence by writing the density as $p(X/\Theta)$. Θ is not a random vector. However, Θ may be unknown.

EXAMPLE 2-5 Let **x** be a normally distributed random variable with expected value m. Then we may write the density of **x** as

$$p(x/m) = (2\pi)^{-1/2}\sigma^{-1}\exp\{-\tfrac{1}{2}(x - m)^2/\sigma^2\} \tag{2-23}$$

This type of density is important in the problem of estimating nonrandom parameters.

Parameters of Distributions

A random vector **X** is fully characterized by its distribution or density function. Often, however, these functions cannot be easily determined or they are mathematically too complex to be of practical use. Therefore, it is sometimes preferable to adopt a less complete, but more computable, characterization.

Expected Vector

One of the most important parameters is the expected vector or mean of a random vector **X**.

Definition The expected vector of a random vector **X** is defined by

$$M = E\{\mathbf{X}\} = \int_{\mathscr{S}} Xp(X)\,dX \tag{2-24}$$

where $\mathscr{S}$ means the entire X space.

The ith component of M, m_i, can be calculated by

$$m_i = \int_{\mathscr{S}} x_i p(X)\,dX = \int_{-\infty}^{+\infty} x_i p(x_i)\,dx_i \tag{2-25}$$

where $p(x_i)$ is the *marginal density* of the ith component of **X** as

$$p(x_i) = \underbrace{\int_{-\infty}^{+\infty} \cdots \int_{-\infty}^{+\infty}}_{n-1} p(X)\,dx_1 \cdots dx_{i-1}\,dx_{i+1} \cdots dx_n \tag{2-26}$$

Thus, each component of M is actually calculated as the expected value of an individual variable with the marginal one-dimensional density.

Definition The conditional expected vector of a random vector **X**, assuming Y, is the integral

$$M = E\{\mathbf{X}/Y\} = \int_{\mathscr{S}} Xp(X/Y)\,dX \tag{2-27}$$

$p(X/Y)$ is used instead of $p(X)$ in (2-24).

Dispersion

Another important set of parameters is that which indicates the dispersion of the distribution.

Definition The *covariance matrix* is defined by

$$\Sigma = E\{(\mathbf{X} - M)(\mathbf{X} - M)^T\} = E\left\{\begin{bmatrix} \mathbf{x}_1 - m_1 \\ \vdots \\ \mathbf{x}_n - m_n \end{bmatrix} [\mathbf{x}_1 - m_1 \cdots \mathbf{x}_n - m_n]\right\}$$

$$= E\left\{\begin{bmatrix} (\mathbf{x}_1 - m_1)(\mathbf{x}_1 - m_1) & \cdots & (\mathbf{x}_1 - m_1)(\mathbf{x}_n - m_n) \\ \vdots & & \vdots \\ (\mathbf{x}_n - m_n)(\mathbf{x}_1 - m_1) & \cdots & (\mathbf{x}_n - m_n)(\mathbf{x}_n - m_n) \end{bmatrix}\right\}$$

$$= \begin{bmatrix} E\{(\mathbf{x}_1 - m_1)(\mathbf{x}_1 - m_1)\} & \cdots & E\{(\mathbf{x}_1 - m_1)(\mathbf{x}_n - m_n)\} \\ \vdots & & \vdots \\ E\{(\mathbf{x}_n - m_n)(\mathbf{x}_1 - m_1)\} & \cdots & E\{(\mathbf{x}_n - m_n)(\mathbf{x}_n - m_n)\} \end{bmatrix}$$

$$= \begin{bmatrix} \sigma_{11}^2 & \cdots & \sigma_{1n}^2 \\ & \vdots & \\ \sigma_{n1}^2 & \cdots & \sigma_{nn}^2 \end{bmatrix} \tag{2-28}$$

The components of this matrix σ_{ij}^2 are

$$\sigma_{ij}^2 = E\{(\mathbf{x}_i - m_i)(\mathbf{x}_j - m_j)\} \qquad (i, j = 1, 2, \ldots, n) \tag{2-29}$$

Thus, the diagonal components of the covariance matrix are the *variances* of individual random variables and the off-diagonal components are the *covariance* of two random variables, $\mathbf{x}_i$ and $\mathbf{x}_j$. Also, it should be noted that all covariance matrices are symmetric. This property allows us to employ results from the theory of symmetric matrices as an important analytical tool.

Equation (2-28) is often converted into the following form:

$$\Sigma = E\{\mathbf{X}\mathbf{X}^T\} - E\{\mathbf{X}\}M^T - ME\{\mathbf{X}^T\} + MM^T = S - MM^T \tag{2-30}$$

where

$$S = E\{\mathbf{X}\mathbf{X}^T\} = \begin{bmatrix} E\{\mathbf{x}_1\mathbf{x}_1\} & \cdots & E\{\mathbf{x}_1\mathbf{x}_n\} \\ \vdots & & \vdots \\ E\{\mathbf{x}_n\mathbf{x}_1\} & \cdots & E\{\mathbf{x}_n\mathbf{x}_n\} \end{bmatrix} \tag{2-31}$$

Derivation of (2-30) is straightforward since $M = E\{\mathbf{X}\}$. S of (2-31) is called the *autocorrelation matrix*, or sometimes the *scatter matrix*, of $\mathbf{X}$. Equation (2-30) gives the relationship between the covariance matrix and the autocorrelation matrix and shows that both essentially contain the same amount of information.

Sometimes it is convenient to normalize covariance matrices by converting the individual covariance terms to *correlation coefficients* as

$$r_{ij} = \frac{\sigma_{ij}^2}{\sigma_{ii}\sigma_{jj}} \tag{2-32}$$

Then

$$\Sigma = \Gamma R \Gamma \tag{2-33}$$

where

$$\Gamma = \begin{bmatrix} \sigma_{11} & 0 & \cdots & 0 \\ 0 & \sigma_{22} & & \vdots \\ \vdots & & \ddots & \\ 0 & \cdots & & \sigma_{nn} \end{bmatrix} \tag{2-34}$$

and

$$R = \begin{bmatrix} 1 & & r_{ij} \\ & \ddots & \\ r_{ij} & & 1 \end{bmatrix} \qquad (|r_{ij}| \leq 1) \tag{2-35}$$

Thus, Σ can be expressed by the combination of two types of matrices: one is the diagonal matrix of variances and the other is the matrix of the correlation coefficients. We will call R a *correlation matrix*. Since variances depend on the scales of the coordinate system, the correlation matrix retains the essential information of the relationship between random variables.

Uncorrelated, Orthogonal, Independent Random Vectors

Definition Two random vectors $\mathbf{X}_i$ and $\mathbf{X}_j$ are called

uncorrelated if $E\{\mathbf{X}_i^T\mathbf{X}_j\} = E\{\mathbf{X}_i^T\}E\{\mathbf{X}_j\}$ (2-36)

orthogonal if $E\{\mathbf{X}_i^T\mathbf{X}_j\} = 0$ (2-37)

independent if $p(X_i, X_j) = p(X_i)p(X_j)$ (2-38)

Several important relationships between these three conditions are:

(1) Independence is a stronger condition than uncorrelatedness. The first implies the equality of (2-38) for every X_i and X_j; while the second is only an integral property of $p(X_i, X_j)$. If $\mathbf{X}_i$ and $\mathbf{X}_j$ are independent, then

they are uncorrelated, since

$$E\{\mathbf{X}_i^T\mathbf{X}_j\} = \int_{\mathscr{S}}\int_{\mathscr{S}} X_i^T X_j p(X_i, X_j)\, dX_i\, dX_j$$
$$= \left\{\int_{\mathscr{S}} X_i^T p(X_i)\, dX_i\right\}\left\{\int_{\mathscr{S}} X_j p(X_j)\, dX_j\right\} = E\{\mathbf{X}_i^T\}E\{\mathbf{X}_j\} \quad (2\text{-}39)$$

The converse is not true.

(2) If the expected vector of either $\mathbf{X}_i$ or $\mathbf{X}_j$ is a zero vector, "uncorrelated" is equivalent to "orthogonal."

(3) If **X**'s are all mutually orthogonal, then

$$E\left\{\left\| \sum_{i=1}^{N} \mathbf{X}_i \right\|^2\right\} = \sum_{i=1}^{N} E\{\| \mathbf{X}_i \|^2\} + \sum_{\substack{i=1 \\ i\neq j}}^{N} \sum_{j=1}^{N} E\{\mathbf{X}_i^T\mathbf{X}_j\} = \sum_{i=1}^{N} E\{\| \mathbf{X}_i \|^2\} \quad (2\text{-}40)$$

where $\| \cdot \|$ is the *length* or *norm* of a vector. Unless stated otherwise, we will use the norm defined by

$$\| X \|^2 = X^T X = \sum_{i=1}^{n} x_i^2 \quad (2\text{-}41)$$

The $E\{\mathbf{X}_i^T\mathbf{X}_j\}$'s for $i \neq j$ are all zero because of the orthogonality condition of (2-37).

(4) If **X**'s are all mutually uncorrelated, then

$$E\left\{\left\| \sum_{i=1}^{N} (\mathbf{X}_i - M_i) \right\|^2\right\}$$
$$= \sum_{i=1}^{N} E\{\| \mathbf{X}_i - M_i \|^2\} + \sum_{\substack{i=1 \\ i\neq j}}^{N} \sum_{j=1}^{N} E\{(\mathbf{X}_i - M_i)^T(\mathbf{X}_j - M_j)\}$$
$$= \sum_{i=1}^{N} E\{\| \mathbf{X}_i - M_i \|^2\} \quad (2\text{-}42)$$

(5) If **X**'s are all mutually independent, then

$$E\left[\left\{\sum_{i=1}^{N} (\mathbf{X}_i - M_i)\right\}\left\{\sum_{j=1}^{N} (\mathbf{X}_j - M_j)^T\right\}\right]$$
$$= \sum_{i=1}^{N} E\{(\mathbf{X}_i - M_i)(\mathbf{X}_i - M_i)^T\} + \sum_{\substack{i=1 \\ i\neq j}}^{N} \sum_{j=1}^{N} E\{\mathbf{X}_i - M_i\}E\{\mathbf{X}_j^T - M_j^T\}$$
$$= \sum_{i=1}^{N} E\{(\mathbf{X}_i - M_i)(\mathbf{X}_i - M_i)^T\} = \sum_{i=1}^{N} \Sigma_i \quad (2\text{-}43)$$

2.2 Properties of Distributions

Characteristic Functions

Definition The characteristic function of a random variable **x** is defined by

$$\varphi(\omega) = E\{\exp(j\omega\mathbf{x})\} = \int_{-\infty}^{+\infty} p(x)\exp(j\omega x)\,dx \tag{2-44}$$

Equation (2-44) shows that, except for the sign of ω, $\varphi(\omega)$ is actually the Fourier transform of $p(x)$. Thus, the use of the characteristic function in the study of distributions corresponds to the frequency analysis of time functions. The inverse Fourier transform, again, except the sign of ω, converts $\varphi(\omega)$ back to $p(x)$ as

$$p(x) = (2\pi)^{-1}\int_{-\infty}^{+\infty} \varphi(\omega)\exp(-j\omega x)\,d\omega \tag{2-45}$$

Definition The characteristic function of a random vector **X** is defined by

$$\varphi(\Omega) = E\{\exp(j\Omega^T\mathbf{X})\} = \int_{\mathscr{S}} p(X)\exp(j\Omega^T X)\,dX \tag{2-46}$$

where

$$\Omega = [\omega_1\omega_2\cdots\omega_n]^T \tag{2-47}$$

Thus (2-46) corresponds to an n-dimensional Fourier transform.

The characteristic function is a very convenient tool for some applications. Let us look at a few examples.

EXAMPLE 2-6 Assume that all **x**'s are mutually independent, and that we would like to obtain the density function of

$$\mathbf{y} = \sum_{i=1}^{n} g_i(\mathbf{x}_i) \tag{2-48}$$

The characteristic function of **y** can be calculated by

$$\begin{aligned}\varphi_{\mathbf{y}}(\omega) &= E\{\exp(j\omega\mathbf{y})\} = \int_{-\infty}^{+\infty} p(y)\exp(j\omega y)\,dy \\ &= \int_{-\infty}^{+\infty}\cdots\int_{-\infty}^{+\infty} p(X)\exp[j\omega\Sigma g_i(x_i)]\,dx_1\cdots dx_n \\ &= \prod_{i=1}^{n}\int_{-\infty}^{+\infty} p(x_i)\exp[j\omega g_i(x_i)]\,dx_i = \prod_{i=1}^{n}\varphi_{g_i(\mathbf{x}_i)}(\omega)\end{aligned} \tag{2-49}$$

The characteristic function of $\mathbf{y}$ is the product of the characteristic functions of $g_i(\mathbf{x}_i)$'s. Since $\varphi_{g_i(\mathbf{x}_i)}(\omega)$ is a one-dimensional Fourier transform, it is usually manageable. Once $\varphi(\omega)$ is found by (2-49), the density function of $\mathbf{y}$, $p(y)$, can be derived by the inverse Fourier transform of (2-45).

EXAMPLE 2-7 As a special case of Example 2-6, let $\mathbf{y}$ be given as

$$\mathbf{y} = \sum_{i=1}^{n} \mathbf{x}_i \tag{2-50}$$

Then from (2-49)

$$\varphi_{\mathbf{y}}(\omega) = \prod_{i=1}^{n} \varphi_{\mathbf{x}_i}(\omega) \tag{2-51}$$

If we recall that $\varphi_{\mathbf{x}_i}(\omega)$ is the Fourier transform of $p(x_i)$, except the sign of ω, the product of the $\varphi_{\mathbf{x}_i}(\omega)$'s corresponds to taking the convolution of $p(x_i)$'s.

EXAMPLE 2-8 Once the characteristic function is found by (2-46), the *moments* of $p(X)$ can be calculated as follows:

$$\begin{aligned} \mu_{k_1\cdots k_n} &= E\{\mathbf{x}_1^{k_1}\mathbf{x}_2^{k_2} \cdots \mathbf{x}_n^{k_n}\} \\ &= (j)^{-(k_1+k_2+\cdots+k_n)} \left. \frac{\partial^{k_1+\cdots+k_n}\varphi(\Omega)}{\partial\omega_1^{k_1} \cdots \partial\omega_n^{k_n}} \right|_{\omega_1=0,\ldots,\omega_n=0} \end{aligned} \tag{2-52}$$

Normal Distributions

An explicit expression of $p(X)$ for normal distributions is

$$N(X, M, \Sigma) = (2\pi)^{-n/2} \,|\, \Sigma \,|^{-1/2} \exp\{-\tfrac{1}{2}\, d^2(X, M, \Sigma)\} \tag{2-53}$$

where $N(X, M, \Sigma)$ is a shorthand notation for a normal distribution with expected vector M and covariance matrix Σ, and

$$\begin{aligned} d^2(X, M, \Sigma) &= (X - M)^T\Sigma^{-1}(X - M) = \mathrm{tr}\{\Sigma^{-1}(X - M)(X - M)^T\} \\ &= \sum_{i=1}^{n} \sum_{j=1}^{n} h_{ij}(x_i - m_i)(x_j - m_j) \end{aligned} \tag{2-54}$$

$$h_{ij}: \text{ component of } \Sigma^{-1} \tag{2-55}$$

The term $\mathrm{tr}\{A\}$ is the trace of a matrix A and is equal to the summation of the diagonal terms of A. As shown in (2-53) and (2-54), normal distributions are simple exponential functions of a distance function (2-54) which is a positive definite quadratic function of the x's. The coefficient $(2\pi)^{-n/2} |\Sigma|^{-1/2}$ is selected to satisfy the probability condition

$$\int_{\mathscr{S}} p(X)\, dX = 1 \tag{2-56}$$

Normal distributions are widely used because of many important properties. Some of these are as follows.

(1) *Parameters Which Specify the Distribution.* The expected vector M and covariance matrix Σ are sufficient to characterize the distribution uniquely. All moments of a normal distribution can be calculated as functions of these parameters.

(2) *Uncorrelated–Independent.* If the $\mathbf{x}_i$'s are mutually uncorrelated, then they are also independent.

From (2-29) and (2-36), if the $\mathbf{x}_i$'s are uncorrelated

$$\sigma_{ij}^2 = E\{(\mathbf{x}_i - m_i)\}\, E\{(\mathbf{x}_j - m_j)\} = 0 \qquad \text{for} \quad i \neq j \tag{2-57}$$

Thus Σ becomes a diagonal matrix as

$$\Sigma = \begin{bmatrix} \sigma_{11}^2 & & 0 \\ & \ddots & \\ 0 & & \sigma_{nn}^2 \end{bmatrix} \quad \text{and} \quad \Sigma^{-1} = \begin{bmatrix} 1/\sigma_{11}^2 & & 0 \\ & \ddots & \\ 0 & & 1/\sigma_{nn}^2 \end{bmatrix} \tag{2-58}$$

Therefore, from (2-53) and (2-54),

$$\begin{aligned} p(X) &= (2\pi)^{-n/2} \left(\prod_{i=1}^{n} \sigma_{ii}^2 \right)^{-1/2} \exp\left\{ -\frac{1}{2} \sum_{i=1}^{n} \frac{(x_i - m_i)^2}{\sigma_{ii}^2} \right\} \\ &= \prod_{i=1}^{n} (2\pi)^{-1/2} \sigma_{ii}^{-1} \exp\left\{ -\frac{1}{2} \frac{(x_i - m_i)^2}{\sigma_{ii}^2} \right\} = \prod_{i=1}^{n} p(x_i) \end{aligned} \tag{2-59}$$

and the condition for independence of (2-38) is satisfied.

(3) *Normal Marginal Densities and Normal Conditional Densities.* The marginal densities and the conditional densities of a normal distribution are all normal. We will show this only for the two-dimensional case. The general case can be proved by a similar procedure, but the discussion is omitted because of its complexity.

For the marginal density:

$$p(x_1) = \int_{-\infty}^{+\infty} p(x_1, x_2)\, dx_2$$

$$= \frac{1}{2\pi|\Sigma|^{1/2}} \int_{-\infty}^{+\infty} \exp\Big[-\frac{1}{2|\Sigma|}\{\sigma_{22}^2(x_1 - m_1)^2 + \sigma_{11}^2(x_2 - m_2)^2$$

$$-2\sigma_{12}^2(x_1 - m_1)(x_2 - m_2)\}\Big]\, dx_2$$

$$= \frac{1}{(2\pi)^{1/2}\sigma_{11}} \exp\left[-\frac{(x_1 - m_1)^2}{2\sigma_{11}^2}\right]$$

$$\times \frac{\sigma_{11}}{(2\pi)^{1/2}|\Sigma|^{1/2}} \int_{-\infty}^{+\infty} \exp\Big[-\frac{\sigma_{11}^2}{2|\Sigma|}$$

$$\times \left\{(x_2 - m_2) - \frac{\sigma_{12}^2(x_1 - m_1)}{\sigma_{11}^2}\right\}^2\Big]\, dx_2$$

$$= \frac{1}{(2\pi)^{1/2}\sigma_{11}} \exp\left[-\frac{(x_1 - m_1)^2}{2\sigma_{11}^2}\right] \tag{2-60}$$

where

$$|\Sigma| = \sigma_{11}^2\sigma_{22}^2 - \sigma_{12}^4 \tag{2-61}$$

For the conditional density,

$$p(x_1/x_2) = p(x_1, x_2)/p(x_2)$$

$$= \frac{(2\pi)^{1/2}\sigma_{22}}{2\pi|\Sigma|^{1/2}} \exp\Big[-\frac{1}{2|\Sigma|}$$

$$\times \{\sigma_{22}^2(x_1 - m_1)^2 + \sigma_{11}^2(x_2 - m_2)^2 - 2\sigma_{12}^2(x_1 - m_1)(x_2 - m_2)\}$$

$$+ \frac{1}{2\sigma_{22}^2}(x_2 - m_2)^2\Big]$$

$$= \frac{\sigma_{22}}{(2\pi)^{1/2}|\Sigma|^{1/2}} \exp\left[-\frac{\sigma_{22}^2}{2|\Sigma|}\left\{(x_1 - m_1) - \frac{\sigma_{12}^2}{\sigma_{22}^2}(x_2 - m_2)\right\}^2\right] \tag{2-62}$$

Equation (2-62) shows a normal distribution with the mean $m_1 + \sigma_{12}^2(x_2 - m_2)/\sigma_{22}^2$ and variance $|\Sigma| / \sigma_{22}^2$.

(4) *Normal Characteristic Functions.* For one random variable, the characteristic function of a normal $p(x)$ can be calculated as

$$\begin{aligned}\varphi(\omega) &= \int_{-\infty}^{+\infty} \frac{1}{(2\pi)^{1/2}\sigma} \exp\left\{-\frac{(x-m)^2}{2\sigma^2}\right\} \exp(j\omega x)\, dx \\ &= \exp\left\{-\frac{\omega^2\sigma^2}{2} + j\omega m\right\} \\ &\quad \times \frac{1}{(2\pi)^{1/2}\sigma} \int_{-\infty}^{+\infty} \exp\left[-\frac{1}{2\sigma^2}\{x-(m+j\omega\sigma^2)\}^2\right] dx \\ &= \exp\left\{-\frac{\omega^2\sigma^2}{2} + j\omega m\right\} \end{aligned} \tag{2-63}$$

That is, $\varphi(\omega)$ is also normal and its variance is the inverse of the variance of $p(x)$. This is a reasonable result since $\varphi(\omega)$ is the frequency characteristic of $p(x)$. When $p(x)$ is concentrated in a small region, $\varphi(\omega)$ should be spread out over a large region with more high frequency components, and vice versa.

The characteristic function of a random vector (2-53) is an extension of (2-63). We present the result here without proof:

$$\varphi(\Omega) = \exp\{-\tfrac{1}{2}\Omega^T\Sigma\Omega + j\Omega^T M\} \tag{2-64}$$

(5) *Linear Transformations.* Under any nonsingular linear transformation, the distance function of (2-54) keeps its quadratic form and also does not lose the positive definiteness. Therefore, after a nonsingular linear transformation, a normal distribution becomes just another normal distribution with different parameters.

Also, it is always possible to find a set of nonsingular linear transformations which makes the new covariance matrix diagonal. Since a diagonal covariance matrix means uncorrelated variables and particularly independent variables for a normal distribution, we can always find a set of axes such that random variables are independent in the new coordinate system. These subjects will be discussed in detail in a later section.

(6) *Physical Justification.* The assumption of normality is a reasonable approximation for many real data sets. This is, in particular, true for processes where the random variables are sums of many independent variables. This problem will be discussed in the next section in relation to the central limit theorem. However, normality should not be assumed without good justification. More often than not this leads to meaningless conclusions.

Stochastic Convergence

A sequence $\{\mathbf{X}_i\}$ of random vectors may converge to a limit $\mathbf{Z}$ which is also a random vector. For example, suppose the sequence $\{\mathbf{Y}_i\}$ consists of independent, identically distributed random vectors with expected vector M and covariance matrix Σ. From $\{\mathbf{Y}_i\}$ we define a sequence of summations as

$$\mathbf{X}_N = (1/N) \sum_{i=1}^{N} \mathbf{Y}_i \tag{2-65}$$

Then we have

$$E\{\mathbf{X}_N\} = (1/N) \sum_{i=1}^{N} E\{\mathbf{Y}_i\} = M \tag{2-66}$$

and

$$\begin{aligned} E\{(\mathbf{X}_N - M)(\mathbf{X}_N - M)^T\} &= (1/N^2) \sum_{i=1}^{N} E\{(\mathbf{Y}_i - M)(\mathbf{Y}_i - M)^T\} \\ &= \Sigma/N \end{aligned} \tag{2-67}$$

Thus, in some sense, the sequence $\{\mathbf{X}_N\}$ converges to M. Let us clarify further what we mean by convergence of random vectors.

Definition If the event

$$\lim_{N \to \infty} \mathbf{X}_N = \mathbf{Z} \tag{2-68}$$

has probability equal to 1, then we write

$$\Pr\{\mathbf{X}_N \to \mathbf{Z}\} = 1 \qquad \text{for} \quad N \to \infty \tag{2-69}$$

and say that the sequence $\mathbf{X}_N$ *converges* to $\mathbf{Z}$ with *probability* 1.

Definition If

$$E\{\| \mathbf{X}_N - \mathbf{Z} \|^2\} \to 0 \qquad \text{for} \quad N \to \infty \tag{2-70}$$

we say that the sequence $\mathbf{X}_N$ tends to $\mathbf{Z}$ *in the mean-square sense.*

Definition If, for all ε, $\varepsilon > 0$,

$$\Pr\{\| \mathbf{X}_N - \mathbf{Z} \| > \varepsilon\} \to 0 \qquad \text{for} \quad N \to \infty \tag{2-71}$$

we say that $\mathbf{X}_N$ tends to $\mathbf{Z}$ *in probability.*

Definition If

$$P(X_N) \to P(Z) \quad \text{as} \quad N \to \infty \tag{2-72}$$

we say that $\mathbf{X}_N$ tends to $\mathbf{Z}$ *in distribution.*

The central limit theorem is an example of convergence in distribution and stated as follows:

Central Limit Theorem If $\mathbf{X}_N$ is of the form $(1/N)$ times the sum of N independent, identically distributed random vectors which have a finite covariance matrix Σ and expected vector M, as in (2-65), then the distribution of $(\mathbf{X}_N - M)$ tends to the normal distribution with zero expected vector and covariance matrix Σ/N. Also $\mathbf{X}_N$ converges to M in probability. (The proof is omitted.)

The sum of independent random vectors means that $p(X_N)$ is the convolution of $Np(Y_i)$'s. Therefore the central limit theorem is merely a property of convolutions involving a large number of positive functions.

The central limit theorem provides a strong justification for the use of normal distributions in many applications because our observations may be generated, in many cases, by the sum of many unobserved random vectors.

Cauchy Criterion Suppose that $\mathbf{X}_N$ tends to $\mathbf{Z}$ in some sense. In general, the target random vector $\mathbf{Z}$ is not known. In this case, we can replace $\mathbf{Z}$ by $\mathbf{X}_{N+k}$ in (2-69) through (2-72) and test for convergence; k can be any positive number.

2.3 Transformation of Random Vectors

Jacobian

Let a random vector $\mathbf{Y}$ be a function of another random vector $\mathbf{X}$ as

$$\mathbf{Y} = G(X) \tag{2-73}$$

or

$$\mathbf{y}_i = g_i(\mathbf{X}) = g_i(\mathbf{x}_1, \mathbf{x}_2, \ldots, \mathbf{x}_n) \qquad (i = 1, 2, \ldots, n) \tag{2-74}$$

Also, let us assume a one-to-one correspondence between $\mathbf{X}$ and $\mathbf{Y}$. Then the density functions of these random vectors are related by

$$p_{\mathbf{Y}}(Y) = \frac{p_{\mathbf{X}}(X)}{|J|} = \frac{p_{\mathbf{X}}[G^{-1}(Y)]}{|J|} \tag{2-75}$$

where $|J|$ is the absolute value of the Jacobian

$$J = \begin{vmatrix} \dfrac{\partial g_1}{\partial x_1} & \cdots & \dfrac{\partial g_1}{\partial x_n} \\ \vdots & & \vdots \\ \dfrac{\partial g_n}{\partial x_1} & \cdots & \dfrac{\partial g_n}{\partial x_n} \end{vmatrix} \tag{2-76}$$

The Jacobian is needed in the transformation because an area $dy_1 \cdots dy_n$ in the Y coordinate system corresponds to an area $|J| \, dx_1 \cdots dx_n$ in the X coordinate system.

EXAMPLE 2-9 The physical meaning of the Jacobian can be shown easily in the two-dimensional case (Fig. 2-3):

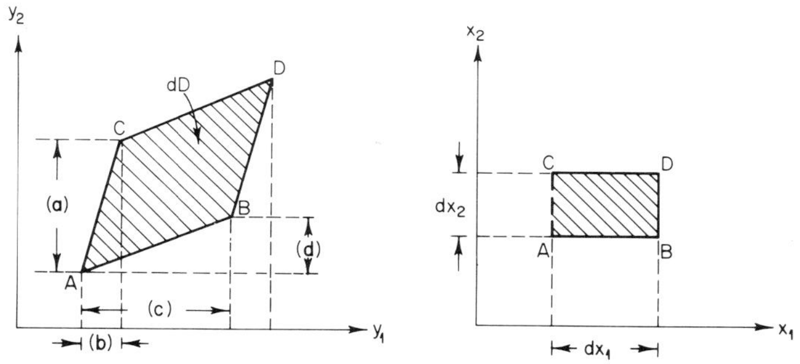

Fig. 2-3 Two-dimensional Jacobian:

(a) $\dfrac{\partial g_2}{\partial x_2} dx_2$, (b) $\dfrac{\partial g_1}{\partial x_2} dx_2$, (c) $\dfrac{\partial g_1}{\partial x_1} dx_1$, (d) $\dfrac{\partial g_2}{\partial x_1} dx_1$

Let us select a rectangular region $dx_1 \, dx_2$ in the original X coordinate system. Then we can find the corresponding region dD in the Y coordinate system according to

$$dy_1 = \frac{\partial g_1}{\partial x_1} dx_1 + \frac{\partial g_1}{\partial x_2} dx_2 \tag{2-77}$$

$$dy_2 = \frac{\partial g_2}{\partial x_1} dx_1 + \frac{\partial g_2}{\partial x_2} dx_2 \tag{2-78}$$

That is, $dx_1(AB)$ produces $(\partial g_1/\partial x_1) \, dx_1$ as dy_1 and $(\partial g_2/dx_1) \, dx_1$ as dy_2. The area of dD can be calculated by simple geometry as

$$dD = \left| \frac{\partial g_1}{\partial x_1} \frac{\partial g_2}{\partial x_2} - \frac{\partial g_1}{\partial x_2} \frac{\partial g_2}{\partial x_1} \right| dx_1 \, dx_2 = |J| \, dx_1 \, dx_2 \tag{2-79}$$

Since the probabilities for the corresponding areas should be the same in both coordinate systems:

$$p(y_1, y_2)\, dD = p(y_1, y_2) \mid J \mid dx_1\, dx_2 = p(x_1, x_2)\, dx_1\, dx_2 \tag{2-80}$$

or

$$p(y_1, y_2) = p(x_1, x_2)/\mid J \mid \tag{2-81}$$

Thus, the Jacobian is a coefficient which accounts for scale changes brought about by the transformation.

Linear Transformation

When the transformation is linear, (2-73) can be replaced by

$$\mathbf{Y} = A\mathbf{X} \tag{2-82}$$

where A is an $n \times n$ matrix. In this case the determinant $\mid A \mid$ is the Jacobian for the linear transformation. The expected vector and covariance matrix of $\mathbf{Y}$ are

$$D = E\{\mathbf{Y}\} = AE\{\mathbf{X}\} = AM \tag{2-83}$$

$$\begin{aligned} K &= E\{(\mathbf{Y} - D)(\mathbf{Y} - D)^T\} = E[\{A(\mathbf{X} - M)\}\{A(\mathbf{X} - M)\}^T] \\ &= AE\{(\mathbf{X} - M)(\mathbf{X} - M)^T\}A^T = A\Sigma A^T \end{aligned} \tag{2-84}$$

where the following rule of matrices (matrices need not be square) is used

$$(AB)^T = B^T A^T \tag{2-85}$$

A similar rule, which holds for the inversion of matrices, is

$$(AB)^{-1} = B^{-1}A^{-1} \tag{2-86}$$

This time, the existence of $(AB)^{-1}$, A^{-1}, and B^{-1} is required.

EXAMPLE 2-10 For normal distributions, the distance function of (2-54) for Y can be calculated as

$$\begin{aligned} d^2(Y, D, K) &= (Y - D)^T K^{-1}(Y - D) \\ &= \{A(X - M)\}^T\{A\Sigma A^T\}^{-1}\{A(X - M)\} \\ &= (X - M)^T\Sigma^{-1}(X - M) \\ &= d^2(X, M, \Sigma) \end{aligned} \tag{2-87}$$

In addition to the fact that we retain a quadratic form for the distance function after a linear transformation, d^2 is invariant under a linear transformation. Thus, from (2-75) and (2-53), the density function of **Y** is

$$p(Y) = (2\pi)^{-n/2} |\Sigma|^{-1/2} \exp\{-\tfrac{1}{2} d^2(X, M, \Sigma)\}/|A| \tag{2-88}$$

Recalling (2-84) and a determinant rule

$$K = A\Sigma A^T \rightarrow |K| = |A|\,|\Sigma|\,|A^T| = |\Sigma|\,|A|^2 \tag{2-89}$$

$p(Y)$ becomes

$$p(Y) = (2\pi)^{-n/2} |K|^{-1/2} \exp\{-\tfrac{1}{2} d^2(Y, D, K)\} \tag{2-90}$$

Thus, **Y** has a normal distribution with the expected vector D and covariance matrix K.

Orthonormal Transformation

Let us shift our coordinate system to bring the expected vector M to the origin. We use **Z** for the new coordinate system.

$$\mathbf{Z} = \mathbf{X} - M \tag{2-91}$$

Then the quadratic form of (2-54) becomes

$$d^2(Z, 0, \Sigma) = Z^T \Sigma^{-1} Z \tag{2-92}$$

Let us find a vector Z which maximizes $d^2(Z, 0, \Sigma)$ subject to the condition $Z^T Z = 1$ (constant). This is obtained by

$$(\partial/\partial Z)\{Z^T\Sigma^{-1}Z - \mu\,(Z^TZ - 1)\} = 2\Sigma^{-1}Z - 2\mu Z = 0 \tag{2-93}$$

where μ is a Lagrangian multiplier. The term $\partial/\partial Z$ consists of n partial differentiations $[\partial/\partial z_1\ \partial/\partial z_2 \cdots \partial/\partial z_n]^T$. The result is

$$\Sigma^{-1}Z = \mu Z \qquad \text{or} \qquad \Sigma Z = \lambda Z \qquad (\lambda = 1/\mu) \tag{2-94}$$

$$Z^T Z = 1 \tag{2-95}$$

In order that a nonnull Z may exist, λ must be chosen to satisfy the determinant equation

$$|\Sigma - \lambda I| = 0 \tag{2-96}$$

This is called the *characteristic equation* of the matrix Σ. Any value of λ which satisfies this equation is called an *eigenvalue*, and the Z corresponding to a given λ is called an *eigenvector*. When Σ is a nonsingular symmetric $n \times n$ matrix we have n real eigenvalues $\lambda_1, \ldots, \lambda_n$ and n eigenvectors $\Phi_1, \Phi_2, \ldots, \Phi_n$. The eigenvectors corresponding to two different eigenvalues are orthogonal. This can be proved as follows:

For λ_i, Φ_i and λ_j, Φ_j $(\lambda_i \neq \lambda_j)$,

$$\Sigma\Phi_i = \lambda_i\Phi_i, \quad \Sigma\Phi_j = \lambda_i\Phi_j \tag{2-97}$$

Multiplying the first equation by Φ_j, the second by Φ_i, and subtracting the second gives

$$(\lambda_i - \lambda_j)\Phi_j^T\Phi_i = \Phi_j^T\Sigma\Phi_i - \Phi_i^T\Sigma\Phi_j = 0 \tag{2-98}$$

as Σ is a symmetric matrix. Since $\lambda_i \neq \lambda_j$,

$$\Phi_j^T\Phi_i = 0 \tag{2-99}$$

Thus, (2-94), (2-95), and (2-99) can be rewritten as

$$\Sigma\Phi = \Phi\Lambda \tag{2-100}$$

$$\Phi^T\Phi = I \tag{2-101}$$

where Φ is an $n \times n$ matrix, consisting of n eigenvectors as

$$\Phi = [\Phi_1\Phi_2\cdots\Phi_n] \tag{2-102}$$

The term Λ is a diagonal matrix of eigenvalues as

$$\Lambda = \begin{bmatrix} \lambda_1 & & 0 \\ & \ddots & \\ 0 & & \lambda_n \end{bmatrix} \tag{2-103}$$

and I is a unity matrix. The terms Φ and Λ will be called the *eigenvector matrix* and the *eigenvalue matrix*, respectively.

Let us use Φ^T as the transformation matrix A of (2-82) as

$$\mathbf{Y} = \Phi^T X \tag{2-104}$$

Then, from (2-84),

$$K = \Phi^T\Sigma\Phi = \Lambda \tag{2-105}$$

where the following relationships are used:

$$(\Phi^T)^T = \Phi \tag{2-106}$$

$$\Phi^{-1} = \Phi^T \qquad \text{[from (2-101)]} \tag{2-107}$$

Equation (2-105) leads to the following important conclusions:

(1) We can find a linear transformation to *diagonalize* the covariance matrix in the new coordinate system. It means that we can obtain uncorrelated random variables in general and independent random variables for normal distributions.

(2) The transformation matrix is the transpose of the eigenvector matrix of Σ. Since the eigenvectors are the ones which maximize $d^2(Z, 0, \Sigma)$, we are actually selecting the principal components of the distribution as the new coordinate axes. A two-dimensional example is given in Fig. 2-4.

(3) The eigenvalues are the variances of the transformed distribution.

(4) This transformation is called an *orthonormal transformation* because (2-101) is satisfied. In orthonormal transformations, Euclidean distances are preserved since

$$\| Y \|^2 = Y^T Y = X^T \Phi \Phi^T X = X^T X = \| X \|^2 \tag{2-108}$$

Whitening Transformation

After applying the orthonormal transformation of (2-104), we can add another transformation $\Lambda^{-1/2}$ that will make the covariance matrix equal to I.

$$\mathbf{Y} = \Lambda^{-1/2} \Phi^T \mathbf{X} \tag{2-109}$$

$$K = \Lambda^{-1/2} \Phi^T \Sigma \Phi \Lambda^{-1/2} = \Lambda^{-1/2} \Lambda \Lambda^{-1/2} = I \tag{2-110}$$

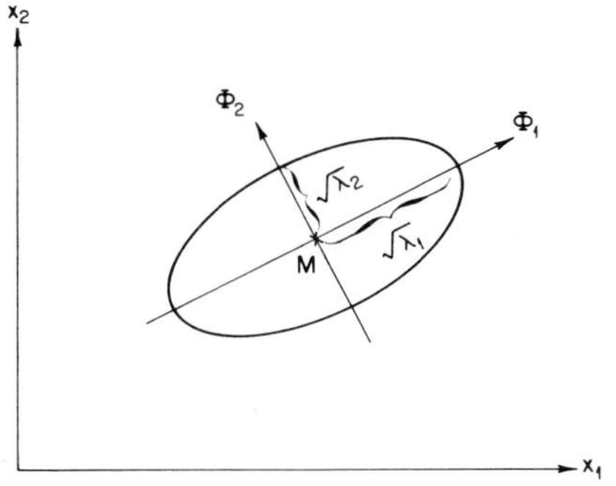

Fig. 2-4 Eigenvalues and eigenvectors of a distribution.

This transformation $\Lambda^{-1/2}\Phi^T$ is called the *whitening transformation* or the *whitening process*. The purpose of the second transformation $\Lambda^{-1/2}$ is to change the scales of the principal components in proportion to $1/\sqrt{\lambda_i}$. Figure 2-5 shows a two-dimensional example.

EXAMPLE 2-11 Whitening transformations are not orthonormal transformations, because

$$(\Lambda^{-1/2}\Phi^T)^T(\Lambda^{-1/2}\Phi^T) = \Phi\Lambda^{-1}\Phi^T \neq I \tag{2-111}$$

Therefore, the Euclidean distance is not preserved:

$$\| Y \|^2 = Y^T Y = X^T \Phi\Lambda^{-1}\Phi^T X \neq \| X \|^2 \tag{2-112}$$

EXAMPLE 2-12 After applying a whitening transformation, the covariance matrix is invariant under any orthonormal transformation, because

$$\Psi I \Psi^T = \Psi\Psi^T = I \tag{2-113}$$

This property will be used for simultaneous diagonalization of two matrices.

EXAMPLE 2-13 In pattern recognition experiments it is often necessary to generate samples which are to be normally distributed according to a given expected vector and covariance matrix. In general, the variables are correlated and this makes the generation of samples complex. However, the generation of normally distributed samples with the covariance matrix I is easy because the variables are independent and identically distributed with the variance 1. Therefore, after generating these samples, we transform the samples **Y** to **X** by

$$\mathbf{X} = (\Lambda^{-1/2}\Phi^T)^{-1}\mathbf{Y} = \Phi\Lambda^{1/2}\mathbf{Y} \tag{2-114}$$

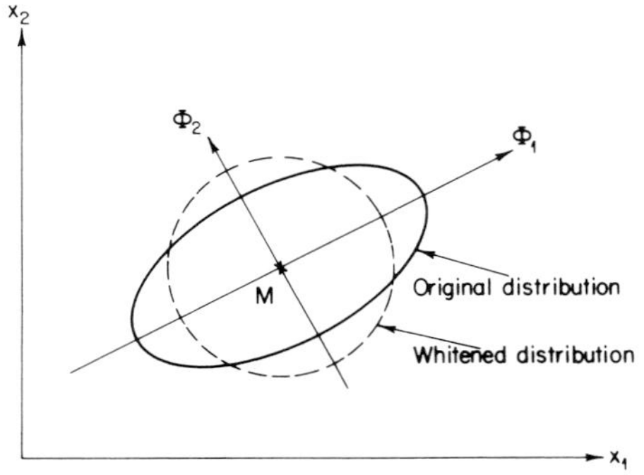

Fig. 2-5 Whitening process.

where Φ and Λ are the eigenvector and eigenvalue matrices of the given covariance matrix.

Simultaneous Diagonalization

We can diagonalize two symmetric matrices Σ_1 and Σ_2 simultaneously by a linear transformation. The process is as follows:

(1) First, we whiten Σ_1 by

$$\mathbf{Y} = \Theta^{-1/2}\Phi^T\mathbf{X} \tag{2-115}$$

where Θ and Φ are the eigenvalue and eigenvector matrices of Σ_1 as

$$\Sigma_1\Phi = \Phi\Theta \quad \text{and} \quad \Phi^T\Phi = I \tag{2-116}$$

Then Σ_1 and Σ_2 are transformed to

$$\Theta^{-1/2}\Phi^T\Sigma_1\Phi\Theta^{-1/2} = I \tag{2-117}$$

$$\Theta^{-1/2}\Phi^T\Sigma_2\Phi\Theta^{-1/2} = K \tag{2-118}$$

In general, K is not a diagonal matrix.

(2) Second, we apply the orthonormal transformation to diagonalize K. That is,

$$\mathbf{Z} = \Psi^T\mathbf{Y} \tag{2-119}$$

where Ψ and Λ are the eigenvector and eigenvalue matrices of K as

$$K\Psi = \Psi\Lambda \quad \text{and} \quad \Psi^T\Psi = I \tag{2-120}$$

As shown in (2-113), the first matrix I (2-117) is invariant under this transformation. Thus,

$$\Psi^T I \Psi = \Psi^T\Psi = I \tag{2-121}$$

$$\Psi^T K \Psi = \Lambda \tag{2-122}$$

Thus, both matrices are diagonalized; Fig. 2-6 shows a two-dimensional example of this process. The combination of step 1 and 2 gives the overall transformation matrix $\Psi^T\Theta^{-1/2}\Phi^T$. The terms $\Psi^T\Theta^{-1/2}\Phi^T$ and Λ can be calculated directly from Σ_1 and Σ_2 without going through the two steps above. This is done as follows:

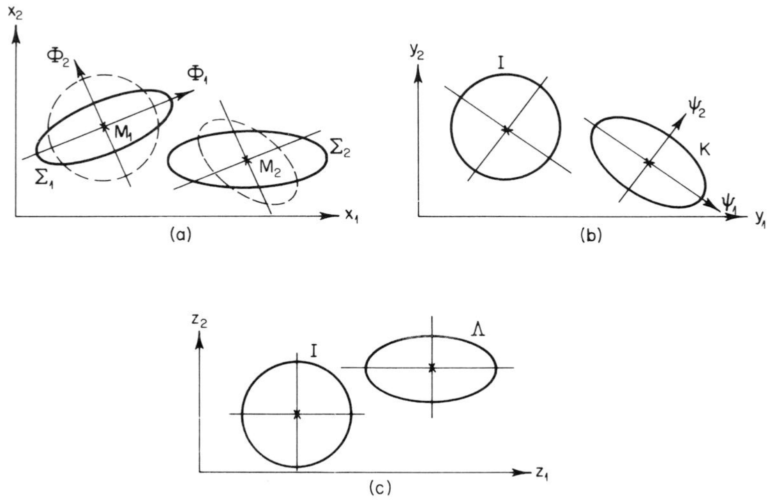

Fig. 2-6 Simultaneous diagonalization.

Theorem We can diagonalize two symmetric matrices as

$$A\Sigma_1 A^T = I \qquad \text{and} \qquad A\Sigma_2 A^T = \Lambda \tag{2-123}$$

where Λ and A^T are the eigenvalue and eigenvector matrices of $\Sigma_1^{-1}\Sigma_2$.

$$\Sigma_1^{-1}\Sigma_2 A^T = A^T \Lambda \tag{2-124}$$

PROOF Since λ's are the eigenvalues of K from (2-120),

$$|\, K - \lambda I \,| = 0 \tag{2-125}$$

Replacing K and I by (2-117) and (2-118),

$$|\, \Theta^{-1/2}\Phi^T \,|\,|\, \Sigma_2 - \lambda\Sigma_1 \,|\,|\, \Phi\Theta^{-1/2} \,| = 0 \tag{2-126}$$

Since the transformation matrix $\Theta^{-1/2}\Phi^T$ is nonsingular, $|\, \Theta^{-1/2}\Phi^T \,| \neq 0$ and $|\, \Phi\, \Theta^{-1/2} \,| \neq 0$. Therefore,

$$|\, \Sigma_2 - \lambda\Sigma_1 \,| = 0 \qquad \text{or} \qquad |\, \Sigma_1^{-1}\Sigma_2 - \lambda I \,| = 0 \tag{2-127}$$

Thus, λ's are the eigenvalues of $\Sigma_1^{-1}\Sigma_2$.

For the eigenvectors, inserting (2-118) into (2-120) yields

$$\Theta^{-1/2}\Phi^T \Sigma_2 \Phi\Theta^{-1/2}\Psi = \Psi\Lambda \tag{2-128}$$

or

$$\Sigma_2 \Phi \Theta^{-1/2} \Psi = (\Theta^{-1/2} \Phi^T)^{-1} \Psi \Lambda \tag{2-129}$$

By (2-117), $(\Theta^{-1/2}\Phi^T)^{-1}$ can be replaced by $\Sigma_1 \Phi\, \Theta^{-1/2}$.

$$\Sigma_2(\Phi \Theta^{-1/2} \Psi) = \Sigma_1(\Phi \Theta^{-1/2} \Psi)\Lambda \tag{2-130}$$

or

$$\Sigma_1^{-1}\Sigma_2(\Psi^T \Theta^{-1/2} \Phi^T)^T = (\Psi^T \Theta^{-1/2} \Phi^T)^T \Lambda \tag{2-131}$$

Thus, the transformation matrix $\Psi^T \Theta^{-1/2} \Phi^T$ is calculated as the eigenvector matrix of $\Sigma_1^{-1}\Sigma_2$.

One fact should be mentioned here. Usually an eigenvector matrix automatically satisfies the orthonormal condition of (2-101). However, in simultaneous diagonalization, the normalization should be made such as to satisfy the first equation of (2-123) rather than (2-101). This can be done by changing the scale of each eigenvector as follows:

(1) Find the orthonormal eigenvectors of $\Sigma_1^{-1}\Sigma_2$ as

$$\Sigma_1^{-1}\Sigma_2 L_i = \lambda_i L_i \qquad (i = 1, 2, \ldots, n) \tag{2-132}$$

$$L_i^T L_j = \delta_{ij} \tag{2-133}$$

(2) Change the scale of L_i to satisfy

$$a^2 L_i^T \Sigma_1 L_i = 1 \qquad \text{or} \qquad a = 1/(L_i^T \Sigma_1 L_i)^{1/2} \tag{2-134}$$

Therefore, the ith component of $(\Psi^T \Theta^{-1/2} \Phi^T)^T$ of (2-131) is

$$(\Psi^T \Theta^{-1/2} \Phi^T)_i^T = L_i/(L_i^T \Sigma_1 L_i)^{1/2} \tag{2-135}$$

Simultaneous diagonalization of two matrices is a very powerful tool in pattern recognition because many problems of pattern recognition consider two distributions for classification purposes. Also, there are many possible modifications of the above discussion. These depend on what kind of properties we are interested in, what kind of matrices are used, etc. In this section we will show one of the modifications which will be used in later chapters.

Modification

Theorem Let a matrix Q be given by a linear combination of two symmetric matrices Q_1 and Q_2 as

$$Q = a_1 Q_1 + a_2 Q_2 \tag{2-136}$$

where a_1 and a_2 are assumed to be positive. If we normalize the eigenvectors with respect to Q as the first equation of (2-123), Q_1 and Q_2 have the same eigenvectors, and their eigenvalues are ordered as

$$\lambda_1^{(1)} > \lambda_2^{(1)} > \cdots > \lambda_n^{(1)} \qquad \text{for} \quad Q_1 \tag{2-137}$$

$$\lambda_1^{(2)} < \lambda_2^{(2)} < \cdots < \lambda_n^{(2)} \qquad \text{for} \quad Q_2 \tag{2-138}$$

PROOF Let Q and Q_1 be diagonalized simultaneously such that

$$AQA^T = I \qquad \text{and} \qquad AQ_1A^T = \Lambda^{(1)} \tag{2-139}$$

where

$$Q^{-1}Q_1A^T = A^T\Lambda^{(1)} \tag{2-140}$$

Then Q_2 is also diagonalized because, from (2-136) and (2-139),

$$AQ_2A^T = (1/a_2)[I - a_1\Lambda^{(1)}] = \Lambda^{(2)} \tag{2-141}$$

or

$$\lambda_i^{(2)} = (1/a_2)(1 - a_1\lambda_i^{(1)}) \tag{2-142}$$

Therefore, Q_1 and Q_2 share the same eigenvectors which are normalized with respect to Q as the first equation of (2-123) and, if $\lambda_i^{(1)} > \lambda_j^{(1)}$, then $\lambda_i^{(2)} < \lambda_j^{(2)}$ from (2-142).

EXAMPLE 2-14 Let S be the mixture autocorrelation matrix of two distributions whose autocorrelation matrices are S_1 and S_2. Then

$$\begin{aligned} S &= E\{\mathbf{X}\mathbf{X}^T\} \\ &= P(\omega_1)E\{\mathbf{X}\mathbf{X}^T/\omega_1\} + P(\omega_2)E\{\mathbf{X}\mathbf{X}^T/\omega_2\} = P(\omega_1)S_1 + P(\omega_2)S_2 \end{aligned} \tag{2-143}$$

Thus, by the above theorem, we can diagonalize S_1 and S_2 with the same set of eigenvectors. Since the eigenvalues are ordered in reverse, the eigenvector with the largest eigenvalue for the first distribution has the least eigenvalue for the second, and vice versa [Fukunaga, 1970c]. This property is helpful for classifying two distributions and will be used in later chapters.

2.4 Various Properties of Eigenvalues and Eigenvectors

As we saw in the diagonalization processes, the eigenvalues and eigenvectors of symmetric matrices play an important role. In this section, we review various properties of eigenvalues and eigenvectors, which will simplify discussion in later chapters. Most of the matrices we will be dealing with are covariance and autocorrelation matrices, which are symmetric. Therefore, unless specially stated, we assume that matrices are symmetric, with real eigenvalues and eigenvectors.

Orthonormal Transformations

Theorem An eigenvalue matrix Λ is invariant under any orthonormal linear transformation.

PROOF Let A be an orthonormal transformation matrix and let it satisfy

$$A^T A = I \qquad \text{or} \qquad A^T = A^{-1} \tag{2-144}$$

By this transformation, Q is converted to AQA^T [see (2-84)]. If the eigenvalue and eigenvector matrices of AQA^T are Λ and Φ.

$$\Phi^T(AQA^T)\Phi = \Lambda \tag{2-145}$$

$$(A^T\Phi)^T Q(A^T\Phi) = \Lambda \tag{2-146}$$

Thus, Λ and $A^T\Phi$ should be the eigenvalue and eigenvector matrices of Q. The term $A^T\Phi$ satisfies the orthonormal condition as

$$(A^T\Phi)^T(A^T\Phi) = \Phi^T AA^T\Phi = \Phi^T\Phi = I \tag{2-147}$$

Positive Definiteness

Theorem If all eigenvalues are positive, Q is a positive definite matrix.

PROOF Consider the quadratic form

$$d^2 = X^T Q X \tag{2-148}$$

We can rewrite X as ΦY, where Φ is any orthonormal matrix, without loss of generality. In particular, let Φ be the eigenvector matrix of Q. Then

$$d^2 = (\Phi Y)^T Q(\Phi Y) = Y^T\Phi^T Q\Phi Y = Y^T\Lambda Y = \sum_{i=1}^{n} \lambda_i y_i^2 \tag{2-149}$$

where the λ's are the eigenvalues of Q. If these eigenvalues are all positive, then d^2 is positive, unless Y is a zero vector. But from the relation between Y and X, we see that d^2 must be positive for all nonzero X as well. Therefore, Q is positive definite.

EXAMPLE 2-15 When Q is a covariance or an autocorrelation matrix, the λ's are the variance or second moments of the samples after the orthonormal transformation to diagonalize Q. Therefore, all λ's should be positive for both cases, and both covariance and autocorrelation matrices are positive definite.

Trace

Theorem The trace of Q is the summation of all eigenvalues and is invariant under any orthonormal transformation. That is,

$$\operatorname{tr} Q = \sum_{i=1}^{n} \lambda_i \tag{2-150}$$

PROOF First for general rectangular matrices $A_{n\times m}$ and $B_{m\times n}$,

$$\operatorname{tr}[A_{n\times m} \cdot B_{m\times n}] = \operatorname{tr}[B_{m\times n} \cdot A_{n\times m}] \tag{2-151}$$

because

$$\sum_{i=1}^{n} \sum_{j=1}^{m} a_{ij} b_{ji} = \sum_{j=1}^{m} \sum_{i=1}^{n} b_{ji} a_{ij} \tag{2-152}$$

where a_{ij} and b_{ji} are the components of $A_{n\times m}$ and $B_{m\times n}$. Using (2-151),

$$\sum_{i=1}^{n} \lambda_i = \operatorname{tr} \Lambda = \operatorname{tr}(\Phi^T Q \Phi) = \operatorname{tr}(Q \Phi \Phi^T) = \operatorname{tr} Q \tag{2-153}$$

As we proved before, the eigenvalues are invariant under any orthonormal transformation. Therefore, any function of eigenvalues is also invariant.

EXAMPLE 2-16 When Q is a covariance or an autocorrelation matrix, the above theorem states that the summation of the variances or second moments of individual variables $E\{\mathbf{x}_1^2\}$ is invariant under any orthonormal transformation.

Theorem The trace of Q^m is the summation of λ_i^m's, and invariant under any orthonormal transformation. That is,

$$\operatorname{tr} Q^m = \operatorname{tr} \Lambda^m = \sum_{i=1}^{n} \lambda_i^m \tag{2-154}$$

PROOF Using $Q\Phi = \Phi\Lambda$,

$$Q^m \Phi = Q^{m-1} \Phi \Lambda = Q^{m-2} \Phi \Lambda^2 = \cdots = \Phi \Lambda^m \tag{2-155}$$

Therefore,

$$\operatorname{tr} Q^m = \operatorname{tr} \Lambda^m = \sum_{i=1}^{n} \lambda_i^m \tag{2-156}$$

EXAMPLE 2-17 Let us look at n eigenvalues, $\lambda_1, \ldots, \lambda_n$, as the samples drawn from the distribution of a random variable $\boldsymbol{\lambda}$. Then we can calculate all moments of the distribution of $\boldsymbol{\lambda}$ by

$$E\{\boldsymbol{\lambda}^m\} = (1/n) \sum_{i=1}^{n} \lambda_i^m = (1/n) \operatorname{tr} Q^m \tag{2-157}$$

Particularly, we may use

$$E\{\boldsymbol{\lambda}\} = (1/n) \operatorname{tr} Q = (1/n) \sum_{i=1}^{n} q_{ii} \tag{2-158}$$

$$\begin{aligned} \sigma_{\boldsymbol{\lambda}}^2 &= (1/n) \operatorname{tr} Q^2 - \{(1/n) \operatorname{tr} Q\}^2 \\ &= (1/n) \sum_{i=1}^{n} \sum_{j=1}^{n} q_{ij}^2 - (1/n^2)\Big(\sum_{i=1}^{n} q_{ii}\Big)^2 \end{aligned} \tag{2-159}$$

EXAMPLE 2-18 Equation (2-154) is used to find the largest eigenvalue because

$$\lambda_1^m + \lambda_2^m + \cdots + \lambda_n^m \cong \lambda_1^m \qquad \text{for} \quad m \gg 1 \tag{2-160}$$

where λ_1 is assumed to be the largest eigenvalue. For example, if we select $m = 16$, we need to multiply matrices four times as $Q \to Q^2 \to Q^4 \to Q^8 \to Q^{16}$ and take the trace of Q^{16} to pick up the largest eigenvalue.

Determinant and Rank

Theorem The determinant of Q is equal to the product of all eigenvalues and is invariant under any orthonormal transformation. That is

$$|Q| = |\Lambda| = \prod_{i=1}^{n} \lambda_i \tag{2-161}$$

PROOF Since the determinant of the product of matrices is the product of the determinants of the matrices

$$|\Lambda| = |\Phi^T|\,|Q|\,|\Phi| = |Q|\,|\Phi^T|\,|\Phi| = |Q| \tag{2-162}$$

Theorem The rank of Q is equal to the number of nonzero eigenvalues.

PROOF Q can be expressed by

$$Q = \Phi \Lambda \Phi^T = \sum_{i=1}^{n} \lambda_i \Phi_i \Phi_i^T \tag{2-163}$$

where Φ_i's are linearly independent vectors with mutually orthonormal relations. Therefore, if we have $n - r$ zero λ's, we can express Q by r linearly independent vectors, which is the definition of rank r.

Three applications of the above theorems are given as follows:

EXAMPLE 2-19 We show the relation between the determinants of the covariance and autocorrelation matrices [from (2-30)]:

$$| S | = | \Sigma + MM^T | = | \Sigma | \, | I + \Sigma^{-1} MM^T | \tag{2-164}$$

Let $\lambda_1, \ldots, \lambda_n$ be the eigenvalues of $\Sigma^{-1}MM^T$. Since $\Sigma^{-1}MM^T$ is a non-symmetric matrix, the λ_i's could be complex numbers. The eigenvalues of $I + \Sigma^{-1}MM^T$ are $(1 + \lambda_i)$'s. Therefore,

$$| S | = | \Sigma | \prod_{i=1}^{n} (1 + \lambda_i) \tag{2-165}$$

On the other hand, the rank of $\Sigma^{-1}MM^T$ is one. Therefore, the λ_i's should satisfy the following conditions

$$\lambda_1 \neq 0, \qquad \lambda_2 = \lambda_3 = \cdots = \lambda_n = 0 \tag{2-166}$$

$$\sum_{i=1}^{n} \lambda_i = \lambda_1 = \operatorname{tr} \Sigma^{-1}MM^T = M^T \Sigma^{-1} M \tag{2-167}$$

Thus,

$$| S | = | \Sigma | \, (1 + M^T \Sigma^{-1} M) \tag{2-168}$$

EXAMPLE 2-20 When only m samples are available in an n-dimensional vector space with $m < n$, the autocorrelation matrix S is calculated from the samples as

$$S = (1/m) \sum_{i=1}^{m} X_i X_i^T \tag{2-169}$$

That is, S is a function of m or of less linearly independent vectors. Therefore, the rank should be m, or less. The same conclusion can be obtained for covariance matrices. This problem, which is called a small sample size problem, is often encountered in pattern recognition, particularly when n

is very large. For this type of problem, instead of calculating eigenvalues and eigenvectors from $n \times n$ matrices, the following procedure is more efficient [McLaughlin, 1968].

Let $X_1, \ldots, X_m$ $(m < n)$ be samples. The autocorrelation matrix of these samples is

$$S_{n\times n} = (1/m) \sum_{i=1}^{m} X_i X_i^T = (1/m)(WW^T)_{n\times n} \tag{2-170}$$

where $W_{n\times m}$ is an $n \times m$ matrix as

$$W = [X_1 X_2 \cdots X_m]_{n\times m} \tag{2-171}$$

Instead of using an $n \times n$ matrix $S_{n\times n}$ of (2-170), let us calculate the eigenvalues and eigenvectors of an $m \times m$ matrix $(W^T W)_{m\times m}$ as

$$(1/m)(W^T W)_{m\times m} \Phi_{m\times m} = \Phi_{m\times m} \Lambda_{m\times m} \tag{2-172}$$

Multiplying W to (2-172) from the left side, we obtain

$$(1/m)(WW^T)_{n\times n}(W\Phi)_{n\times m} = (W\Phi)_{n\times m} \Lambda_{m\times m} \tag{2-173}$$

Thus, $(W\Phi)_{n\times m}$ and $\Lambda_{m\times m}$ are the m eigenvectors and eigenvalues of $S = (1/m)(WW^T)_{n\times n}$. The other $n - m$ eigenvalues are all zero and their eigenvectors are indefinite. The advantage of this calculation is that only an $m \times m$ matrix is used for calculating m eigenvalues and eigenvectors. The term $(W\Phi)_{n\times m}$ represents orthogonal vectors but not orthonormal ones. In order to obtain orthonormal eigenvectors V_i, we have to divide each column vector of $(W\Phi)_{n\times m}$ by $(m\lambda_i)^{1/2}$ as

$$V_i = W\Phi_i/(m\lambda_i)^{1/2} \quad \text{or} \quad V_{n\times m} = (W\Phi\Lambda^{-1/2})_{n\times m}/m^{1/2} \tag{2-174}$$

because, from (2-172),

$$V^T V = \Lambda^{-1/2}\Phi^T W^T W \Phi \Lambda^{-1/2}/m = \Lambda^{-1/2}\Phi^T \Phi \Lambda \Lambda^{-1/2} = \Lambda^{-1/2}\Lambda\Lambda^{-1/2} = I \tag{2-175}$$

EXAMPLE 2-21 In many pattern recognition problems, n may be very large, for example, 1000. However, only a few eigenvalues, such as 10, are dominant, that is,

$$\lambda_1 + \lambda_2 + \cdots + \lambda_n \cong \lambda_1 + \lambda_2 + \cdots + \lambda_k \qquad (k \ll n) \tag{2-176}$$

This means that in a practical sense we are handling S or Σ with rank k, even though the mathematical rank of S or Σ is still n. Therefore, it is very inefficient to use $n \times n$ matrices to find k eigenvalues and eigenvectors, even when we have a sample size greater than n. In addition to this inefficiency, we face some computational difficulty in handling large, near-singular matrices. For example, let us consider the calculation of S^{-1} or Σ^{-1}, or $|S|$ or $|\Sigma|$. The terms $|S|$ or $|\Sigma|$ are $\prod_{i=1}^{n} \lambda_i$ and $n-k$ λ's are very close to zero. If we have $n = 1000$, $k = 10$, and $\lambda_1 + \lambda_2 + \cdots + \lambda_{10} = 0.9$ out of $\lambda_1 + \lambda_2 + \cdots + \lambda_{1000} = 1$, the term $|S|$ or $|\Sigma|$ becomes $\prod_{i=1}^{10} \lambda_i \times \prod_{j=11}^{1000} \lambda_j = \prod_{i=1}^{10} \lambda_i \times (0.1/991)^{991}$ for the assumption of $\lambda_{11} = \lambda_{12} = \cdots = \lambda_{1000}$. The technique of the previous example could be used. However, to form W of (2-171), further discussion is needed to relate the estimation accuracy of the eigenvalues to the sample size.

Matrix Inversion

Diagonalization of matrices is particularly useful when we would like to invert the matrices.

EXAMPLE 2-22 From (2-54), a distance function is expressed by

$$d^2(X, M, \Sigma) = (X - M)^T \Sigma^{-1} (X - M) = (Y - D)^T \Lambda^{-1} (Y - D)$$
$$= \sum_{i=1}^{n} (y_i - d_i)^2 / \lambda_i \tag{2-177}$$

If we have two distributions, the two distance functions are, by simultaneous diagonalization,

$$d_1^2(X, M_1, \Sigma_1) = (Y - D_1)^T I^{-1} (Y - D_1) = \sum_{i=1}^{n} (y_i - d_{1i})^2 \tag{2-178}$$

$$d_2^2(X, M_2, \Sigma_2) = (Y - D_2)^T \Lambda^{-1} (Y - D_2) = \sum_{i=1}^{n} (y_i - d_{2i})^2 / \lambda_i \tag{2-179}$$

EXAMPLE 2-23 We show the inverse matrix of an autocorrelation matrix in terms of the covariance matrix and expected vector. From (2-30),

$$S^{-1} = (\Sigma + MM^T)^{-1} = (I + \Sigma^{-1} MM^T)^{-1} \Sigma^{-1} \tag{2-180}$$

Using an orthonormal transformation to diagonalize $\Sigma^{-1} MM^T$, we have

$$\Phi^T \Sigma^{-1} MM^T \Phi = \Lambda \qquad \text{and} \qquad \Phi^T I \Phi = I \tag{2-181}$$

where Λ is given in (2-166), and (2-167). Therefore,

$$(I+\Lambda)^{-1} = \begin{bmatrix} 1+\lambda_1 & & & 0 \\ & 1 & & \\ & & \ddots & \\ 0 & & & 1 \end{bmatrix}^{-1} = \begin{bmatrix} \dfrac{1}{1+\lambda_1} & & & 0 \\ & 1 & & \\ & & \ddots & \\ 0 & & & 1 \end{bmatrix}$$

$$= \begin{bmatrix} 1-\dfrac{\lambda_1}{1+\lambda_1} & & & 0 \\ & 1 & & \\ & & \ddots & \\ 0 & & & 1 \end{bmatrix} = I - \frac{1}{1+\lambda_1}\Lambda \tag{2-182}$$

Combining (2-180), (2-181), and (2-182),

$$\begin{aligned} S^{-1} &= [\Phi(I+\Lambda)\Phi^T]^{-1}\Sigma^{-1} = \Phi(I+\Lambda)^{-1}\Phi^T\Sigma^{-1} \\ &= \Phi\left(I - \frac{1}{1+\lambda_1}\Lambda\right)\Phi^T\Sigma^{-1} = \left(I - \frac{1}{1+\lambda_1}\Sigma^{-1}MM^T\right)\Sigma^{-1} \\ &= \Sigma^{-1} - \frac{\Sigma^{-1}MM^T\Sigma^{-1}}{1+M^T\Sigma^{-1}M} \end{aligned} \tag{2-183}$$

If we would like to calculate $M^TS^{-1}M$ in terms of $M^T\Sigma^{-1}M$,

$$M^TS^{-1}M = M^T\Sigma^{-1}M - \frac{(M^T\Sigma^{-1}M)^2}{1+M^T\Sigma^{-1}M} \tag{2-184}$$

The other equation is

$$M^T\Sigma^{-1}M = \frac{M^TS^{-1}M}{1-M^TS^{-1}M} \tag{2-185}$$

EXAMPLE 2-24 One way of calculating the pseudoinverse of a singular matrix is as follows. Let Q be a singular matrix with rank r, then Q can be expressed by the eigenvalues and eigenvectors as

$$Q = \Phi\Lambda\Phi^T = \sum_{i=1}^{r} \lambda_i \Phi_i \Phi_i^T \tag{2-186}$$

If we express Q^* by

$$Q^* = \sum_{i=1}^{r} \frac{1}{\lambda_i} \Phi_i \Phi_i^T \tag{2-187}$$

Then

$$QQ^* = \sum_{i=1}^{r} \sum_{j=1}^{r} \frac{\lambda_i}{\lambda_j} \Phi_i \Phi_i^T \Phi_j \Phi_j^T = \sum_{i=1}^{r} \Phi_i \Phi_i^T$$

$$= \left[\begin{array}{cccc|ccc} 1 & & 0 & & & & \\ & 1 & & & & 0 & \\ & & \ddots & & & & \\ 0 & & & 1 & & & \\ \hline & & & & 0 & & \\ & & 0 & & & \ddots & \\ & & & & & & 0 \end{array}\right] \tag{2-188}$$

Therefore Q^* is the inverse matrix of Q in the subspace spanned by r eigenvectors, and satisfies

$$QQ^*Q = Q \tag{2-189}$$

Example 2-25 Equation (2-189) suggests a general way to define the "inverse" of a singular matrix [Penrose, 1955]. The *generalized inverse* of an $m \times n$ matrix R of rank r is an $n \times m$ matrix $R^{\#}$ satisfying

$$RR^{\#}R = R \tag{2-190}$$

$$O^{\#} = O^T \tag{2-191}$$

The column vectors of R, R_i, are eigenvectors of the $m \times m$ matrix $(RR^{\#})$, among which the r's are linearly independent with eigenvalues equal to 1. Also, $m - r$ eigenvalues of $(RR^{\#})$ must be zero. The matrix $(RR^{\#})$ has the properties of a projection matrix and is useful in linear regression analysis [Deutch, 1965].

A particular form of $R^{\#}$ is most often used. Let B be an $m \times r$ matrix whose columns are the linearly independent columns of R. Then R can be expressed by

$$R_{m\times n} = B_{m\times r} C_{r\times n} \tag{2-192}$$

Since $B^T B$ is an $r \times r$ nonsingular matrix, C can be obtained by

$$C = (B^T B)^{-1} B^T R \tag{2-193}$$

From (2-193), C has rank r so that CC^T is also an $r \times r$ nonsingular matrix. The *pseudoinverse* R^* of R is defined by

$$R^* = C^T (CC^T)^{-1} (B^T B)^{-1} B^T \tag{2-194}$$

It can be shown that R^* satisfies (2-190) and is therefore a generalized inverse. Further, R^* is unique [Penrose, 1955]. The pseudoinverse is the most often used generalized inverse.

Perturbation Theory

In this subsection, we derive first-order approximations for the eigenvectors and eigenvalues of a perturbed matrix in terms of those of the nonperturbed matrix.

Let Q_0 be a real, symmetric $n \times n$ matrix and let ΔQ be a real, symmetric perturbation matrix. Let Φ_i and λ_i, $i = 1, \ldots, n$, be the eigenvectors and eigenvalues, respectively, of Q_0. Assume that the λ_i's are distinct. We wish to obtain a first-order approximation of the eigenvectors and eigenvalues of Q in terms of Φ_i's and λ_i's, where

$$Q = Q_0 + \Delta Q \tag{2-195}$$

These may be obtained by retaining the terms of first order or lower of the equation

$$(Q_0 + \Delta Q)(\Phi_i + \Delta\Phi_i) = (\lambda_i + \Delta\lambda_i)(\Phi_i + \Delta\Phi_i) \tag{2-196}$$

where

$$Q_0\Phi_i = \lambda_i\Phi_i \tag{2-197}$$

The resulting equation is

$$Q_0\,\Delta\Phi_i + \Delta Q\Phi_i \cong \lambda_i\,\Delta\Phi_i + \Delta\lambda_i\Phi_i \tag{2-198}$$

To calculate $\Delta\lambda_i$, we premultiply (2-198) by Φ_i^T and, since $\Phi_i^T Q_0 = \lambda_i\Phi_i^T$ and $\Phi_i^T\Phi_j = \delta_{ij}$, we have

$$\Delta\lambda_i \cong \Phi_i^T\,\Delta Q\Phi_i \tag{2-199}$$

We can write $\Delta\Phi_i$ as a linear combination of the Φ_j's as follows:

$$\Delta\Phi_i = \sum_{j=1}^{n} b_{ij}\Phi_j \tag{2-200}$$

where

$$b_{ij} = \Phi_j^T\,\Delta\Phi_i \tag{2-201}$$

If we premultiply (2-198) by Φ_j^T and rearrange, we have for $i \neq j$

$$b_{ij} \cong (\Phi_i^T \Delta Q \Phi_i)/(\lambda_i - \lambda_j) \qquad (i \neq j) \tag{2-202}$$

To determine b_{ii} we impose a first-order normalization condition on $\Phi_i + \Delta\Phi_i$, that is we require

$$\| \Phi_i + \Delta\Phi_i \|^2 = 1 \cong \| \Phi_i \|^2 + 2\Phi_i^T \Delta\Phi_i = 1 + 2\Phi_i^T \Delta\Phi_i \tag{2-203}$$

and it follows that

$$\Phi_i^T \Delta\Phi_i = b_{ii} \cong 0 \tag{2-204}$$

Noting that $\Phi_i^T Q_0 \Phi_i = \lambda_i$ and $\Phi_i^T Q_0 \Phi_j = 0$ for $i \neq j$, we summarize this section as follows:

$$\lambda_i + \Delta\lambda_i \cong \Phi_i^T Q \Phi_i \tag{2-205}$$

and

$$b_{ij} \cong \begin{cases} (\Phi_i^T Q \Phi_j)/(\lambda_i - \lambda_j) & i \neq j \\ 0 & i = j \end{cases} \tag{2-206}$$

Standard Data

Throughout this book, the following data will be referred to as Standard Data [Marill, 1963].

1. Type of distribution—Normal

2. Dimension—8

3. Number of classes—4

4. Number of samples—200 per class (unless otherwise stated, generate 200 samples per class according to the following parameters).

5. Distribution parameters

$$M_1 = [7.825 \quad 6.750 \quad 5.835 \quad 8.525 \quad 6.615 \quad 7.065 \quad 7.865 \quad 4.435]^T$$

$$M_2 = [5.760 \quad 5.715 \quad 5.705 \quad 4.150 \quad 6.225 \quad 6.960 \quad 6.750 \quad 3.910]^T$$

$$M_4 = [6.610 \quad 5.060 \quad 5.980 \quad 3.975 \quad 9.020 \quad 14.685 \quad 10.640 \quad 4.175]^T$$

$$M_5 = [6.120 \quad 6.285 \quad 5.850 \quad 4.365 \quad 6.340 \quad 4.675 \quad 6.260 \quad 4.440]^T$$

$$\Sigma_1 = \begin{bmatrix} 1.034 & 1.281 & 0.351 & -0.293 & 0.098 & 0.301 & 0.141 & 1.336 \\ & 1.967 & 0.664 & -0.219 & 0.259 & 0.556 & 0.276 & 2.094 \\ & & 7.138 & 1.192 & 2.726 & 1.116 & 0.678 & 2.097 \\ & & & 2.269 & 1.367 & 0.146 & 0.201 & -0.308 \\ & & & & 5.727 & 1.280 & 0.933 & 2.107 \\ & & & & & 2.941 & 1.949 & 2.197 \\ & & & & & & 1.577 & 1.229 \\ & & & & & & & 6.606 \end{bmatrix}$$

$$\Sigma_2 = \begin{bmatrix} 4.792 & 4.417 & 4.244 & 2.406 & 1.798 & 0.790 & 0.785 & 2.993 \\ & 5.074 & 4.636 & 2.798 & 1.824 & 0.639 & 0.644 & 2.799 \\ & & 5.428 & 3.224 & 2.111 & 0.903 & 1.131 & 2.943 \\ & & & 5.287 & 3.006 & 1.326 & 1.897 & 2.648 \\ & & & & 3.574 & 2.229 & 2.471 & 1.915 \\ & & & & & 4.008 & 2.405 & 1.106 \\ & & & & & & 4.507 & 1.727 \\ & & & & & & & 3.972 \end{bmatrix}$$

$$\Sigma_3 = \begin{bmatrix} 1.638 & 2.153 & 1.482 & 1.695 & -0.557 & --2.443 & -0.710 & 1.983 \\ & 3.596 & 2.461 & 2.436 & -0.591 & -3.711 & -0.493 & 2.434 \\ & & 2.500 & 2.834 & -0.665 & -2.621 & 0.248 & 1.738 \\ & & & 4.704 & -0.629 & -2.913 & 0.576 & 2.471 \\ & & & & 19.000 & 0.896 & 8.622 & -0.254 \\ & & & & & 5.856 & 1.357 & -2.915 \\ & & & & & & 20.800 & -0.622 \\ & & & & & & & 3.214 \end{bmatrix}$$

$$\Sigma_4 = \begin{bmatrix} 5.116 & 4.736 & 4.058 & 1.821 & 1.109 & 1.289 & 1.029 & 2.232 \\ & 5.684 & 4.523 & 2.311 & 1.273 & 1.328 & 1.151 & 2.425 \\ & & 6.117 & 2.525 & 1.321 & 1.501 & 1.274 & 2.191 \\ & & & 4.432 & 2.481 & 2.179 & 1.080 & 1.784 \\ & & & & 2.134 & 2.325 & 1.017 & 1.030 \\ & & & & & 4.099 & 2.019 & 1.803 \\ & & & & & & 1.872 & 2.081 \\ & & & & & & & 3.806 \end{bmatrix}$$

Computer Projects

Write the following programs:

2-1 Generate 200 samples according to the parameters of a normal distribution.

Data: Standard Data $i = 1$.

2-2 Calculate the expected vector and the covariance, autocorrelation, and correlation matrices.

Data: 200 samples generated in Project 2-1.

2-3 Calculate the distance of X from M_i by (2-54). Also, calculate the values of the density and distribution functions of $\mathbf{X}$.

Data: Standard Data $i = 1$.

2-4 Calculate the eigenvalues and eigenvectors of the autocorrelation and covariance matrices.

Data: Standard Data $i = 1$.

2-5 Whiten Standard Data $i = 1$.

2-6 Diagonalize Standard Data $i = 1, 2$ simultaneously.

Problems

2-1 The terms $\mathbf{x}_1$ and $\mathbf{x}_2$ are independent random variables, and uniformly distributed between 1 and 3 for $\mathbf{x}_1$ and 2 and 4 for $\mathbf{x}_2$. Three events are defined as $A = \{1 \leq \mathbf{x}_1 \leq 2, 2 \leq \mathbf{x}_2 \leq 4\}$, $B = \{1 \leq \mathbf{x}_1 \leq 3, 2 \leq \mathbf{x}_2 \leq 3\}$ and $C = \{(\mathbf{x}_1 - 2)^2 + (\mathbf{x}_2 - 3)^2 \leq 1\}$.

Calculate the following:

(a) $\Pr\{(B - A) \cdot C\}$; (b) $P(2,3/C)$; (c) $E\{\mathbf{x}_2/B\}$;

(d) $\varphi_{\mathbf{x}_2}(\omega)$; (e) $\Pr\{\mathbf{x}_2 < \mathbf{x}_1\}$.

2-2 In a telegraph system, marks are transmitted with probability 0.4 and spaces with probability 0.6. Because of atmospheric disturbances, marks are received as spaces with probability 0.001, and spaces are received as marks with probability 0.002. Compute the probability that an error is made in any particular transmission.

2-3 Calculate the expected vector and the covariance, autocorrelation, and correlation matrices of the data given by

$$X_1 = [2 \quad 1]^T, \qquad X_2 = [3 \quad 2]^T, \qquad X_4 = [2 \quad 3]^T, \qquad X_4 = [1 \quad 2]^T$$

2-4 Prove the following equalities:

(a) $E\{E\{\mathbf{x}_1/\mathbf{x}_2, \ldots, \mathbf{x}_n\}\} = E\{\mathbf{x}_1\}$;

(b) $E\{\mathbf{x}_1\mathbf{x}_2/\mathbf{x}_3\} = E\{\mathbf{x}_2 E\{\mathbf{x}_1/\mathbf{x}_2, \mathbf{x}_3\}/\mathbf{x}_3\}$.

2-5 The terms $\mathbf{x}_1, \ldots, \mathbf{x}_{100}$ are 100 random variables, mutually independent, indentically distributed, whose density function is normal, with the mean $\eta = 4$ and variance $\sigma = 2$. Find the density function of the sample mean of these random variables

$$\bar{\mathbf{x}} = (\mathbf{x}_1 + \mathbf{x}_2 + \cdots + \mathbf{x}_{100})/100$$

2-6 Find the expected value and variance of a random variable given by $\mathbf{s} = \sum_{i=1}^{\mathbf{n}} \mathbf{x}_i$, where the $\mathbf{x}_i$ are mutually independent, identically distributed, and $\mathbf{n}$ is a random variable ($\mathbf{s}$ is called a random sum).

2-7 The random variables $\mathbf{x}_i$ are independent and their density functions are Cauchy densities as

$$p_i(x) = (\alpha_i/\pi)/(\alpha_i^2 + x^2)$$

Find the density function of $\mathbf{x}_1 + \mathbf{x}_2 + \cdots + \mathbf{x}_n$. (Hint: Use the characteristic functions.)

2-8 The random variables $\mathbf{x}_i$ are independent and uniformly distributed in the $(0, T)$ interval. Calculate and plot the density function of $\mathbf{x}_1 + \mathbf{x}_2 + \mathbf{x}_3$, and see how the central limit theorem works.

2-9 Show the procedure for transforming two symmetric matrices Q_1 and Q_2 to two diagonal matrices $(I + \Lambda)/2$ and $(I - \Lambda)/2$.

2-10 Let Q be a matrix given by $Q = a_1 M_1 M_1^T + a_2 M_2 M_2^T$ where M_1 and M_2 are vectors and a_1 and a_2 are constants: (a) prove that the rank of Q is two; (b) calculate the eigenvalues of Q, using (a); (c) calculate the determinant of Q, using (a).

2-11 The mixture of two distributions is normalized by a linear transformation as

$$P(\omega_1)(\Sigma_1 + M_1 M_1^T) + P(\omega_2)(\Sigma_2 + M_2 M_2^T) \Rightarrow I$$
$$P(\omega_1)M_1 + P(\omega_2)M_2 \Rightarrow 0$$

(a) Calculate $[P(\omega_1)\Sigma_1 + P(\omega_2)\Sigma_2]^{-1}$;

(b) calculate $(M_2 - M_1)^T[P(\omega_1)\Sigma_1 + P(\omega_2)\Sigma_2]^{-1}(M_2 - M_1)$;

(c) calculate $| P(\omega_1)\Sigma_1 + P(\omega_2)\Sigma_2 |$.

Chapter 3

HYPOTHESIS TESTING

The purpose of pattern recognition is to determine to which category or class a given sample belongs. Through an observation or measurement process, we obtain a set of numbers which make up the observation vector. The observation vector serves as the input to a decision rule by which we assign the sample to one of the given classes. Let us assume that the observation vector is a random vector whose conditional density function depends on its class. If the conditional density function for each class is known, then the pattern recognition problem becomes a problem in statistical hypothesis testing.

3.1 Simple Hypothesis Tests

In this section, we discuss the two-class problem, which arises because each sample belongs to one of two classes, ω_1 or ω_2. The conditional density functions and the *a priori* probabilities are assumed to be known.

When $\Sigma_1 = \Sigma_2 = \Sigma$, the boundary becomes a linear function of x_i as

$$h(X) = (M_2 - M_1)^T \Sigma^{-1} X + \tfrac{1}{2}(M_1{}^T \Sigma^{-1} M_1 - M_2{}^T \Sigma^{-1} M_2) \lessgtr \ln \frac{P(\omega_1)}{P(\omega_2)} \rightarrow X \in \begin{cases} \omega_1 \\ \omega_2 \end{cases} \qquad \text{(3-11)}$$

Figure 3-1 shows two-dimensional examples for $\Sigma_1 \neq \Sigma_2$ and $\Sigma_1 = \Sigma_2$.

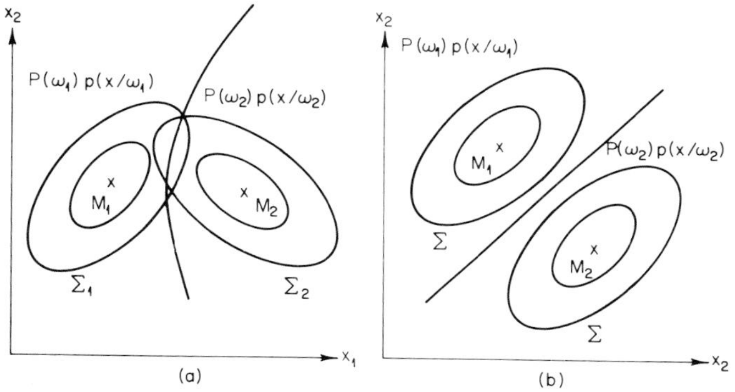

Fig. 3-1 Decision boundaries for normal distributions: (a) $\Sigma_1 \neq \Sigma_2$; (b) $\Sigma_1 = \Sigma_2$.

The Bayes Decision Rule for Minimum Risk

The decision rule of (3-1) was derived by arguing that we should choose the class whose *a posteriori* probability is largest. We also may formulate our decision rule using somewhat different reasoning. Suppose, for a given decision, that we must pay a cost depending on the true class of the sample. There are, then, four such costs:

$$\begin{aligned} c_{11} &= \text{cost of deciding } X \in \omega_1 \quad \text{when} \quad X \in \omega_1 \\ c_{12} &= \text{cost of deciding } X \in \omega_2 \quad \text{when} \quad X \in \omega_1 \\ c_{21} &= \text{cost of deciding } X \in \omega_1 \quad \text{when} \quad X \in \omega_2 \\ c_{22} &= \text{cost of deciding } X \in \omega_2 \quad \text{when} \quad X \in \omega_2 \end{aligned} \qquad \text{(3-12)}$$

We assume that a wrong decision is more expensive than a correct decision, that is,

$$c_{12} > c_{11} \qquad \text{and} \qquad c_{21} > c_{22} \qquad \text{(3-13)}$$

Let Γ_1 and Γ_2 be the regions in the domain of X for which we decide

$X \in \omega_1$ and $X \in \omega_2$, respectively. We want to choose Γ_1 and Γ_2 so as to minimize the *expected cost* or the *risk* r.

$$\begin{aligned}
r &= E\{\text{cost}\} \\
&= \int_{\Gamma_1} c_{11} P(\omega_1/X) p(X)\, dX + \int_{\Gamma_2} c_{12} P(\omega_1/X) p(X)\, dX \\
&\quad + \int_{\Gamma_1} c_{21} P(\omega_2/X) p(X)\, dX + \int_{\Gamma_2} c_{22} P(\omega_2/X) p(X)\, dX \\
&= \int_{\Gamma_1} \{c_{11} P(\omega_1) p(X/\omega_1) + c_{21} P(\omega_2) p(X/\omega_2)\}\, dX \\
&\quad + \int_{\Gamma_2} \{c_{12} P(\omega_1) p(X/\omega_1) + c_{22} P(\omega_2) p(X/\omega_2)\}\, dX
\end{aligned} \tag{3-14}$$

Since Γ_1 and Γ_2 do not overlap and cover the entire domain,

$$\int_{\Gamma_1} p(X/\omega_i)\, dX = 1 - \int_{\Gamma_2} p(X/\omega_i)\, dX \tag{3-15}$$

Using (3-15), (3-14) becomes

$$\begin{aligned}
r &= c_{12} P(\omega_1) + c_{22} P(\omega_2) \\
&\quad + \int_{\Gamma_1} \{-(c_{12} - c_{11}) P(\omega_1) p(X/\omega_1) + (c_{21} - c_{22}) P(\omega_2) p(X/\omega_2)\}\, dX
\end{aligned} \tag{3-16}$$

Now our problem becomes one of choosing Γ_1 such that r is minimized. Suppose, for a given value of X, that the integrand of (3-16) is negative. Then we can decrease r by assigning X to Γ_1. If the integrand is positive, we can decrease r by assigning X to Γ_2. Thus the *minimum risk decision rule* is to assign to Γ_1 those X's, and only those X's, for which the integrand of (3-16) is negative. This decision rule can be stated by the following inequality:

$$(c_{21} - c_{22}) P(\omega_2) p(X/\omega_2) \lessgtr (c_{12} - c_{11}) P(\omega_1) p(X/\omega_1) \qquad \text{for} \quad X \in \begin{cases} \Gamma_1 \\ \Gamma_2 \end{cases} \tag{3-17}$$

or

$$\frac{p(X/\omega_1)}{p(X/\omega_2)} \gtrless \frac{(c_{21} - c_{22}) P(\omega_2)}{(c_{12} - c_{11}) P(\omega_1)} \qquad \text{for} \quad X \in \begin{cases} \Gamma_1 \\ \Gamma_2 \end{cases} \tag{3-18}$$

where $(c_{21} - c_{22})$ and $(c_{12} - c_{11})$ are both positive, from (3-13). This decision rule is called the *Bayes test for minimum risk.*

Comparing (3-18) with (3-4), we notice that the Bayes test for minimum risk is a likelihood ratio test with a different threshold than (3-4) and that the selection of the cost functions is equivalent to the change of *a priori* probabilities $P(\omega_i)$. Equation (3-18) is equal to (3-4) for the special selection of the cost functions

$$c_{12} - c_{11} = c_{21} - c_{22} \tag{3-19}$$

This is called a *symmetrical cost function.* For a symmetrical cost function, the cost becomes the probability of error, and the test of (3-4) minimizes the probability of error.

Different cost functions are used when a wrong decision for one class is more critical than one for the other class.

The Neyman–Pearson Test

The Neyman–Pearson test follows from a third formulation of the hypothesis test problem. Recall that we can commit two types of errors in a two-class decision problem. Let the probabilities of these two errors again be ε_1 and ε_2. The *Neyman–Pearson decision rule* is the one which minimizes ε_1, subject to ε_2 being equal to a constant, say ε_0. To determine this decision rule, we must find the minimum of

$$r = \varepsilon_1 + \mu(\varepsilon_2 - \varepsilon_0) \tag{3-20}$$

where μ is a Lagrange multiplier. Inserting ε_1 and ε_2 of (3-7) into (3-20),

$$\begin{aligned} r &= \int_{\Gamma_2} p(X/\omega_1)\, dX + \mu\left\{\int_{\Gamma_1} p(X/\omega_2)\, dX - \varepsilon_0\right\} \\ &= (1 - \mu\varepsilon_0) + \int_{\Gamma_1} \{\mu p(X/\omega_2) - p(X/\omega_1)\}\, dX \end{aligned} \tag{3-21}$$

Using the same argument as in the derivation of (3-17) from (3-16), r can be minimized by selecting Γ_1 and Γ_2 as

$$\mu p(X/\omega_2) \lesseqgtr p(X/\omega_1) \qquad \text{for} \quad X \in \begin{cases} \Gamma_1 \\ \Gamma_2 \end{cases} \tag{3-22}$$

or

$$\frac{p(X/\omega_1)}{p(X/\omega_2)} \gtrless \mu \qquad \text{for} \quad X \in \begin{cases} \Gamma_1 \\ \Gamma_2 \end{cases} \tag{3-23}$$

Comparing (3-23) with (3-18), we can conclude that the Neyman–Pearson test does not offer any new decision rule but relies on the likelihood ratio test, as did the Bayes test. However, the preceding discussion shows that the likelihood ratio test is the test which minimizes the error for one class, while maintaining the error for the other class constant.

The threshold μ is the solution, for a given ε_0, of the following equation:

$$\varepsilon_2 = \int_{\Gamma_1} p(X/\omega_2)\, dX = \varepsilon_0 \tag{3-24}$$

Or, using the density function of the likelihood ratio,

$$\varepsilon_2 = \int_{\mu}^{+\infty} p(l/\omega_2)\, dl = \varepsilon_0 \tag{3-25}$$

Since $p(l/\omega_2) \geq 0$, ε_2 of (3-25) is a monotonic function of μ, that is, as μ increases ε_2 decreases. Therefore, after calculating ε_2's for several μ's, we can find the μ which gives a specified ε_0 as ε_2. However, it is not easy to obtain the explicit solution of (3-25).

EXAMPLE 3-2 Let us consider two-dimensional normal distributions with $M_1 = [-1,0]^T$, $M_2 = [+1,0]^T$, $\Sigma_1 = \Sigma_2 = I$, and $P(\omega_1) = P(\omega_2) = 0.5$. Then, from (3-11) and (3-23), the decision boundaries can be expressed by

$$\begin{aligned} h(X) &= \{[+1 \quad 0] - [-1 \quad 0]\}\begin{bmatrix} x_1 \\ x_2 \end{bmatrix} \\ &\quad + \frac{1}{2}\left\{[-1 \quad 0]\begin{bmatrix} -1 \\ 0 \end{bmatrix} - [+1 \quad 0]\begin{bmatrix} +1 \\ 0 \end{bmatrix}\right\} \\ &= 2x_1 \lessgtr \ln \mu \end{aligned} \tag{3-26}$$

The decision boundaries for various μ's are the lines parallel to the x_2 axis, as is shown in Fig. 3-2, and the corresponding errors ε_2 are given in

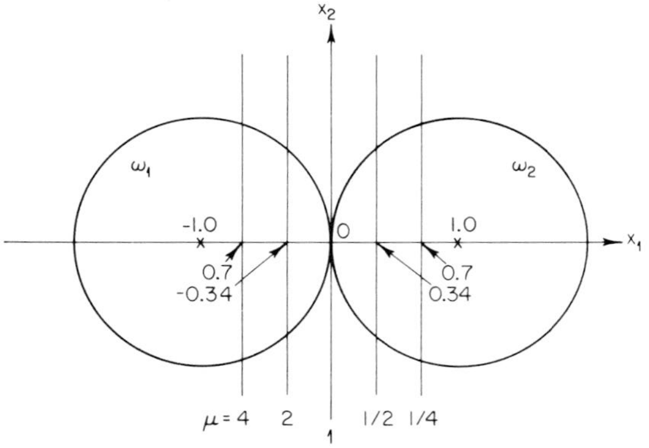

Fig. 3-2 Neyman–Pearson boundaries.

TABLE 3-1

RELATION BETWEEN μ AND ε_2

μ:	4	2	1	$\frac{1}{2}$	$\frac{1}{4}$
ε_2:	0.04	0.09	0.16	0.25	0.38

Table 3-1. For example, if we would like to maintain $\varepsilon_2 = 0.09$, then μ becomes 2 from Table 3-1, and the decision boundary passes (—0.34) of x_1.

The Minimax Test

In the Bayes test for minimum risk, we notice that we computed the likelihood ratio and compared the result with a threshold value which is a function of $P(\omega_i)$. Therefore, as long as the $P(\omega_i)$'s do not vary, our decision rule always gives the minimum risk. However, if the $P(\omega_i)$'s vary, the fixed threshold value no longer gives the minimum attainable risk. The *minimax test* is used to design the threshold value so that, even if the $P(\omega_i)$'s vary, we can minimize the maximum possible risk.

First, let us express the expected cost r of (3-14) in terms of $P(\omega_i)$. Since $P(\omega_1) + P(\omega_2) = 1$, $P(\omega_2)$ is uniquely determined by $P(\omega_1)$. Using (3-15),

$$r = c_{22} + (c_{21} - c_{22}) \int_{\Gamma_1} p(X/\omega_2)\, dX + P(\omega_1)\Big[(c_{11} - c_{22}) + (c_{12} - c_{11}) \times \int_{\Gamma_2} p(X/\omega_1)\, dX - (c_{21} - c_{22}) \int_{\Gamma_1} p(X/\omega_2)\, dX\Big] \tag{3-27}$$

Equation (3-27) shows that, once Γ_1 and Γ_2 are determined, r is a linear function of $P(\omega_1)$. In Fig. 3-3a, the curved line represents the Bayes risk plotted against $P(\omega_1)$, where Γ_1 and Γ_2 are selected for each $P(\omega_1)$. Fixing Γ_1 and Γ_2 means that the decision will be optimum only for one value of $P(\omega_1)$ which we shall designate $P^*(\omega_1)$. With Γ_1 and Γ_2 fixed, r changes with $P(\omega_1)$ as the straight line shown in Fig. 3-3a. This line is the tangent of the Bayes risk curve at $P^*(\omega_1)$. If we select Γ_1 and Γ_2 to make the coefficient of $P(\omega_1)$ zero in (3-27), the straight line becomes the tangent at the point where the Bayes risk curve is maximum, as shown in Fig. 3-3b. This selection of Γ_1 and Γ_2 also guarantees that the maximum Bayes risk is minimized after the threshold value is fixed, regardless of the change of $P(\omega_1)$.

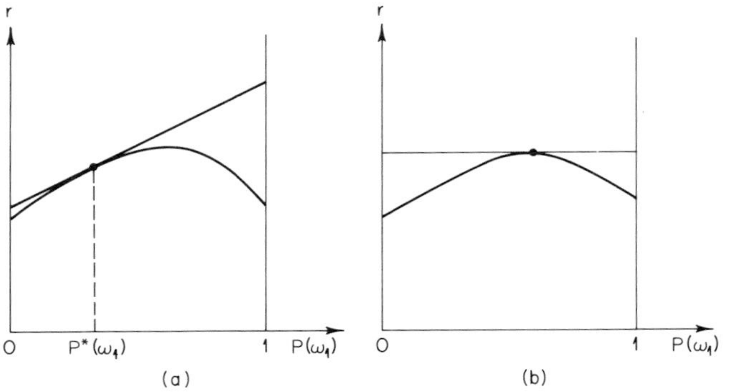

Fig. 3-3 The Bayes risk vs $P(\omega_1)$.

Thus, in the minimax test, the boundary is designed to satisfy

$$(c_{11} - c_{22}) + (c_{12} - c_{11}) \int_{\Gamma_2} p(X/\omega_1)\, dX - (c_{21} - c_{22}) \int_{\Gamma_1} p(X/\omega_2)\, dX = 0 \tag{3-28}$$

If we select the special set of cost functions

$$c_{11} = c_{22} = 0 \qquad \text{and} \qquad c_{12} = c_{21} \tag{3-29}$$

(3-28) becomes

$$\int_{\Gamma_2} p(X/\omega_1)\, dX = \int_{\Gamma_1} p(X/\omega_2)\, dX \tag{3-30}$$

That is, the decision boundary is selected such that the errors from both classes are equal.

When the decision boundary which satisfies (3-28) does not exist, the maximum risk exists for either $P(\omega_1) = 0$ or $P(\omega_1) = 1$. Therefore, we can

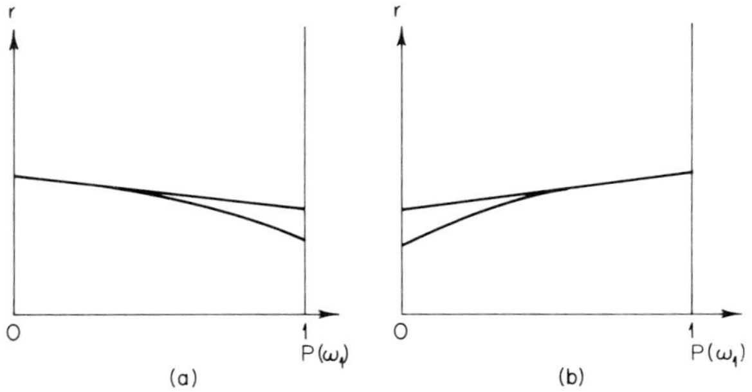

Fig. 3-4. $P(\omega_1) = 0$ or 1 for the minimax test.

design the Bayes boundary for either $P(\omega_1) = 0$ or $P(\omega_1) = 1$, whichever gives the larger risk, and automatically minimize the maximum risk. Examples are shown in Fig. 3-4a and b.

3.2 Error Probability in Hypothesis Testing

Associated with any decision rule is a *probability of error*. The probability of error is the most effective measure of a decision rule's usefulness. In general, the calculation of error probability is very difficult, although the concept is quite simple. In order to evaluate (3-6) and (3-7), we must perform an n-dimensional integration. On the other hand, if we want to evaluate (3-8) and (3-9), we need to know the density function of the likelihood ratio. Neither approach generally leads to straightforward calculations. Thus, in many practical problems, we either employ experimental techniques, such as Monte Carlo simulation, or we seek bounds on the error probabilities. We will discuss error bounds in the next section.

Linear Boundaries

When the distributions are normal, with equal covariance matrices $\Sigma_1 = \Sigma_2 = \Sigma$, the minus-log-likelihood ratio becomes a linear function of X; this was shown in (3-11). Since (3-11) is a linear transformation from an n-dimensional space to one dimension, $h(\mathbf{X})$ is a normal random variable, when $\mathbf{X}$ is a normally distributed random vector. The expected value and variance of $h(\mathbf{X})$ can be calculated as follows:

$$\begin{aligned}\eta_i &= E\{h(\mathbf{X})/\omega_i\} \\ &= (M_2 - M_1)^T\Sigma^{-1}E\{\mathbf{X}/\omega_i\} + \tfrac{1}{2}(M_1{}^T\Sigma^{-1}M_1 - M_2{}^T\Sigma^{-1}M_2) \qquad (3\text{-}31)\end{aligned}$$

Since $E\{\mathbf{X}/\omega_i\} = M_i$, (3-31) becomes

$$\eta_1 = -\tfrac{1}{2}(M_2 - M_1)^T\Sigma^{-1}(M_2 - M_1) = -\eta \qquad (3\text{-}32)$$

$$\eta_2 = +\tfrac{1}{2}(M_2 - M_1)^T\Sigma^{-1}(M_2 - M_1) = +\eta \qquad (3\text{-}33)$$

Also,

$$\begin{aligned}\sigma_i^2 &= E[\{h(\mathbf{X}) - \eta_i\}^2/\omega_i] \\ &= E[\{(M_2 - M_1)^T\Sigma^{-1}(\mathbf{X} - M_i)\}^2/\omega_i] \\ &= (M_2 - M_1)^T\Sigma^{-1}E\{(\mathbf{X} - M_i)(\mathbf{X} - M_i)^T/\omega_i\}\Sigma^{-1}(M_2 - M_1) \\ &= (M_2 - M_1)^T\Sigma^{-1}(M_2 - M_1) = 2\eta \qquad (3\text{-}34)\end{aligned}$$

The above holds because $E\{(\mathbf{X} - M_i)(\mathbf{X} - M_i)^T/\omega_i\}$ is $\Sigma_i(= \Sigma)$, as was shown in (2-28).

Figure 3-5 shows the density functions of $h(\mathbf{X})$ for ω_1 and ω_2, and the hatched parts correspond to the error probabilities which are due to the Bayes test for minimum error. Therefore,

$$\varepsilon_1 = \int_t^{\infty} p(h/\omega_1)\, dh = \int_{(\eta+t)/\sigma}^{+\infty} (2\pi)^{-1/2} \exp(-\xi^2/2)\, d\xi = \tfrac{1}{2} - \operatorname{erf}[(\eta + t)/\sigma] \tag{3-35}$$

$$\varepsilon_2 = \int_{-\infty}^{t} p(h/\omega_2)\, dh = \int_{(\eta-t)/\sigma}^{+\infty} (2\pi)^{-1/2} \exp(-\xi^2/2)\, d\xi = \tfrac{1}{2} - \operatorname{erf}[(\eta - t)/\sigma] \tag{3-36}$$

where

$$t = \ln\{P(\omega_1)/P(\omega_2)\} \tag{3-37}$$

$$\sigma^2 = \sigma_1^{\,2} = \sigma_2^{\,2} = 2\eta \tag{3-38}$$

Thus, when the density function of the likelihood ratio is normal, the probabilities of error can be obtained from the table of erf($\cdot$)—the *error function*—since the likelihood ratio is a one-dimensional normal random variable.

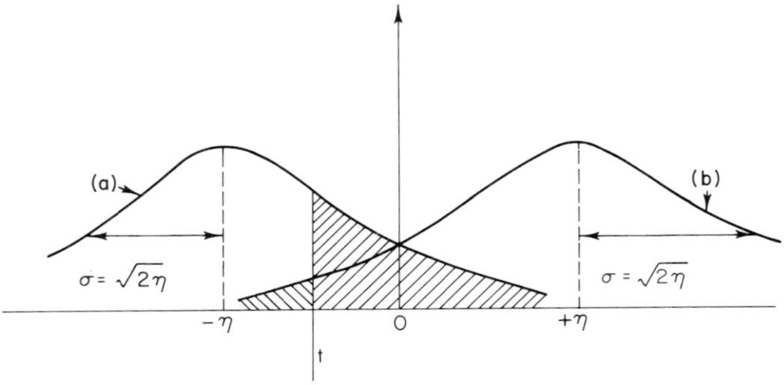

Fig. 3-5 Density function of $h(\mathbf{X})$, where $t = \ln\{P(\omega_1)/P(\omega_2)\}$: (a) $p(h/\omega_1)$; (b) $p(h/\omega_2)$.

Independent Random Variables

When the n random variables of the vector $\mathbf{X}$ are independent, the density function of $\mathbf{X}$ can be expressed as the product of the density functions of the individual random variables:

$$p(X/\omega_i) = \prod_{l=1}^{n} p(x_l/\omega_i) \tag{3-39}$$

Therefore, the minus-log–likelihood ratio $h(\mathbf{X})$ is

$$h(\mathbf{X}) = \sum_{l=1}^{n} h(\mathbf{x}_l) \tag{3-40}$$

where

$$h(\mathbf{x}_l) = -\ln \frac{p(\mathbf{x}_l/\omega_1)}{p(\mathbf{x}_l/\omega_2)} \tag{3-41}$$

The random variable $h(\mathbf{X})$ is the summation of n random variables $h(\mathbf{x}_l)$'s.

According to the central limit theorem, the density function of $h(\mathbf{X})$ tends toward a normal distribution regardless of the density functions of $h(\mathbf{x}_l)$ when n is large. Hence, we can approximately calculate the errors by (3-35) and (3-36), if we obtain the expected value and variance of $h(\mathbf{X})$ by

$$\eta_i = E\{h(\mathbf{X})/\omega_i\} = \sum_{l=1}^{n} E\{h(\mathbf{x}_l)/\omega_i\} = \sum_{l=1}^{n} \eta_{il} \qquad (i = 1, 2) \tag{3-42}$$

$$\begin{aligned} \sigma_i^2 &= E[\{h(\mathbf{X}) - \eta_i\}^2/\omega_i] = \sum_{l=1}^{n} E[\{h(\mathbf{x}_l) - \eta_{il}\}^2/\omega_i] \\ &= \sum_{l=1}^{n} \sigma_{il}^2 \qquad (i = 1, 2) \end{aligned} \tag{3-43}$$

Since η_{il} and σ_{il}^2 are functions of one random variable $\mathbf{x}_l$, the calculation of these parameters is, in most cases, relatively easy, even for nonnormal cases.

When n is small and the central limit theorem does not hold, we calculate the density function of $h(\mathbf{X})$, and subsequently the errors, by using the characteristic function as follows. The characteristic function of $h(\mathbf{X})$ for $\mathbf{X} \in \omega_i$, $\varphi_i(\omega)$, is the product of the characteristic functions of $h(\mathbf{x}_l)$'s for $\mathbf{X} \in \omega_i$, $\varphi_{il}(\omega)$'s, when $h(X)$ is expressed by (3-40):

$$\varphi_i(\omega) = \prod_{l=1}^{n} \varphi_{il}(\omega) \tag{3-44}$$

where

$$\varphi_{il}(\omega) = E\{\exp[j\omega h(\mathbf{x}_l)]/\omega_i\} = \int_{-\infty}^{+\infty} \exp[j\omega h(x_l)] p(x_l/\omega_i)\, dx_l \tag{3-45}$$

By using the absolute values and phase angles of these complex functions of ω,

$$|\varphi_i(\omega)| \exp[j \angle\varphi_i(\omega)] = \left\{\prod_{l=1}^{n} |\varphi_{il}(\omega)|\right\} \exp\left\{j \sum_{l=1}^{n} \angle\varphi_{il}(\omega)\right\} \tag{3-46}$$

Therefore, when we calculate $|\varphi_{il}(\omega)|$ and $\angle\varphi_{il}(\omega)$ from (3-45), $|\varphi_i(\omega)|$ and $\angle\varphi_i(\omega)$ can be computed by (3-46).

Once the characteristic function of $h(\mathbf{X})$ is obtained, the density function of $h(\mathbf{X})$ is the inverse Fourier transform (except for the sign of ω).

$$p(h/\omega_i) = (2\pi)^{-1} \int_{-\infty}^{+\infty} \varphi_i(\omega) \exp(-j\omega h)\, d\omega \tag{3-47}$$

On the other hand, the probabilities of errors, from (3-8) and (3-9), are

$$\varepsilon_1 = \int_t^{+\infty} p(h/\omega_1)\, dh = \left\{1 - \int_{-\infty}^t p(h/\omega_1)\, dh\right\} \tag{3-48}$$

$$\varepsilon_2 = \int_{-\infty}^t p(h/\omega_2)\, dh \tag{3-49}$$

where

$$t = \ln\{P(\omega_1)/P(\omega_2)\} \tag{3-50}$$

The integration in (3-48) and (3-49) can also be performed in the frequency domain. By a familiar rule of the Fourier transform,

$$\begin{aligned}\int_{-\infty}^t p(h/\omega_i)\, dh &= \frac{\varphi_i(0)}{2} + \frac{1}{2\pi} \int_{-\infty}^{+\infty} \frac{\varphi_i(\omega)}{j\omega} \exp(-\, j\omega t)\, d\omega \\ &= \frac{\varphi_i(0)}{2} + \frac{1}{\pi} \int_0^{+\infty} \frac{\text{Im}[\varphi_i(\omega) \exp(-\, j\omega t)]}{\omega}\, d\omega \end{aligned} \tag{3-51}$$

where the real and imaginary parts of $\varphi_i(\omega) \exp(-j\omega t)$ are even and odd functions, respectively. Since $\varphi_i(0) = 1$ from (3-44) and (3-45), (3-51) can be reduced to

$$\int_{-\infty}^t p(h/\omega_i)\, dh = \frac{1}{2} + \frac{1}{\pi} \int_0^{\infty} \frac{\prod_{l=1}^{n} |\varphi_{il}(\omega)|}{\omega} \sin\left\{\left[\sum_{l=1}^{n} \angle\varphi_{il}(\omega)\right] - \omega t\right\} d\omega \tag{3-52}$$

In most applications, integration in (3-52) would be carried out numerically, even if $\varphi_i(\omega)$ could be obtained in an explicit mathematical expression. However, the integral is one dimensional, and hence the above calculation is manageable.

Probability of Error for Normal X

When the distributions are normal, we can always find a linear transformation which diagonalizes the two covariance matrices simultaneously. Therefore, we can always satisfy the independent assumption in the transformed coordinate system. Besides, the errors are invariant under any transformation because the likelihood ratio is independent of any coordinate systems. Let D_1, D_2, and I, Λ be the expected vectors and covariance matrices of ω_1 and ω_2, respectively, for a new random vector **Y** after the transformation. From (3-10),

$$\begin{aligned} h(Y) &= \tfrac{1}{2}(Y - D_1)^T I^{-1}(Y - D_1) - \tfrac{1}{2}(Y - D_2)^T \Lambda^{-1}(Y - D_2) + \tfrac{1}{2}\ln\{|I|/|\Lambda|\} \\ &= \sum_{l=1}^{n} [\tfrac{1}{2}(y_l - d_{1l})^2 - \tfrac{1}{2}(y_l - d_{2l})^2/\lambda_l - \tfrac{1}{2}\ln\lambda_l] \end{aligned} \tag{3-53}$$

where d_{il} is the lth component of D_i.

Hence,

$$h(y_l) = \tfrac{1}{2}[(y_l - d_{1l})^2 - (y_l - d_{2l})^2/\lambda_l - \ln\lambda_l] \tag{3-54}$$

The characteristic function φ_{1l} is

$$\begin{aligned} \varphi_{1l}(\omega) &= \int_{-\infty}^{+\infty} \exp\left[\frac{j\omega}{2}\left\{(y_l - d_{1l})^2 - \frac{(y_l - d_{2l})^2}{\lambda_l} - \ln\lambda_l\right\}\right] \\ &\quad \times \frac{1}{(2\pi)^{1/2}} \exp\left[-\frac{(y_l - d_{1l})^2}{2}\right] dy_l \\ &= \frac{1}{(1 - j\omega a_{1l})^{1/2}} \exp\left[\frac{-b_{1l}^2\omega^2}{2(1 - j\omega a_{1l})} - \frac{j\omega}{2} h_{1l}\right] \\ &\quad \times \frac{(1 - j\omega a_{1l})^{1/2}}{(2\pi)^{1/2}} \int_{-\infty}^{+\infty} \exp\left[-\tfrac{1}{2}(1 - j\omega a_{1l})\right. \\ &\quad \times \left.\left\{(y_l - d_{1l}) - \frac{j\omega b_{1l}}{1 - j\omega a_{1l}}\right\}^2\right] dy_l \\ &= \frac{1}{(1 - j\omega a_{1l})^{1/2}} \exp\left[\frac{-b_{1l}^2\omega^2}{2(1 - j\omega a_{1l})} - \frac{j\omega}{2} h_{1l}\right] \end{aligned} \tag{3-55}$$

where

$$a_{1l} = 1 - 1/\lambda_l \tag{3-56}$$

$$b_{1l} = (1/\lambda_l)(d_{2l} - d_{1l}) \tag{3-57}$$

$$h_{1l} = b_{1l}^2/(1 - a_{1l}) + \ln\lambda_l \tag{3-58}$$

The absolute value and phase angle of (3-55) are

$$|\varphi_{1l}(\omega)| = (1 + \omega^2 a_{1l}^2)^{-1/4} \exp[\tfrac{1}{2}(-b_{1l}^2\omega^2)/(1 + \omega^2 a_{1l}^2)] \tag{3-59}$$

$$\angle\varphi_{1l} = \tfrac{1}{2}\tan^{-1}(a_{1l}\omega) - \tfrac{1}{2}\omega[h_{1l} + (a_{1l}b_{1l}^2\omega^2)/(1 + \omega^2 a_{1l}^2)] \tag{3-60}$$

For $\varphi_{2l}(\omega)$,

$$\varphi_{2l}(\omega) = \int_{-\infty}^{+\infty} \exp\left[\frac{j\omega}{2}\left\{(y_l - d_{1l})^2 - \frac{(y_l - d_{2l})^2}{\lambda_l} - \ln \lambda_l\right\}\right] \times \frac{1}{(2\pi)^{1/2}\lambda_l} \exp\left[-\frac{(y_l - d_{2l})^2}{2\lambda_l}\right] dy_l$$

$$= \frac{1}{(1 - j\omega a_{2l})^{1/2}} \exp\left[\frac{-b_{2l}^2\omega^2}{2(1 - j\omega a_{2l})} - \frac{j\omega}{2} h_{2l}\right] \tag{3-61}$$

where

$$a_{2l} = \lambda_l - 1 \tag{3-62}$$

$$b_{2l} = (\lambda_l)^{1/2}(d_{2l} - d_{1l}) \tag{3-63}$$

$$h_{2l} = -b_{2l}^2/(1 + a_{2l}) + \ln \lambda_l \tag{3-64}$$

Equation (3-61) is identical with (3-55), except that a_{1l}, b_{1l}, and h_{1l} are replaced by a_{2l}, b_{2l}, and h_{2l}. Therefore, we can have the same functional form for $|\varphi_{2l}(\omega)|$ and $\angle\varphi_{2l}(\omega)$ as $|\varphi_{1l}(\omega)|$ and $\angle\varphi_{1l}(\omega)$, except for these parameters.

Thus, when the distributions are normal, we can calculate the error probabilities by the following procedure [Fukunaga, 1969].

(1) Apply a linear transformation to diagonalize the covariance matrices of ω_1 and ω_2 simultaneously.

(2) Calculate the characteristic functions of $h(\mathbf{x}_l)$ for ω_1 and ω_2 by (3-55) and (3-61).

(3) Compute the errors by (3-48), (3-49), and (3-52). (A one-dimensional numerical integral is involved for the error from each class.)

When $\Sigma_1 \cong \Sigma$ and $\Sigma_2 \cong \Sigma$, Λ approaches I and both a_{1l} and a_{2l} ($l = 1, 2, \ldots, n$) approach 0. Then,

$$\varphi_1(\omega) \cong \exp\left[-\tfrac{1}{2}\omega^2 \sum_{l=1}^{n} (d_{2l} - d_{1l})^2 - \tfrac{1}{2} j\omega \sum_{l=1}^{n} (d_{2l} - d_{1l})^2\right] \tag{3-65}$$

$$\varphi_2(\omega) \cong \exp\left[-\tfrac{1}{2}\omega^2 \sum_{l=1}^{n} (d_{2l} - d_{1l})^2 + \tfrac{1}{2} j\omega \sum_{l=1}^{n} (d_{2l} - d_{1l})^2\right] \tag{3-66}$$

Both $\varphi_1(\omega)$ and $\varphi_2(\omega)$ are the characteristic functions of normal distributions whose expected values and variances are

$$\eta_1 = -\tfrac{1}{2}\| D_2 - D_1 \|^2 = -\tfrac{1}{2}(M_2 - M_1)^T\Sigma^{-1}(M_2 - M_1) \tag{3-67}$$

$$\eta_2 = +\tfrac{1}{2}\| D_2 - D_1 \|^2 = +\tfrac{1}{2}(M_2 - M_1)^T\Sigma^{-1}(M_2 - M_1) \tag{3-68}$$

$$\sigma_1^2 = \sigma_2^2 = \| D_2 - D_1 \|^2 = (M_2 - M_1)^T\Sigma^{-1}(M_2 - M_1) \tag{3-69}$$

where the right side of each of the above equations shows the distance function before the transformation. These results are identical with those of (3-32), (3-33), and (3-34).

Even when Σ_1 and Σ_2 are fairly different, we still may obtain a rough approximation of the error probability, by assuming that $h(\mathbf{X})$ is normally distributed. The expected values and variances can be calculated since we have the characteristic functions. The results are

$$E\{h(\mathbf{X})/\omega_1\} = \tfrac{1}{2}\operatorname{tr}\{I - \Sigma_2^{-1}\Sigma_1\} - \tfrac{1}{2}(M_1 - M_2)^T\Sigma_2^{-1}(M_1 - M_2) + \tfrac{1}{2}\ln\{|\Sigma_1|/|\Sigma_2|\} \tag{3-70}$$

$$E\{h(\mathbf{X})/\omega_2\} = \tfrac{1}{2}\operatorname{tr}\{\Sigma_1^{-1}\Sigma_2 - I\} + \tfrac{1}{2}(M_1 - M_2)^T\Sigma_1^{-1}(M_1 - M_2) + \tfrac{1}{2}\ln\{|\Sigma_1|/|\Sigma_2|\} \tag{3-71}$$

$$\operatorname{Var}\{h(\mathbf{X})/\omega_1\} = \tfrac{1}{2}\operatorname{tr}\{(I - \Sigma_2^{-1}\Sigma_1)^2\} + (M_1 - M_2)^T\Sigma_2^{-1}\Sigma_1\Sigma_2^{-1}(M_1 - M_2) \tag{3-72}$$

$$\operatorname{Var}\{h(\mathbf{X})/\omega_2\} = \tfrac{1}{2}\operatorname{tr}\{(\Sigma_1^{-1}\Sigma_2 - I)^2\} + (M_1 - M_2)^T\Sigma_1^{-1}\Sigma_2\Sigma_1^{-1}(M_1 - M_2) \tag{3-73}$$

Or, in terms of λ_i and $(d_{2i} - d_{1i})$,

$$E\{h(\mathbf{X})/\omega_1\} = \tfrac{1}{2}\sum_{l=1}^{n}[(1 - 1/\lambda_l) - (d_{2l} - d_{1l})^2/\lambda_l + \ln(1/\lambda_l)] \tag{3-74}$$

$$E\{h(\mathbf{X})/\omega_2\} = \tfrac{1}{2}\sum_{l=1}^{n}[(\lambda_l - 1) + (d_{2l} - d_{1l})^2 + \ln(1/\lambda_l)] \tag{3-75}$$

$$\operatorname{Var}\{h(\mathbf{X})/\omega_1\} = \tfrac{1}{2}\sum_{l=1}^{n}[(1 - 1/\lambda_l)^2 + (d_{2l} - d_{1l})^2/\lambda_l^2] \tag{3-76}$$

$$\operatorname{Var}\{h(\mathbf{X})/\omega_2\} = \tfrac{1}{2}\sum_{l=1}^{n}[(\lambda_l - 1)^2 + \lambda_l(d_{2l} - d_{1l})^2] \tag{3-77}$$

Substituting these results into (3-35) and (3-36), the probabilities of error can be roughly approximated.

Since the higher-order moments are also available from the characteristic function, it is theoretically possible to improve the approximation by using a series of Hermite polynomials whose coefficients are functions of the moments [Fisher, 1923; Papoulis, 1965]. However, our experience has shown that the convergence of the series is very slow and that many higher-order moments are required in order to reach convergence, unless all λ_i's are close to 1.

EXAMPLE 3-3 Let us examine Standard Data $i = 1, 2$, whose parameters after the transformation are given in Table 3-2. The λ's are widely distributed from 12.06 to 0.12. Assuming $P(\omega_1) = P(\omega_2) = 0.5$, the density functions of

TABLE 3-2

STANDARD DATA $i = 1, 2$ AFTER SIMULTANEOUS DIAGONALIZATION

l:	1	2	3	4	5	6	7	8
λ_l:	8.41	12.06	0.12	0.22	1.49	1.77	0.35	2.73
$d_{2l} - d_{1l}$:	3.86	3.10	0.84	0.84	1.64	1.08	0.26	0.01

$h(\mathbf{X})$ for ω_1 and ω_2 are calculated by (3-47), and are shown in Fig. 3-6. As seen in Fig. 3-6, these density functions are skewed from a normal distribution. Table 3-3 shows the comparison between the exact calculation of the errors by (3-48), (3-49), and (3-52) and the results of normal approximation by using the parameters of (3-74) through (3-77).

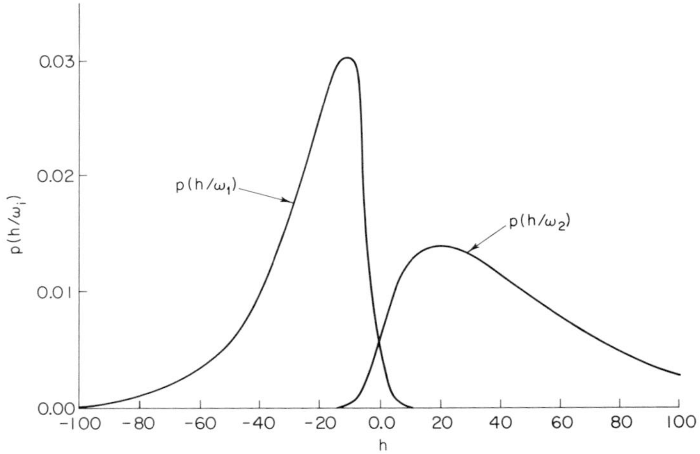

Fig. 3-6 Density functions of h ($\mathbf{X}$) [Fukunaga, 1969].

TABLE 3-3

COMPARISON OF ERROR CALCULATIONS[a]

	ε_1 (%)	ε_2 (%)	$\frac{1}{2}(\varepsilon_1 + \varepsilon_2)$
Exact calculation	1.6	2.2	1.9
Normal approximation	10.0	10.2	10.1

[a] [Fukunaga, 1969].

3.3 Upper Bounds on Error Probability

It is evident from the preceding discussion that calculation of error probability is, in general, a difficult task. Even when the observation vectors have a normal distribution, we must resort to numerical techniques. However, a closed-form expression for the error probability is the most desirable solution for a number of reasons. Not only is the computational effort greatly reduced, since we need only to evaluate a formula, but, more importantly, the use of the closed-form solution provides insight into the mechanisms causing the errors. This information is useful later when we consider the problem of feature selection.

When we cannot obtain a closed-form expression for the error probability, we may take some other approach. We may seek either an approximate expression for the error probability, or an upper bound on the error probability. In this section, we will discuss some *upper bound of error probability*.

The Chernoff Bound

Let us consider the characteristic function of $h(\mathbf{X})$ for ω_1, $\varphi_1(\omega)$:

$$\varphi_1(\omega) = \int_{-\infty}^{+\infty} \exp(j\omega h)p(h/\omega_1)\, dh \tag{3-78}$$

We may also get the *moment-generating function* of $h(\mathbf{X})$ by replacing $j\omega$ of (3-78) by a real number s:

$$\varphi_1(s) = \int_{-\infty}^{+\infty} \exp(sh)p(h/\omega_1)\, dh \tag{3-79}$$

Or, taking the minus logarithm of $\varphi_1(s)$,

$$\mu(s) = -\ln \varphi_1(s) = -\ln \int_{-\infty}^{+\infty} \exp(sh)p(h/\omega_1)\, dh \tag{3-80}$$

Let us introduce a new random variable $\mathbf{g}$ with the following density function:

$$p_{\mathbf{g}}(g = h/\omega_1) = [\exp(sh)/\varphi_1(s)]p(h/\omega_1) = \exp[sh + \mu(s)]p(h/\omega_1) \tag{3-81}$$

From (3-79), we can confirm that (3-81) is a density function because

$$\int_{-\infty}^{+\infty} p_{\mathbf{g}}(g = h/\omega_1)\, dh = [1/\varphi_1(s)] \int_{-\infty}^{+\infty} \exp(sh)p(h/\omega_1)\, dh = 1 \tag{3-82}$$

Also, $\mathbf{g}$ has the expected value and variance given by

$$E\{\mathbf{g}/\omega_1\} = \int_{-\infty}^{+\infty} hp_{\mathbf{g}}(g = h/\omega_1)\, dh = -d\mu(s)/ds \tag{3-83}$$

$$\sigma_{\mathbf{g}}^2 = -d^2\mu(s)/ds^2 \tag{3-84}$$

Now we rewrite ε_1 of (3-48) in terms of $p_{\mathbf{g}}(g = h/\omega_1)$.

$$\begin{aligned}\varepsilon_1 &= \int_t^{+\infty} p(h/\omega_1)\, dh = \int_t^{+\infty} \exp[-\mu(s) - sh]p_{\mathbf{g}}(g = h/\omega_1)\, dh \\ &= \exp[-\mu(s)] \int_t^{+\infty} \exp(-sh)p_{\mathbf{g}}(g = h/\omega_1)\, dh \end{aligned} \tag{3-85}$$

We now can obtain an upper bound of ε_1. For $s \geq 0$

$$\exp(-sh) \leq \exp(-st) \qquad \text{for} \quad h \geq t \tag{3-86}$$

Therefore,

$$\varepsilon_1 \leq \exp[-\mu(s) - st] \int_t^{+\infty} p_{\mathbf{g}}(g = h/\omega_1)\, dh \tag{3-87}$$

Since the integral of (3-87) is less than 1,

$$\varepsilon_1 \leq \exp[-\mu(s) - st] \tag{3-88}$$

Although (3-88) gives the upper boundary of ε_1 for any $s \geq 0$, the optimum boundary can be found by minimizing $-\mu(s) - st$ with respect to s.

That is, the optimum s should satisfy

$$-d\mu(s)/ds = t \tag{3-89}$$

The upper bound of (3-88) with the optimum s is called the *Chernoff bound* [Chernoff, 1962]. Equations (3-83) and (3-89) show that s is chosen to make the expected value of $\mathbf{g}$ equal to the threshold value.

The same reasoning applies for ε_2. Let us express $\varphi_1(s)$ and $\varphi_2(s)$ in terms of $p(X/\omega_1)$ and $p(X/\omega_2)$:

$$\begin{aligned}\varphi_1(s) &= \int_{\mathscr{S}} \exp\left[-s \ln \frac{p(X/\omega_1)}{p(X/\omega_2)}\right] p(X/\omega_1)\, dX \\ &= \int_{\mathscr{S}} \left[\frac{p(X/\omega_1)}{p(X/\omega_2)}\right]^{-s} p(X/\omega_1)\, dX \\ &= \int_{\mathscr{S}} p(X/\omega_1)^{1-s}\, p(X/\omega_2)^s\, dX \end{aligned} \tag{3-90}$$

$$\begin{aligned}\varphi_2(s) &= \int_{\mathscr{S}} \exp\left[-s \ln \frac{p(X/\omega_1)}{p(X/\omega_2)}\right] p(X/\omega_2)\, dX \\ &= \int_{\mathscr{S}} p(X/\omega_1)^{-s}\, p(X/\omega_2)^{1+s}\, dX \end{aligned} \tag{3-91}$$

Comparing (3-90) and (3-91), we notice that both integrands are related by

$$p(X/\omega_1)^{-s} p(X/\omega_2)^{1+s} = p(X/\omega_1)^{1-s} p(X/\omega_2)^{s} \left[\frac{p(X/\omega_1)}{p(X/\omega_2)}\right]^{-1} \tag{3-92}$$

Or, in terms of $p(h/\omega_1)$ and $p(h/\omega_2)$:

$$p(h/\omega_2) = e^h p(h/\omega_1) \tag{3-93}$$

Therefore, from (3-49),

$$\begin{aligned}\varepsilon_2 &= \int_{-\infty}^{t} p(h/\omega_2)\, dh = \int_{-\infty}^{t} e^h p(h/\omega_1)\, dh \\ &= \int_{-\infty}^{t} \exp[-\mu(s) + (1-s)h] p_{\mathbf{g}}(g = h/\omega_1)\, dh \end{aligned} \tag{3-94}$$

For $s \le 1$

$$\exp[(1-s)h] \le \exp[(1-s)t] \qquad \text{for} \quad h \le t \tag{3-95}$$

Thus,

$$\begin{aligned}\varepsilon_2 &\le \exp[-\mu(s) + (1-s)t] \int_{-\infty}^{t} p_g(g = h/\omega_1)\, dh \\ &\le \exp[-\mu(s) + (1-s)t] \qquad \text{for} \quad s \le 1\end{aligned} \tag{3-96}$$

Again, the optimum s can be obtained by

$$-d\mu(s)/ds = t \tag{3-97}$$

Thus, the same s gives the minimum upper bound for both ε_1 and ε_2.

When we are interested in the total error rather than individual class errors, we can obtain a better upper bound by recalling that the threshold value t is $\ln P(\omega_1)/P(\omega_2)$ from (3-50), and rewriting (3-87) and (3-96) as

$$\varepsilon_1 \le \{P(\omega_2)/P(\omega_1)\}^s \exp[-\mu(s)] \int_{t}^{+\infty} p_g(g = h/\omega_1)\, dh \tag{3-98}$$

$$\varepsilon_2 \le \{P(\omega_1)/P(\omega_2)\}^{1-s} \exp[-\mu(s)] \int_{-\infty}^{t} p_g(g = h/\omega_1)\, dh \tag{3-99}$$

Therefore,

$$\begin{aligned}\varepsilon &= P(\omega_1)\varepsilon_1 + P(\omega_2)\varepsilon_2 \\ &\le P(\omega_1)^{1-s} P(\omega_2)^s \exp[-\mu(s)] \\ &\quad \times \left[\int_{t}^{+\infty} p_g(g = h/\omega_1)\, dh + \int_{-\infty}^{t} p_g(g = h/\omega_1)\, dh\right] \\ &= P(\omega_1)^{1-s} P(\omega_2)^s \exp[-\mu(s)]\end{aligned} \tag{3-100}$$

The optimum s should be found by minimizing the last line of (3-100) with respect to s. That is,

$$-d\mu(s)/ds = \ln P(\omega_1)/P(\omega_2) = t \tag{3-101}$$

which is the same as (3-89) and (3-97).

Upper Bounds for Normal Distributions

For normal distributions, an explicit mathematical expression for $\mu(s)$ can be obtained.

According to (3-90) and (2-90), $\varphi_1(s)$ can be expressed in the diagonalized coordinate system as follows:

$$\begin{aligned}
\varphi_1(s) &= \int_{\mathscr{S}} \frac{1}{(2\pi)^{n/2} \mid I \mid^{(1-s)/2} \mid \Lambda \mid^{s/2}} \\
&\quad \times \exp[-\tfrac{1}{2}\{(1-s)(Y-D_1)^T(Y-D_1)+s(Y-D_2)^T\Lambda^{-1}(Y-D_2)\}]\,dY \\
&= \prod_{l=1}^{n} \int_{-\infty}^{+\infty} \frac{1}{(2\pi)^{1/2}\lambda_l^{s/2}} \\
&\quad \times \exp[-\tfrac{1}{2}\{(1-s)(y_l-d_{1l})^2+(s/\lambda_l)(y_l-d_{2l})^2\}]\,dy_l \\
&= \prod_{l=1}^{n} \frac{1}{\lambda_l^{s/2}\{(1-s)+s/\lambda_l\}^{1/2}} \exp\left[-\frac{s(1-s)}{2}\,\frac{(d_{2l}-d_{1l})^2}{s+(1-s)\lambda_l}\right] \\
&\quad \times \int_{-\infty}^{+\infty} \frac{\{(1-s)+s/\lambda_l\}^{1/2}}{(2\pi)^{1/2}} \\
&\quad \times \exp\left[-\frac{\{(1-s)+s/\lambda_l\}}{2}\left\{(y_l-d_{1l})-\frac{(s/\lambda_l)(d_{2l}-d_{1l})}{(1-s)+s/\lambda_l}\right\}^2\right]dy_l \\
&= \prod_{l=1}^{n} \frac{\lambda^{(1-s)/2}}{\{s+(1-s)\lambda_l\}^{1/2}} \exp\left[-\frac{s(1-s)}{2}\,\frac{(d_{2l}-d_{1l})^2}{s+(1-s)\lambda_l}\right] \\
&= \frac{\mid I \mid^{s/2} \mid \Lambda \mid^{(1-s)/2}}{\mid sI+(1-s)\Lambda \mid^{1/2}} \\
&\quad \times \exp\left[-\frac{s(1-s)}{2}(D_2-D_1)^T\{sI+(1-s)\Lambda\}^{-1}(D_2-D_1)\right]
\end{aligned} \tag{3-102}$$

In the original coordinate system:

$$\begin{aligned}
\varphi_1(s) &= \frac{\mid \Sigma_1 \mid^{s/2} \mid \Sigma_2 \mid^{(1-s)/2}}{\mid s\Sigma_1+(1-s)\Sigma_2 \mid^{1/2}} \\
&\quad \times \exp\left[-\frac{s(1-s)}{2}(M_2-M_1)^T\{s\Sigma_1+(1-s)\Sigma_2\}^{-1}(M_2-M_1)\right]
\end{aligned} \tag{3-103}$$

Therefore $\mu(s)$ is, from (3-80),

$$\begin{aligned}
\mu(s) &= \frac{s(1-s)}{2}(M_2-M_1)^T[s\Sigma_1+(1-s)\Sigma_2]^{-1}(M_2-M_1) \\
&\quad + \tfrac{1}{2}\ln\frac{\mid s\Sigma_1+(1-s)\Sigma_2 \mid}{\mid \Sigma_1 \mid^{s} \mid \Sigma_2 \mid^{1-s}}
\end{aligned} \tag{3-104}$$

Or, in the diagonalized coordinate system,

$$\mu(s) = \frac{1}{2}\sum_{l=1}^{n}\left[\frac{s(1-s)(d_{2l}-d_{1l})^2}{s+(1-s)\lambda_l} + \ln\{s+(1-s)\lambda_l\} - (1-s)\ln\lambda_l\right] \tag{3-105}$$

Unfortunately, it is not easy to solve (3-101) to obtain the optimum s. As shown in (3-106), $d\mu(s)/ds$ is a very complicated function of s.

$$\frac{d\mu(s)}{ds} = \frac{1}{2}\sum_{l=1}^{n}\left[\frac{(1-s)^2\lambda_l - s^2}{\{s+(1-s)\lambda_l\}^2}(d_{2l}-d_{1l})^2 + \frac{1-\lambda_l}{s+(1-s)\lambda_l} + \ln\lambda_l\right] \tag{3-106}$$

If we do not insist on the optimum selection of s, we may obtain less complicated upper bounds for ε_1, ε_2, and ε, because ε_1, ε_2, and ε are bounded by (3-88), (3-96), and (3-100) for any s. One of the possibilities is to select $s = \frac{1}{2}$. Then, for normal distributions, $\mu(\frac{1}{2})$ becomes

$$\mu(\tfrac{1}{2}) = \tfrac{1}{8}(M_2 - M_1)^T\left(\frac{\Sigma_1+\Sigma_2}{2}\right)^{-1}(M_2 - M_1) + \tfrac{1}{2}\ln\frac{|(\Sigma_1+\Sigma_2)/2|}{|\Sigma_1|^{1/2}|\Sigma_2|^{1/2}} \tag{3-107}$$

and, from (3-88), (3-96), and (3-100), ε_1, ε_2, and ε are bounded by

$$\varepsilon_1 \le [P(\omega_2)/P(\omega_1)]^{1/2}\exp[-\mu(\tfrac{1}{2})] \tag{3-108}$$

$$\varepsilon_2 \le [P(\omega_1)/P(\omega_2)]^{1/2}\exp[-\mu(\tfrac{1}{2})] \tag{3-109}$$

$$\varepsilon \le [P(\omega_1)P(\omega_2)]^{1/2}\exp[-\mu(\tfrac{1}{2})] \tag{3-110}$$

The term $\mu(\frac{1}{2})$ is called the *Bhattacharyya distance* and will be used as an important measure of the separability of two distributions [Bhattacharyya, 1943].

When $\Sigma_1 = \Sigma_2 = \Sigma$, (3-104) becomes

$$\mu(s) = [s(1-s)/2](M_2 - M_1)^T\Sigma^{-1}(M_2 - M_1) \tag{3-111}$$

Therefore, the optimum s can be obtained by solving

$$-d\mu(s)/ds = -[(1-2s)/2](M_2 - M_1)^T\Sigma^{-1}(M_2 - M_1) = \ln\{P(\omega_1)/P(\omega_2)\} \tag{3-112}$$

When $P(\omega_1) = P(\omega_2) = 0.5$, $d\mu(s)/ds$ becomes zero, and 0.5 is the optimum s.

TABLE 3-4

ERROR PROBABILITIES AND THEIR UPPER BOUNDS[a]

	True value (%)	Normal approximation (%)	$\exp[-\mu(\frac{1}{2})]$ (%)	$\exp[-\mu(s_0)]$ (%)
ε_1	1.6	10.0	9.5	9.1
ε_2	2.2	10.2	9.5	9.1
ε	1.9	10.1	4.8	4.6

[a] $\mu(\frac{1}{2}) = 2.35;\quad s_0 = 0.58;\quad \mu(s_0) = 2.39.$

EXAMPLE 3-4 Let us use the data given in Table 3-2 again. Since $P(\omega_1) = P(\omega_2) = 0.5$, $t = 0$. Table 3-4 compares the upper bounds of ε_1, ε_2, and ε using $\mu(\frac{1}{2})$ and $\mu(s_0)$ (s_0 is the optimum s). The true errors and those resulting from the normal approximation are also given. The results for this particular example indicate that the upper bounds are better than the normal approximations. Also, since these bounds are insensitive to s, the use of $\mu(\frac{1}{2})$ is justified. The curve $\mu(s)$ vs s is plotted in Fig. 3-7.

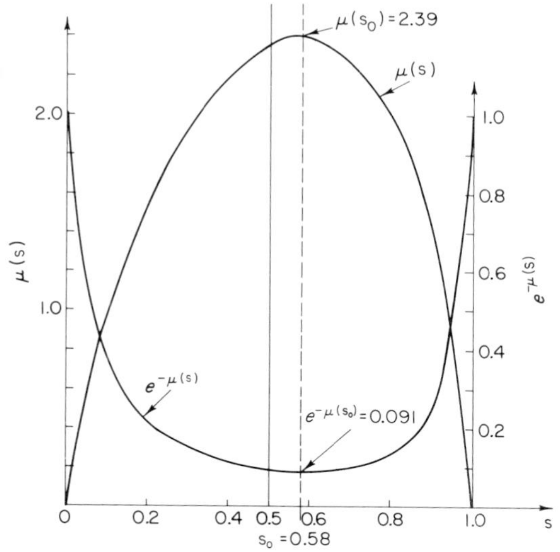

Fig. 3-7 Error bound vs s.

3.4 Other Hypothesis Tests

In this section, we will discuss two more complex hypothesis tests, multihypotheses tests and composite hypothesis tests.

Multihypothesis Tests

When the samples are known to come from M classes, we can generalize the binary hypothesis testing problem.

First, if our decision is simply based on probabilities, the decision rule is

$$P(\omega_i/X) > P(\omega_j/X) \qquad \text{for all } j \text{ except } i \quad \rightarrow X \in \omega_i \tag{3-113}$$

or, by Bayes' theorem,

$$P(\omega_i)p(X/\omega_i) > P(\omega_j)p(X/\omega_j) \qquad \text{for all } j \text{ except } i \quad \rightarrow X \in \omega_i \tag{3-114}$$

When we would like to consider cost functions, we extend (3-12) to

$$c_{ij} = \text{cost of deciding } X \text{ to } \omega_j \qquad \text{for} \quad X \in \omega_i \qquad (X \in \omega_i \quad \text{and} \quad X \in \Gamma_j) \tag{3-115}$$

The expected cost is

$$\begin{aligned} r &= \sum_{j=1}^{M} \sum_{i=1}^{M} \int_{\Gamma_j} c_{ij} P(\omega_i/X) p(X)\, dX \\ &= \sum_{j=1}^{M} \sum_{i=1}^{M} \int_{\Gamma_j} c_{ij} P(\omega_i) p(X/\omega_i)\, dX \end{aligned} \tag{3-116}$$

where the Γ_j's satisfy the following condition:

$$\int_{\Gamma_j} p(X/\omega_j)\, dX = 1 - \sum_{\substack{i=1 \\ i \neq j}}^{M} \int_{\Gamma_i} p(X/\omega_j)\, dX \tag{3-117}$$

Using (3-117), r can be rewritten as

$$r = \sum_{j=1}^{M} c_{jj} P(\omega_j) + \sum_{j=1}^{M} \int_{\Gamma_j} \left\{ \sum_{i=1}^{M} (c_{ij} - c_{ii}) P(\omega_i) p(X/\omega_i) \right\} dX \tag{3-118}$$

The risk r can be minimized if we select the Γ's such that

$$\sum_{i=1}^{M} (c_{ij} - c_{ii}) P(\omega_i) p(X/\omega_i) < \sum_{i=1}^{M} (c_{ik} - c_{ii}) P(\omega_i) p(X/\omega_i)$$
$$\text{for all } k \text{ except } j \quad \rightarrow X \in \Gamma_j \tag{3-119}$$

or,

$$\sum_{i=1}^{M} c_{ij}P(\omega_i)p(X/\omega_i) < \sum_{i=1}^{M} c_{ik}P(\omega_i)p(X/\omega_i)$$
$$\text{for all } k \text{ except } j \quad \rightarrow X \in \Gamma_j \tag{3-120}$$

When $c_{ii} = 0$ and $c_{ij} = 1$ $(i \neq j)$ are used as the cost functions, (3-120) becomes

$$\sum_{i=1}^{M} P(\omega_i)p(X/\omega_i) - P(\omega_j)p(X/\omega_j) < \sum_{i=1}^{M} P(\omega_i)p(X/\omega_i) - P(\omega_k)p(X/\omega_k) \tag{3-121}$$

or

$$P(\omega_j)p(X/\omega_j) > P(\omega_k)p(X/\omega_k) \qquad \text{for all } k \text{ except } j \quad \rightarrow X \in \Gamma_j \tag{3-122}$$

Equation (3-122) is the same as (3-114).

Composite Hypothesis Tests

Sometimes $p(X/\omega_i)$ is not given directly, but is given by the combination of $p(X/\Theta_i)$ and $p(\Theta_i/\omega_i)$, where $p(X/\Theta_i)$ is the conditional density function of X assuming a set of parameters or a parameter vector Θ_i, and $p(\Theta_i/\omega_i)$ is the conditional density function of $\mathbf{\Theta}_i$ assuming class ω_i. In this case, we can calculate $p(X/\omega_i)$ by

$$p(X/\omega_i) = \int_{\mathscr{S}} p(X/\Theta_i)p(\Theta_i/\omega_i)\, d\Theta_i \tag{3-123}$$

where $\mathscr{S}$ is the entire domain of $\mathbf{\Theta}_i$.

Once $p(X/\omega_i)$ is obtained, the likelihood ratio test can be carried out for $p(X/\omega_1)$ and $p(X/\omega_2)$, as described in the previous sections. That is,

$$l(X) = \frac{p(X/\omega_1)}{p(X/\omega_2)} = \frac{\int_{\mathscr{S}} p(X/\Theta_1)p(\Theta_1/\omega_1)\, d\Theta_1}{\int_{\mathscr{S}} p(X/\Theta_2)p(\Theta_2/\omega_2)\, d\Theta_2} \tag{3-124}$$

This is the *composite hypothesis test.*

EXAMPLE 3-5 Two distributions are known to be normal, with fixed covariance matrices Σ_1 and Σ_2 for given expected vectors M_1 and M_2. The terms $\mathbf{M}_1$ and $\mathbf{M}_2$ are also known to be normally distributed, with the expected vectors M_{10} and M_{20} and covariance matrices K_1 and K_2. Then, according to (3-124),

$$p(X/\omega_i) = \int_{\mathscr{S}} (2\pi)^{-n} | \Sigma_i |^{-1/2} | K_i |^{-1/2} \exp[- \tfrac{1}{2}(X - M_i)^T \Sigma_i^{-1} (X - M_i) - \tfrac{1}{2}(M_i - M_{i0})^T K_i^{-1} (M_i - M_{i0})] \, dM_i \tag{3-125}$$

This can be calculated by the same procedure as used in (3-102), diagonalizing Σ_i and K_i simultaneously. The result is

$$p(X/\omega_i) = (2\pi)^{-n/2} | \Sigma_i + K_i |^{-1/2} \times \exp[-\tfrac{1}{2}(X - M_{10})^T (\Sigma_i + K_i)^{-1} (X - M_{10})] \tag{3-126}$$

Knowing that $p(X/\omega_i)$ is normal when $p(X/M_i)$ and $p(M_i/\omega_i)$ are normal, we can simply calculate the expected vector and covariance matrix of $\mathbf{X}$ assuming ω_i that:

$$\begin{aligned} E\{\mathbf{X}/\omega_i\} &= \int_{\mathscr{S}} X p(X/\omega_i) \, dX = \int_{\mathscr{S}} \int_{\mathscr{S}} X p(X/M_i) p(M_i/\omega_i) \, dX \, dM_i \\ &= \int_{\mathscr{S}} \left[\int_{\mathscr{S}} X p(X/M_i) \, dX \right] p(M_i/\omega_i) \, dM_i \\ &= \int_{\mathscr{S}} M_i p(M_i/\omega_i) \, dM_i \\ &= M_{i0} \end{aligned} \tag{3-127}$$

$$\begin{aligned} E\{(\mathbf{X} - M_{i0})(\mathbf{X} - M_{i0})^T/\omega_i\} \\ &= \int_{\mathscr{S}} \left[\int_{\mathscr{S}} (X - M_{i0})(X - M_{i0})^T p(X/M_i) \, dX \right] p(M_i/\omega_i) \, dM_i \\ &= \int_{\mathscr{S}} [\Sigma_i + (M_i - M_{i0})(M_i - M_{i0})^T] p(M_i/\omega_i) \, dM_i \\ &= \Sigma_i + K_i \end{aligned} \tag{3-128}$$

The result is the same as (3-126).

3.5 Sequential Hypothesis Testing

In the problems considered so far, all of the information about the sample to be classified is presented at one instant. The classifier uses the single observation vector to make a decision via Bayes' rule since no further observations will be made, and, as a result, we essentially have no control over the error, unless we can modify the observation process.

In many practical problems, however, the observations are sequential in nature, and more and more information becomes available as time procedes. For example, the vibration of a machine is observed to determine whether the machine is in good or bad condition. In this case, a sequence of observed waveforms should belong to the same category: either "good" or "bad" condition. Another popular example is a radar detection problem. Again the sequence of return pulses over a certain period of time should be from the same class: either existence or nonexistence of a target. A basic approach to problems of this type is the averaging of the sequence of observation vectors. This has the effect of filtering the noise and reducing the observed vectors down to the expected vector. Thus, it is possible, at least theoretically, to achieve zero error, provided that the expected vectors of the two classes are not the same. However, since obtaining an infinite number of observation vectors is obviously not feasible, it is necessary to have a condition, or rule, which helps us decide when to terminate the observations. The *sequential hypothesis test*, the subject of this section, is a mathematical tool for this type of problem.

The Wald Sequential Test

The Wald sequential hypothesis test can be carried out as follows. Let $\mathbf{X}_1, \mathbf{X}_2, \ldots$ be the random vectors observed in sequence. These are assumed to be independent and identically distributed. For each $\mathbf{X}_j$, we can calculate the likelihood ratio

$$\mathbf{z}_j = -\ln \frac{p(\mathbf{X}_j/\omega_1)}{p(\mathbf{X}_j/\omega_2)} \tag{3-129}$$

which is a random variable. After k samples have been observed, the likelihood ratio of k samples is

$$\mathbf{u}_k = -\ln \frac{p(\mathbf{X}_1, \ldots, \mathbf{X}_k/\omega_1)}{p(\mathbf{X}_1, \ldots, \mathbf{X}_k/\omega_2)} = -\sum_{j=1}^{k} \ln \frac{p(\mathbf{X}_j/\omega_1)}{p(\mathbf{X}_j/\omega_2)} = \sum_{j=1}^{k} \mathbf{z}_j \tag{3-130}$$

The expected values and variances of $\mathbf{u}_k$ for ω_1 and ω_2 are

$$\eta_{ik} = E\{\mathbf{u}_k/\omega_i\} = \sum_{j=1}^{k} E\{\mathbf{z}_j/\omega_i\} = k\eta_i \tag{3-131}$$

$$\sigma_{ik}^2 = \sum_{j=1}^{k} E\{(\mathbf{z}_j - \eta_i)^2/\omega_i\} = k\sigma_i^2 \tag{3-132}$$

since the $\mathbf{z}_j$'s are also independent and identically distributed. Thus, as k increases, η_{ik} increases for $\eta_i > 0$, and η_{ik} decreases for $\eta_i < 0$. The increase of σ_{ik} is proportional to $\sqrt{k}$ and is slower than the increase of η_{ik}. Also, by the central limit theorem, the density function of $\mathbf{u}_k$ tends toward a normal distribution with large k. Figure 3-8 shows the trend of η_{ik} and σ_{ik} in terms of k.

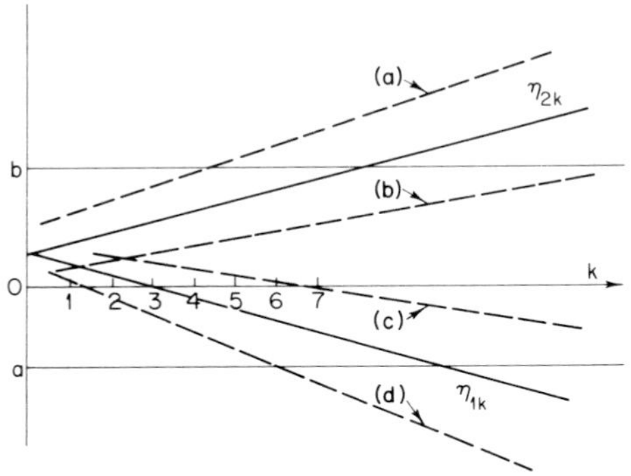

Fig. 3-8 Expected value and variance of $\mathbf{u}_k$ vs k: (a) $\eta_{2k} + \sigma_{2k}$; (b) $\eta_{2k} - \sigma_{2k}$; (c) $\eta_{1k} + \sigma_{1k}$; (d) $\eta_{1k} - \sigma_{1k}$.

Therefore, if we set up a decision rule as

$$\begin{aligned} &u_k \leq a \rightarrow X\text{'s} \in \omega_1 \\ &a < u_k < b \rightarrow \text{take the next sample} \\ &b \leq u_k \rightarrow X\text{'s} \in \omega_2 \end{aligned} \tag{3-133}$$

we can classify $\mathbf{X}$'s as either ω_1 or ω_2 with probability 1 [Wald, 1947]. Also, the errors are controlled by a and b; that is, as the absolute values of a and b increase, the errors decrease, while the number of observations required to reach the decision increases. The relation between the threshold value and the errors can be expressed by

$$\varepsilon_1 = \sum_{j=1}^{\infty} \int_b^{+\infty} p(u_j/\omega_1)\, du_j \tag{3-134}$$

$$\varepsilon_2 = \sum_{j=1}^{\infty} \int_{-\infty}^{a} p(u_j/\omega_2)\, du_j \tag{3-135}$$

Theoretically, we should be able to find a and b from (3-134) and (3-135) for any given ε_1 and ε_2.

A simpler way to find the threshold values has been developed by Wald. The procedure is as follows: At the kth observation, the likelihood ratio is tested as

$$l_k = \frac{p(X_1, \ldots, X_k/\omega_1)}{p(X_1, \ldots, X_k/\omega_2)} \geq A \rightarrow X\text{'s} \in \omega_1$$
$$\leq B \rightarrow X\text{'s} \in \omega_2 \tag{3-136}$$

Therefore,

$$\sum_{k=1}^{\infty} \int_{l_k \geq A} p(X_1, \ldots, X_k/\omega_1)\, dX_1 \cdots dX_k$$
$$\geq A \sum_{k=1}^{\infty} \int_{l_k \geq A} p(X_1, \ldots, X_k/\omega_2)\, dX_1 \cdots dX_k \tag{3-137}$$

$$\sum_{k=1}^{\infty} \int_{l_k \leq B} p(X_1, \ldots, X_k/\omega_1)\, dX_1 \cdots dX_k$$
$$\leq B \sum_{k=1}^{\infty} \int_{l_k \leq B} p(X_1, \ldots, X_k/\omega_2)\, dX_1 \cdots dX_k \tag{3-138}$$

The left side of (3-137) includes all X's which belong to ω_1 and are classified correctly; hence, it should be $1 - \varepsilon_1$. On the other hand, the right side of (3-137) includes all X's which belong to ω_2 and are misclassified as ω_1; hence, it should be ε_2. By the same argument, the left and right sides of (3-138) become ε_1 and $1 - \varepsilon_2$, respectively. Therefore, (3-137) and (3-138) are rewritten as

$$1 - \varepsilon_1 \geq A\varepsilon_2 \tag{3-139}$$

$$\varepsilon_1 \leq B(1 - \varepsilon_2) \tag{3-140}$$

or

$$(1 - \varepsilon_1)/\varepsilon_2 \geq A \tag{3-141}$$

$$\varepsilon_1/(1 - \varepsilon_2) \leq B \tag{3-142}$$

Thus, for any given ε_1 nd ε_2, A and B are obtained by (3-141) and (3-142). When the minus-log–likelihood ratio is used, A and B should be converted to

$$a = -\ln A \geq -\ln (1 - \varepsilon_1)/\varepsilon_2 \tag{3-143}$$

$$b = -\ln B \leq -\ln \varepsilon_1(1 - \varepsilon_2) \tag{3-144}$$

When the increments $\mathbf{z}_j$ are small, the likelihood ratio will exceed the threshold values A and B by only a small amount at the stage where ω_1 is chosen.

Thus, the inequalities of the above equations become approximate equalities, and A and B are approximately determined by $(1 - \varepsilon_1)/\varepsilon_2$ and $\varepsilon_1/(1 - \varepsilon_2)$. Or, ε_1 and ε_2 can be expressed in terms of A and B as

$$\varepsilon_1 \cong B(A - 1)/(A - B) \tag{3-145}$$

$$\varepsilon_2 \cong (1 - B)/(A - B) \tag{3-146}$$

A few remarks concerning the properties of the Wald sequential test are in order.

(1) For the derivation of (3-141) and (3-142), $\mathbf{X}_1, \mathbf{X}_2, \ldots$ do not need independent and identically distributed.

(2) It can be proved that the Wald test terminates with probability 1 [Wald, 1947].

(3) The Wald test minimizes the average number of observations to achieve a given set of errors, ε_1 and ε_2 [Wald, 1948].

(4) The Wald test is independent of *a priori* probabilities $P(\omega_i)$, although the error probabilities necessarily depend on $P(\omega_i)$.

Performance of the Wald Sequential Test

Two appropriate evaluation functions are available for the performance of the Wald sequential test. One is the average number of observations. The other is the operating characteristic function which describes how well the test achieves its objective of making correct decisions when the true value of the unknown parameter is different from the assumed value.

First, let $\mathbf{k}$ be the number of observations needed to reach the upper or lower threshold value. (The term $\mathbf{k}$ is a random variable.) If we introduce a new random variable $\mathbf{v}$ as follows:

$$\mathbf{v} = \sum_{j=1}^{\mathbf{k}} \mathbf{z}_j \tag{3-147}$$

then $\mathbf{v}$ should be either a or b of (3-133), with

$$\begin{array}{llll}
\mathbf{v} = a & (\text{accept } \omega_1) \text{ with probability } 1 - \varepsilon_1 & \text{when} & X\text{'s} \in \omega_1 \\
\mathbf{v} = a & (\text{accept } \omega_1) \text{ with probability } \varepsilon_2 & \text{when} & X\text{'s} \in \omega_2 \\
\mathbf{v} = b & (\text{accept } \omega_2) \text{ with probability } \varepsilon_1 & \text{when} & X\text{'s} \in \omega_1 \\
\mathbf{v} = b & (\text{accept } \omega_2) \text{ with probability } 1 - \varepsilon_2 & \text{when} & X\text{'s} \in \omega_2
\end{array} \tag{3-148}$$

Therefore,

$$E\{\mathbf{v}/\omega_1\} = a(1 - \varepsilon_1) + b\varepsilon_1 \tag{3-149}$$

$$E\{\mathbf{v}/\omega_2\} = a\varepsilon_2 + b(1 - \varepsilon_2) \tag{3-150}$$

On the other hand, since (3-147) is a random sum, it is known that

$$E\{\mathbf{v}/\omega_i\} = E\{E\{\mathbf{v}/\mathbf{k}, \omega_i\}\} = E\{\mathbf{k}\eta_i/\omega_i\} = E\{\mathbf{k}/\omega_i\}\eta_i \tag{3-151}$$

where $E\{\mathbf{z}_j/\omega_i\}$ is equal to η_i, regardless of j. Thus, the *average number of observations* needed to reach the decisions is

$$E\{\mathbf{k}/\omega_1\} = [a(1 - \varepsilon_1) + b\varepsilon_1]/\eta_1 \tag{3-152}$$

$$E\{\mathbf{k}/\omega_2\} = [a\varepsilon_2 + b(1 - \varepsilon_2)]/\eta_2 \tag{3-153}$$

EXAMPLE 3-6 Let us consider an example with normal distributions. Then, from (3-129) and (3-10),

$$\begin{aligned}\mathbf{z}_j = \tfrac{1}{2}(\mathbf{X}_j - M_1)^T \Sigma_1^{-1}(\mathbf{X}_j - M_1) - \tfrac{1}{2}(\mathbf{X}_j - M_2)^T \Sigma_2^{-1}(\mathbf{X}_j - M_2) \\ + \tfrac{1}{2}\ln\{|\Sigma_1|/|\Sigma_2|\}\end{aligned} \tag{3-154}$$

By taking the expectation of (3-154),

$$\begin{aligned}\eta_1 = E\{\mathbf{z}_j/\omega_1\} = -\tfrac{1}{2}(M_1 - M_2)^T \Sigma_2^{-1}(M_1 - M_2) + \tfrac{1}{2}\ln\{|\Sigma_1|/|\Sigma_2|\} \\ + \tfrac{1}{2}\operatorname{tr}\{I - \Sigma_2^{-1}\Sigma_1\}\end{aligned} \tag{3-155}$$

$$\begin{aligned}\eta_2 = E\{\mathbf{z}_j/\omega_2\} = +\tfrac{1}{2}(M_2 - M_1)^T \Sigma_1^{-1}(M_2 - M_1) + \tfrac{1}{2}\ln\{|\Sigma_1|/|\Sigma_2|\} \\ + \tfrac{1}{2}\operatorname{tr}\{\Sigma_1^{-1}\Sigma_2 - I\}\end{aligned} \tag{3-156}$$

On the other hand, we can select ε_1 and ε_2 as we like, and a, b, $a(1 - \varepsilon_1) + b\varepsilon_1$, and $a\varepsilon_2 + b(1 - \varepsilon_2)$ are subsequently determined, as shown in Table 3-5.

In order to get an idea of how many observations are needed, let us consider one-dimensional distributions with equal variances. In this case, (3-155) and (3-156) become

$$\eta_1 = -\tfrac{1}{2}(m_2 - m_1)^2/\sigma^2 \quad \text{and} \quad \eta_2 = +\tfrac{1}{2}(m_2 - m_1)^2/\sigma^2 \tag{3-157}$$

If we assume $(m_2 - m_1)/\sigma = 1$, then we have heavy overlap with $\varepsilon_1 = \varepsilon_2 = 0.31$ by the observation of one sample. However, we can achieve 10^{-6}

as ε_1 and ε_2 by observing an average of 27.6 samples. As the dimension of the samples n increases, $(M_2 - M_1)^T \Sigma_i^{-1}(M_2 - M_1)$ becomes larger because we take the sum of n distance components. Therefore, we can see how errors can be significantly reduced by using a relatively small number of observations.

TABLE 3-5

AVERAGE NUMBER OF OBSERVATIONS

$\varepsilon_1 = \varepsilon_2$:	10^{-2}	10^{-3}	10^{-4}	10^{-5}	10^{-6}
$-a = b$:	4.6	6.9	9.2	11.5	13.8
$a(1 - \varepsilon_1) + b\varepsilon_1$:	−4.6	−6.9	−9.2	−11.5	−13.8
$a\varepsilon_2 + b(1 - \varepsilon_2)$:	4.6	6.9	9.2	11.5	13.8

The design of the Wald sequential test is often governed only by a set of parameters which characterize the density of the observed samples under each hypothesis. If some of these parameters vary after the design is completed, the performance of the test also will vary. We will now describe this variation quantitatively.

Suppose we are testing class ω_1 with parameters Θ_1 against class ω_2 with parameters Θ_2. Then the sequential decision rule T is

$$\frac{p(X_1, \ldots, X_k/\Theta_1)}{p(X_1, \ldots, X_k/\Theta_2)} \begin{array}{l} \geq A \rightarrow X\text{'s} \in \omega_1 \\ \leq B \rightarrow X\text{'s} \in \omega_2 \end{array} \tag{3-158}$$

We would like to evaluate the performance of this decision rule when ω_1 is characterized by Θ instead of Θ_1. To do this, we rewrite T as

$$\begin{aligned} &\frac{p(X_1, \ldots, X_k/\Theta)}{g(X_1, \ldots, X_k/\Theta)} \\ &= \frac{p(X_1, \ldots, X_k/\Theta)}{[p(X_1, \ldots, X_k/\Theta_2)/p(X_1, \ldots, X_k/\Theta_1)]^h p(X_1, \ldots, X_k/\Theta)} \begin{array}{l} \geq A^h \\ \leq B^h \end{array} \\ &\rightarrow \begin{cases} X\text{'s} \in \omega_1 \\ X\text{'s} \in \omega_2 \end{cases} \end{aligned} \tag{3-159}$$

Since the numerator of (3-159) is cancelled by $p(X_1, \ldots, X_k/\Theta)$ in the denominator, and since the remaining terms of (3-159) define an inequality equivalent to (3-158), (3-159) is clearly the same as T of (3-158). Also, (3-159) can be viewed as a sequential decision rule T' to test hypothesis ω characterized by parameters Θ against hypothesis ω^* characterized by $g(X_1, \ldots, X_k/\Theta)$.

Now assume hypothesis ω is true. Then, since T' is a Wald sequential test, we can use (3-136) and (3-145) to calculate the probability that T' rejects hypothesis ω as

$$\varepsilon(\Theta) \cong B^h(A^h - 1)/(A^h - B^h) \tag{3-160}$$

But, because of the equivalence between (3-158) and (3-159), any sequence of observed samples which leads to rejection of ω by T' at some stage leads to rejection of ω_1 by T at the same stage. Therefore, $\varepsilon(\Theta)$ of (3-160) is also the probability that class ω_1 is rejected by T when hypothesis ω is true. Since, by our premise, we would like for T to accept class ω_1 when ω is true, $\varepsilon(\Theta)$ is an error probability.

The above argument depends on $g(X_1, \ldots, X_k/\Theta)$ being a probability density function. Therefore, h must be chosen so that

$$\begin{aligned} &\int_{\mathscr{S}} g(X_1, \ldots, X_k/\Theta)\, dX_1 \cdots dX_k \\ &= \int_{\mathscr{S}} \left[\frac{p(X_1, \cdots, X_k/\Theta_2)}{p(X_1, \cdots, X_k/\Theta_1)}\right]^h p(X_1, \ldots, X_k/\Theta)\, dX_1 \cdots dX_k = 1 \end{aligned} \tag{3-161}$$

It has been shown that such an h exists and is unique [Wald, 1947].

When Θ is equal to Θ_1 or Θ_2, h should be $+1$ or -1 to satisfy (3-161). Therefore, from (3-160),

$$\varepsilon(\Theta_1) = B(A - 1)/(A - B) = \varepsilon_1 \tag{3-162}$$

$$\varepsilon(\Theta_2) = B^{-1}(A^{-1} - 1)/(A^{-1} - B^{-1}) = 1 - \varepsilon_2 \tag{3-163}$$

Thus, $\varepsilon(\Theta)$ represents the error when a set of parameters varies after the decision rule is fixed, and is called the *operating characteristic function* of the Wald sequential test.

In general, it is not easy to find h by solving (3-161), but it is possible to calculate h for some specific cases as in the following example.

EXAMPLE 3-7 Consider the case where $\Theta_i = M_i (i = 1, 2)$ for normal distribution with equal covariance matrices which are fixed ($\Sigma_1 = \Sigma_2 = \Sigma$).

Then, by using M for Θ, (3-161) becomes

$$\prod_{j=1}^{k}\left[\int_{\mathscr{S}}[\exp\{-\tfrac{1}{2}h(X_j-M_2)^T\Sigma^{-1}(X_j-M_2) + \tfrac{1}{2}h(X_j-M_1)^T\Sigma^{-1}(X_j-M_1)\} \times (2\pi)^{-n/2}|\Sigma|^{-1/2}\exp\{-\tfrac{1}{2}(X_j-M)\Sigma^{-1}(X_j-M)\}]\,dX_j\right]$$

$$= \prod_{j=1}^{k}\exp[-\tfrac{1}{2}h\{(M_2-M)^T\Sigma^{-1}(M_2-M)-(M_1-M)^T\Sigma^{-1}(M_1-M) - h(M_2-M_1)\Sigma^{-1}(M_2-M_1)\}] \times (2\pi)^{-n/2}|\Sigma|^{-1/2}\int_{\mathscr{S}}\exp[-\tfrac{1}{2}\{(X_j-M) - h(M_2-M_1)\}^T\Sigma^{-1}\{(X_j-M)-h(M_2-M_1)\}]\,dX_j$$

$$= \exp[-\tfrac{1}{2}hk\{(M_2-M)^T\Sigma^{-1}(M_2-M)-(M_1-M)^T\Sigma^{-1}(M_1-M) - h(M_2-M_1)^T\Sigma^{-1}(M_2-M_1)\}] = 1 \tag{3-164}$$

In order to satisfy (3-164), the power term of the exponential function should be zero. Therefore,

$$h = \frac{(M_2-M)^T\Sigma^{-1}(M_2-M)-(M_1-M)^T\Sigma^{-1}(M_1-M)}{(M_2-M_1)^T\Sigma^{-1}(M_2-M_1)} \tag{3-165}$$

Thus, h and subsequently $\varepsilon(M)$ of (3-160) can easily be calculated for a given M.

The Bayes Sequential Test

The sequential test might be applied to the case where the individual variables within a sample are tested in sequence, in order to reduce the number of observed variables required to reach a decision. However, in this application, we face many difficult problems.

(1) The observed variables are mutually correlated and have different distributions.

(2) The threshold values should be changed at each observation. Figure 3-9 shows a two-dimensional example. When $\mathbf{x}_1$ is observed, we can set up the threshold values A_1 and B_1 for the likelihood ratio to classify samples to ω_1 or ω_2. However, when both $\mathbf{x}_1$ and $\mathbf{x}_2$ are observed, A_2 should be equal to B_2 because we cannot postpone the decision to the next variable.

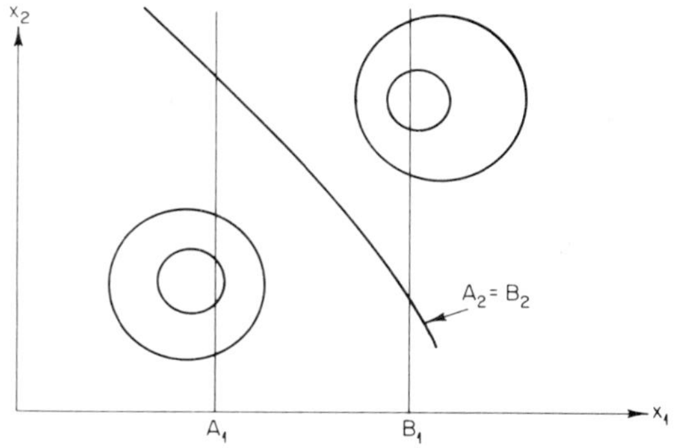

Fig. 3-9 Sequential test within one sample.

In general, the threshold values A_k and B_k are expected to approach one value as k increases.

(3) The probability of error is determined by $p(X/\omega_1)$ and $p(X/\omega_2)$ with the observation of the entire set of n variables.

The sequential test does not improve the error but helps to reduce the number of variables required to reach the decision. Therefore, the procedure may be justified when the cost of observing each variable is an important factor.

Although the procedure is very complicated, the general Bayes sequential test is used for sequentially testing the variables of a sample. The Bayes risk can be expressed by

$$r = \sum_{i=1}^{M} p(\omega_i) \sum_{j=1}^{n} \int_{\mathscr{S}_j} [c_j + L(\omega_i, d_j(x_1, \ldots, x_j))] \times p(x_1, \ldots, x_j/\omega_i)\, dx_1 \cdots dx_j \tag{3-166}$$

where

(1) c_j is the cost of observations $x_1, x_2, \ldots, x_j$;

(2) $L(\omega_i, d_j(x_1, \ldots, x_j))$ is the expected cost for the case where $(x_1, \ldots, x_j) \in \omega_i$ and the decision rule $d_j(x_1, \ldots, x_j)$ is used;

(3) $\mathscr{S}_j$ is the region of $\mathbf{X}$ for which the sequential test terminates at the jth observation.

In the Bayes test, we have to find $d_j(x_1, \ldots, x_j)$ $(j = 1, 2, \ldots, n)$ to minimize r for a given set of costs.

A few remarks follows:

(1) Dynamic programming gives a computational procedure to find $d_j(x_1, \ldots, x_j)$ to minimize r [Fu, 1968].

(2) The threshold values of the likelihood ratios become constant regardless of the number of observations, when the following three conditions are satisfied: (a) the cost of measuring each variable is the same; (b) $\mathbf{x}_j$ are independent and identically distributed; (c) the number of variables n is unbounded. These conditions are satisfied when we observe samples in sequence as was discussed at the beginning of this section. Even for this simplified case the computation of the threshold values is fairly complicated and must be carried out numerically [Helstrom, 1968; Blackwell, 1954].

Computer Projects

Write the following programs:

3-1 Program to perform the Bayes test for minimum risk.
Data: Standard Data $i = 1, 2$

Cost function $c_{11} = c_{22} = 0$ and $c_{12} = c_{21} = 1$

3-2 Calculate the probability of error due to the Bayes test with $c_{11} = c_{22} = 0$ and $c_{12} = c_{21} = 1$.
Data: Standard Data $i = 1, 2$

3-3 Calculate $\mu(s)$ of (3-104) and plot $\mu(s)$ vs s to determine the optimum s. Calculate the Chernoff bound.
Data: Standard Data $i = 1, 2$

3-4 Program to perform the Neyman–Pearson test. (The program of Project 3-2 is needed.)
Data: Standard Data $i = 1, 2$; $\varepsilon_0 = 0.01$

3-5 Program to perform the minimax test. (The program of Project 3-2 is needed.)
Data: Standard Data $i = 1, 2$

3-6 Program to perform the Bayes test for minimum risk for multiclass problems.
Data: Standard Data $i = 1, 2, 3, 4$
Cost function $c_{ii} = 0$ and $c_{ij} = 1$

3-7 Program to perform the Wald sequential test and plot the error vs the number of tests.
Data: Standard Data $i = 1, 2$; $\varepsilon_1 = \varepsilon_2 = 10^{-8}$

Problems

3-1 Two normal distributions are characterized by

$$P(\omega_1) = P(\omega_2) = 0.5$$

$$M_1 = \begin{bmatrix} +1 \\ 0 \end{bmatrix}, \quad M_2 = \begin{bmatrix} -1 \\ 0 \end{bmatrix}, \quad \Sigma_1 = \Sigma_2 = \begin{bmatrix} 1 & 0.5 \\ 0.5 & 1 \end{bmatrix}$$

(a) Draw the contour lines of the two distributions for

$$(X - M_i)^T \Sigma^{-1} (X - M_i) = 1, 2, 3$$

(b) Draw the Bayes decision boundary to minimize the probability of error.

(c) Draw the Bayes decision boundary to minimize the expected risk with $c_{11} = c_{22} = 0$ and $c_{12} = 2c_{21}$.

3-2 Repeat Problem 3-1 for

$$\Sigma_1 = \begin{bmatrix} 1 & 0.5 \\ 0.5 & 1 \end{bmatrix} \quad \text{and} \quad \Sigma_2 = \begin{bmatrix} 1 & -0.5 \\ -0.5 & 1 \end{bmatrix}$$

3-3 Assuming that $c_{11} = c_{22} = 0$ and $c_{12} = c_{21}$ in Problem 3-1, plot the relationship between the threshold values of the likelihood ratio and the probabilities of errors.

(a) Find the total error when the Neyman–Pearson test is performed with $\varepsilon_1 = 0.05$.

(b) Find the threshold value and the total error for the minimax test.

3-4 The random variable $l(\mathbf{X})$ is defined by (3-4). Prove the following:

(a) $E\{l^n(\mathbf{X})/\omega_1\} = E\{l^{n+1}(\mathbf{X})/\omega_2\}$

(b) $E\{l(\mathbf{X})/\omega_2\} = 1$

(c) $E\{l(\mathbf{X})/\omega_1\} - E\{l(\mathbf{X})/\omega_2\} = \text{Var}\{l(\mathbf{X})/\omega_2\}$

3-5 The terms $\mathbf{x}_j (j = 1, 2, \ldots, n)$ are n independent random variables with

$$E\{\mathbf{x}_j/\omega_i\} = ij\eta, \ \text{Var}\{\mathbf{x}_j/\omega_j\} = i^2 j^2 \sigma^2 \qquad (i = 1, 2)$$

Calculate the probability of error due to the Bayes test with $c_{11} = c_{22} = 0$ and $c_{12} = c_{21} = 1$. (Hint: Use the central limit theorem.)

3-6 Let two distributions be normal with equal covariance matrices Σ_1

$= \Sigma_2 = \Sigma$. Plot the probability of error due to the Bayes test with $c_{11} = c_{22} = 0$ and $c_{12} = c_{21} = 1$ and the Chernoff upper bound as the functions of

$$\eta = \tfrac{1}{2}(M_1 - M_2)^T \Sigma^{-1} (M_1 - M_2)$$

3-7 Three distributions are normal with

$$M_1 = M_2 = M_3 = \begin{bmatrix} 0 \\ 0 \end{bmatrix}, \qquad \Sigma_1 = \begin{bmatrix} \sigma_n^2 & 0 \\ 0 & \sigma_n^2 \end{bmatrix}$$

$$\Sigma_2 = \begin{bmatrix} \sigma_n^2 + \sigma_s^2 & 0 \\ 0 & \sigma_n^2 \end{bmatrix}, \qquad \Sigma_3 = \begin{bmatrix} \sigma_n^2 & 0 \\ 0 & \sigma_n^2 + \sigma_s^2 \end{bmatrix}$$

The cost matrix is

$$\begin{bmatrix} 0 & 1 & 1 \\ 1 & 0 & \alpha \\ 1 & \alpha & 0 \end{bmatrix}$$

where $0 \le \alpha < 1$ and $P(\omega_2) = P(\omega_3) = p$.

(a) Find the Bayes boundary and plot it in the X coordinate system.

(b) Write an expression for the probabilities of errors. (Do not evaluate the integrals.)

3-8 Two distributions are normal with

$$P(\omega_1) = P(\omega_2) = 0.5, \qquad M_1 = \begin{bmatrix} 0 \\ 0 \end{bmatrix}, \qquad M_2 = \begin{bmatrix} 1 \\ 0 \end{bmatrix}$$

$$\Sigma_1 = \Sigma_2 = \begin{bmatrix} 1 & 0.5 \\ 0.5 & 1 \end{bmatrix}$$

(a) Calculate the threshold values for the Wald sequential test for $\varepsilon_1 = \varepsilon_2 = 10^{-3}$, 10^{-5}, and 10^{-7}.

(b) Find the average number of observations required.

(c) Plot the operating characteristic function for

$$M = \begin{bmatrix} \xi \\ 0 \end{bmatrix} \qquad (0 \le \xi \le 1)$$

3-9 For Problem 3-8, calculate the probabilities of correct decisions and the probabilities of errors at each observation.

Chapter 4

LINEAR CLASSIFIERS

The Bayes likelihood ratio test has been shown to be optimal in the sense that it minimizes the expected cost or the probability of error. However, in order to construct the likelihood ratio, we must have the conditional probability density function for each class. In most applications, we must estimate these density functions using a finite number of sample observation vectors. Estimation procedures are available, but they may be very complex or require a large number of samples to give accurate results.

Even if we can obtain the densities, the likelihood ratio test may be difficult to implement; time and storage requirements for the classification process may be excessive. Therefore, we are often led to consider a simpler procedure for designing a pattern classifier. In particular, we may specify the mathematical form of the classifier, leaving a finite set of parameters to be determined. The simplest and most common choice is the linear, or piecewise linear, classifier which we will discuss in this chapter. First, we will consider a special case where the Bayes classifier is linear. We will then develop alternative methods for deriving "good" linear classifiers.

The reader should remember, however, that the Bayes classifier is the best classifier in all cases. No linear classifier will exceed the performance of the likelihood ratio test.

4.1 The Bayes Linear Classifier

For two normal distributions, the Bayes decision rule can be expressed as a quadratic function of the observation vector X as

$$\tfrac{1}{2}(X - M_1)^T\Sigma_1^{-1}(X - M_1) - \tfrac{1}{2}(X - M_2)^T\Sigma_2^{-1}(X - M_2) + \tfrac{1}{2}\ln\frac{|\Sigma_1|}{|\Sigma_2|}$$
$$\lessgtr \ln\frac{P(\omega_1)}{P(\omega_2)} \rightarrow X \in \begin{cases}\omega_1\\ \omega_2\end{cases} \tag{4-1}$$

When both covariance matrices are equal, that is when $\Sigma_1 = \Sigma_2 = \Sigma$, (4-1) reduces to a linear function of X as

$$(M_2 - M_1)^T\Sigma^{-1}X + \tfrac{1}{2}(M_1{}^T\Sigma^{-1}M_1 - M_2{}^T\Sigma^{-1}M_2) \lessgtr \ln\{P(\omega_1)/P(\omega_2)\}$$
$$\rightarrow X \in \begin{cases}\omega_1\\ \omega_2\end{cases} \tag{4-2}$$

We will first consider the special case where $\Sigma = I$ and then show that (4-2) can be viewed as a modification.

White Observation Noise

If the covariance matrix is the identity matrix, then we can view $\mathbf{X}$ as an observation corrupted by *white noise*. The components of $\mathbf{X}$ are uncorrelated and have unit variance. The Bayes decision rule reduces to

$$(M_2 - M_1)^TX + \tfrac{1}{2}(M_1{}^TM_1 - M_2{}^TM_2) \lessgtr \ln\{P(\omega_1)/P(\omega_2)\} \rightarrow X \in \begin{cases}\omega_1\\ \omega_2\end{cases} \tag{4-3}$$

Correlation Classifier

The product $M_i{}^T\mathbf{X}$ is called the *correlation* between M_i and $\mathbf{X}$. When $\mathbf{X}$ consists of time-sampled values taken from a continuous random process, we can write the correlation as

$$M_i{}^T\mathbf{X} = \sum_{j=1}^{n} m_i(t_j)\mathbf{x}(t_j) \tag{4-4}$$

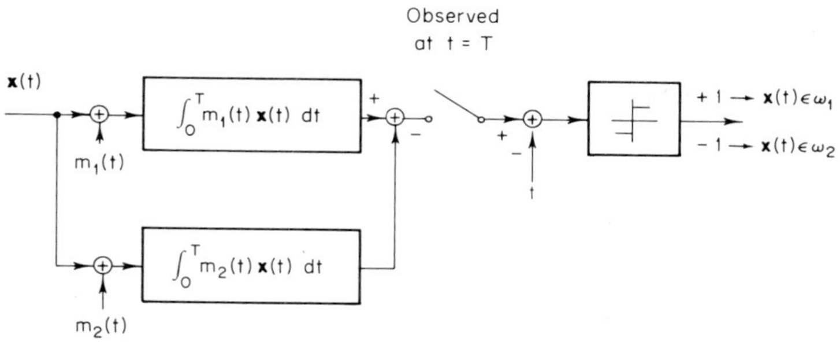

Fig. 4-1 Block diagram of a correlation classifier, where

$$t = \tfrac{1}{2}\int_0^T \{m_1^2(t) - m_2^2(t)\}\,dt - \ln\{P(\omega_1)/P(\omega_2)\}.$$

In the continuous case, the correlation becomes an integral, that is

$$\sum_{j=1}^{n} m_i(t_j)\mathbf{x}(t_j) \to \int_0^T m_i(t)\mathbf{x}(t)\,dt \tag{4-5}$$

We can see that the classifier compares the difference in the correlation of $\mathbf{X}$ with M_1 and M_2 with a threshold to make a decision. Thus, we may call it a *correlation classifier*. The structure of the correlation classifier is shown in Fig. 4-1.

Matched Filter

The correlation between M_i and $\mathbf{X}$ can also be considered as the output of a linear filter. Suppose we construct functions $g_i(t)$ such that

$$g_i(T - t) = m_i(t) \tag{4-6}$$

The relation between $g_i(t)$ and $m_i(t)$ is illustrated in Fig. 4-2. Then, clearly,

$$\int_0^T m_i(t)\mathbf{x}(t)\,dt = \int_0^T g_i(T - t)\mathbf{x}(t)\,dt \tag{4-7}$$

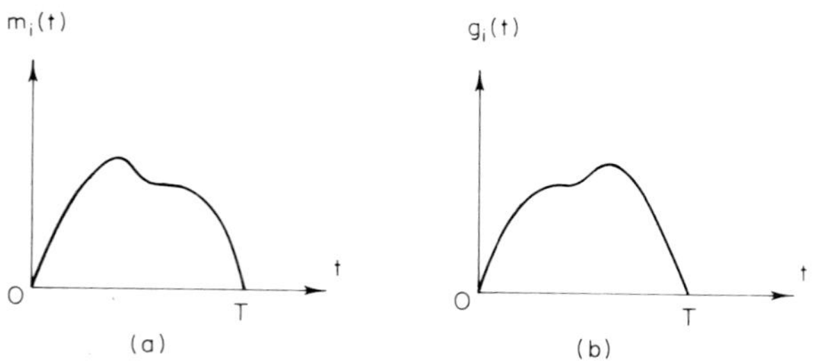

Fig. 4-2 Relationship between (a) $m_i(t)$ and (b) $g_i(t)$.

Thus, the correlation is the output of a linear filter whose impulse response is $g_i(t)$. This filter is called a *matched filter*. The matched filter classifier, which performs the same function as the correlation classifier, is shown in Fig. 4-3.

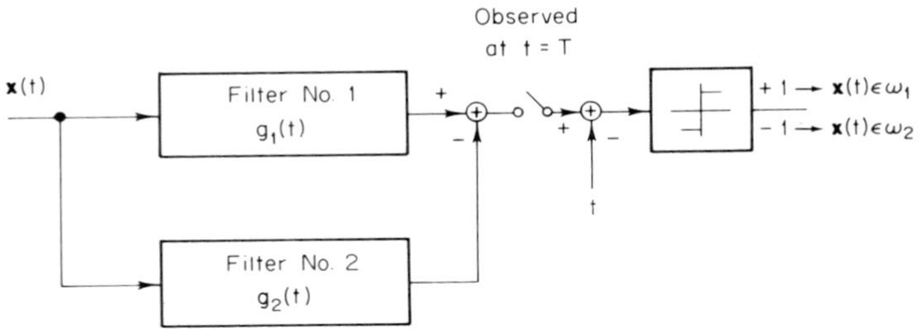

Fig. 4-3 Block diagram of a matched filter detector.

Distance Classifier

Suppose we multiply (4-3) by 2, add and then substract X^TX from the left-hand side. The resulting decision rule is

$$(X^TX - 2M_1{}^TX + M_1{}^TM_1) - (X^TX - 2M_2{}^TX + M_2{}^TM_2) \lesseqgtr 2\ln\{P(\omega_1)/P(\omega_2)\} \rightarrow X \in \begin{cases}\omega_1\\ \omega_2\end{cases} \tag{4-8}$$

or

$$\| X - M_1 \|^2 - \| X - M_2 \|^2 \lesseqgtr 2\ln\{P(\omega_1)/P(\omega_2)\} \rightarrow X \in \begin{cases}\omega_1\\ \omega_2\end{cases} \tag{4-9}$$

Now the decision rule has the geometrical interpretation of comparing the distances from X to M_1 and M_2 according to a threshold. When $P(\omega_1) = P(\omega_2) = 0.5$, the decision boundary is the perpendicular *bisector* of the line joining M_1 and M_2, as shown in Fig. 4-4.

Nonwhite Observation Noise

In the more general case where $\Sigma \neq I$, the observation noise is correlated and is often called *colored noise*. The Bayes classifier is not as readily interpreted in this case. However, it is still useful to view the decision rule as a correlation classifier or a distance classifier. To do this, we introduce the "whitening" transformation, $\mathbf{Y} = A\mathbf{X}$, where

$$A\Sigma A^T = I \tag{4-10}$$

It is important to note that as long as Σ is positive definite, A exists and is nonsingular. Thus, the whitening transformation is reversible, and the observation $\mathbf{Y}$ can be classified as effectively as $\mathbf{X}$.

The expected vector of $\mathbf{Y}$ is

$$D_i = E\{\mathbf{Y}/\omega_i\} = AM_i \qquad (i = 1, 2) \tag{4-11}$$

for class ω_i, and the covariance of $\mathbf{Y}$ is I for both classes. Hence, all of the discussion of the preceding section applies to $\mathbf{Y}$ if we replace M_i[or $m_i(t)$] with D_i[or $d_i(t)$].

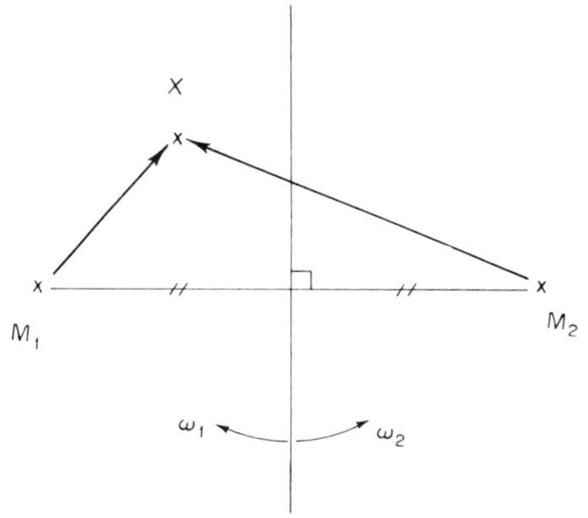

Fig. 4-4 A classifier by Euclidean distances.

In the continuous time case, the transformation becomes an integral as

$$\mathbf{Y} = A\mathbf{X} \rightarrow \mathbf{y}(t) = \int_0^T a(t, \tau)\mathbf{x}(\tau)\, d\tau \tag{4-12}$$

The kernel, $a(t, \tau)$, can be viewed as the impulse response of a *whitening filter*. A possible structure for the Bayes classifier is shown in Fig. 4-5. We see that we have the correlation classifier of Fig. 4-1 modified by the addition of whitening filters.

EXAMPLE 4-1 Figure 4-6 shows a two-dimensional example in which a whitening transformation is effective. Although the two distributions of

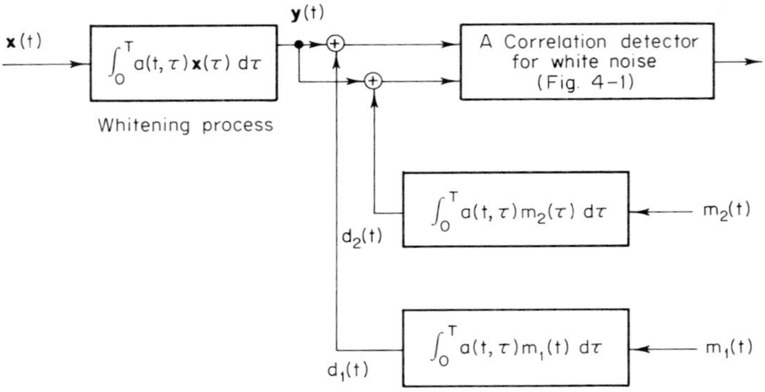

Fig. 4-5 A correlation classifier for colored noise.

Fig. 4-6a are very much separable by the Bayes classifier, the bisector classifier or simple correlation gives a poor classification. The narrow distributions of Fig. 4-6a are seen when $\mathbf{x}_1$ and $\mathbf{x}_2$ are highly correlated. Particularly, when $\mathbf{x}_1, \mathbf{x}_2, \ldots$ are the time-samples values of waveforms, adjacent $\mathbf{x}$'s are usually highly correlated and show this type of distribution. The whitening transformation changes these two distributions to the circular ones of Fig. 4-6b, such that the Bayes classifier becomes the bisector.

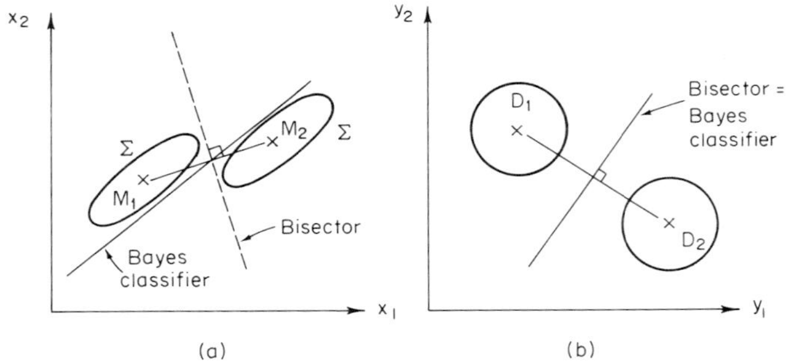

Fig. 4-6 Effect of a whitening process.

4.2 Linear Discriminant Function for Minimum Error

Linear classifiers are the simplest ones as far as implementation is concerned and are directly related to many known techniques, such as correlations and Euclidean distances. However, in the Bayes sense, linear classifiers are optimum only for normal distributions with equal covariance matrices. In some applications, such as signal detection in communication systems, equal covariance is a reasonable assumption because the properties of noise do not change very much from one signal to another. However, in many other applications of pattern recognition, the assumption of equal covariance is not valid.

Many attempts have been made to design the best linear classifiers for normal distributions with unequal covariance matrices and non-normal distributions. Of course, these are not optimum, but in many cases the simplicity of the linear classifier more than compensates for the loss in performance. In this section, we will discuss how linear classifiers are designed for these more complicated cases. Since it is predetermined that we use a linear classifier regardless of the given distributions, our decision rule should be

$$h(X) = V^T X + v_0 \lessgtr 0 \rightarrow X \in \begin{cases} \omega_1 \\ \omega_2 \end{cases} \tag{4-13}$$

The term $h(X)$ is a linear function of X and is called a *linear discriminant function.* Our design work is to find the optimum coefficients $V^T = [v_1 \cdots v_n]$ and the threshold value v_0 for given distributions under various criteria. The linear discriminant function becomes the log–likelihood ratio when given distributions are normal with equal covariance matrices.

Linear Discriminant Function for Minimum Error

When the random variable $h(\mathbf{X})$ is normal, or close to normal, we can use the expected values and variances of $h(\mathbf{X})$ for ω_1 and ω_2 to calculate the probabilities of error. Then we adjust V and v_0 to minimize the error. Since $h(\mathbf{X})$ is the summation of n $\mathbf{x}_i$'s.

(1) if $\mathbf{X}$ is normally distributed, $h(\mathbf{X})$ is normal, and

(2) even if $\mathbf{X}$ is not normally distributed, $h(\mathbf{X})$ could be close to normal for large n, under the conditions where the central limit theorem holds.

The expected values and variances of $h(\mathbf{X})$ are

$$\eta_i = E\{h(\mathbf{X})/\omega_i\} = V^T E\{\mathbf{X}/\omega_i\} + v_0 = V^T M_i + v_0 \tag{4-14}$$

$$\begin{aligned}\sigma_i^2 = \operatorname{Var}\{h(\mathbf{X})/\omega_i\} &= V^T E\{(\mathbf{X} - M_i)(\mathbf{X} - M_i)^T\} V \\ &= V^T \Sigma_i V\end{aligned} \tag{4-15}$$

Therefore, the probability of error can be written as

$$\varepsilon = P(\omega_1) \int_{-\eta_1/\sigma_1}^{+\infty} \frac{1}{(2\pi)^{1/2}} \exp\left(-\frac{\xi^2}{2}\right) d\xi + P(\omega_2) \int_{-\infty}^{-\eta_2/\sigma_2} \frac{1}{(2\pi)^{1/2}} \exp\left(-\frac{\xi^2}{2}\right) d\xi \qquad (4\text{-}16)$$

When the expected cost is to be minimized, $c_{12}P(\omega_1)$ and $c_{21}P(\omega_2)$ should be used in place of $P(\omega_1)$ and $P(\omega_2)$ in (4-16). This assumes that $c_{11} = c_{22} = 0$.

Differentiating (4-16) with respect to V and v_0,

$$\begin{aligned}\frac{\partial \varepsilon}{\partial V} &= -P(\omega_1) \frac{1}{(2\pi)^{1/2}} \exp\left(-\frac{\eta_1^2}{2\sigma_1^2}\right) \frac{\partial}{\partial V}\left(-\frac{\eta_1}{\sigma_1}\right) \\ &\quad + P(\omega_2) \frac{1}{(2\pi)^{1/2}} \exp\left(-\frac{\eta_2^2}{2\sigma_2^2}\right) \frac{\partial}{\partial V}\left(-\frac{\eta_2}{\sigma_2}\right) \\ &= \frac{P(\omega_1)}{(2\pi)^{1/2}\sigma_1} \exp\left(-\frac{\eta_1^2}{2\sigma_1^2}\right)\left(M_1 - \frac{\eta_1}{\sigma_1^2} \Sigma_1 V\right) \\ &\quad - \frac{P(\omega_2)}{(2\pi)^{1/2}\sigma_2} \exp\left(-\frac{\eta_2^2}{2\sigma_2^2}\right)\left(M_2 - \frac{\eta_2}{\sigma_2^2} \Sigma_2 V\right) = 0 \end{aligned} \qquad (4\text{-}17)$$

$$\begin{aligned}\frac{\partial \varepsilon}{\partial v_0} &= -P(\omega_1) \frac{1}{(2\pi)^{1/2}} \exp\left(-\frac{\eta_1^2}{2\sigma_1^2}\right) \frac{\partial}{\partial v_0}\left(-\frac{\eta_1}{\sigma_1}\right) \\ &\quad + P(\omega_2) \frac{1}{(2\pi)^{1/2}} \exp\left(-\frac{\eta_2^2}{2\sigma_2^2}\right) \frac{\partial}{\partial v_0}\left(-\frac{\eta_2}{\sigma_2}\right) \\ &= \frac{P(\omega_1)}{(2\pi)^{1/2}\sigma_1} \exp\left(-\frac{\eta_1^2}{2\sigma_1^2}\right) - \frac{P(\omega_2)}{(2\pi)^{1/2}\sigma_2} \exp\left(-\frac{\eta_2^2}{2\sigma_2^2}\right) = 0 \end{aligned} \qquad (4\text{-}18)$$

where

$$\frac{\partial}{\partial V}\left(\frac{\eta_i}{\sigma_i}\right) = \frac{(\partial\eta_i/\partial V)\sigma_i - \eta_i(\partial\sigma_i/\partial V)}{\sigma_i^2} = \frac{M_i}{\sigma_i} - \frac{\eta_i}{\sigma_i^3} \Sigma_i V \qquad (4\text{-}19)$$

Equation (4-18) shows that both $P(\omega_1)p(h/\omega_1)$ and $P(\omega_2)p(h/\omega_2)$ should have the same value at $h = 0$, that is

$$P(\omega_1) \frac{1}{(2\pi)^{1/2}\sigma_1} \exp\left(-\frac{\eta_1^2}{2\sigma_1^2}\right) = P(\omega_2) \frac{1}{(2\pi)^{1/2}\sigma_2} \exp\left(-\frac{\eta_2^2}{2\sigma_2^2}\right) \qquad (4\text{-}20)$$

as shown in Fig. 4-7.

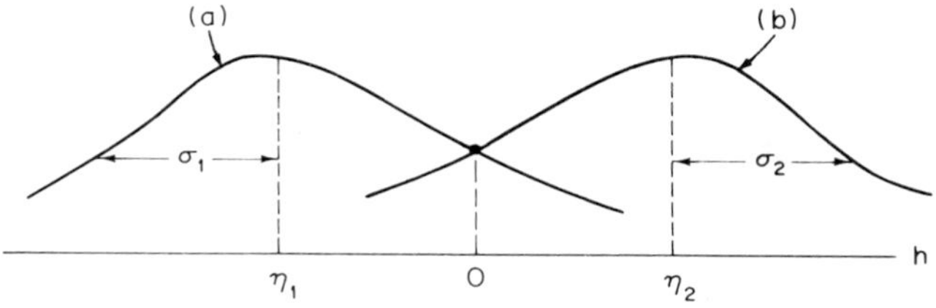

Fig. 4-7 Distributions of $h(\mathbf{X})$: (a) $P(\omega_1)p(h/\omega_1)$; (b) $P(\omega_2)p(h/\omega_2)$.

In addition to this condition, (4-17) should be satisfied; that is,

$$M_2 - M_1 = [(\eta_2/\sigma_2^2)\Sigma_2 - (\eta_1/\sigma_1^2)\Sigma_1]V \tag{4-21}$$

Thus, if we can find V's and v_0's which satisfy (4-20) and (4-21), these V and v_0 minimize the probability of error of (4-16) [Anderson, 1962]. Unfortunately, since η_i and σ_i^2 are functions of V and v_0, the explicit solution of these equations has not been found. Thus, we must use an iterative procedure to find the solution.

A simple iterative process has been proposed [Peterson, 1966]. Instead of solving (4-20) and (4-21), the minimum of ε is sought under the condition of (4-21) as follows:

$$V = a[s\Sigma_1 + (1 - s)\Sigma_2]^{-1}(M_2 - M_1) \tag{4-22}$$

where

$$1/a = (\eta_2/\sigma_2^2) - (\eta_1/\sigma_1^2) \tag{4-23}$$

$$s = \frac{-\eta_1/\sigma_1^2}{\eta_2/\sigma_2^2 - \eta_1/\sigma_1^2} \qquad (0 \leq s \leq 1) \tag{4-24}$$

Since $\eta_i = V^T M_i + v_0$ and $s\sigma_1^2\eta_2 + (1 - s)\sigma_2^2\eta_1 = 0$ from (4-24), v_0 can be calculated as

$$v_0 = \frac{-\{s\sigma_1^2 V^T M_2 + (1 - s)\sigma_2^2 V^T M_1\}}{s\sigma_1^2 + (1 - s)\sigma_2^2} \tag{4-25}$$

That is, if V is multiplied by a, v_0 also increases by a factor of a. Recall that the decision made by $V^T X + v_0 \gtrless 0$ is equivalent to the decision of $aV^T X + av_0 \gtrless 0$ and that ε of (4-16) is also invariant under scale change because

$$\frac{\eta_i}{\sigma_i} = \frac{aV^T M_i + av_0}{[(aV)^T \Sigma_i (aV)]^{1/2}} = \frac{V^T M_i + v_0}{(V^T \Sigma_i V)^{1/2}} \tag{4-26}$$

Therefore, ignoring a scale factor a in (4-22), we can plot ε as a function of one parameter s as follows:

(1) Calculate V for a given s by (4-22) with $a = 1$.

(2) Using the V obtained, calculate σ_1^2, σ_2^2, $V^T M_1$, $V^T M_2$, and v_0 by (4-15) and (4-25).

(3) Calculate ε by (4-16).

(4) Change s from 0 to 1.

The s which minimized ε can be found from the ε vs s plot.

The advantage of this process is that we have only one parameter s to adjust. That makes the process very much simpler than solving (4-20) and (4-21) with $n + 1$ variables. Also, in order to save computer time, it is suggested to diagonalize Σ_1 and Σ_2 simultaneously at the beginning of the process and to work in the transformed coordinate system. Thus, the calculations of σ_i^2 and the inverse matrix of (4-22) become very simple.

EXAMPLE 4-2 The data of Example 3-3 is used, and ε vs s is plotted in Fig. 4-8. As seen in Fig. 4-8, ε is not particularly sensitive to s around the

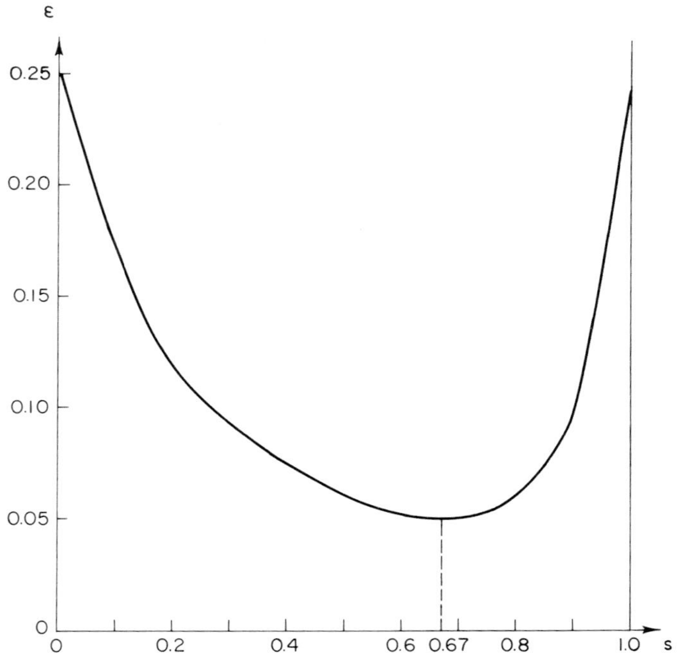

Fig. 4-8 The probability of error vs s.

optimum point. The optimized error is 5% by the best linear discriminant function, while the Bayes classifier with a quadratic form gives 1.9%, as shown in Example 3-3.

Generalized Formula for Various Criteria

Although we have discussed the minimization of error, this concept can be generalized as follows [Peterson, 1966].

Let $f(\eta_1, \eta_2, \sigma_1^2, \sigma_2^2)$ be any criterion to be minimized or maximized for the determination of the optimum coefficients of a linear discriminant function. Then

$$\frac{\partial f}{dV} = \frac{\partial f}{\partial \sigma_1^2}\frac{\partial \sigma_1^2}{\partial V} + \frac{\partial f}{\partial \sigma_2^2}\frac{\partial \sigma_2^2}{\partial V} + \frac{\partial f}{\partial \eta_1}\frac{\partial \eta_1}{\partial V} + \frac{\partial f}{\partial \eta_2}\frac{\partial \eta_2}{\partial V} \tag{4-27}$$

$$\frac{\partial f}{\partial v_0} = \frac{\partial f}{\partial \sigma_1^2}\frac{\partial \sigma_1^2}{\partial v_0} + \frac{\partial f}{\partial \sigma_2^2}\frac{\partial \sigma_2^2}{\partial v_0} + \frac{\partial f}{\partial \eta_1}\frac{\partial \eta_1}{\partial v_0} + \frac{\partial f}{\partial \eta_2}\frac{\partial \eta_2}{\partial v_0} \tag{4-28}$$

From (4-14) and (4-15),

$$\partial \sigma_i^2/\partial V = 2\Sigma_i V \tag{4-29}$$

$$\partial \eta_i/\partial V = M_i \tag{4-30}$$

$$\partial \sigma_i^2/\partial v_0 = 0 \tag{4-31}$$

$$\partial \eta_i/\partial v_0 = 1 \tag{4-32}$$

Substituting (4-29) through (4-32) into (4-27) and (4-28),

$$2[(\partial f/\partial \sigma_1^2)\Sigma_1 + (\partial f/\partial \sigma_2^2)\Sigma_2]V = (M_1 - M_2)\partial f/\partial \eta_2 \tag{4-33}$$

$$\partial f/\partial \eta_1 + \partial f/\partial \eta_2 = 0 \tag{4-34}$$

The terms V and v_0 are found as the solution of these simultaneous equations.

EXAMPLE 4-3 Let us consider the *Fisher criterion* which is given by

$$f = (\eta_1 - \eta_2)^2/(\sigma_1^2 + \sigma_2^2) \tag{4-35}$$

This criterion is a measure that indicates how far the two distributions of the discriminant function for ω_1 and ω_2 are separated. Therefore, we have to find the V and v_0 which maximize this criterion in order to achieve the best separability. According to (4-33) and (4-34),

$$2[(\eta_1 - \eta_2)/(\sigma_1^2 + \sigma_2^2)](\tfrac{1}{2}\Sigma_1 + \tfrac{1}{2}\Sigma_2)V = M_1 - M_2 \tag{4-36}$$

As discussed earlier, we can ignore a scale factor of V. Therefore, V can be determined by

$$V = (\tfrac{1}{2}\Sigma_1 + \tfrac{1}{2}\Sigma_2)^{-1}(M_1 - M_2) \tag{4-37}$$

Comparing (4-37) with (4-22), we notice that the optimum s for the Fisher criterion is 0.5. Therefore, substituting $s = 0.5$ and the V of (4-37) into (4-25), v_0 can be calculated as

$$v_0 = \frac{(M_2 - M_1)^T(\tfrac{1}{2}\Sigma_1 + \tfrac{1}{2}\Sigma_2)^{-1}(\sigma_1{}^2 M_2 + \sigma_2{}^2 M_1)}{\sigma_1{}^2 + \sigma_2{}^2} \tag{4-38}$$

4.3 Linear Discriminant Function for Minimum Mean-Square Error

In the previous section, we assumed that the density functions of the linear discriminant function for ω_1 and ω_2 are normal, or close to a normal distribution, in order to find an optimum discriminant function in the sense of minimum error. Even for the generalized formula for various criteria, we assumed that the criteria are functions of the expected values and variances of the discriminant function. Similar results can be obtained even without the assumption of normal distributions, if we take a mean-square error approach. Instead of making assumptions about the distribution of **X**, we will suppose that we have a finite sample of N X's available.

Linear Discriminant Functions

Instead of (4-13), we can write a linear discriminant function as

$$h(X) = V^T X + v_0 \geq 0 \qquad \text{for} \quad X \in \omega_1 \tag{4-39}$$

$$h(X) = -V^T X - v_0 > 0 \qquad \text{for} \quad X \in \omega_2 \tag{4-40}$$

Furthermore, if we introduce a new form to express sample vectors as

$$Z = [+1\ x_1\ x_2 \cdots x_n]^T \qquad \text{for} \quad X \in \omega_1 \tag{4-41}$$

$$Z = [-1\ -x_1\ -x_2 \cdots -x_n]^T \qquad \text{for} \quad X \in \omega_2 \tag{4-42}$$

then the discriminant function becomes simply

$$h(Z) = W^T Z = \sum_{i=0}^{n} w_i z_i \geq 0 \tag{4-43}$$

where z_0 is either $+1$ or -1.

Thus our design procedure is

(1) to generate a new set of vectors, Z's from X's, and
(2) to find W^T so as to satisfy (4-43) for as many Z's as possible.

Suppose $\gamma(Z)$ is the best discriminant function for separating the two classes. Then $\gamma(Z)$ can be viewed as the *desired output* of the discriminant function $h(Z)$. Usually, we do not know the precise form of $\gamma(Z)$, but, given our knowledge of the classification of the training samples, we can postulate reasonable values for $\gamma(Z)$. From (4-43), $\gamma(Z)$ should be a positive number for each Z. Then the mean-square error between the desired and actual output of the discriminant function is

$$\bar{\varepsilon}^2 = E\{(W^T\mathbf{Z} - \gamma(\mathbf{Z}))^2\} \tag{4-44}$$

Or, if the sample mean of the available N samples is used instead of the expected value,

$$\begin{aligned} \bar{\varepsilon}^2 &= (1/N) \sum_{j=1}^{N} (W^T Z_j - \gamma(Z_j))^2 \\ &= (1/N)(W^T U - \Gamma^T)(U^T W - \Gamma) \end{aligned} \tag{4-45}$$

where

$$\begin{aligned} U &= [Z_1 Z_2 \cdots Z_N]_{(n+1)\times N} \\ &= \underbrace{\left[\begin{array}{cccc|cccc} \multicolumn{4}{c|}{\underbrace{\begin{matrix} +1 & +1 & \cdots & +1 \\ X_1 & X_2 & \cdots & X_{N_1} \end{matrix}}_{N_1}} & \multicolumn{4}{c}{\underbrace{\begin{matrix} -1 & \cdots & -1 \\ -X_{N_1+1} & \cdots & -X_N \end{matrix}}_{N_2}} \end{array}\right]}_{N} \begin{matrix} \}\,1 \\ \}\,n \end{matrix} \end{aligned} \tag{4-46}$$

$$\Gamma = [\gamma(Z_1) \cdots \gamma(Z_N)]^T_{1\times N} \tag{4-47}$$

That is, U consists of N sample vectors, among which N_1 samples belong to ω_1, and N_2 samples belong to ω_2, and is called a *sample matrix*. The term Γ is called a *desired output vector*.

In order to minimize ε^2 of (4-45) for a given desired output, we differentiate ε^2 with respect to W and equate the result to zero.

$$\partial\bar{\varepsilon}^2/\partial W = (2/N)U(U^T W - \Gamma) = 0 \tag{4-48}$$

or

$$W = (UU^T)^{-1} U\Gamma \tag{4-49}$$

This equation is the well-known *normal equation* from linear least-square estimation theory. Thus W can be calculated by (4-49), minimizing the mean-square error between the desired and actual output of the discriminant function.

In order to better appreciate this solution, let us consider UU^T.

$$UU^T = n+1\left\{\underbrace{\left[\begin{array}{ccc|ccc} +1 & \cdots & +1 & -1 & \cdots & -1 \\ \hline X_1 & \cdots & X_{N_1} & -X_{N_1+1} & \cdots & -X_N \end{array}\right]}_{N}\right. \underbrace{\left[\begin{array}{c|c} +1 & X_1^T \\ \vdots & \vdots \\ +1 & X_{N_1}^T \\ \hline -1 & -X_{N_1+1}^T \\ \vdots & \vdots \\ -1 & -X_N^T \end{array}\right]}_{n+1}\left.\vphantom{\begin{array}{c}1\\1\\1\\1\\1\\1\end{array}}\right\}N$$

$$= N\left[\begin{array}{c|c} 1 & M_0^T \\ \hline M_0 & S \end{array}\right]\begin{array}{l}\}\,1 \\ \}\,n\end{array} \qquad \text{(columns: } 1,\ n\text{)} \tag{4-50}$$

where

$$M_0 = (1/N)\sum_{j=1}^{N} X_j \tag{4-51}$$

is the sample mean vector of the mixture of two distributions and

$$S = (1/N)\sum_{j=1}^{N} X_j X_j^T \tag{4-52}$$

is the sample autocorrelation matrix of the mixture.

Let us use a linear transformation such that

$$(1/N)\sum_{j=1}^{N} Y_j = 0 \qquad \text{and} \qquad (1/N)\sum_{j=1}^{N} Y_j Y_j^T = I \tag{4-53}$$

where

$$\begin{aligned} Y_j &= AX_j + B \qquad (B:\ \text{a vector}) \\ D_i &= AM_i + B \qquad \text{and} \qquad K_i = A\Sigma_i A^T \end{aligned} \tag{4-54}$$

Then, since UU^T is transformed to NI, (4-49) becomes

$$W' = \frac{1}{N}\,U'\Gamma' = \frac{1}{N}\left[\begin{array}{ccc|ccc} +1 & \cdots & +1 & -1 & \cdots & -1 \\ \hline Y_1 & \cdots & Y_{N_1} & -Y_{N_1+1} & \cdots & -Y_N \end{array}\right]\left[\begin{array}{c} \gamma'(Z_1') \\ \vdots \\ \gamma'(Z_N') \end{array}\right] \tag{4-55}$$

where the prime shows the vectors and variables in the transformed coordinate system.

Thus, W' is

$$W' = (1/N) \sum_{j=1}^{N} \gamma'(Z_j')Z_j' \tag{4-56}$$

or

$$w_0' = (1/N)\left[\sum_{j=1}^{N_1} \gamma'(Z_j') - \sum_{j=N_1+1}^{N} \gamma'(Z_j') \right] \tag{4-57}$$

$$[w_1' \cdots w_n']^T = (1/N)\left[\sum_{j=1}^{N_1} \gamma'(Z_j')Y_j - \sum_{j=N_1+1}^{N} \gamma'(Z_j')Y_j \right] \tag{4-58}$$

Equation (4-58) shows that $[w_1' \cdots w_n']^T$ is determined by the correlation between the desired output and Y.

A simpler result can be obtained if we assume

$$\gamma'(Z_j') = +1 \qquad (j = 1, 2, \ldots, N) \tag{4-59}$$

In this case

$$w_0' = v_0' = N_1/N - N_2/N = P(\omega_1) - P(\omega_2) \tag{4-60}$$

$$[w_1' \cdots w_n']^T = V' = P(\omega_1)D_1 - P(\omega_2)D_2 \tag{4-61}$$

where it is assumed that the sample *a priori* probabilities and sample means are equal to the true *a priori* probabilities and expected vectors.

Furthermore, from (4-53) and (4-54), $P(\omega_i)$, D_i, and K_i are related in the transformed coordinate system as

$$P(\omega_1)(K_1 + D_1D_1^T) + P(\omega_2)(K_2 + D_2D_2^T) = I \tag{4-62}$$

$$P(\omega_1)D_1 + P(\omega_2)D_2 = 0 \tag{4-63}$$

Therefore,

$$D_1 = -[P(\omega_2)/P(\omega_1)]D_2 \tag{4-64}$$

$$D_2 - D_1 = [1/P(\omega_1)]D_2 \tag{4-65}$$

Substituting (4-64) into (4-61), we have

$$V' = -2P(\omega_2)D_2 \tag{4-66}$$

Thus, in the transformed coordinate system, V' is perpendicular to the mean-difference vector $D_2 - D_1[= D_2/P(\omega_1)]$, as shown in Fig. 4-9a. When

$P(\omega_1) = P(\omega_2)$, the threshold value of (4-60) becomes zero, as shown in Fig. 4-9b.

The transformation of (4-53) and (4-54) can be determined using only the information of the mixture of the two distributions. Information of individual class distributions is not needed. Therefore, we will call this transformation a *mixture normalization*. The mixture normalization will play an important role, when we would like to separate given samples into two groups without having any knowledge of class distributions [Fukunaga, 1970c, d]. This type of classification is called *unsupervised classification* or *clustering* and will be discussed in a later chapter. This is contrasted with *supervised classification* which uses a knowledge of class distributions to design the classifier.

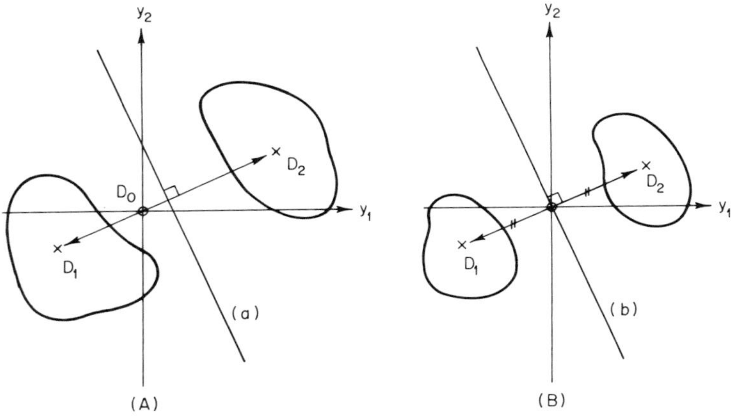

Fig. 4-9 Mean-square error classifier:

(A) $P(\omega_1) \neq P(\omega_2)$: (a) $2P(\omega_2)\, D_2{}^T Y + \{P(\omega_2) - P(\omega_1)\} = 0$

(B) $P(\omega_1) = P(\omega_2)$: (b) $D_2{}^T Y = 0$.

Thus, the conclusions of this subsection are:

(1) When we apply the mixture normalization, the linear discriminant function, which minimizes the mean-square error between the desired and actual output of the function, is determined by the correlation between the desired output and Y. This is true for any distribution.

(2) In particular, when the desired outputs are all $+1$, the classifier becomes a hyperplane which is perpendicular to the mean-difference vector. This is the same condition that was observed in (4-3), where the correlation classifier, or Euclidean distance classifier, was used. However, since (4-3)

and Fig. 4-9a have a different expression for the threshold value, the selection of the threshold value depends on which method is preferred for a particular application. When $P(\omega_1) = P(\omega_2)$, the threshold values are equal.

Mixture Normalization for Normal Distributions

The combination of the mixture normalization and a correlation classifier can be derived from a different viewpoint. Let us consider the case where two distributions have different expected vectors and covariance matrices. An intuitive approach for designing a linear discriminant function for these distributions is as follows:

(1) Assume two distributions with equal covariance matrices which are the average of the actual covariance matrices, $P(\omega_1)\Sigma_1 + P(\omega_2)\Sigma_2$.

(2) Apply the Bayes classifier. Since the covariance matrices are assumed to be equal, the Bayes classifier is linear, if the distributions are normal.

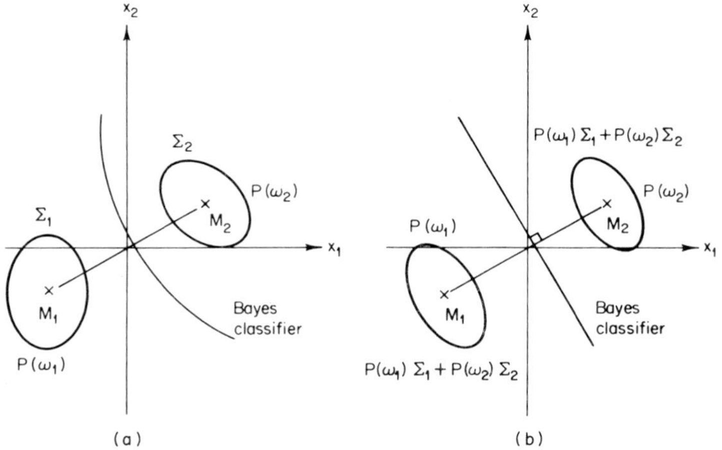

Fig. 4-10 Use of average covariance matrices.

Figure 4-10 shows an example of this process. From (4-2), the Bayes classifier for the above artificial distributions is

$$(M_2 - M_1)^T\{P(\omega_1)\Sigma_1 + P(\omega_2)\Sigma_2\}^{-1}X$$
$$- \tfrac{1}{2}(M_2 - M_1)^T\{P(\omega_1)\Sigma_1 + P(\omega_2)\Sigma_2\}^{-1}(M_2 + M_1)$$
$$\lessgtr \ln \{P(\omega_1)/P(\omega_2)\} \to X \in \begin{cases} \omega_1 \\ \omega_2 \end{cases} \tag{4-67}$$

Applying the mixture normalization of (4-62) and (4-63), (4-67) becomes

$$
\begin{aligned}
&(D_2 - D_1)^T\{P(\omega_1)K_1 + P(\omega_2)K_2\}^{-1}Y \\
&\qquad - \tfrac{1}{2}(D_2 - D_1)^T\{P(\omega_1)K_1 + P(\omega_2)K_2\}^{-1}(D_2 + D_1) \\
&= \frac{D_2^T}{P(\omega_1)}\left\{I - \frac{P(\omega_2)}{P(\omega_1)} D_2 D_2^T\right\}^{-1} Y \\
&\qquad - \frac{D_2^T}{2P(\omega_1)}\left\{I - \frac{P(\omega_2)}{P(\omega_1)} D_2 D_2^T\right\}^{-1} \frac{P(\omega_1) - P(\omega_2)}{P(\omega_1)} D_2 \\
&= \frac{D_2^T}{P(\omega_1)}\left\{I + \frac{[P(\omega_2)/P(\omega_1)]D_2 D_2^T}{1 - [P(\omega_2)/P(\omega_1)]D_2^T D_2}\right\} Y \\
&\qquad - \frac{P(\omega_1) - P(\omega_2)}{2P(\omega_1)^2} D_2^T\left\{I + \frac{[P(\omega_2)/P(\omega_1)]D_2 D_2^T}{1 - [P(\omega_2)/P(\omega_1)]D_2^T D_2}\right\} D_2 \\
&= \frac{1}{P(\omega_1) - P(\omega_2) D_2^T D_2}\left\{D_2^T Y - \frac{P(\omega_1) - P(\omega_2)}{2P(\omega_1)} D_2^T D_2\right\} \\
&\lessgtr \ln \frac{P(\omega_1)}{P(\omega_2)}
\end{aligned}
\tag{4-68}
$$

The hyperplane of the classifier is perpendicular to the mean-difference vector $D_2 - D_1$ [$= D_2/P(\omega_2)$]. The threshold value is given by

$$
\frac{P(\omega_1) - P(\omega_2)}{2P(\omega_1)} D_2^T D_2 - \{P(\omega_1) - P(\omega_2) D_2^T D_2\} \ln \frac{P(\omega_1)}{P(\omega_2)} \tag{4-69}
$$

When $P(\omega_1) = P(\omega_2)$, the threshold value of (4-69) is zero, and the classifier intersects the expected vector of the mixture distribution, which is the origin in the transformed coordinate system.

As was shown in (4-37), the linear discriminant function which maximizes the Fisher criterion has $V^T = (M_2 - M_1)^T(0.5\Sigma_1 + 0.5\Sigma_2)^{-1}$. Therefore, by the mixture normalization with $P(\omega_1) = P(\omega_2) = 0.5$, the optimum hyperplane in the Fisher sense should be perpendicular to the mean-difference vector $D_2 - D_1$, such that the correlation classifier can be used after the transformation.

4.4 Desired Output and Mean-Square Error

In pattern recognition, the classifier must be designed by using the samples near the decision boundary. The samples, which are far from the decision boundary, are less important to the design. However, if we fix the desired output $\gamma(Z)$ and try to minimize the mean-square error between $W^T\mathbf{Z}$ and $\gamma(Z)$, the larger $W^T\mathbf{Z}$ contributes more to the mean-square error. This has long been recognized as a disadvantage of the mean-square error approach in pattern recognition. In this section, we discuss a modification which reduces this effect.

Desired Output and Search Techniques

The modification is to use the following criteria, rather than those of (4-45):

(1)
$$\bar{\varepsilon}^2 = (1/N) \sum_{j=1}^{N} \{| W^T Z_j | - W^T Z_j\}^2 \tag{4-70}$$

(2)
$$\bar{\varepsilon}^2 = (1/N) \sum_{j=1}^{N} \{1 - \text{sign}(W^T Z_j)\}^2 \tag{4-71}$$

(3)
$$\bar{\varepsilon}^2 = (1/N) \sum_{j=1}^{N} \{\gamma(Z_j) - W^T Z_j\}^2$$

$$\gamma(Z_j)\text{: a variable with constraint } \gamma(Z_j) > 0 \tag{4-72}$$

where sign $(\cdot)$ is either $+1$ or -1, depending on the sign of $W^T Z_j$. In (4-70), $\gamma(Z_j)$ is selected as $| W^T Z_j |$, such that, only when $W^T Z_j < 0$, the contribution to $\bar{\varepsilon}^2$ is made with $(W^T Z)^2$ weighting. On the other hand, (4-71) counts the number of samples which give $W^T Z < 0$. In the third criterion, we adjust $\gamma(Z_j)$ as variables along with W. However, the $\gamma(Z_j)$'s are constrained to be positive.

These criteria perform well, but, because of the nonlinear functions such as $| \cdot |$, sign $(\cdot)$, and $\gamma(Z_j) > 0$, the explicit solutions of W which minimize these criteria are hard to obtain. Therefore, a search technique, such as the gradient method, must be used to find the optimum W.

The gradient method for minimizing a criterion is given by

$$W(l + 1) = W(l) - \varrho \, (\partial \bar{\varepsilon}^2 / \partial W) \,|_{W(l)} \tag{4-73}$$

where l indicates the lth iterative step, and ϱ is a positive constant.

Again, we cannot calculate $\partial \bar{\varepsilon}^2 / \partial W$ because of the nonlinear functions involved in $\bar{\varepsilon}^2$. However, by analogy to the linear case of (4-48), the following correction terms have been suggested for the criteria [Ho, 1966]:

(1) $$W(l+1) = W(l) + (2\varrho/N)U[\,|U^T W(l)| - U^T W(l)] \tag{4-74}$$

(2) $$W(l+1) = W(l) + (2\varrho/N)U[\Gamma_0 - \text{sign}\{U^T W(l)\}] \tag{4-75}$$

(3) $$W(l+1) = W(l) + (2\varrho/N)U[\Gamma(l) - U^T W(l)] \tag{4-76}$$

$$\Gamma(l+1) = \Gamma(l) + (2\varrho/N)[U^T W(l) - \Gamma(l)] + L(l) \tag{4-77}$$

where

(a) $|U^T W|$ is a vector whose components are the absolute values of the corresponding components of $U^T W$;

(b) $\text{sign}(U^T W)$ is a vector whose components are $+1$ or -1 depending on the signs of the corresponding components of $U^T W$;

(c) $\Gamma_0 = [1 \quad 1 \cdots 1]^T$;

(d) $L(l)$ is a penalty vector whose components are the functions of the corresponding components of $\Gamma(l)$.

A different approach is to treat the problem as that of finding a feasible solution of (4-43) to a linear programming problem with an artificially created cost vector. For this approach, it is suggested that readers refer to a text in linear programming.

Convergence Proof for Linearly Separable Case

When two distributions are known to be separable without errors by a linear discriminant function, there is a search process to optimize a criterion with convergence guaranteed [Ho, 1965, 1966].

Let us consider the third criterion of (4-72), in which $\gamma(Z_j)$ are adjusted along with W with the constraint $\gamma(Z_j) > 0$. Also, let us assume that our coordinate system has been already transformed to satisfy (4-53) and (4-54), such that

$$UU^T = NI \tag{4-78}$$

Since convergence does not depend on coordinate systems, this transformation simplifies discussion without losing generality. Then (4-72) becomes

$$\bar{\varepsilon}^2 = (1/N)(W^T U - \Gamma^T)(U^T W - \Gamma) = W^T W - (2/N)W^T U\Gamma + (1/N)\Gamma^T\Gamma \tag{4-79}$$

The gradients of $\bar{\varepsilon}^2$ with respect to W and Γ are

$$\partial\bar{\varepsilon}^2/\partial W = 2(W - (1/N)U\Gamma) \tag{4-80}$$

$$\partial\bar{\varepsilon}^2/\partial \Gamma = (2/N)(\Gamma - U^T W) \tag{4-81}$$

In order to satisfy the constraint $\gamma(Z_j) > 0$, a modification is made as follows:

(1) Positiveness of the γ's can be guaranteed if we start with positive numbers and never decrease their values.

This can be done by modifying Γ in proportion to

$$\Delta\Gamma = C + |C| \tag{4-82}$$

instead of C, where

$$C = U^T W - \Gamma \tag{4-83}$$

Thus, the components of the vector $\Delta\Gamma$ are positive or zero, depending on whether corresponding components of C are positive or negative. Thus, $\Gamma(l+1)$ is

$$\Gamma(l+1) = \Gamma(l) + \varrho\,\Delta\Gamma = \Gamma(l) + \varrho(C + |C|) \tag{4-84}$$

where ϱ is a properly selected positive constant. In this process γ's are always increased at each iterative step, and W is adjusted to reduce the error between $\gamma(Z_j)$ and $W^T Z_j$. However, one should be reminded that the scale of γ's and, subsequently, the scale of W does not change the essential structure of the classifier. That is, $W^T Z_j$ is the same classifier as $aW^T Z_j$.

(2) On the other hand, there are no restrictions on W. Therefore, for a given Γ, we can select W to satisfy $\partial\bar{\varepsilon}^2/\partial W = 0$ in (4-80).

$$W = (1/N)U\Gamma \tag{4-85}$$

or,

$$\begin{aligned} W(l+1) &= (1/N)U\Gamma(l+1) = (1/N)\{U\Gamma(l) + \varrho U\,\Delta\Gamma(l)\} \\ &= W(l) + (\varrho/N)U\,\Delta\Gamma(l) \end{aligned} \tag{4-86}$$

$W(l+1)$ minimizes $\bar{\varepsilon}^2$ for a given $\Gamma(l+1)$ at this iterative step.

In order to prove the convergence of the optimization process (4-84) and (4-86), let us study the norm of C. The term C is the vector which makes the correction for both Γ and W. Also, from (4-83) and (4-79),

$$\|C\|^2 = 0 \quad \rightarrow \quad U^T W = \Gamma \quad \rightarrow \quad \bar{\varepsilon}^2 = 0 \tag{4-87}$$

As l increases, the change of $\| C(l) \|^2$ can be calculated by substituting (4-84) and (4-86) into (4-83). The result is

$$\| C(l+1) \|^2 - \| C(l) \|^2$$
$$= -2\varrho C^T(l)[I - (U^T U/N)] \Delta\Gamma(l) + \varrho^2 \Delta\Gamma^T(l)[I - (U^T U/N)] \Delta\Gamma(l) \tag{4-88}$$

On the other hand, from (4-83), (4-85), and (4-78),

$$C^T U^T U = (W^T U - \Gamma^T) U^T U = (N W^T - \Gamma^T U^T) U = 0 \tag{4-89}$$

and

$$\begin{aligned} 2C^T \Delta\Gamma &= \{(C + | C |)^T + (C - | C |)^T\}(C + | C |) \\ &= (C + | C |)^T (C + | C |) = \Delta\Gamma^T \Delta\Gamma \end{aligned} \tag{4-90}$$

Therefore, (4-88) can be simplified as

$$\begin{aligned} \| C(l+1) \|^2 - \| C(l) \|^2 &= -\Delta\Gamma^T(l)[\varrho^2(U^T U/N) + (\varrho - \varrho^2) I] \Delta\Gamma(l) \\ &= -[\varrho^2(\| U \Delta\Gamma(l) \|^2/N) + (\varrho - \varrho^2) \| \Delta\Gamma(l) \|^2] \leq 0 \\ &\quad \text{for} \quad 0 < \varrho < 1 \end{aligned} \tag{4-91}$$

Equality holds only when $\| \Delta\Gamma \|^2 = 0$. Thus, as l increases, $\| C(l) \|^2$ decreases monotonically, until $\| \Delta\Gamma \|^2$ equals zero.

On the other hand, $\| \Delta\Gamma \|^2$ can be zero only when $\| C \|^2 = 0$ or $C = -| C |$. Now we will show that $C = -| C |$ never happens for linearly separable cases. $C = -| C |$ means

$$U^T W \leq \Gamma \tag{4-92}$$

where $<$ shows that this inequality holds for all components of these vectors. Assuming linear separability, we have

$$U^T W > 0 \tag{4-93}$$

Therefore, we can find some constant $a (\geq 1)$, such that

$$U^T W \leq U^T(aW) \leq \Gamma \tag{4-94}$$

This contradicts the fact that W is selected to minimize $\bar{\varepsilon}^2$ of (4-79) for a given Γ. Thus, the equality of (4-91) holds only when $\| C \|^2 = 0$. That is, $\| C(l) \|^2$ continues to decrease monotonically with l until $\| C \|^2$ equals zero. This completes the proof of convergence for linearly separable cases.

In linearly nonseparable cases, (4-93) and, hence, (4-94) does not hold. Therefore, we cannot extend the proof to linearly nonseparable cases. The only thing we can say is that the optimization process stops at either $\| C \|^2 = 0$ or $C = -| C |$.

4.5 Other Discriminant Functions

Linear Discriminant Functions for Binary Inputs

Often, in pattern recognition, the inputs to the recognition network are binary, either $+1$ or -1. Since binary inputs can be considered as a special case of the general input form, all of the previous discussion holds for binary inputs. However, binary inputs have some specific properties which simplify the discussion for some points. In this section, we will discuss those properties which are related to linear discriminant functions.

Independent Binary Inputs

When variables are independent, the density functions of a random input vector $\mathbf{X}$ for ω_1 and ω_2 are given by

$$p(X/\omega_i) = \prod_{j=1}^{n} p(x_j/\omega_i) \tag{4-95}$$

If $\mathbf{x}_j$'s are binary random variables, $+1$ or -1, the density function $p(x_j/\omega_i)$ for a discrete variable is replaced by a probability as follows:

$$\Pr\{\mathbf{x}_j = x_j/\omega_i\} = P_{ij}^{(1+x_j)/2}(1 - P_{ij})^{(1-x_j)/2} \tag{4-96}$$

where

$$P_{ij} = \Pr\{\mathbf{x}_j = 1/\omega_i\} \tag{4-97}$$

Taking the minus logarithm of $\Pr\{\mathbf{X} = X/\omega_1\}/\Pr\{\mathbf{X} = X/\omega_2\}$, instead of the conventional likelihood ratio $p(X/\omega_1)/p(X/\omega_2)$,

$$\begin{aligned} h(X) &= -\sum_{j=1}^{n}\left[\frac{1+x_j}{2}\ln\frac{P_{1j}}{P_{2j}} + \frac{1-x_j}{2}\ln\frac{1-P_{1j}}{1-P_{2j}}\right] \\ &= -\frac{1}{2}\left\{\sum_{j=1}^{n}\left[\ln\frac{P_{1j}(1-P_{2j})}{P_{2j}(1-P_{1j})}\right]x_j + \sum_{j=1}^{n}\ln\frac{P_{1j}(1-P_{1j})}{P_{2j}(1-P_{2j})}\right\} \end{aligned} \tag{4-98}$$

This is a linear function of x_j. Therefore, the Bayes classifier is linear if we have independent binary inputs. The discussion of dependent binary variables will be given in a later chapter.

Orthonormality of Inputs

When we have n binary inputs forming an input vector X, the number of all possible inputs is 2^n, $\{X_0, \ldots, X_{2^n-1}\}$. Then the components of X_j, x_{jl} $(l = 1, 2, \ldots, n)$, satisfy

$$(1/2^n) \sum_{j=0}^{2^n-1} x_{jl} = 0 \tag{4-99}$$

$$(1/2^n) \sum_{j=0}^{2^n-1} x_{jl}^2 = 1 \tag{4-100}$$

$$(1/2^n) \sum_{j=0}^{2^n-1} x_{jl}x_{jk} = 0 \qquad (l \neq k) \tag{4-101}$$

Thus, if we define the sample matrix as

$$U = \underbrace{\left.\begin{bmatrix} 1 & 1 & \cdots & 1 \\ X_0 & X_1 & \cdots & X_{2^n-1} \end{bmatrix}\right\}}_{2^n} n+1 \tag{4-102}$$

then the row vectors of U are mutually orthonormal, that is

$$UU^T = 2^n I \tag{4-103}$$

EXAMPLE 4-4 Table 4-1 shows an example of three binary inputs. We can easily see that (4-99)–(4-103) are all satisfied.

Let $\gamma(X_j)$ be the desired output of a pattern recognition network for the inputs X_j. The $\gamma(X_j)$'s are not necessarily binary numbers. One of the design procedures which may be used to realize this network by a linear discriminant function is to minimize the mean-square error between $\gamma(X_j)$ and $V^TX_j + v_0$. The mean-square error can be expressed by

$$\bar{\varepsilon}^2 = (1/2^n) \sum_{j=0}^{2^n-1} \{\gamma(X_j) - (V^TX_j + v_0)\}^2 = (1/2^n)(W^TU - \Gamma^T)(U^TW - \Gamma) \tag{4-104}$$

where W and Γ are the same as the ones used in (4-45). Therefore, the W which minimizes $\bar{\varepsilon}^2$ is

$$\partial\bar{\varepsilon}^2/\partial W = (2/2^n)U(U^TW - \Gamma) = 2[W - (1/2^n)U\Gamma] = 0 \tag{4-105}$$

$$W = (1/2^n)U\Gamma \tag{4-106}$$

TABLE 4-1

ALL POSSIBLE BINARY INPUTS

	X_0	X_1	X_2	X_3	X_4	X_5	X_6	X_7
x_0	1	1	1	1	1	1	1	1
x_1	−1	1	−1	1	−1	1	−1	1
x_2	−1	−1	1	1	−1	−1	1	1
x_3	−1	−1	−1	−1	1	1	1	1
$x_1 x_2$	1	−1	−1	1	1	−1	−1	1
$x_1 x_3$	1	−1	1	−1	−1	1	−1	1
$x_2 x_3$	1	1	−1	−1	−1	−1	1	1
$x_1 x_2 x_3$	−1	1	1	−1	1	−1	−1	1

Thus, the coefficients of the linear discriminant function are given by the correlation between the desired outputs and the input X's. The above discussion is identical to that of the general linear discriminant functions. However, it should be noted that for binary inputs $UU^T = NI$ is automatically satisfied without transformation.

As an example of $\gamma(X_j)$, let us use

$$\gamma(X_j) = p(X_j)\{P(\omega_1/X_j) - P(\omega_2/X_j)\} = P(\omega_1)p(X_j/\omega_1) - P(\omega_2)p(X_j/\omega_2) \tag{4-107}$$

The term $\gamma(X_j)$ would be positive for $P(\omega_1)p(X_j/\omega_1) > P(\omega_2)p(X_j/\omega_2)$ or $P(\omega_1/X_j) > P(\omega_2/X_j)$, and be negative otherwise. Also, the absolute value of $\gamma(X_j)$ depends on $p(X_j/\omega_1)$ and $p(X_j/\omega_2)$. When n is large, but the number of observed samples N is far less than 2^n, $p(X_j/\omega_1)$ and $p(X_j/\omega_2)$ become nonzero only for the observed X_j. Therefore, the correlation of (4-106) can be carried out only by N multiplications and additions, instead of 2^n [Fukunaga, 1965].

Table 4–1 suggests that we can extend our vector $X_j = [x_{j1} \cdots x_{jn}]^T$ to

$$Y_j = [\underbrace{1 \quad x_{j1} \cdots x_{jn}\, (x_{j1}x_{j2}) \cdots (x_{j1}x_{j2} \cdots x_{jn})}_{2^n}] \tag{4-108}$$

Then the sample matrix for this extended vector becomes a square matrix as

$$U' = [\underbrace{Y_0 \quad Y_1 \cdots Y_{2^n-1}}_{2^n}]\} \, 2^n \tag{4-109}$$

The row vectors of U' are also orthonormal, such that

$$U'U'^T = 2^n I \tag{4-110}$$

A linear discriminant function for Y is

$$\sum_{j=0}^{2^n-1} w_j y_j = w_0 + \sum_{j=1}^{n} w_j x_j + \sum_i \sum_j w_l x_i x_j + \cdots + w_{2^n-1} x_1 \cdots x_n \tag{4-111}$$

In accordance with the reasoning applied to derive (4-106), we can determine W of (4-111) by

$$W = (1/2^n) U' \Gamma \tag{4-112}$$

The following should be noted here:

(1) any desired output is expressed by $W^T Y$ without error;

(2) since y_l's are mutually orthonormal, $\bar{\varepsilon}^2$ due to the elimination of $w_l y_l$ from $W^T Y$ is w_l^2;

(3) The $\bar{\varepsilon}^2$ determined by the linear discriminant function of $V^T X + v_0$ is

$$\bar{\varepsilon}^2 = \sum_{j=n+1}^{2^n-1} w_j^2 \tag{4-113}$$

Piecewise Linear Discriminant Functions

If we limit our discussion to two-class problems, linear discriminant functions have wide applications, although some sacrifice in performance is unavoidable. However, when we have to handle three or more classes, we find many cases where the performance of a linear discriminant function becomes unacceptably poor. This also can even be observed in two-class problems when each class consists of several clusters. For these cases, a set of linear discriminant functions, which is called a *piecewise linear discriminant function*, gives increased flexibility in designing a classifier. Fig. 4-11 shows an example of four classes.

For multiclass or multicluster problems, the multihypotheses test in the Bayes sense gives the best classifier with regard to minimizing the expected cost or the probability of error. In the test, the density function of each class, or its logarithm, should be compared with the ones of other classes, as shown in (3-114). Figure 4-11a shows these boundaries. When the estimation of density functions is too complicated, or when the boundaries determined by this process are too complicated, we may replace the complex boundaries by a simple set of linear boundaries. This, of course, results in

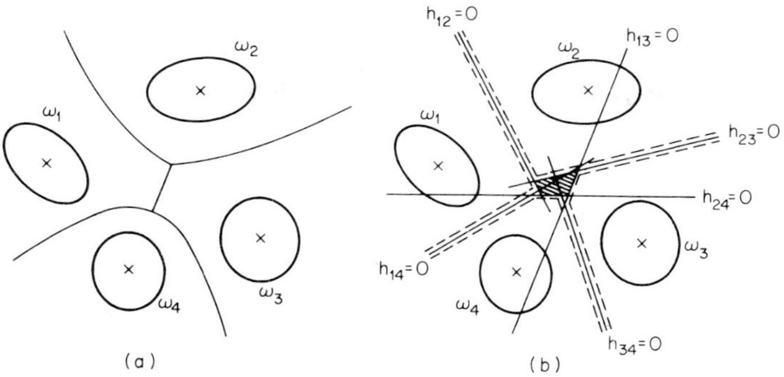

Fig. 4-11 Four distributions: (a) Bayes classifier; (b) piecewise linear classifier.

some sacrifice in performance. However, the use of linear boundaries is particularly effective for multiclass problems, as complexity increases rapidly with the number of classes, and some simplification of the entire process is desirable. For example, Fig. 4-11b shows the replacement of the Bayes boundaries of Fig. 4-11a by piecewise linear boundaries.

For piecewise linear discriminant functions, a set of linear functions is given by

$$h_{ij}(X) = V_{ij}^T X + v_{ij0} \qquad (i, j = 1, 2, \ldots, M; \quad i \neq j) \tag{4-114}$$

where M is the number of classes. The signs of V_{ij} are selected such that the distribution of class i is located on the positive side of $h_{ij}(X)$ and class j on the negative side. Therefore,

$$h_{ij}(X) = -h_{ji}(X) \tag{4-115}$$

Let us assume that the region for each class is convex, as shown in Fig. 4-11b. Then the region of class i can be simply specified by

$$h_{i1}(X) > 0, \ldots, h_{iM}(X) > 0 \rightarrow X \in \omega_i \qquad [h_{ii}(X) \text{ is excluded}] \tag{4-116}$$

As evidenced by the hatched part of Fig. 4-11b, the M regions given by (4-116) do not necessarily cover the entire space. When a sample falls in this region, the piecewise linear classifier cannot decide the class of this sample; we call this a *reject region*. Implementation of (4-116) consists of $M - 1$ linear discriminant functions and a logical AND circuit with $M - 1$ inputs of sign$\{h_{ij}(X)\}$, as is shown in Fig. 4-12. Since the network has two cascaded circuits, the piecewise linear classifier is sometimes called a *layered machine*. When the assumption of convexity does not hold, we have to cal-

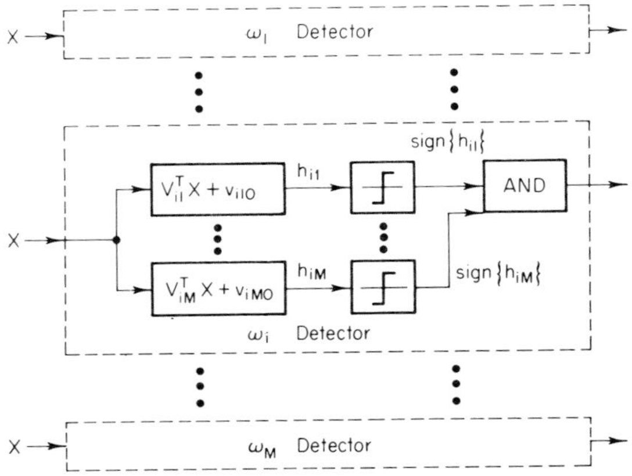

Fig. 4-12 Implementation of a piecewise linear classifier.

culate the intersections of these $M - 1$ hyperplanes and assign the decision logic according to these intersections. Consequently, the classifier becomes too complicated to be practical. Therefore, we will limit our discussion to convex regions in this book.

The probability of error for each class ε_i can be expressed in terms of the $M - 1$ dimensional distribution function as

$$\begin{aligned}\varepsilon_i &= 1 - \Pr\{h_{i1}(\mathbf{X}) > 0, \ldots, h_{iM}(\mathbf{X}) > 0/\mathbf{X} \in \omega_i\} \\ &= 1 - \int_0^\infty \cdots \int_0^\infty p(h_{i1}, \ldots, h_{iM}/\omega_i)\, dh_{i1} \cdots dh_{iM} \\ &\qquad [h_{ii}(X) \text{ is excluded}]\end{aligned} \tag{4-117}$$

The total error is

$$\varepsilon = \sum_{i=1}^{M} P(\omega_i)\varepsilon_i \tag{4-118}$$

Knowing the structure of piecewise linear classifiers, our problem is how to design the V's and v_0's for a given set of M distributions. Because of the complexity involved, solutions for this problem are not as clear-cut as in a linear classifier.

Three approaches are mentioned briefly:

(1) We can adjust the V's and v_0's so as to minimize ε of (4-118). Since it is difficult to get an explicit mathematical expression for ε, the error should be calculated numerically each time when we adjust the V's and v_0's. When $\mathbf{X}$ is distributed normally for all classes, some simplification can be achieved, since the $\mathbf{h}$'s are also normally distributed and $p(h_{i1}, \ldots, h_{iM}/\omega_i)$

is given by an explicit mathematical expression. Even for this case, the integration of an $M-1$ dimensional normal distribution in the first quadrant must be carried out in a numerical way, using techniques such as the Monte Carlo method.

(2) Design a linear discriminant function between a pair of classes according to one of the methods discussed previously for two-class problems. $\binom{M}{2}$ discriminant functions are calculated. Then use them as a piecewise linear discriminant function without further modification. With M normal distributions having all equal covariance matrices ($\Sigma_1 = \cdots = \Sigma_M$), this procedure is equivalent to using the Bayes classifier. When distributions are quite different, further modification can result in less error. However, in many applications, the decrease in error is found to be relatively minor by the further adjustment of V's and v_0's.

(3) We can assign the desired output $\gamma(\mathbf{X})$ for a piecewise linear discriminant function and minimize the mean-square error between the desired and actual outputs in order to find the optimum V's and v_0's. The desired outputs could be fixed or could be adjusted as variables with constraints. Unfortunately, even for piecewise linearly separable data, there is no proof of convergence.

EXAMPLE 4-5 An example is given here for four normal distributions which are presented as Standard Data in Computer Projects of Chapter 2. Since these four distributions are normal, we can calculate the optimum linear classifier between each pair of classes in the sense of minimum errors. Table 4-2 shows the pairwise errors by $\varepsilon_{ij}(i, j = 1, 2, 3, 4)$ due to these opti-

TABLE 4-2

THE PROBABILITY OF ERROR FOR A FOUR-CLASS PROBLEM[a]

$\varepsilon_{ij}(\%)$ \ i	1	2	3	4	
ε_{i1}	—	6.7	2.3	4.7	
ε_{i2}	3.3	—	2.5	12.3	
ε_{i3}	1.3	3.6	—	0.9	
ε_{i4}	3.5	24.5	1.1	—	
$\sum_{j=1}^{4} \varepsilon_{ij}$	8.1	34.8	5.9	17.9	
ε_i	5.2	30.4	3.4	16.0	$\varepsilon_T = \frac{1}{4} \sum_{i=1}^{4} \varepsilon_i = 13.75$

[a] [Fukunaga, 1970a].

mum linear classifiers. The summations of the pairwise errors are also given as $\Sigma\varepsilon_{ij}$. When piecewise linear classifiers are set up, by using these linear classifiers without further modification, the error is calculated by (4-117) and (4-118) and is shown in Table 4-2 as ε_i and ε_T.

In order to make sure that ε_T of Table 4-2 is close to the optimum value, ε_T's have been calculated by changing the V's and v_0's. As one of the results, Fig. 4-13 shows the effect of V_{24} on ε_T. This example was selected because ε_{24} and ε_{42} are the dominant errors in ε_T. As is seen in Fig. 4-13, the totally optimum value of V_{24} is shifted from the pairwise optimum of V_{24}. However the change of ε_T is within 0.3%. The effect of the other V's is much smaller. This result justifies the use of the pairwise optimum classifiers, without readjustment, for this particular example.

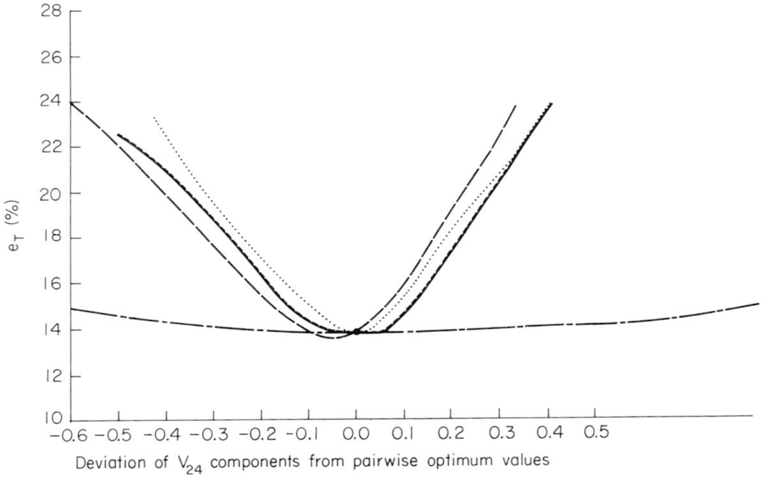

Fig. 4-13 Total error ε_T vs changes of V_{24} components: (— - —) V_{240}; (——) V_{241}; (- - - -) V_{243}; (– – –) V_{245}; (······) V_{247}. Note: V_{24i} is the ith component of V_{24} [Fukunaga, 1970a].

Generalized Linear Discriminant Functions

Thus far there has been considerable discussion about linear discriminant functions ignoring some nonlinear discriminant functions. One of the reasons for this is that for high dimensional observation vectors only linear or piecewise linear discriminant functions give a reasonable compromise between performance and simplicity. However, another important aspect is that even a nonlinear discriminant function can be interpreted as a linear discriminant function in a *functional space*. That is,

$$h(X) = \sum_{j=1}^{r} w_j g_j(X) \gtrless 0 \rightarrow X \in \begin{cases} \omega_1 \\ \omega_2 \end{cases} \tag{4-119}$$

is a linear discriminant function in a functional space where the r $g_j(X)$'s are variables, instead of n x's in the original space. An example is (4-111) for binary inputs, where 2^n new variables are used.

Another important example is the implementation of a quadratic surface, where we define the r $g_j(X)$'s such that the first n components are x_i^2 ($i = 1, 2, \ldots, n$), the next $n(n-1)/2$ components are all pairs $x_i x_j$ ($i, j = 1, 2, \ldots, n$, $i \neq j$), and the last n components are x_i ($i = 1, 2, \ldots, n$). The result of this transformation is that for every quadratic discriminant function of X there is a corresponding linear discriminant function of the $g_j(X)$'s.

The term $g_j(X)$ could be called a *feature*. Selection of effective features is an independent subject and will be discussed in Chapters 8, 9, and 10.

Computer Projects

Write the following programs:

4-1 Design the linear classifier which minimizes the probability of error for normal distributions.

Data: Standard Data $i = 1, 2$. (Answer: Fig. 4-8)

4-2 Normalize the mixture of two normal distributions. After normalization, apply the correlation technique to classify the generated data. Check the effect of the threshold value on the probability of error.

Data: Standard Data $i = 1,2$.

4-3 Minimize the mean-square error between the desired and actual outputs of a linear discriminant function for the following:

(a) Use (4-45) where $\Gamma = [1 \quad 1 \cdots 1]^T$;
(b) Use (4-75) where $\Gamma = [1 \quad 1 \cdots 1]^T$;
(c) Use (4-76) and (4-77) with a proper $L(l)$;
(d) Use (4-74).

Data: Standard Data $i = 1, 2$.

4-4 Minimize the mean-square error between the desired and actual outputs of a linear discriminant function for binary inputs. The desired outputs are to be assigned according to $P(\omega_1)p(X/\omega_1) - P(\omega_2)p(X/\omega_2)$. Check how the linear discriminant function is designed for three inputs. Also, see the effect of the threshold value on the probability of error.

4-5 Use Computer Project 4-3b to design pairwise linear classifiers, and calculate the multiclass error.

Data: Standard Data $i = 1, 2, 3, 4$.

Problems

4-1 Pearson type II and VII distributions are given by

$$p(Y/\omega_i) = A\left(\prod_{j=1}^{n} \alpha_{ij}\right)\left\{1 - \sum_{j=1}^{n} \alpha_{ij}^2(y_j - d_{ij})^2\right\}^{m} \qquad \text{(Type II)}$$

$$p(Y/\omega_i) = A\left(\prod_{j=1}^{n} \alpha_{ij}\right)\left\{1 + \sum_{j=1}^{n} \alpha_{ij}^2(y_j - d_{ij})^2\right\}^{-m} \qquad \text{(Type VII)}$$

(a) Show that the Bayes classifiers for these distributions are quadratic.

(b) Extending the above result, what is the general form of distributions for which the Bayes classifier is quadratic?

4-2 List all cases where the Bayes test gives a linear discriminant function.

4-3 Two distributions are given by

$$P(\omega_1) = P(\omega_2) = 0.5, \qquad M_1 = \begin{bmatrix} -1 \\ 0 \end{bmatrix}, \qquad M_2 = \begin{bmatrix} +1 \\ 0 \end{bmatrix}$$

$$\Sigma_1 = \Sigma_2 = \begin{bmatrix} 4 & 3 \\ 3 & 4 \end{bmatrix}$$

Calculate the errors due to the Bayes classifier and the bisector.

4-4 Using the same data as in Problem 4-3, except

$$\Sigma_1 = \begin{bmatrix} 4 & 3 \\ 3 & 4 \end{bmatrix} \quad \text{and} \quad \Sigma_2 = \begin{bmatrix} 4 & -3 \\ -3 & 4 \end{bmatrix}$$

find the optimum linear discriminant function which minimizes the probability of error.

4-5 Using the same data as in Problem 4-4, find the linear discriminant function which maximizes the Fisher criterion.

4-6 In "Linear Discriminant Functions" (Section 4.3), we discuss the discriminant function, which minimizes the mean-square error, based on a finite number of available samples. Rewrite this part, assuming that we have two density functions given instead of samples.

4-7 Find the result of the mixture normalization for the data given in Problem 4-3.

4-8 Propose a proper penalty function for $L(l)$ of (4-77).

4-9 Two coins have different probabilities, 0.55 and 0.45, for the occurrence of heads. Assuming n tosses, find the discriminant function which separates these two coins. Discuss the relation between the number of tosses n and the probability of error of this classification.

4-10 Design a linear discriminant function for the data given in following Table, assuming $P(\omega_1) = P(\omega_2) = 0.5$.

x_1	x_2	x_3	$P(X/\omega_1)$	$P(X/\omega_2)$
-1	-1	-1	1/3	0
$+1$	-1	-1	1/24	1/8
-1	$+1$	-1	1/8	1/24
$+1$	$+1$	-1	0	1/3
-1	-1	$+1$	1/3	0
$+1$	-1	$+1$	1/24	1/8
-1	$+1$	$+1$	1/8	1/24
$+1$	$+1$	$+1$	0	1/3

4-11 In the design of a piecewise linear classifier, propose a way to assign the desired output so that we can apply the technique of minimizing the mean-square error.

Chapter 5

PARAMETER ESTIMATION

As discussed in the previous chapters, once we know the density functions of the distributions, we can design the boundary to partition the space to classify samples. The next question is how to estimate these density functions from available samples. This problem is very complex when we cannot assume any structure for the multivariate density function. However, if we can assume the functional form of the density function, our problem becomes one of estimating a finite number of parameters, and we can use well-known techniques of *parameter estimation*. Estimating the parameters of known density functions and classifying samples on the basis of the estimated densities is called a *parametric approach*.

Our first concern in parameter estimation is that of estimating the key parameters that characterize a density function, such as the expected vector and covariance matrix, etc., where these parameters are assumed to be nonrandom. Then our discussion will be extended to the case where these parameters are random. These problems are called *point estimation*.

Other important quantities in pattern recognition are the probability of error, likelihood ratio, eigenvalues and eigenvectors. Since the probability of error and likelihood ratio are complicated functions, straightforward application of standard estimation techniques is not adequate. In this chapter, we discuss methods of estimating these quantities from available samples. The estimation of eigenvalues and eigenvectors is strongly related to feature selection and will, therefore, be discussed in Chapter 8.

The third subject in this chapter is the estimation of the confidence interval containing, with a given probability, the true value of a parameter. This is the study of statistical inference, called *interval estimation.*

5.1 Estimation of Nonrandom Parameters

Before we discuss various estimates, we should introduce the terminology of nonrandom parameter estimation which often appears in the literature.

Terminologies

Let Θ and $\hat{\mathbf{\Theta}}$ be the true parameter vector and its estimate, respectively. The term $\hat{\mathbf{\Theta}}$ is a function G of observed n-dimensional random sample vectors $\mathbf{X}_1, \mathbf{X}_2, \ldots, \mathbf{X}_N$, which are drawn from a distribution to be estimated. Thus, the estimate becomes a random vector. Unless otherwise stated, the $\mathbf{X}_i$'s are assumed to be independent and identically distributed. Thus,

$$\hat{\mathbf{\Theta}} = G(\mathbf{X}_1, \ldots, \mathbf{X}_N) = G(\mathbf{Z}) \tag{5-1}$$

where $\mathbf{Z}$ is a vector with $n \times N$ components as

$$\mathbf{Z} = [\mathbf{X}_1^T \, \mathbf{X}_2^T \cdots \mathbf{X}_N^T]^T \tag{5-2}$$

and is used to simplify expressions. Since the observed samples are random vectors, $\hat{\mathbf{\Theta}}$ is also a random vector and is written as either $\hat{\mathbf{\Theta}}$ or $\hat{\Theta}(\mathbf{Z})$.

(1) *Unbiased estimate*

If

$$\begin{aligned} E\{\hat{\mathbf{\Theta}}\} &= \int_{\mathscr{S}} \cdots \int_{\mathscr{S}} G(X_1, \ldots, X_N) p(X_1, \ldots, X_N) \, dX_1 \cdots dX_N \\ &= \int_{\mathscr{S}} G(Z) p(Z) \, dZ = \Theta \end{aligned} \tag{5-3}$$

then $\hat{\mathbf{\Theta}}$ is termed an *unbiased estimate* of Θ; otherwise it is a *biased estimate.*

(2) *Consistent estimate*

If the estimate of (5-1) converges in probability to Θ as $N \to \infty$, that is,

$$\lim_{N\to\infty} \Pr\{\| \hat{\mathbf{\Theta}} - \Theta \| < \varepsilon\} = 1 \tag{5-4}$$

The term $\hat{\mathbf{\Theta}}$ is called a *consistent estimate* of Θ.

(3) *Efficient estimate*

When two estimates of Θ based on the same observed samples are compared, the *efficiency* of the second estimate $\hat{\mathbf{\Theta}}_2$ relative to the first estimate $\hat{\mathbf{\Theta}}_1$ is defined by

$$\eta = E\{ \| \hat{\mathbf{\Theta}}_1 - \Theta \|^2 \} / E\{ \| \hat{\mathbf{\Theta}}_2 - \Theta \|^2 \} \tag{5-5}$$

When $\hat{\mathbf{\Theta}}_1$ is found such that η is always less than or equal to 1 for all possible $\hat{\mathbf{\Theta}}_2$, $\hat{\mathbf{\Theta}}_1$ is termed an *efficient estimate.*

(4) *Sufficient estimate*

An estimate is called sufficient for Θ if it contains all information about Θ which is contained in the set of observed samples. In other words, $\hat{\Theta}_1(\mathbf{Z})$ is a sufficient estimate if, and only if, for any other estimates $\hat{\Theta}_2(\mathbf{Z}), \ldots, \hat{\Theta}_N(\mathbf{Z})$ (for which the Jacobian of the associated transformation is not identically zero) the conditional density function of $\hat{\Theta}_2(\mathbf{Z}), \ldots, \hat{\Theta}_N(\mathbf{Z})$, given $\hat{\Theta}_1(\mathbf{Z})$, does not depend on Θ.

$$p(\hat{\Theta}_2, \ldots, \hat{\Theta}_N / \hat{\Theta}_1, \Theta) = f(\hat{\Theta}_1, \ldots, \hat{\Theta}_N) \tag{5-6}$$

Thus, the best estimate we can find should be unbiased, consistent, efficient, and sufficient.

Moment Estimates

The fundamental parameters that characterize a density function are the moments, and they are usually estimated by the *sample moments.* A general $(i_1 + i_2 + \cdots + i_n)$th order sample moment is defined by the average of the $(i_1 + i_2 + \cdots + i_n)$th order moments of individual random samples as

$$\hat{\mathbf{m}}_{i_1\cdots i_n} = (1/N) \sum_{j=1}^{N} \mathbf{x}_{j_1}^{i_1}\mathbf{x}_{j_2}^{i_2} \cdots \mathbf{x}_{j_n}^{i_n} \tag{5-7}$$

where $\mathbf{x}_{jk}$ is the kth component of the jth sample. Since the $\mathbf{X}_j$'s are selected randomly from a distribution, it is reasonable to assume that the $\mathbf{X}_j$'s are mutually independent and identically distributed. Therefore,

$$\begin{aligned} E\{\hat{\mathbf{m}}_{i_1 i_2 \cdots i_n}\} &= (1/N) \sum_{j=1}^{N} E\{\mathbf{x}_{j_1}^{i_1} \mathbf{x}_{j_2}^{i_2} \cdots \mathbf{x}_{j_n}^{i_n}\} \\ &= (1/N) \sum_{j=1}^{N} m_{i_1 i_2 \cdots i_n} = m_{i_1 i_2 \cdots i_n} \end{aligned} \tag{5-8}$$

where $m_{i_1 i_2 \cdots i_n}$ is the true $(i_1 + \cdots + i_n)$th moment of this distribution. Thus, the sample moment is an unbiased estimate.

The variance of this estimate can be calculated as

$$\begin{aligned} \mathrm{Var}[\hat{\mathbf{m}}_{i_1 i_2 \cdots i_n}] &= E\{(\hat{\mathbf{m}}_{i_1 \cdots i_n} - m_{i_1 \cdots i_n})^2\} \\ &= (1/N^2) \sum_{j=1}^{N} E\{(\mathbf{x}_{j_1}^{i_1} \cdots \mathbf{x}_{j_n}^{i_n} - m_{i_1 \cdots i_n})^2\} \\ &= (1/N)\, \mathrm{Var}[\mathbf{x}_1^{i_1} \cdots \mathbf{x}_n^{i_n}] \end{aligned} \tag{5-9}$$

That is, the variance of the estimate is $1/N$ times the variance of the moment of individual random sample. The estimate, therefore, is consistent if the variance of the moment is bounded.

In most applications, our attention is focused on the first-and second-order moments, the *sample mean vector* and *sample autocorrelation matrix*, respectively. These are defined by

$$\hat{\mathbf{M}} = (1/N) \sum_{j=1}^{N} \mathbf{X}_j \tag{5-10}$$

and

$$\hat{\mathbf{S}} = (1/N) \sum_{j=1}^{N} \mathbf{X}_j \mathbf{X}_j^T \tag{5-11}$$

All components of (5-10) and (5-11) are specific examples of (5-8) and (5-9). Therefore, the estimates (5-10) and (5-11) are unbiased and consistent because their variances are reduced to $1/N$ times the original bounded ones.

The situation is somewhat different when we discuss central moments, such as variances and covariance matrices. Let us define an estimate of a covariance matrix as

$$\hat{\boldsymbol{\Sigma}} = (1/N) \sum_{j=1}^{N} (\mathbf{X}_j - \hat{\mathbf{M}})(\mathbf{X}_j - \hat{\mathbf{M}})^T \tag{5-12}$$

Since the true expected vector M is not available, we use the sample mean vector $\hat{\mathbf{M}}$ instead. Then

$$\hat{\mathbf{\Sigma}} = (1/N) \sum_{j=1}^{N} \{(\mathbf{X}_j - M) - (\hat{\mathbf{M}} - M)\}\{(\mathbf{X}_j - M) - (\hat{\mathbf{M}} - M)\}^T$$
$$= (1/N) \sum_{j=1}^{N} (\mathbf{X}_j - M)(\mathbf{X}_j - M)^T - (\hat{\mathbf{M}} - M)(\hat{\mathbf{M}} - M)^T \qquad (5\text{-}13)$$

Thus, taking the expectation of $\hat{\mathbf{\Sigma}}$,

$$E\{\hat{\mathbf{\Sigma}}\} = \Sigma - E\{(\hat{\mathbf{M}} - M)(\hat{\mathbf{M}} - M)^T\}$$
$$= \Sigma - (1/N)\Sigma = \frac{N-1}{N}\Sigma \qquad (5\text{-}14)$$

That is, (5-14) shows that $\hat{\mathbf{\Sigma}}$ is a biased estimate of Σ. This bias can be eliminated by using a modified estimate for the covariance matrix as

$$\hat{\mathbf{\Sigma}} = \frac{1}{N-1} \sum_{j=1}^{N} (\mathbf{X}_j - \hat{\mathbf{M}})(\mathbf{X}_j - \hat{\mathbf{M}})^T \qquad (5\text{-}15)$$

Both (5-12) and (5-15) are termed a *sample covariance matrix*. However, let us use (5-15) as the estimate of a covariance matrix unless otherwise stated, because of its unbiasedness. When N is large, both are practically the same.

When $\mathbf{X}$ is normally distributed, the density function of $\hat{\mathbf{M}}$ is also normal. Even when $\mathbf{X}$ is not normal, the density function of $\hat{\mathbf{M}}$ tends to be normal with large N, by the central limit theorem. The dispersion of this estimate can be calculated by

$$E\{(\hat{\mathbf{M}} - M)(\hat{\mathbf{M}} - M)^T\} = (1/N)\Sigma \qquad (5\text{-}16)$$

regardless of the distribution of $\mathbf{X}$.

On the other hand, the density function of $\hat{\mathbf{\Sigma}}$ is very complex. When $\mathbf{X}$ is a normal distribution, the density function of $\hat{\mathbf{\Sigma}}$ has been shown to be the *Wishart distribution*, which is given by

$$p(\hat{\Sigma}) = \frac{(N-1)^n \,|\, \hat{\Sigma} \,|^{(N-n-2)/2} \exp\{-\frac{1}{2}(N-1) \operatorname{tr} \Sigma^{-1}\hat{\Sigma}\}}{2^{(N-1)n/2}\pi^{n(n-1)/4} \,|\, \Sigma \,|^{(N-1)/2} \prod_{i=1}^{n} \Gamma[\frac{1}{2}(N-i)]} \qquad (5\text{-}17)$$

Various properties of the Wishart distribution are discussed in the literature [Anderson, 1958]. However, since in most instances we are primarily concerned with some measure of the dispersion of the estimate, but not with the precise density, we may use the variance of each component of

$\hat{\mathbf{\Sigma}}$ as the measure.

$$\text{Var}\{\hat{\boldsymbol{\sigma}}_{kl}\} \cong (1/N)\,\text{Var}\{(\mathbf{x}_k - m_k)(\mathbf{x}_l - m_l)\} \tag{5-18}$$

where the approximation is due to the use of $\hat{\mathbf{m}}_k$ on the left side and m_k on the right side. Both sides are practically the same for $N \gg 1$.

The Maximum Likelihood Estimate

A more general method of point estimation is to select, for the observed value of Z, the Θ which maximizes $p(Z/\Theta)$ or $\ln p(Z/\Theta)$. This means that we select the value of Θ for which Z is the most likely result. It should be clear that this estimate is a function of Z. The logarithm is taken for computational convenience and does not change the maximum point because of its monotonicity. This estimate is termed the *maximum likelihood estimate.* The maximum likelihood estimate is the solution of the following equivalent equations:

$$\left.\frac{\partial p(Z/\Theta)}{\partial \Theta}\right|_{\Theta=\hat{\Theta}(Z)} = 0 \quad \text{or} \quad \left.\frac{\partial \ln p(Z/\Theta)}{\partial \Theta}\right|_{\Theta=\hat{\Theta}(Z)} = 0 \tag{5-19}$$

These equations are termed the *likelihood equations.*

EXAMPLE 5-1 Let us find the maximum likelihood estimate of the expected vector for a normal distribution, based on N available samples. Equation (5-19) becomes

$$\begin{aligned}
&\frac{\partial \ln p(X_1, \ldots, X_N/M)}{\partial M} \\
&\quad = \sum_{i=1}^{N} \frac{\partial \ln p(X_i/M)}{\partial M} \\
&\quad = \sum_{i=1}^{N} \frac{\partial}{\partial M}\left[-\tfrac{1}{2}(X_i - M)^T\Sigma^{-1}(X_i - M) - \tfrac{1}{2}\ln|\Sigma| - \tfrac{1}{2}n\ln(2\pi)\right] \\
&\quad = \Sigma^{-1}\left\{\sum_{i=1}^{N}(X_i - M)\right\}
\end{aligned} \tag{5-20}$$

Therefore,

$$\left.\frac{\partial \ln p(Z/M)}{\partial M}\right|_{M=\hat{M}(Z)} = \Sigma^{-1}\left.\left\{\sum_{i=1}^{N}(X_i - M)\right\}\right|_{M=\hat{M}(Z)} = 0 \tag{5-21}$$

and the solution of (5-21) is

$$\hat{M}(\mathbf{Z}) = (1/N)\sum_{i=1}^{N}\mathbf{X}_i \tag{5-22}$$

which is the sample mean vector.

We shall now show a lower bound on the variance of any unbiased estimate and shall show that, if the lower bound is achieved, it will be by a maximum likelihood estimate. For simplicity's sake, the proof is given for one parameter.

Theorem Let $\hat{\theta}(\mathbf{Z})$ be any unbiased estimate of a parameter θ. Then the lower bound of the variance of the estimate is given by

$$\operatorname{Var}\{\hat{\theta}(\mathbf{Z})\} \geq \left(E\left\{\left[\frac{\partial \ln p(\mathbf{Z}/\theta)}{\partial \theta}\right]^2\right\}\right)^{-1} = \left(-E\left\{\frac{\partial^2 \ln p(\mathbf{Z}/\theta)}{\partial \theta^2}\right\}\right)^{-1} \tag{5-23}$$

where $\partial p(Z/\theta)/\partial\theta$ and $\partial^2 p(Z/\theta)/\partial\theta^2$ are assumed to exist and to be absolutely integrable.

This inequality is known as the *Cramèr–Rao bound*, and any unbiased estimate that satisfies the bound with an equality is an *efficient estimate.*

PROOF Because $\hat{\theta}(\mathbf{Z})$ is unbiased,

$$E\{\hat{\theta}(\mathbf{Z}) - \theta\} = \int_{\mathscr{S}} p(Z/\theta)(\hat{\theta}(Z) - \theta)\, dZ = 0 \tag{5-24}$$

Differentiating (5-24) with respect to θ we obtain

$$\int_{\mathscr{S}} \left[\frac{\partial p(Z/\theta)}{\partial \theta}(\hat{\theta}(Z) - \theta) - p(Z/\theta)\right] dZ = 0 \tag{5-25}$$

or

$$\int_{\mathscr{S}} \frac{\partial p(Z/\theta)}{\partial \theta}(\hat{\theta}(Z) - \theta)\, dZ = 1 \tag{5-26}$$

Modifying (5-26) and applying the Schwarz inequality yields

$$\begin{aligned}
&\int_{\mathscr{S}} \frac{\partial p(Z/\theta)}{\partial \theta}(\hat{\theta}(Z) - \theta)\, dZ \\
&\quad = \int_{\mathscr{S}} \frac{\partial \ln p(Z/\theta)}{\partial \theta} p(Z/\theta)(\hat{\theta}(Z) - \theta)\, dZ \\
&\quad = \int_{\mathscr{S}} \left\{\frac{\partial \ln p(Z/\theta)}{\partial \theta}[p(Z/\theta)]^{1/2}\right\}\{[p(Z/\theta)]^{1/2}(\hat{\theta}(Z) - \theta)\}\, dZ \\
&\quad \leq \left[\left\{\int_{\mathscr{S}} \left(\frac{\partial \ln p(Z/\theta)}{\partial \theta}\right)^2 p(Z/\theta)\, dZ\right\}\left\{\int_{\mathscr{S}} p(Z/\theta)(\hat{\theta}(Z) - \theta)^2\, dZ\right\}\right]^{1/2}
\end{aligned} \tag{5-27}$$

The second term of the last line of (5-27) is the variance of the estimate. The combination of (5-27) and (5-26) gives the first inequality of (5-23).

The second bound of (5-23) can be proved by calculating the second derivative of

$$\int_{\mathscr{S}} p(Z/\theta)\, dZ = 1 \tag{5-28}$$

Differentiating (5-28) twice with respect to θ gives

$$\int_{\mathscr{S}} \frac{\partial p(Z/\theta)}{\partial\theta}\, dZ = \int_{\mathscr{S}} \frac{\partial \ln p(Z/\theta)}{\partial\theta} p(Z/\theta)\, dZ = 0 \tag{5-29}$$

and

$$\int_{\mathscr{S}} \frac{\partial^2 \ln p(Z/\theta)}{\partial\theta^2} p(Z/\theta)\, dZ + \int_{\mathscr{S}} \left[\frac{\partial \ln p(Z/\theta)}{\partial\theta}\right]^2 p(Z/\theta)\, dZ = 0 \tag{5-30}$$

Thus, the first and second terms of (5-30) have the same magnitudes and different signs, which proves the equality of the first and second bound of (5-23).

Next, let us consider the condition under which the equality of the Schwarz inequality holds. In (5-27) the equality holds if, and only if,

$$\frac{\partial \ln p(Z/\theta)}{\partial\theta} = (\hat{\theta}(Z) - \theta) f(\theta) \tag{5-31}$$

where $f(\theta)$ does not depend on Z. Since (5-31) must hold for all θ, we may insert the maximum likelihood estimate $\hat{\theta}_{ml}(Z)$ into θ of (5-31) without violating the equality. From (5-19), $\partial \ln p(Z/\theta)/\partial\theta = 0$ for $\theta = \hat{\theta}_{ml}(Z)$. This leads us to

$$0 = \left.\frac{\partial \ln p(Z/\theta)}{\partial\theta}\right|_{\theta=\hat{\theta}_{ml}(Z)} = (\hat{\theta}(Z) - \theta) f(\theta) \,|_{\theta=\hat{\theta}_{ml}(Z)} \tag{5-32}$$

In order to make the right side of (5-32) equal to zero, $\hat{\theta}(Z)$ should satisfy, for all Z,

$$\hat{\theta}(Z) = \hat{\theta}_{ml}(Z) \tag{5-33}$$

The possibility of $f(\hat{\theta}_{ml}) = 0$ is eliminated, because we want a solution that depends on the data Z, and $f(\theta)$ does not depend on Z.

Thus, if an efficient estimate exists [that is (5-31) is satisfied], it has to be the maximum likelihood estimate.

Example 5-2 As we discussed in Example 5-1, the sample mean vector is the maximum likelihood estimate for a normal distribution. Equation (5-20) shows that (5-31) is satisfied for this example. Since the sample mean vector is unbiased, this is the efficient estimate of the expected vector for a normal distribution.

The Sufficient Estimate

The definition of a sufficient estimate is given in (5-6). However, it may be quite tedious to verify that $\hat{\Theta}_1(\mathbf{Z})$ satisfies (5-6) for other estimates. Therefore, we introduce a more convenient criterion to test sufficiency —the *factorization theorem.*

Theorem The term $\hat{\Theta}_1(\mathbf{Z})$ is sufficient if, and only if, we can find two non-negative functions k and g such that

$$p(Z/\Theta) = k(\hat{\Theta}_1(Z)/\Theta)g(Z) \tag{5-34}$$

where $g(Z)$ does not depend on Θ.

PROOF Let us make the transformation as

$$\hat{\mathbf{\Theta}}_i = G_i(\mathbf{X}_1, \ldots, \mathbf{X}_N) \qquad (i = 1, 2, \ldots, N) \tag{5-35}$$

Then we have the inverse transform

$$\mathbf{X}_i = W_i(\hat{\mathbf{\Theta}}_1, \ldots, \hat{\mathbf{\Theta}}_N) \qquad (i = 1, 2, \ldots, N) \tag{5-36}$$

Assuming (5-34) is true, the joint density function of $\hat{\mathbf{\Theta}}_1, \ldots, \hat{\mathbf{\Theta}}_N$ is then given by

$$\begin{aligned} p(\hat{\Theta}_1, \ldots, \hat{\Theta}_N/\Theta) &= p(X_1, \ldots, X_N/\Theta)/|J| \\ &= k(\hat{\Theta}_1/\Theta)g[W_1(\hat{\Theta}_1, \ldots, \hat{\Theta}_N), \ldots, W_N(\hat{\Theta}_1, \ldots, \hat{\Theta}_N)]/|J| \\ &= k(\hat{\Theta}/\Theta)h(\hat{\Theta}_1, \ldots, \hat{\Theta}_N)/|J| \end{aligned} \tag{5-37}$$

where $|J|$ is the Jacobian of the transformation of (5-35) and does not depend on Θ. The marginal density $p(\hat{\Theta}_1/\Theta)$ can be calculated by

$$\begin{aligned} p(\hat{\Theta}_1/\Theta) &= \int_{\mathscr{S}} \cdots \int_{\mathscr{S}} p(\hat{\Theta}_1, \ldots, \hat{\Theta}_N/\Theta)\, d\hat{\Theta}_2 \cdots d\hat{\Theta}_N \\ &= k(\hat{\Theta}_1/\Theta) \int_{\mathscr{S}} \cdots \int_{\mathscr{S}} (1/|J|)h(\hat{\Theta}_1, \ldots, \hat{\Theta}_N)\, d\hat{\Theta}_2 \cdots d\hat{\Theta}_N \\ &= k(\hat{\Theta}_1/\Theta)m(\hat{\Theta}_1) \end{aligned} \tag{5-38}$$

where $m(\hat{\Theta}_1)$ does not depend upon Θ. Thus, the conditional density function of $\hat{\mathbf{\Theta}}_2, \ldots, \hat{\mathbf{\Theta}}_N$, given $\hat{\Theta}_1$, can be calculated by

$$\begin{aligned} &p(\hat{\Theta}_2, \ldots, \hat{\Theta}_N/\hat{\Theta}_1, \Theta) \\ &\quad = \frac{p(\hat{\Theta}_1, \ldots, \hat{\Theta}_N/\Theta)}{p(\hat{\Theta}_1/\Theta)} = \frac{h(\hat{\Theta}_1, \ldots, \hat{\Theta}_N)}{m(\hat{\Theta}_1)\,|J|} = f(\hat{\Theta}_1, \ldots, \hat{\Theta}_N) \end{aligned} \tag{5-39}$$

Equation (5-39) is identical with (5-6), thus proving that $\hat{\mathbf{\Theta}}$ is a sufficient estimate for Θ.

Conversely, if $\hat{\mathbf{\Theta}}_1$ is a sufficient estimate for Θ, the multiplication of $k(\hat{\Theta}_1/\Theta)$ to both sides of (5-39) leads to a functional form of (5-34). This completes the proof of the theorem.

EXAMPLE 5-3 Let us examine the sample mean vector for a normal distribution again, as in Examples 5-1 and 5-2. Then

$$\begin{aligned} p(Z/M) &= p(X_1, \ldots, X_N/M) \\ &= \prod_{i=1}^{N} (2\pi)^{-n/2} |\Sigma|^{-1/2} \exp[-\tfrac{1}{2}(X_i - M)^T \Sigma^{-1} (X_i - M)] \end{aligned} \tag{5-40}$$

On the other hand, the density function of the sample mean vector is known to be normal with expected vector M and covariance matrix Σ/N. Therefore,

$$\begin{aligned} &p(\hat{M}(X_1, \ldots, X_N)/M) \\ &\quad = (2\pi)^{-n/2} |\Sigma/N|^{-1/2} \exp[-\tfrac{1}{2}(\hat{M} - M)^T (\Sigma/N)^{-1} (\hat{M} - M)] \end{aligned} \tag{5-41}$$

Let us test whether (5-40) divided by (5-41) includes M or not:

$$\begin{aligned} \frac{p(Z/M)}{p(\hat{M}/M)} &= k \exp\Big[-\tfrac{1}{2}\sum_{i=1}^{N} (X_i - M)^T \Sigma^{-1} (X_i - M) \\ &\quad + \tfrac{1}{2}N(\hat{M} - M)^T \Sigma^{-1} (\hat{M} - M)\Big] \\ &= k \exp\Big[-\tfrac{1}{2}\sum_{i=1}^{N} \{(X_i - \hat{M}) + (\hat{M} - M)\}^T \\ &\quad \times \Sigma^{-1}\{(X_i - \hat{M}) + (\hat{M} - M)\} + \tfrac{1}{2}N(\hat{M} - M)^T \Sigma^{-1} (\hat{M} - M)\Big] \\ &= k \exp\Big[-\tfrac{1}{2}\sum_{i=1}^{N} (X_i - \hat{M})^T \Sigma^{-1} (X_i - \hat{M})\Big] \end{aligned} \tag{5-42}$$

where

$$k = (2\pi)^{-n(N-1)/2} |\Sigma|^{-(N-1)/2} N^{-n/2} \tag{5-43}$$

$$\hat{M} = (1/N) \sum_{i=1}^{N} X_i \tag{5-44}$$

Thus, (5-42) does not depend on M, and therefore the sample mean vector for a normal distribution is a sufficient estimate for M.

5.2 Estimation of Random Parameters

When the parameters to be estimated are random, we try to minimize the expected value of the error function between the random parameters and its estimates.

The Bayes Estimate

Let $\mathbf{\Theta}$ and $\hat{\Theta}(\mathbf{Z})$ be the random parameters to be estimated and its estimate based on available samples $\mathbf{Z} = [\mathbf{X}_1{}^T\,\mathbf{X}_2{}^T \cdots \mathbf{X}_N{}^T]^T$. Then we can assign a cost function such that the *expected cost* or *risk of the estimate* can be expressed by

$$r = E\{c(\mathbf{\Theta}, \hat{\Theta}(\mathbf{Z}))\} = \int_{\mathscr{S}}\int_{\mathscr{S}} c(\Theta, \hat{\Theta}(Z))p(Z, \Theta)\, dZ\, d\Theta \tag{5-45}$$

where $c(\cdot)$ is the cost function, depending on both $\mathbf{\Theta}$ and $\hat{\Theta}(\mathbf{Z})$. The term r is called the *Bayes risk* and the estimate which minimizes r is called the *Bayes estimate.*

Although the Bayes estimate is very general and is the optimum in terms of the cost function, it is generally not easy to obtain the explicit form of the estimate. Therefore, the estimates are obtained for some specific cost functions.

The Maximum a Posteriori Estimate

Let us use a uniform function for $c(\mathbf{\Theta}, \hat{\Theta}(\mathbf{Z}))$ as

$$c(\mathbf{\Theta}, \hat{\Theta}(\mathbf{Z})) = \begin{cases} 0 & \text{for } \Delta\mathscr{S} \text{ about } \hat{\Theta}(\mathbf{Z}) \quad \text{where } \| \mathbf{\Theta} - \hat{\Theta}(\mathbf{Z}) \| \leq \delta \\ 1 & \text{elsewhere} \end{cases} \tag{5-46}$$

where δ and subsequently $\Delta\mathscr{S}$ are selected small enough such that $p(\Theta/Z)$ can be considered a constant in the region. Let ΔV be the volume of the region $\Delta\mathscr{S}$. Then (5-45) becomes

$$\begin{aligned} r &= \int_{\mathscr{S}} p(Z)\left[\int_{\mathscr{S}} c(\Theta, \hat{\Theta}(Z))p(\Theta/Z)\, d\Theta\right] dZ \\ &= \int_{\mathscr{S}} p(Z)\left[1 - \int_{\Delta\mathscr{S}} p(\Theta/Z)\, d\Theta\right] dZ \\ &= \int_{\mathscr{S}} p(Z)[1 - p(\hat{\Theta}(Z)/Z)\,\Delta V]\, dZ \end{aligned} \tag{5-47}$$

Since the integrand of (5-47) is non-negative, r can be minimized by selecting $\hat{\Theta}(Z)$ to equal the Θ which maximizes the *a posteriori* density function $p(\Theta/Z)$. That is, the estimate is the solution of

$$\left.\frac{\partial p(\Theta/Z)}{\partial\Theta}\right|_{\Theta=\hat{\Theta}(Z)}=0 \quad \text{or} \quad \left.\frac{\partial \ln p(\Theta/Z)}{\partial\Theta}\right|_{\Theta=\hat{\Theta}(Z)}=0 \tag{5-48}$$

This estimate is termed the *maximum a posteriori estimate.*

As we saw in the previous chapters, it is more convenient to have an expression in terms of an *a priori* density rather than in those of an *a posteriori* density. By using the Bayes theorem, we can convert (5-48) into

$$\ln p(\Theta/Z)=\ln p(Z/\Theta)+\ln p(\Theta)-\ln p(Z) \tag{5-49}$$

$$\left.\frac{\partial \ln p(\Theta/Z)}{\partial\Theta}\right|_{\Theta=\hat{\Theta}(Z)}=\left.\frac{\partial \ln p(Z/\Theta)}{\partial\Theta}\right|_{\Theta=\hat{\Theta}(Z)}+\left.\frac{\partial \ln p(\Theta)}{\partial\Theta}\right|_{\Theta=\hat{\Theta}(Z)}=0 \tag{5-50}$$

If

$$\frac{\partial \ln p(Z/\Theta)}{\partial\Theta}\gg\frac{\partial \ln p(\Theta)}{\partial\Theta} \tag{5-51}$$

or, in other words, $p(\Theta)$ is far more flatly distributed than $p(Z/\Theta)$, we can neglect the second term of (5-50) and the maximum *a posteriori* estimate becomes the maximum likelihood estimate of (5-19).

EXAMPLE 5-4 Let us calculate the maximum *a posteriori* estimate of the expected vector for a normal distribution. Let $p(M)$ be a normal distribution with expected vector M_0 and covariance matrix Σ_0. Then (5-50) becomes

$$\frac{\partial \ln p(M/X_1,\ldots,X_N)}{\partial M}=\Sigma^{-1}\left[\sum_{i=1}^{N}(X_i-M)\right]-\Sigma_0^{-1}(M-M_0) \tag{5-52}$$

Therefore,

$$\hat{M}(\mathbf{X}_1,\ldots,\mathbf{X}_N)=\{I+(1/N)\Sigma\Sigma_0^{-1}\}^{-1}\left\{\left((1/N)\sum_{i=1}^{N}\mathbf{X}_i\right)+(1/N)\Sigma\Sigma_0^{-1}M_0\right\} \tag{5-53}$$

The *a priori* knowledge of $\mathbf{M}$, M_0, is effective when N is small. But as N increases, the effect of M_0 on the estimation of $\mathbf{M}$ decreases, and $\hat{M}(\mathbf{X}_1,\ldots,\mathbf{X}_N)$ tends toward the sample mean vector. The expected value of $\hat{M}(\mathbf{X}_1,\ldots,\mathbf{X}_N)$ equals $E\{\mathbf{M}\}=M_0$ since

$$\begin{aligned}E\{\hat{M}(\mathbf{X}_1,\ldots,\mathbf{X}_N)\}&=\{I+(1/N)\Sigma\Sigma_0^{-1}\}^{-1}\left\{(1/N)\sum_{i=1}^{N}E\{\mathbf{X}_i\}+(1/N)\Sigma\Sigma_0^{-1}M_0\right\}\\&=\{I+(1/N)\Sigma\Sigma_0^{-1}\}^{-1}\{I+(1/N)\Sigma\Sigma_0^{-1}\}M_0=M_0\end{aligned} \tag{5-54}$$

The Minimum Mean-Square Estimate

We can use the norm of the difference between $\mathbf{\Theta}$ and its estimate $\hat{\Theta}(\mathbf{Z})$ as a cost function, that is

$$c(\mathbf{\Theta}, \hat{\Theta}(\mathbf{Z})) = \| \mathbf{\Theta} - \hat{\Theta}(\mathbf{Z}) \|^2 \tag{5-55}$$

Then the Bayes risk r of (5-45) becomes the mean-square error of the estimate.

$$\bar{\varepsilon}^2 = E\{\| \mathbf{\Theta} - \hat{\Theta}(\mathbf{Z}) \|^2\} = \int_{\mathscr{S}} p(Z)\left[\int_{\mathscr{S}} \| \Theta - \hat{\Theta}(Z) \|^2 p(\Theta/Z)\, d\Theta\right] dZ \tag{5-56}$$

Since the integrand of (5-56) is non-negative, $\bar{\varepsilon}^2$ can be minimized by minimizing the *conditional risk*, *given* $\mathbf{Z}$

$$r(\hat{\Theta}/Z) = \int_{\mathscr{S}} \| \Theta - \hat{\Theta}(Z) \|^2 p(\Theta/Z)\, d\Theta \tag{5-57}$$

for every Z. For a given Z, $\hat{\Theta}(Z)$ is a nonrandom vector $\hat{\Theta}(Z) = C$. Therefore we can minimize (5-57) with respect to C by solving

$$(\partial/\partial C) \int_{\mathscr{S}} \| \Theta - C \|^2 p(\Theta/Z)\, d\Theta = -2 \int_{\mathscr{S}} (\Theta - C) p(\Theta/Z)\, d\Theta = 0 \tag{5-58}$$

Hence,

$$C = \int_{\mathscr{S}} \Theta p(\Theta/Z)\, dZ = E\{\mathbf{\Theta}/Z\} \tag{5-59}$$

Since (5-59) is true for all Z's, we conclude that the minimum mean-square estimate $\hat{\Theta}(\mathbf{Z})$ is

$$\hat{\Theta}(\mathbf{Z}) = E\{\mathbf{\Theta}/\mathbf{Z}\} \tag{5-60}$$

Equation (5-59) is also known as the *regression function*. Thus the minimum mean-square estimate is the expected vector of the *a posteriori* density.

Substituting (5-60) into (5-56), we can obtain the mean-square error of the estimate. When we fix Z, the conditional risk of (5-57) becomes $\mathrm{tr}\Sigma_{\mathbf{\Theta}}$, where $\Sigma_{\mathbf{\Theta}}$ is the covariance matrix of $\mathbf{\Theta}$. Since $\Sigma_{\mathbf{\Theta}}$ is a function of $\mathbf{Z}$,

$$\bar{\varepsilon}^2 = \mathrm{tr} \int_{\mathscr{S}} \Sigma_{\mathbf{\Theta}}(Z) p(Z)\, dZ = \mathrm{tr}\, E\{\Sigma_{\mathbf{\Theta}}(\mathbf{Z})\} = \sum_{i=1}^{n} E\{\sigma^2_{\mathbf{\theta}_i}(\mathbf{Z})\} \tag{5-61}$$

where $\mathbf{\theta}_i$ are the components of $\mathbf{\Theta}$.

For the lower bound of the mean-square error, we have a theorem similar to the Cramèr–Rao bound for nonrandom parameters.

Theorem Let $\hat{\theta}(\mathbf{Z})$ be an estimate of a random parameter $\boldsymbol{\theta}$. Then the lower bound of the mean-square error between $\hat{\theta}(\mathbf{Z})$ and $\boldsymbol{\theta}$ is given by

$$E\{(\hat{\theta}(\mathbf{Z})-\boldsymbol{\theta})^2\} \geq \left(E\left\{\left(\frac{\partial \ln p(\mathbf{Z},\theta)}{\partial \theta}\right)^2\right\}\right)^{-1} = \left(-E\left\{\frac{\partial^2 \ln p(\mathbf{Z},\theta)}{\partial \theta^2}\right\}\right)^{-1} \tag{5-62}$$

where $\partial p(Z,\theta)/\partial\theta$ and $\partial^2 p(Z,\theta)/\partial\theta^2$ are absolutely integrable with respect to Z and θ. Also, the following condition must be satisfied.

$$\lim_{\theta\to\pm\infty} p(\theta)\int_{\mathscr{S}} (\hat{\theta}(Z)-\theta)p(Z/\theta)\,dZ = 0 \tag{5-63}$$

The proof is a modification of the Cramèr–Rao bound and is omitted.

In order to satisfy the equality of (5-62), we have to have

$$\frac{\partial \ln p(Z,\theta)}{\partial\theta} = k\cdot(\hat{\theta}(Z)-\theta) \tag{5-64}$$

where k does not depend on either Z or θ.

When we limit our estimate to a linear function of $\mathbf{X}_i$, the minimum mean-square estimate becomes more explicit. Let A_j be an $m \times n$ matrix to form an estimate

$$\hat{\mathbf{\Theta}} = \sum_{j=1}^{N} A_j\mathbf{X}_j = A\mathbf{Z} \tag{5-65}$$

where A is an $m \times nN$ matrix. Then the mean-square error becomes

$$\bar{\varepsilon}^2 = E\{\|\,\mathbf{\Theta} - A\mathbf{Z}\,\|^2\} \tag{5-66}$$

In order to minimize $\bar{\varepsilon}^2$ with respect to A, we have to solve

$$\partial\bar{\varepsilon}^2/\partial A = -2E\{(\mathbf{\Theta} - A\mathbf{Z})\mathbf{Z}^T\} = 0 \tag{5-67}$$

Therefore,

$$A = E\{\mathbf{\Theta}\mathbf{Z}^T\}E\{\mathbf{Z}\mathbf{Z}^T\}^{-1} = S_{\mathbf{\Theta Z}}S_{\mathbf{Z}}^{-1} \tag{5-68}$$

where $S_{\mathbf{\Theta Z}}$ is the cross-correlation matrix between $\mathbf{\Theta}$ and $\mathbf{Z}$ and $S_{\mathbf{Z}}$ is the autocorrelation matrix of $\mathbf{Z}$. This estimate is termed a *linear estimate.*

The mean-square error is calculated by substituting (5-68) into (5-66). The result is

$$\begin{aligned}\bar{\varepsilon}^2 &= \operatorname{tr} E\{(\mathbf{\Theta} - S_{\mathbf{\Theta Z}}S_{\mathbf{Z}}^{-1}\mathbf{Z})(\mathbf{\Theta} - S_{\mathbf{\Theta Z}}S_{\mathbf{Z}}^{-1}\mathbf{Z})^T\} \\ &= \operatorname{tr}[E\{\mathbf{\Theta}\mathbf{\Theta}^T\} - E\{\mathbf{\Theta}\mathbf{Z}^T\}S_{\mathbf{Z}}^{-1}S_{\mathbf{\Theta Z}}^T] \\ &= \operatorname{tr}[S_{\mathbf{\Theta}} - S_{\mathbf{\Theta Z}}S_{\mathbf{Z}}^{-1}S_{\mathbf{\Theta Z}}^T] \\ &= \operatorname{tr}[S_{\mathbf{\Theta}} - S_{\mathbf{Z}}^{-1}S_{\mathbf{\Theta Z}}^T S_{\mathbf{\Theta Z}}]\end{aligned} \tag{5-69}$$

where $S_{\mathbf{Z}} = S_{\mathbf{Z}}^T$ because an autocorrelation matrix is symmetric.

Convex and Symmetric Cost Functions

In (5-60) we showed that the minimum mean-square estimate is always the expected vector of the *a posteriori* density. The same conclusion is derived for a large class of cost functions, whenever the *a posteriori* density is symmetric.

Let us assume that the cost function is convex and symmetric. Thus,

$$c(\Theta) = c(-\Theta) \tag{5-70}$$

and

$$c(\alpha\Theta_1 + (1-\alpha)\Theta_2) \leq \alpha c(\Theta_1) + (1-\alpha)c(\Theta_2) \qquad \text{for} \quad 0 \leq \alpha \leq 1 \tag{5-71}$$

Also, we assume that the *a posteriori* density is symmetric about the conditional expectation, that is,

$$p(\Theta'/Z) = p(-\Theta'/Z) \tag{5-72}$$

where

$$\mathbf{\Theta}' = \mathbf{\Theta} - E\{\mathbf{\Theta}/Z\} \tag{5-73}$$

Then the conditional risk which should be minimized [see (5-57)] is given by

$$\begin{aligned} r(\hat{\Theta}/Z) &= \int_{\mathscr{S}} c(\Theta - \hat{\Theta})p(\Theta/Z)\, d\Theta \\ &= \int_{\mathscr{S}} c(\Theta' - \hat{\Theta} + E\{\mathbf{\Theta}/Z\})p(\Theta'/Z)\, d\Theta' \\ &= \int_{\mathscr{S}} c(-\Theta' + \hat{\Theta} - E\{\mathbf{\Theta}/Z\})p(\Theta'/Z)\, d\Theta' \\ &= \int_{\mathscr{S}} c(-\Theta' + \hat{\Theta} - E\{\mathbf{\Theta}/Z\})p(-\Theta'/Z)\, d\Theta' \\ &= \int_{\mathscr{S}} c(\Theta' + \hat{\Theta} - E\{\mathbf{\Theta}/Z\})p(\Theta'/Z)\, d\Theta' \end{aligned} \tag{5-74}$$

By the convex condition (5-71),

$$\begin{aligned} r(\hat{\Theta}/Z) &= \tfrac{1}{2}E[\{c(\mathbf{\Theta}' - \hat{\Theta} + E\{\mathbf{\Theta}/Z\}) + c(\mathbf{\Theta}' + \hat{\Theta} - E\{\mathbf{\Theta}/Z\})\}/Z] \\ &\geq E[\{c(\tfrac{1}{2}\mathbf{\Theta}' - \tfrac{1}{2}\hat{\Theta} + \tfrac{1}{2}E\{\mathbf{\Theta}/Z\} + \tfrac{1}{2}\mathbf{\Theta}' + \tfrac{1}{2}\hat{\Theta} - \tfrac{1}{2}E\{\mathbf{\Theta}/Z\})\}/Z] \\ &= E[c(\mathbf{\Theta}')/Z] \end{aligned} \tag{5-75}$$

The equality holds only if

$$\hat{\Theta} = E\{\mathbf{\Theta}/Z\} \tag{5-76}$$

Therefore, (5-76) is the estimate which minimizes the Bayes risk for convex and symmetric cost functions. This estimate is the expected vector of the *a posteriori* density of $\mathbf{\Theta}$.

5.3 Interval Estimation

In the previous sections we were primarily concerned with point estimation, that is, the determination of a good estimate for a set of parameters from the available samples. Although we have derived the variances of these estimates, we have not specifically discussed our confidence in the estimate. In this section, we will discuss the probability that the estimated values of a set of parameters will lie within the selected region. This problem is termed *interval estimation.*

Confidence Region

Let us begin with the estimation of the expected value m of a one-dimensional normal distribution with a known variance σ^2. The sample mean of N observations $\hat{\mathbf{m}}$ is a random variable, normally distributed with expected value m and variance σ^2/N as

$$p(\hat{m}/m) = \frac{1}{(2\pi)^{1/2}\sigma/N^{1/2}} \exp\left[-\frac{1}{2}\frac{(\hat{m}-m)^2}{\sigma^2/N}\right] \tag{5-77}$$

Therefore, when many sets of N samples are drawn from the distribution and $\hat{\mathbf{m}}$ is calculated, 95% of the $\hat{\mathbf{m}}$'s should fall between $m - 2\sigma/N^{1/2}$ and $m + 2\sigma/N^{1/2}$. That is

$$\begin{aligned}\Pr\{m - 2\sigma/N^{1/2} < \hat{\mathbf{m}} < m + 2\sigma/N^{1/2}\} \\ = \int_{m-2\sigma/N^{1/2}}^{m+2\sigma/N^{1/2}} \frac{1}{(2\pi)^{1/2}\sigma/N^{1/2}} \exp\left[-\frac{1}{2}\frac{(\hat{m}-m)^2}{\sigma^2/N}\right] d\hat{m} = 0.95\end{aligned} \tag{5-78}$$

Or (5-78) may be rewritten as

$$\Pr\{\hat{\mathbf{m}} - 2\sigma/N^{1/2} < m < \hat{\mathbf{m}} + 2\sigma/N^{1/2}\} = 0.95 \tag{5-79}$$

This expression is read "the probability is 0.95 that the *random interval* $(\hat{\mathbf{m}} - 2\sigma/N^{1/2}, \hat{\mathbf{m}} + 2\sigma/N^{1/2})$ includes m." This random interval is called 95% *confidence interval* for an unknown parameter m. The terms 0.95,

$\hat{\mathbf{m}} + 2\sigma/N^{1/2}$ and $\hat{\mathbf{m}} - 2\sigma/N^{1/2}$ are the *confidence coefficient* and the *upper and lower confidence limits*, respectively. As we see from this example, in order to relate a random interval with the confidence coefficient, we have to know the density function of the estimate and integrate it as in (5-78).

The above discussion can be extended easily to multiparameters. Again, assuming a normal distribution for the observed samples $\mathbf{X}_i$ with unknown expected vector M and known covariance matrix Σ, the sample-expected vector $\hat{\mathbf{M}}$ is also normal with expected vector M and covariance matrix Σ/N. Therefore, the density function of $\hat{\mathbf{M}}$ is

$$p(\hat{M}/M) = (2\pi)^{-n/2}|\,\Sigma/N\,|^{-1/2} \exp[-\tfrac{1}{2}(\hat{M} - M)^T(\Sigma/N)^{-1}(\hat{M} - M)] \tag{5-80}$$

In this case, the confidence region must be designed with

$$\mathbf{d}^2 = (\hat{\mathbf{M}} - M)^T(\Sigma/N)^{-1}(\hat{\mathbf{M}} - M) \tag{5-81}$$

such that

$$\Pr\{0 < \mathbf{d}^2 < a\} = \gamma \tag{5-82}$$

Figure 5-1 shows this multidimensional confidence region.

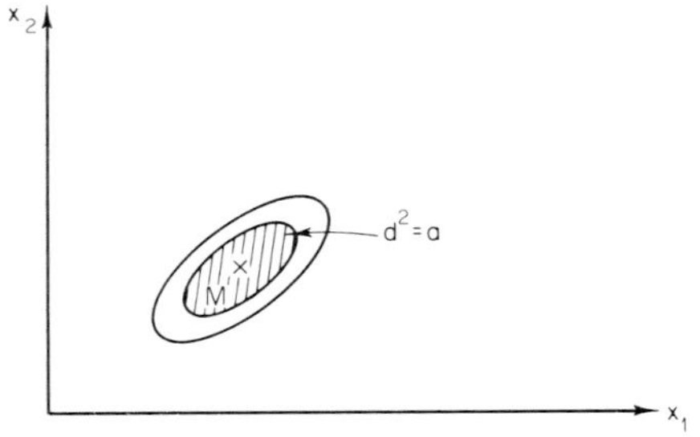

Fig. 5-1 A multidimensional confidence region.

Equation (5-81) can be always whitened, such that

$$\mathbf{d}^2 = \mathbf{Y}^T\mathbf{Y} = \sum_{i=1}^{n} \mathbf{y}_i^2 \tag{5-83}$$

Therefore, when $\hat{\mathbf{M}}$ is normal, $\mathbf{Y}$ is also normal. Consequently, the density function of $\mathbf{d}^2$ becomes a χ^2 distribution with $n - 1$ degrees of freedom given by

$$p(d^2) = \frac{1}{\Gamma[(n-1)/2]} 2^{-(n-1)/2}(d^2)^{(n-1)/2-1} \exp(-\tfrac{1}{2}d^2) \tag{5-84}$$

The confidence coefficient γ and the upper confidence limit a of (5-82) are related by the density function of $\mathbf{d}^2$.

Returning to the one-dimensional normal case, let us next consider the case where both expected value m and variance σ^2 are unknown. We use the sample mean and sample variance as their estimates:

$$\hat{\mathbf{m}} = (1/N) \sum_{i=1}^{N} \mathbf{x}_i \qquad \text{and} \qquad \boldsymbol{\sigma}^2 = (1/N) \sum_{i=1}^{N} (\mathbf{x}_i - \hat{\mathbf{m}})^2 \tag{5-85}$$

Fortunately, the density function of a new random variable

$$\mathbf{t} = (N-1)^{1/2}(\hat{\mathbf{m}} - m)/\hat{\boldsymbol{\sigma}} \tag{5-86}$$

is known as the Student's distribution with $N-1$ degrees of freedom, and is expressed by

$$p(t) = [(N-1)\pi]^{-1/2} \frac{\Gamma(N/2)}{\Gamma[(N-1)/2]} (1 + [t^2/(N-1)])^{-N/2} \tag{5-87}$$

Since the density function of $\mathbf{t}$ is known, it is possible to find the relation between the upper and lower confidence limits and the confidence coefficient as

$$\Pr\{a < \mathbf{t} < b\} = \int_a^b p(t)\, dt = \gamma \tag{5-88}$$

or

$$\Pr[\hat{\mathbf{m}} - b\hat{\boldsymbol{\sigma}}/(N-1)^{1/2} < m < \hat{\mathbf{m}} - a\hat{\boldsymbol{\sigma}}/(N-1)^{1/2}] = \gamma \tag{5-89}$$

Equation (5-89) makes it possible to find the confidence interval for m from N samples without knowing the true values of m and σ^2.

The confidence interval for the variance of a normal distribution can also be calculated for the one-dimensional case. Again, it is assumed that both the expected value m and variance σ^2 are unknown, and the sample mean and sample variance are used as their estimates. Let us define a new random variable by

$$\boldsymbol{\chi}^2 = (1/\sigma^2) \sum_{i=1}^{N} (\mathbf{x}_i - \hat{\mathbf{m}})^2 \tag{5-90}$$

It is well known that $\boldsymbol{\chi}^2$ is distributed according to the chi-square distribution, with $N-1$ degrees of freedom:

$$p(\chi^2) = \frac{1}{\Gamma[(N-1)/2]} 2^{-(N-1)/2}(\chi^2)^{(N-1)/2-1} \exp(-\tfrac{1}{2}\chi^2) \tag{5-91}$$

Since the density function includes neither m nor σ^2, we can find the confidence interval based on N samples as

$$\Pr\{a < \boldsymbol{\chi}^2 < b\} = \int_a^b p(\chi^2)\, d\chi^2 = \gamma \tag{5-92}$$

or

$$\Pr\left\{(1/b) \sum_{i=1}^{N} (\mathbf{x}_i - \hat{\mathbf{m}})^2 < \sigma^2 < (1/a) \sum_{i=1}^{N} (\mathbf{x}_i - \hat{\mathbf{m}})^2\right\} = \gamma \tag{5-93}$$

Order Statistics

In this subsection, a brief discussion of order statistics is given. These statistics play an important role in statistical inference partly because some of their properties do not depend on the distribution from which samples are drawn.

Let us assume that observed samples $\mathbf{x}_1, \mathbf{x}_2, \ldots, \mathbf{x}_N$ are one dimensional. We can order these observed samples according to their magnitude, and define a new random variable $\mathbf{y}_i$ as

$$\mathbf{y}_1 < \mathbf{y}_2 < \cdots < \mathbf{y}_N \tag{5-94}$$

where $\mathbf{y}_1$ is the smallest $\mathbf{x}_i$, $\mathbf{y}_2$ is the second smallest, and so on. Then the joint density function of $\mathbf{y}_1, \ldots, \mathbf{y}_N$ is

$$p(y_1, \ldots, y_N) = \begin{cases} N!\, p(y_1)p(y_2) \cdots p(y_N), & \mathbf{y}_1 < \mathbf{y}_2 < \cdots < \mathbf{y}_N \\ 0 \quad \text{otherwise} \end{cases} \tag{5-95}$$

where the $\mathbf{y}_i$'s are independent.

Equation (5-95) can be derived easily by observing a simple example with $N = 3$. In the transformation, one set of $\mathbf{y}_i$ corresponds to six sets of $\mathbf{x}_j$ as

$$\begin{aligned} &\{\mathbf{x}_1 = \mathbf{y}_1, \quad \mathbf{x}_2 = \mathbf{y}_2, \quad \mathbf{x}_3 = \mathbf{y}_3\} \\ &\{\mathbf{x}_1 = \mathbf{y}_1, \quad \mathbf{x}_2 = \mathbf{y}_3, \quad \mathbf{x}_3 = \mathbf{y}_2\} \\ &\{\mathbf{x}_1 = \mathbf{y}_2, \quad \mathbf{x}_2 = \mathbf{y}_1, \quad \mathbf{x}_3 = \mathbf{y}_3\} \\ &\{\mathbf{x}_1 = \mathbf{y}_2, \quad \mathbf{x}_2 = \mathbf{y}_3, \quad \mathbf{x}_3 = \mathbf{y}_1\} \\ &\{\mathbf{x}_1 = \mathbf{y}_3, \quad \mathbf{x}_2 = \mathbf{y}_1, \quad \mathbf{x}_3 = \mathbf{y}_2\} \\ &\{\mathbf{x}_1 = \mathbf{y}_3, \quad \mathbf{x}_2 = \mathbf{y}_2, \quad \mathbf{x}_3 = \mathbf{y}_1\} \end{aligned} \tag{5-96}$$

The Jacobians of these transformations are all 1. For example, the second set $\{\mathbf{x}_1 = \mathbf{y}_1, \quad \mathbf{x}_2 = \mathbf{y}_3, \quad \mathbf{x}_2 = \mathbf{y}_2\}$ gives

$$J_2 = \begin{vmatrix} 1 & 0 & 0 \\ 0 & 0 & 1 \\ 0 & 1 & 0 \end{vmatrix} = -1 \tag{5-97}$$

and $| J_2 | = +1$. Hence,

$$\begin{aligned} p(y_1, y_2, y_3) &= p(y_1)p(y_2)p(y_3)/|J_1| + p(y_1)p(y_3)p(y_2)/|J_2| \\ &\quad + \cdots + p(y_3)p(y_2)p(y_1)/|J_6| \\ &= \begin{cases} 3!\, p(y_1)p(y_2)p(y_3) & \text{for} \quad \mathbf{y}_1 < \mathbf{y}_2 < \mathbf{y}_3 \\ 0 & \text{elsewhere} \end{cases} \end{aligned} \tag{5-98}$$

In order to simplify the discussion, a further transformation is performed as follows. Let $\mathbf{z}_i$ be defined by

$$\mathbf{z}_i = P(\mathbf{y}_i) \tag{5-99}$$

where $P(\mathbf{y}_i)$ is the distribution function of $\mathbf{y}_i$. Then the density function of $\mathbf{z}_i$ is

$$\begin{aligned} p(z_i) &= \frac{p(y_i)}{|dP(y_i)/dy_i|} = \frac{p(y_i)}{p(y_i)} = 1 \qquad \text{for} \quad 0 < \mathbf{z}_i < 1 \\ &= 0 \qquad\qquad\qquad\qquad\qquad\qquad \text{elsewhere} \end{aligned} \tag{5-100}$$

Therefore, (5-95), in terms of the $\mathbf{z}_i$'s, can be expressed as

$$\begin{aligned} p(z_1, \ldots, z_N) &= N! \qquad \text{for} \quad 0 < \mathbf{z}_1 < \cdots < \mathbf{z}_N < 1 \\ &= 0 \qquad\ \ \text{elsewhere} \end{aligned} \tag{5-101}$$

where the order of the $\mathbf{z}_i$'s is the same as the one of the $\mathbf{y}_i$'s because the distribution function of (5-99) is monotonic.

The marginal density of (5-101) is calculated as

$$\begin{aligned} p(z_k) &= N!\left\{\int_0^{z_k} \cdots \int_0^{z_2} dz_1 \cdots dz_{k-1}\right\}\left\{\int_{z_k}^1 \cdots \int_{z_{N-1}}^1 dz_N \cdots dz_{k+1}\right\} \\ &= k\binom{N}{k} z_k^{k-1}(1 - z_k)^{N-k} \qquad \text{for} \quad 0 < \mathbf{z}_k < 1 \end{aligned} \tag{5-102}$$

Based on the above knowledge, we will discuss confidence intervals related to a set of ordered samples. Let us define the *quantile* ξ *of order* p by

$$\Pr\{\mathbf{x} \leq \xi\} = P(\xi) = p \tag{5-103}$$

For example, when $\mathbf{x}$ is the likelihood ratio and ξ is its threshold value, p corresponds to the probability of error. Then the probability that the kth order statistic is less than the quantile of order p is

$$\Pr\{\mathbf{y}_k \leq \xi\} = \Pr\{P(\mathbf{y}_k) \leq P(\xi)\} = \Pr\{\mathbf{z}_k \leq p\} \tag{5-104}$$

Therefore, using (5-102),

$$\Pr\{\mathbf{y}_k \leq \xi\} = \int_0^p p(z_k)\, dz_k = \int_0^p k\binom{N}{k} z_k^{k-1}(1 - z_k)^{N-k}\, dz_k \tag{5-105}$$

By repeated integration by parts,

$$\Pr\{\mathbf{y}_k \leq \xi\} = \sum_{j=k}^{N} \binom{N}{j} p^j (1 - p)^{N-j} \tag{5-106}$$

This result can be obtained without going through order statistics. Suppose that we draw N independent samples with the probability of (5-103) for $\mathbf{x} \leq \xi$. Then the probability that j samples satisfy $\mathbf{x} \leq \xi$ and $N - j$ samples do not, is given by

$$\Pr\{j \text{ samples satisfy } \mathbf{x} \leq \xi\} = \binom{N}{j} p^j (1 - p)^{N-j} \tag{5-107}$$

On the other hand, $\Pr\{\mathbf{y}_k \leq \xi\}$ means that k or more samples satisfy $\mathbf{x} \leq \xi$. Therefore, $\Pr\{\mathbf{y}_k \leq \xi\}$ is the summation of (5-107) for $j \geq k$, which is (5-106).

Once (5-106) is obtained, we can calculate the confidence interval of the quantile of order p by

$$\Pr\{\mathbf{y}_i \leq \xi < \mathbf{y}_j\} = \Pr\{\mathbf{y}_i \leq \xi\} - \Pr\{\mathbf{y}_j \leq \xi\} = \gamma \tag{5-108}$$

Specifying i, j, N, and p, we can calculate γ by (5-106) and (5-108). Thus the confidence interval for ξ with the confidence coefficient γ is given by the ith and jth sample from the lowest in magnitude. This process does not require the knowledge of the density function and is known as a *distribution-free method of inference*.

EXAMPLE 5-5 Let us draw four samples from a distribution and calculate the confidence coefficients for the quantile of order 0.5 between the largest and smallest samples. From (5-106) and (5-108)

$$\Pr\{\mathbf{y}_1 \le \xi < \mathbf{y}_4\} = \sum_{j=1}^{4} \frac{4!}{j!(4-j)!}\left(\frac{1}{2}\right)^4 - \sum_{j=4}^{4} \frac{4!}{j!(4-j)!}\left(\frac{1}{2}\right)^4$$

$$= \left(\frac{4!}{1!\,3!} + \frac{4!}{2!\,2!} + \frac{4!}{3!\,1!}\right)\left(\frac{1}{2}\right)^4 = 0.875 \qquad (5\text{-}109)$$

We have 87.5% assurance that ξ falls between $\mathbf{y}_1$ and $\mathbf{y}_4$.

Tolerance Limit for Distributions

In the confidence interval method we calculated the probability that a random interval includes a certain point. A somewhat similar approach is to use the following equation:

$$\Pr\{P(\mathbf{y}_j) - P(\mathbf{y}_i) \ge p\} = \gamma \qquad (5\text{-}110)$$

That is, the random interval $(\mathbf{y}_i, \mathbf{y}_j)$ has probability γ of containing at least $100p\%$ of the probability for the distribution of $\mathbf{x}$. Or, $\mathbf{y}_i$ and $\mathbf{y}_j$ are termed $100\gamma\%$ *tolerance limits* for $100p\%$ of the probability for the distribution of $\mathbf{x}$.

Equation (5-110) can be calculated by

$$\gamma = \Pr\{\mathbf{z}_j - \mathbf{z}_i \ge p\} = \int_0^{1-p} \int_{p+z_i}^{1} p(z_i, z_j)\, dz_j\, dz_i \qquad (5\text{-}111)$$

where $p(z_i, z_j)$ is the joint density function of $\mathbf{z}_i$ and $\mathbf{z}_j$ and can be obtained by taking the proper integration of (5-101), as we did for $p(z_i)$ in (5-102). However, we can calculate γ by a simpler method which is obtained by introducing the concept of coverage.

Let us consider a transformation from $\mathbf{z}_i$ to $\mathbf{w}_i$ as

$$\begin{aligned} \mathbf{w}_1 &= \mathbf{z}_1 \\ \mathbf{w}_2 &= \mathbf{z}_2 - \mathbf{z}_1 \\ &\vdots \\ \mathbf{w}_N &= \mathbf{z}_N - \mathbf{z}_{N-1} \end{aligned} \qquad (5\text{-}112)$$

The term $\mathbf{w}_i$ is called a *coverage* of the random interval $(\mathbf{y}_{i-1}, \mathbf{y}_i)$, since

$$\mathbf{w}_i = \mathbf{z}_i - \mathbf{z}_{i-1} = P(\mathbf{y}_i) - P(\mathbf{y}_{i-1}) = \Pr\{\mathbf{y}_{i-1} \le \mathbf{x} < \mathbf{y}_i\} \qquad (5\text{-}113)$$

Since the transformation of (5-112) is one to one and its Jacobian is one, the joint density function of $\mathbf{w}_1, \ldots, \mathbf{w}_N$ is, from (5-101),

$$p(w_1, \ldots, w_N) = N! \quad \text{for} \quad \mathbf{w}_i > 0 \quad \text{and} \quad \mathbf{w}_1 + \cdots + \mathbf{w}_N < 1$$
$$= 0 \quad \text{elsewhere} \tag{5-114}$$

The significance of the coverage is that $\mathbf{w}_i$'s are not required to satisfy the ordered condition $\mathbf{z}_1 < \mathbf{z}_2 < \cdots < \mathbf{z}_N$ of (5-101) and, therefore, $p(w_1, \ldots, w_N)$ is symmetric in $w_1, \ldots, w_N$. This means that we can have the following relation:

$$\Pr\{\mathbf{w}_{i+1} + \cdots + \mathbf{w}_j \geq p\} = \Pr\{\mathbf{w}_1 + \cdots + \mathbf{w}_{j-i} \geq p\} \tag{5-115}$$

Thus, (5-111) becomes

$$\gamma = \Pr\{\mathbf{z}_j - \mathbf{z}_i \geq p\} = \Pr\{\mathbf{w}_{i+1} + \cdots + \mathbf{w}_j \geq p\}$$
$$= \Pr\{\mathbf{w}_1 + \cdots + \mathbf{w}_{j-i} \geq p\} = \Pr\{\mathbf{z}_{j-i} \geq p\} = \int_p^1 p(z_{j-i})\, dz_{j-i} \tag{5-116}$$

Equation (5-116) is no longer the integral of the joint density function of $\mathbf{z}_i$ and $\mathbf{z}_j$ but the integral of the marginal density function of $\mathbf{z}_k$, which is given in (5-102). Therefore, γ is

$$\gamma = \int_p^1 (j-i)\binom{N}{j-i} z^{j-i-1}(1-z)^{N-j+i}\, dz \tag{5-117}$$

EXAMPLE 5-6 Let us draw four samples from a distribution and calculate the probability γ of them containing at least 50% of the probability for the distribution of $\mathbf{x}$ within the largest and smallest samples. Substituting $j = 4$, $i = 1$, $N = 4$, and $p = 0.5$ into (5-117),

$$\gamma = \int_{0.5}^1 3\binom{4}{3} z^2(1-z)\, dz = 0.69 \tag{5-118}$$

Thus, we can have 69% confidence.

5.4 Estimation of the Probability of Error

The probability of error is the very key quantity in pattern recognition, and the estimation of that quantity is very important. Unfortunately, as discussed in the previous chapters, the probability of error is a complex function involving an n-dimensional integral of a density function with a complex boundary. Therefore, we cannot expect much guidance from theoretical results but have to depend on experiments.

In the estimation of the probability of error there are two kinds of problems. The first one is the estimation of the probability of error from available samples, assuming that a classifier is given. This problem is simple and will be discussed first in this section. The second problem is to estimate the probability of error for given distributions. For this problem, the probability of error depends on the classifier to be used as well as on the distributions. Therefore, we first have to specify the nature of the classifier, for example, the Bayes classifier for minimum error. Then the task becomes one of finding a way of using available samples for designing the classifier and evaluating the error. Since we have only a finite number of samples, we cannot design the optimum classifier, and the parameters of the classifier are therefore also random variables. Furthermore, based on this random classifier, we have to estimate the probability of error. The second problem will also be discussed in this section.

Error Estimate for a Given Classifier

Let us assume that both distributions and the classifier are given and that our problem is the estimation of the probability of error from N samples drawn from these distributions [Highleyman, 1962].

(1) *Unknown a Priori Probabilities—Random Sampling*

When we do not know *a priori* probabilities $P(\omega_i)$ $(i = 1, 2)$, we simply draw N samples randomly and test whether the given classifier yields correct decisions for these samples or not. This drawing of samples is termed *random sampling*. Let $\boldsymbol{\tau}$ be the number of samples misclassified by this experiment. The term $\boldsymbol{\tau}$ is a discrete random variable. Using ε for the true error probability, the density function of $\boldsymbol{\tau}$, given ε, is replaced by a probability because of discreteness and is given by the binomial distribution as

$$\Pr\{\boldsymbol{\tau} = \tau/\varepsilon\} = \binom{N}{\tau}\varepsilon^{\tau}(1 - \varepsilon)^{N-\tau} \tag{5-119}$$

The maximum likelihood estimate of ε, $\hat{\boldsymbol{\varepsilon}}$, is the solution of the following likelihood equation:

$$\left.\frac{\partial \ln \Pr\{\boldsymbol{\tau} = \tau/\varepsilon\}}{\partial\varepsilon}\right|_{\varepsilon=\hat{\varepsilon}} = \left.\left(\frac{\tau}{\varepsilon} - \frac{N - \tau}{1 - \varepsilon}\right)\right|_{\varepsilon=\hat{\varepsilon}} = 0 \tag{5-120}$$

Hence,

$$\hat{\boldsymbol{\varepsilon}} = \boldsymbol{\tau}/N \tag{5-121}$$

That is, the ratio of the number of misclassified samples to the total number of samples gives the maximum likelihood estimate.

The properties of a binomial distribution are well known. The characteristic function, the expected value, and variance are given by

$$\varphi(\omega) = \{\varepsilon \exp(j\omega) + (1 - \varepsilon)\}^N \tag{5-122}$$

$$E\{\boldsymbol{\tau}\} = N\varepsilon \tag{5-123}$$

$$\mathrm{Var}\{\boldsymbol{\tau}\} = N\varepsilon(1 - \varepsilon) \tag{5-124}$$

Therefore,

$$E\{\hat{\boldsymbol{\varepsilon}}\} = E\{\boldsymbol{\tau}\}/N = \varepsilon \tag{5-125}$$

$$\mathrm{Var}\{\hat{\boldsymbol{\varepsilon}}\} = \mathrm{Var}\{\boldsymbol{\tau}\}/N^2 = \varepsilon(1 - \varepsilon)/N \tag{5-126}$$

The estimate is unbiased.

Since the density function of $\hat{\boldsymbol{\varepsilon}}$ is known, it is possible to calculate confidence intervals from

$$\Pr\{a < \hat{\boldsymbol{\varepsilon}} < b\} = \sum_{a<\hat{\varepsilon}<b} \Pr\{\hat{\boldsymbol{\varepsilon}} = \hat{\varepsilon}/\varepsilon\} = \gamma \tag{5-127}$$

Unfortunately, the explicit form of the integration of (5-127) is not available. But the relationship among ε, $\hat{\varepsilon}$, N, and γ is tabulated numerically, and Fig. 5-2 shows the relation between ε and $\hat{\varepsilon}$ for $\gamma = 0.95$. When we obtain $\tau = 50$ for $N = 250$, $\hat{\varepsilon}$ is 0.2 and, from Fig. 5-2, the confidence interval of ε for $\gamma = 0.95$ is (0.15, 0.27).

(2) *Known a Priori Probabilities—Selective Sampling*

When we know the *a priori* probabilities of classes $P(\omega_i)$ $(i = 1, 2)$, we can draw $N_1 = P(\omega_1)N$ and $N_2 = P(\omega_2)N$ samples from ω_1 and ω_2, respectively and test these samples by the given classifier. This process is known as *selective sampling*. Let $\boldsymbol{\tau}_1$ and $\boldsymbol{\tau}_2$ be the number of misclassified samples from ω_1 and ω_2. Since $\boldsymbol{\tau}_1$ and $\boldsymbol{\tau}_2$ are mutually independent, the joint density function of $\boldsymbol{\tau}_1$ and $\boldsymbol{\tau}_2$ becomes

$$\begin{aligned}\Pr\{\boldsymbol{\tau}_1 = \tau_1, \boldsymbol{\tau}_2 = \tau_2\} &= \Pr\{\boldsymbol{\tau}_1 = \tau_1\} \Pr\{\boldsymbol{\tau}_2 = \tau_2\} \\ &= \prod_{i=1}^{2} \binom{N_i}{\tau_i} \varepsilon_i^{\tau_i}(1 - \varepsilon_i)^{1-\tau_i}\end{aligned} \tag{5-128}$$

where the ε_i are the true error for the ω_i. A discussion similar to that given in (5-119)–(5-126) leads us to the maximum likelihood estimate of ε, $\hat{\boldsymbol{\epsilon}}'$.

$$\hat{\boldsymbol{\epsilon}}' = \sum_{i=1}^{2} P(\omega_i)\boldsymbol{\tau}_i/N \tag{5-129}$$

Subsequently, the expected value and variance are

$$E\{\hat{\boldsymbol{\epsilon}}'\} = \varepsilon \tag{5-130}$$

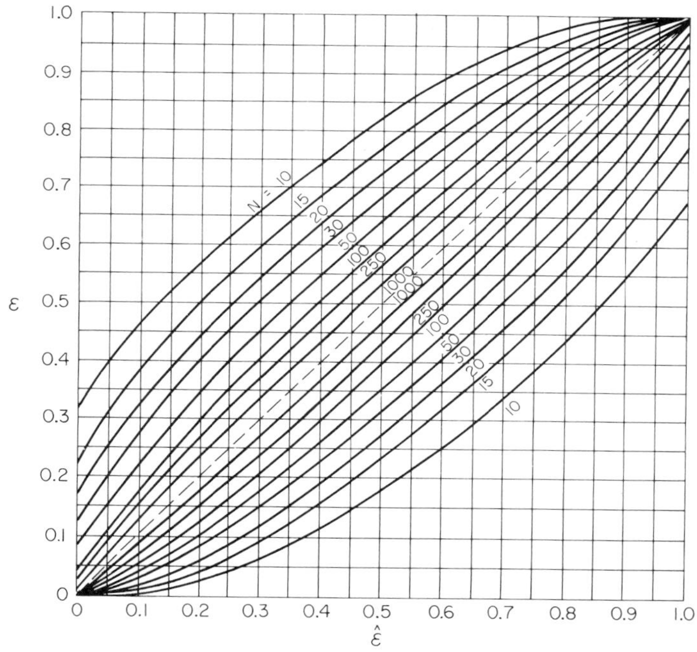

Fig. 5-2 Confidence interval for $\gamma = 0.95$ [Highleyman, 1962]. Copyright, 1962, The American Telephone and Telegraph Co., reprinted by permission.

and

$$\text{Var}\{\hat{\boldsymbol{\epsilon}}'\} = \sum_{i=1}^{2} P(\omega_i)\varepsilon_i(1 - \varepsilon_i)/N \tag{5-131}$$

Thus, the estimate of (5-129) is also unbiased. However, we can show that the variance of (5-131) is less than the variance of (5-126) by the following argument:

$$\begin{aligned}
&\operatorname{Var}\{\hat{\boldsymbol{\varepsilon}}\} - \operatorname{Var}\{\hat{\boldsymbol{\varepsilon}}'\} \\
&\quad = [\varepsilon(1-\varepsilon) - P(\omega_1)\varepsilon_1(1-\varepsilon_1) - P(\omega_2)\varepsilon_2(1-\varepsilon_2)]/N \\
&\quad = [P(\omega_1)\varepsilon_1{}^2 + P(\omega_2)\varepsilon_2{}^2 - \varepsilon^2]/N \\
&\quad = [P(\omega_1)\varepsilon_1{}^2 + P(\omega_2)\varepsilon_2{}^2 - \{P(\omega_1)\varepsilon_1 + P(\omega_2)\varepsilon_2\}^2]/N \\
&\quad = [P(\omega_1)P(\omega_2)(\varepsilon_1 - \varepsilon_2)^2]/N \geq 0
\end{aligned} \tag{5-132}$$

This is a reasonable result since we utilize *a priori* knowledge in selective sampling.

Calculating the confidence interval for this case is much more complicated than in the case of random sampling, since the density function of the estimate is more complex. In fact, the confidence interval depends on the particular set of ε_1 and ε_2—not simply on ε. However, since the density function is known, it is possible to calculate the confidence interval numerically.

The above discussion can easily be extended to multiclass problems. We simply have to change the upper limits of $\prod$ and $\sum$ in (5-128), (5-129), and (5-131) from 2 to M, which is the number of classes.

Error Estimate without Given Classifiers

When N samples are given without a classifier design, we have to use these samples to design a classifier as well as to test the performance of the classifier. Obviously, the probability of error to be estimated depends on the given distributions and on the classifier to be used. In order to simplify the problem, we assume in this section that we always use the Bayes classifier for minimum error. Then the Bayes minimum error to be estimated becomes a fixed parameter for given distributions. Also, the error is the minimum one we can attain for the given distributions.

In general, the probability of error ε is a function of two arguments as follows [Hills, 1966]:

$$\varepsilon(\Theta_1, \Theta_2) \tag{5-133}$$

where Θ_1 is the set of parameters for the distributions used to design the Bayes classifier, and Θ_2 is the set of parameters for the distributions used to test the performance.

For testing the samples from the distributions with Θ_2, the optimum classifier is the Bayes one, which is designed by using the distribution with Θ_2. Therefore,

$$\varepsilon(\Theta_2, \Theta_2) \leq \varepsilon(\Theta_1, \Theta_2) \tag{5-134}$$

For a particular problem, let Θ and $\hat{\mathbf{\Theta}}$ be the set of true parameters and its estimate. Thus, $\hat{\mathbf{\Theta}}$ is a random vector and $\varepsilon_0 = \varepsilon(\Theta, \Theta)$. For any particular value of $\hat{\mathbf{\Theta}}$, $\hat{\Theta}_N$, the following inequalities follow from (5-134):

$$\varepsilon(\Theta, \Theta) \leq \varepsilon(\hat{\Theta}_N, \Theta) \tag{5-135}$$

$$\varepsilon(\hat{\Theta}_N, \hat{\Theta}_N) \leq \varepsilon(\Theta, \hat{\Theta}_N) \tag{5-136}$$

Taking the expectation yields

$$\varepsilon(\Theta, \Theta) \leq E\{\varepsilon(\hat{\mathbf{\Theta}}_N, \Theta)\} \tag{5-137}$$

and

$$E\{\varepsilon(\hat{\mathbf{\Theta}}_N, \hat{\mathbf{\Theta}}_N)\} \leq E\{\varepsilon(\Theta, \hat{\mathbf{\Theta}}_N)\} \tag{5-138}$$

If we have

$$E\{\varepsilon(\Theta, \hat{\mathbf{\Theta}}_N)\} = \varepsilon(\Theta, \Theta) \tag{5-139}$$

then the Bayes error ε_0 is bounded from both sides as

$$E\{\varepsilon(\hat{\mathbf{\Theta}}_N, \hat{\mathbf{\Theta}}_N)\} \leq \varepsilon(\Theta, \Theta) \leq E\{\varepsilon(\hat{\mathbf{\Theta}}_N, \Theta)\} \tag{5-140}$$

The left inequality of (5-140) is based on the "if" statement of (5-139) and has not been proven for arbitrary true densities. However, this inequality has been verified many experimental evidences. By referring to (3-7) we see that (5-139) holds when the estimate of the test density based on N samples is unbiased, since the classifier is fixed. Also, it should be pointed out that the lower bound is less important than the upper bound.

Both bounds of the Bayes error $\varepsilon(\Theta, \Theta)$ are interpreted as follows:

(1) $\varepsilon(\hat{\Theta}_N, \hat{\Theta}_N)$: N samples are used to design the Bayes classifier and the same N samples are tested. We call this the *C method*. From (5-140), we see that the C method yields an optimistic bias.

(2) $\varepsilon(\hat{\Theta}_N, \Theta)$: N samples are used to design the Bayes classifier, and the samples from the true distributions are used for testing. We call this the *U method*. The U method is also a biased estimate of ε_0, but the bias is such that the expected value is an upper bound on ε_0. The samples from the true distribution may be replaced by the samples which are not used to design the classifier and are independent of design samples. As the number of test samples increases, the distributions of the test samples tend toward the true distributions.

In order to realize the U method, there are many possibilities. Here we describe two typical procedures:

(1) *The Sample-Partitioning Method*

The first method is to divide available samples into two groups and use one of them for designing the classifier and the other one for testing. We call this the *sample-partitioning method.* For this method, the question is how to divide the samples. In order to answer this question, we will study the effects of the numbers of test and design samples on the variance of the error estimate in the next subsection.

(2) *The Leaving-One-Out Method*

In the second method, we try to utilize the available samples more effectively than in the sample partition method.

In order to estimate $E\{\varepsilon(\hat{\mathbf{\Theta}}_N, \Theta)\}$, we have to draw many sample sets to design many classifiers, test the performance of each classifier by unused samples, and take an average of these performances. A similar operation can be carried out by using only the available N samples as follows [Lachenbruch, 1965].

Let us take out one sample, design a classifier by using $N - 1$ samples, and test the unused sample. Then, let us repeat this operation N times and count the number of misclassified samples. This is called the *leaving-one-out method.* This method utilizes available samples effectively and estimates $E\{\varepsilon(\hat{\mathbf{\Theta}}_{N-1}, \Theta)\}$. One of the disadvantages of this method is that we have to design N classifiers. However, this problem is easily overcome for normal distributions by the procedure which we will discuss in a later subsection.

The Sample-Partitioning Method

In order to see how available samples should be divided into design and test samples, let us study how these samples affect the variance of the error estimate.

First, let us assume that we have an infinite number of design samples and N test samples. With infinite samples, the classifier converges to the one for the true distributions and its contribution to the variance is zero. Then we can apply selective sampling for a fixed classifier, and the distribution of the error estimate is binomial with variance

$$\mathrm{Var}\{\hat{\boldsymbol{\varepsilon}}\} = \sum_{i=1}^{2} P(\omega_i)\varepsilon_i(1 - \varepsilon_i)/N \tag{5-141}$$

where ε_i is the true error for class i [see (5-131)].

On the other hand, if we have N design samples and an infinite number of test samples, the error estimate is expressed by

$$\hat{\boldsymbol{\varepsilon}} = P(\omega_1) \int_{\hat{\boldsymbol{\Gamma}}_2} p(X/\omega_1)\, dX + P(\omega_2) \int_{\hat{\boldsymbol{\Gamma}}_1} p(X/\omega_2)\, dX \tag{5-142}$$

where $\hat{\boldsymbol{\Gamma}}_i$ is the region where class i is chosen. In this case, the integrands are fixed but the boundary of these regions varies each time when a set of N samples is drawn. The variance of $\hat{\boldsymbol{\varepsilon}}$, for general densities, is too complex to calculate. However, when the density functions are normal with equal covariance matrices, (5-142) can be converted to a one-dimensional integral as

$$\begin{aligned} \hat{\boldsymbol{\varepsilon}} = P(\omega_1) &\int_{(t-\hat{\eta}_1)/\hat{\sigma}_1}^{+\infty} \frac{1}{(2\pi)^{1/2}} \exp(-\xi^2/2)\, d\xi \\ +P(\omega_2) &\int_{(\hat{\eta}_2-t)/\hat{\sigma}_2}^{+\infty} \frac{1}{(2\pi)^{1/2}} \exp(-\xi^2/2)\, d\xi \end{aligned} \tag{5-143}$$

where $\hat{\boldsymbol{\eta}}_i$ and $\hat{\boldsymbol{\sigma}}_i^2$ are given by the conditional expectations.

$$\begin{aligned} \hat{\boldsymbol{\eta}}_i = E\{&(\hat{\mathbf{M}}_1 - \hat{\mathbf{M}}_2)^T \hat{\boldsymbol{\Sigma}}^{-1} \mathbf{X} \\ &- \tfrac{1}{2}(\hat{\mathbf{M}}_1^T \hat{\boldsymbol{\Sigma}}^{-1} \hat{\mathbf{M}}_1 - \hat{\mathbf{M}}_2^T \hat{\boldsymbol{\Sigma}}^{-1} \hat{\mathbf{M}}_2)/\mathbf{X} \in \omega_i, \hat{\mathbf{M}}_1, \hat{\mathbf{M}}_2, \hat{\boldsymbol{\Sigma}}\} \end{aligned} \tag{5-144}$$

$$\begin{aligned} \hat{\boldsymbol{\sigma}}_i^2 = \operatorname{Var}\{&(\hat{\mathbf{M}}_1 - \hat{\mathbf{M}}_2)^T \hat{\boldsymbol{\Sigma}}^{-1} \mathbf{X} \\ &- \tfrac{1}{2}(\hat{\mathbf{M}}_1^T \hat{\boldsymbol{\Sigma}}^{-1} \hat{\mathbf{M}}_1 - \hat{\mathbf{M}}_2^T \hat{\boldsymbol{\Sigma}}^{-1} \hat{\mathbf{M}}_2)/\mathbf{X} \in \omega_i, \hat{\mathbf{M}}_1, \hat{\mathbf{M}}_2, \hat{\boldsymbol{\Sigma}}\} \end{aligned} \tag{5-145}$$

$$t = \ln\{P(\omega_1)/P(\omega_2)\} \tag{5-146}$$

This conversion is based on the facts that the Bayes classifier is linear for normal distributions with equal covariances and that the distribution of the likelihood ratio is also normal. Similar expressions were seen in (3-35) through (3-38). Even when two true covariance matrices are the same, their estimates are different. However, for simplicity's sake let us assume that both estimates are the same and given by

$$\begin{aligned} \hat{\boldsymbol{\Sigma}} = [1/(N_1 + N_2 - 2)]\Big\{ &\sum_{j=1}^{N_2} (\mathbf{X}_j^{(1)} - \hat{\mathbf{M}}_1)(\mathbf{X}_j^{(1)} - \hat{\mathbf{M}}_1)^T \\ &+ \sum_{j=1}^{N_2} (\mathbf{X}_j^{(2)} - \hat{\mathbf{M}}_2)(\mathbf{X}_j^{(2)} - \hat{\mathbf{M}}_2)^T \Big\} \end{aligned} \tag{5-147}$$

where N_i is the number of design samples of class i, $X_j^{(i)}$.

Although it is still complicated, the variation of $\hat{\boldsymbol{\varepsilon}}$ in (5-143) is now manageable and the expected value of $\hat{\boldsymbol{\varepsilon}}$ has been reported [Okamoto, 1963].

Since $E\{\hat{\varepsilon}\}$ is lengthy, let us present here the simplest case with $P(\omega_1) = P(\omega_2)$ and $N_1 = N_2$ as

$$E\{\Delta\hat{\varepsilon}\} = E\{\hat{\varepsilon}\} - \varepsilon_0 = \gamma/N \tag{5-148}$$

$$\gamma = \{\tfrac{1}{2}(n-1)/d + \tfrac{1}{8}nd\}(2\pi)^{-1/2}\exp[-\tfrac{1}{2}(d/2)^2] \tag{5-149}$$

where d is the distance between two expected vectors given by

$$d^2 = (M_1 - M_2)^T \Sigma^{-1}(M_1 - M_2) \tag{5-150}$$

The term ε_0 is the Bayes minimum error.

Since ε_0 is the minimum value of $\hat{\varepsilon}$, the distribution of $\Delta\hat{\varepsilon}$ is causal. Therefore, we may provide an estimate of the variance of $\Delta\hat{\varepsilon}$ based on its expected value. Let us assume the gamma density for the distribution of $\Delta\hat{\varepsilon}$. The gamma density covers a wide range of causal distributions and is expressed by

$$p(\Delta\hat{\varepsilon}) = [c^{b+1}/\Gamma(b+1)](\Delta\hat{\varepsilon})^b \exp(-c\,\Delta\hat{\varepsilon}) \qquad \text{for} \quad \Delta\varepsilon > 0$$
$$(b \geq 0 \qquad \text{and} \qquad c > 0) \tag{5-151}$$

The expected value and variance of (5-151) are

$$E\{\Delta\hat{\varepsilon}\} = (b+1)/c \tag{5-152}$$

$$\mathrm{Var}\{\Delta\hat{\varepsilon}\} = (b+1)/c^2 \tag{5-153}$$

Therefore, eliminating c, we obtain an upper bound of $\mathrm{Var}\{\Delta\hat{\varepsilon}\}$ as

$$\mathrm{Var}\{\Delta\hat{\varepsilon}\} = [1/(b+1)]E^2\{\Delta\hat{\varepsilon}\} \leq E^2\{\Delta\hat{\varepsilon}\} \qquad \text{for} \quad b \geq 0 \tag{5-154}$$

Thus, a measure of effect of the number of design samples on the estimate of the probability of error ε_0 is

$$s_d = E\{\Delta\hat{\varepsilon}\} + (\mathrm{Var}\{\Delta\hat{\varepsilon}\})^{1/2} \leq 2\gamma/N \tag{5-155}$$

for normal distributions with equal covariance matrices and equal *a priori* probabilities. The term s_d of (5-155) should be compared with s_t, which is the effect of the number of test samples. The term s_t is obtained by inserting $P(\omega_1) = P(\omega_2) = 0.5$ and $\varepsilon_1 = \varepsilon_2 = \varepsilon_0$ into (5-141).

$$s_t = [\varepsilon_0(1-\varepsilon_0)/N]^{1/2} \tag{5-156}$$

The terms $d/2$ and $(2\pi)^{-1/2}\exp[-\tfrac{1}{2}(d/2)^2]$ of (5-149) and ε_0 of (5-156) are uniquely related. Therefore, we can compare 2γ in s_d with $[\varepsilon_0(1 - \varepsilon_0)]^{1/2}$ in s_t. This relationship is plotted in Fig. 5-3.

From Fig. 5-3 we see that $2\gamma(n)$ depends to a great extent on both the number of dimensions n and the separation of the classes as measured by the distance d. For any particular n, d and number of design and test samples s_d and s_t may be evaluated from (5-155), (5-156), and Fig. 5-3. Since s_d decreases as $1/N$ and s_t decreases only as $1/\sqrt{N}$, we see for many cases that more samples should be used for testing than for design.

EXAMPLE 5-7 In order to extend the above conclusion to normal distributions with unequal covariance matrices, an experiment was run for

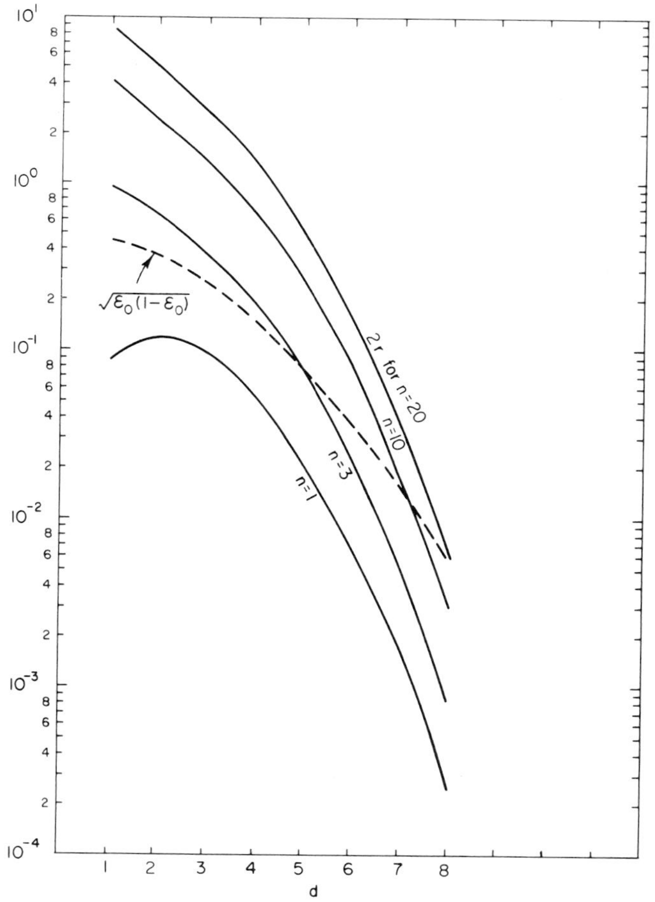

Fig. 5-3 $2\gamma(n)$ and $[\varepsilon_0(1 - \varepsilon_0)]^{1/2}$ vs d.

Standard Data $i = 1, 2$. The *sample size* for design was chosen as $N_1 = N_2 = 12$, 50, 100, 200, and 400 ($N = N_1 + N_2$) for each class. Four hundred samples per class, which were generated independently of the design samples, were used for testing the performance of the classifier. For each sample size, the experiment was repeated 40 times to calculate the sample mean and standard deviation of the error estimate. The result is shown in Table 5-1. We note that these results are consistent with the previous discussion with regard to both the bias and s_d which decrease very rapidly with increasing number of design samples. Since s_d was estimated by using only 400 test samples per class, most of the contribution to s_d at moderate and high numbers of design samples actually represented a deviation due not to design but to testing.

TABLE 5-1

SAMPLING EXPERIMENT TO CALCULATE BIAS AND STANDARD DEVIATION DUE TO DESIGN[a]

No. of samples per class $N_1 = N_2$	s_t: theoretical (%) $[0.5\{\varepsilon_1(1-\varepsilon_1)+\varepsilon_2(1-\varepsilon_2)\}/N]^{1/2}$	s_d: experimental (%)	
		$E\{\Delta\hat{\varepsilon}\}$	$(\mathrm{Var}\{\Delta\hat{\varepsilon}\})^{1/2}$
12	2.75	10.7	5.4
50	1.35	0.78	0.59
100	0.95	0.35	0.57
200	0.67	0.16	0.50
400	0.48	0	0.36

[a] $n = 8$; $\varepsilon_1 = 1.6\%$; $\varepsilon_2 = 2.2\%$.

Highleyman also concluded that the design requires relatively few samples as compared to the testing, if the object is to provide a minimum variance unbiased estimate of ε_0 [Highleyman, 1962]. His approach holds for any density, but with quite restrictive conditions on the form of the error estimate.

Elimination of Class Assignment for Test Samples

In order to estimate the error, we need the samples to be identified according to class both for designing and testing. In some cases, the class identification of samples is expensive. We will discuss hereafter a way to eliminate the class assignment for the test samples [Chow, 1970]. When the number of test samples is larger in the optimum sample partitioning than the number of design samples, this elimination is more effective.

Let us introduce a *reject region* for M class problems as

$$\max_i P(\omega_i)p(X/\omega_i) \lesseqgtr (1-t)p(X) \rightarrow X \in \begin{cases} \Gamma_r(t) \\ \Gamma_a(t) \end{cases} \quad (i = 1, 2, \ldots, M) \qquad (5\text{-}157)$$

where $p(X)$ is the mixture density function and t is the *rejection threshold* with $0 \leq t \leq 1$. Equation (5-157) states that, if no individual $P(\omega_i)p(X/\omega_i)$ for X exceeds $(1 - t)$ times the mixture density $p(X)$, we reject X; otherwise we accept X and classify X into class i. Then the entire region of X is divided into a *reject region* $\Gamma_r(t)$ and an *acceptance region* $\Gamma_a(t)$, where both are functions of the rejection threshold t. By this decision rule, the *probability of error* $\varepsilon(t)$, *reject rate* $r(t)$, and *correct recognition rate* $c(t)$ are given by

$$c(t) = \int_{\Gamma_a(t)} \max_i P(\omega_i)p(X/\omega_i)\, dX \qquad (5\text{-}158)$$

$$r(t) = \int_{\Gamma_r(t)} p(X)\, dX \qquad (5\text{-}159)$$

and

$$\varepsilon(t) = 1 - c(t) - r(t) \qquad (5\text{-}160)$$

Suppose we increase the reject region by an amount $\Delta\Gamma_r(t)$ by changing t to $t - \Delta t$. Then for those X's, which were accepted previously but are now rejected:

$$\begin{aligned}(1 - t)p(X) &\leq \max_i P(\omega_i)p(X/\omega_i) \\ &< (1 - t + \Delta t)p(X) \qquad \text{for} \quad X \in \Delta\Gamma_r(t)\end{aligned} \qquad (5\text{-}161)$$

By integrating (5-161) over the region $\Delta\Gamma_r(t)$, we have

$$(1 - t)\, \Delta r(t) \leq -\Delta c(t) < (1 - t + \Delta t)\, \Delta r(t) \qquad (5\text{-}162)$$

where $\Delta r(t)$ and $\Delta c(t)$ are the increments of $r(t)$ and $c(t)$ induced by the change of t. From (5-160), (5-162) can be rewritten as

$$-t\, \Delta r(t) \leq \Delta\varepsilon(t) < -(t - \Delta t)\, \Delta r(t) \qquad (5\text{-}163)$$

Summing over discrete values of t from 0 to t gives

$$-\Sigma t\, \Delta r(t) \leq \varepsilon(t) < -\Sigma(t - \Delta t)\, \Delta r(t) \qquad (5\text{-}164)$$

Letting $\Delta t \rightarrow 0$ gives the Stieltjes integral

$$\varepsilon(t) = -\int_{t=0}^{t} t\, dr(t) = \int_{t=t}^{0} t\, dr(t) \qquad (5\text{-}165)$$

Equation (5-165) shows that the probability of error $\varepsilon(t)$ can be calculated once we know the relationship between t and $r(t)$. From (5-157), we see that there is no rejection region for $t = 1 - 1/M$, so that the Bayes error ε_0 equals $\varepsilon(1 - 1/M)$. Also, we can discuss from (5-165) the *tradeoff between the error and reject rate*, since the change of the error can be calculated as a function of the change of the reject rate.

In order to use (5-165) for eliminating the class assignment of test samples, we proceed as follows:

(1) Use the relatively expensive classified samples to determine $\Delta\Gamma_r(kt_0)$'s for $t = kt_0$ $[k = 0, 1, \ldots, m = (1 - 1/M)/t_0]$, as shown in Fig. 5-4, where t_0 is a discrete step of t.

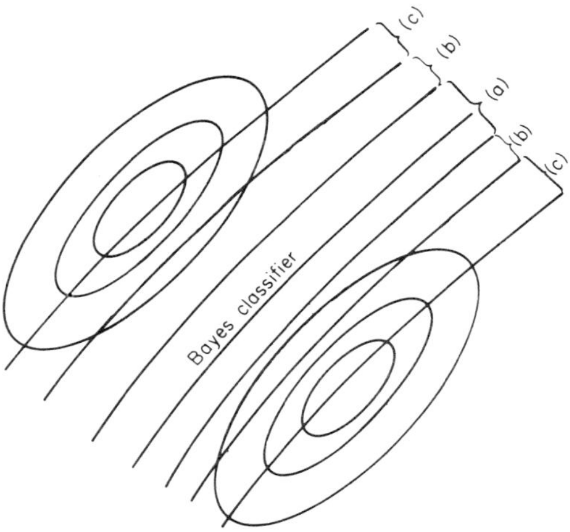

Fig. 5-4 Incremental reject regions:
(a) $\Delta\Gamma_r(mt_0)$; (b) $\Delta\Gamma_r((m-1)t_0)$; (c) $\Delta\Gamma_r((m-2)t_0)$

(2) Count the number of unclassified test samples which fall in $\Delta\Gamma_r(kt_0)$, divide the number by the total number of samples, and call this ratio $\Delta r(kt_0)$.

(3) Then, from (5-165), the error estimate is

$$\varepsilon(mt_0) = \sum_{k=m}^{0} (kt_0)\, \Delta r(kt_0) \tag{5-166}$$

In this process, we used the property of the reject rate being only a function of the mixture density but not of individual class densities. Therefore, once we design the incremental reject regions from classified samples, we no longer need classified samples for evaluating $\Delta r(t)$ and, subsequently, the probability of error $\varepsilon(t)$.

The Leaving-One-Out Method for Normal Distributions

In this subsection, we discuss a simple way of implementing the leaving-one-out method for normal distributions, namely the elimination of the N Bayes classifier calculation [Fukunaga, 1971c].

For normal distributions, the Bayes classifier is given by

$$h(X, \Theta) = \tfrac{1}{2}(X - M_1)^T \Sigma_1^{-1}(X - M_1) - \tfrac{1}{2}(X - M_2)^T \Sigma_2^{-1}(X - M_2) + \ln\{|\Sigma_1|/|\Sigma_2|\} - \ln\{P(\omega_1)/P(\omega_2)\} \lesseqgtr 0 \rightarrow X \in \begin{cases} \omega_1 \\ \omega_2 \end{cases} \tag{5-167}$$

where Θ is a set of parameters, M_1, M_2, Σ_1, Σ_2, $P(\omega_1)$, and $P(\omega_2)$.

Let $\hat{\Theta}_N = \{\hat{M}_i, \hat{\Sigma}_i, \hat{P}(\omega_i)\ (i = 1, 2)\}$ be the set of parameters estimated from the available N samples, and let $\hat{\Theta}_{N-1}^{(k)} = \{\hat{M}_{ik}, \hat{\Sigma}_{ik}, \hat{P}_k(\omega_i)\ (i = 1, 2)\}$ be the set of parameters estimated from $N - 1$ samples left when a sample X_k is excluded. Assuming that the N independent samples consist of N_1 samples from ω_1 and N_2 samples from ω_2, these parameters are given and related as follows for $X_j \in \omega_i$:

$$\hat{M}_i = \frac{1}{N_i} \sum_{j=1}^{N_i} X_j \tag{5-168}$$

$$\hat{M}_{ik} = \frac{1}{N_i - 1} \left\{ \left(\sum_{j=1}^{N_i} X_j \right) - X_k \right\} = \hat{M}_i - \frac{1}{N_i - 1}(X_k - \hat{M}_i) \tag{5-169}$$

$$\hat{\Sigma}_i = \frac{1}{N_i - 1} \sum_{j=1}^{N_i} (X_j - \hat{M}_i)(X_j - \hat{M}_i)^T \tag{5-170}$$

$$\begin{aligned} \hat{\Sigma}_{ik} &= \frac{1}{N_i - 2} \left[\left\{ \sum_{j=1}^{N_i} (X_j - \hat{M}_{ik})(X_j - \hat{M}_{ik})^T \right\} - (X_k - \hat{M}_{ik})(X_k - \hat{M}_{ik})^T \right] \\ &= \hat{\Sigma}_i + \frac{1}{N_i - 2} \left[\hat{\Sigma}_i - \frac{N_i}{N_i - 1}(X_k - \hat{M}_i)(X_k - \hat{M}_i)^T \right] \end{aligned} \tag{5-171}$$

$$\hat{P}(\omega_i) = \frac{N_i}{N} \tag{5-172}$$

$$\hat{P}_k(\omega_i) = \frac{N_i - 1}{N - 1} \quad \text{and} \quad \hat{P}_k(\omega_j) = \frac{N_j}{N - 1} \quad \text{for} \quad X_k \in \omega_i \quad \text{and} \quad X_k \notin \omega_j \tag{5-173}$$

According to (5-167), in the leaving-one-out method we have to calculate

$$h(X_k, \hat{\Theta}_{N-1}^{(k)}) = \tfrac{1}{2}(X_k - \hat{M}_{1k})^T \hat{\Sigma}_{1k}^{-1}(X_k - \hat{M}_{1k}) - \tfrac{1}{2}(X_k - \hat{M}_2)^T \hat{\Sigma}_2^{-1}(X_k - \hat{M}_2)$$
$$+ \tfrac{1}{2} \ln\{|\hat{\Sigma}_{1k}| / |\hat{\Sigma}_2|\} - \ln\{\hat{P}_k(\omega_1)/\hat{P}_k(\omega_2)\}$$
$$\text{for} \quad X_k \in \omega_1 \tag{5-174}$$

A similar expression can be obtained for $X_k \in \omega_2$.

As is shown in Appendix 5-1, using (5-168) through (5-173), $h(X_k, \hat{\Theta}_{N-1}^{(k)})$ of (5-174) can be expressed as the deviation from $h(X_k, \hat{\Theta}_N)$, which is the estimate of the likelihood ratio by the C method, as follows:

$$h(X_k, \hat{\Theta}_{N-1}^{(k)}) - h(X_k, \hat{\Theta}_N) = \begin{cases} +g[N_1, \hat{d}_1^2(X_k)] & \text{for} \quad X_k \in \omega_1 \\ -g[N_2, \hat{d}_2^2(X_k)] & \text{for} \quad X_k \in \omega_2 \end{cases} \tag{5-175}$$

where

$$g[N_i, \hat{d}_i^2(X_k)] = \frac{1}{2} \frac{(N_i^2 - 3N_i + 1)\hat{d}_i^2(X_k)/(N_i - 1) + N_i \hat{d}_i^4(X_k)}{(N_i - 1)^2 - N_i \hat{d}_i^2(X_k)}$$
$$+ \frac{1}{2} \ln\left[1 - \frac{N_i}{(N_i - 1)^2} \hat{d}_i^2(X_k)\right]$$
$$+ \ln \frac{N_i}{N_i - 1} + \frac{n}{2} \ln \frac{N_i - 1}{N_i - 2} > 0 \tag{5-176}$$

and

$$\hat{d}_i^2(X_k) = (X_k - \hat{M}_i)^T \hat{\Sigma}_i^{-1}(X_k - \hat{M}_i) \tag{5-177}$$

From (5-175), (5-176), and (5-177) the following three observations can be made:

(1) When the C method is used to calculate the probability of error, $h(X_k, \hat{\Theta}_N)$ and $\hat{d}_i^2(X_k)$ $(i = 1, 2)$ must be computed for $k = 1, 2, \ldots, N$. Therefore, the additional computation of the scalar function of (5-176) for each k is a negligible load for a computer in comparison with the computation of $h(X_k, \hat{\Theta}_N)$ for each k. Thus, the computation time of both the C method and the leaving-one-out method becomes almost equivalent to the computation time of the C method alone. Remember that, in the C method, we are required to design only one classifier.

(2) As is proved in Appendix 5-1, $g(\cdot)$ of (5-176) is always positive no matter what N_i, $\hat{d}_i^2(X_k)$, and n are. Therefore, from (5-175),

$$h(X_k, \hat{\Theta}_{N-1}^{(k)}) > h(X_k, \hat{\Theta}_N) \qquad \text{for} \quad X_k \in \omega_1 \tag{5-178}$$

and

$$h(X_k, \hat{\Theta}_{N-1}^{(k)}) < h(X_k, \hat{\Theta}_N) \qquad \text{for} \quad X_k \in \omega_2 \tag{5-179}$$

According to the decision rule of (5-167), we can conclude that

(i) if X_k is misclassified by the C method, X_k is also misclassified by the leaving-one-out method, and

(ii) there may be some X_k's which are correctly classified by the C method but misclassified by the leaving-one-out method.

This conclusion for normal distributions is a stronger statement than the inequality of (5-140), because the inequality of (5-140) holds only for the expectations of errors, while the above statement is for individual samples of individual tests.

(3) For $N_i \gg 1$ and $\hat{d}_i^2(X_k)/N_i \ll 1$, a simpler approximation of (5-176) can be obtained as follows:

$$g[N_i, \hat{d}_i^2(X_k)] \simeq \tfrac{1}{2}\, \hat{d}_i^4(X_k)/N_i \tag{5-180}$$

EXAMPLE 5-8 Both the C method and the leaving-one-out method were tested for generated normal data according to Standard Data $i = 1, 2$. This was done for sample sizes $N_1 = N_2 = 12$, 50, 100, 200, and 400 for each class. Each time a set of data was generated, the sample mean vectors and covariance matrices $\hat{M}_i$ and $\hat{\Sigma}_i$ were calculated, and the C method and the leaving-one-out method were applied to calculate the estimates of the error probabilities. Forty sets of samples were generated for $N_1 = N_2 = 12$, 50, 100, 200, and 400 to calculate the experimental means and variances of these estimates. The results are shown in Table 5-2. The theoretical error ε_0 for this example is 1.9% from Table 3-3.

TABLE 5-2

ESTIMATION OF ERROR

No. of samples per class $N_1 = N_2$	C Method		Leaving-one-out method		Bias between two means (%)
	Mean (%)	Standard deviation (%)	Mean (%)	Standard deviation (%)	
12	0.21	1.3	18.54	7.6	18.33
50	1.22	0.9	2.97	1.7	1.75
100	1.44	0.8	2.15	1.0	0.71
200	1.56	0.7	2.00	0.7	0.44
400	1.83	0.5	1.97	0.5	0.14

In (5-180) we saw that the difference of the estimates for likelihood ratios between the two methods is proportional to $1/N$. Although we do not have any theoretical result for error estimation, Table 5-2 shows that the bias between the two error estimates decreases roughly as $1/N$, and the standard deviations of the error estimates decrease as $1/N^{1/2}$.

Appendix 5-1 Calculation of the Bias between the *C* Method and the Leaving-One-Out Method

The proof of (5-175) consists of three parts: the quadratic term, the determinant term, and the *a priori* probability term in (5-174).

(1) *Quadratic Terms*

We rewrite (5-171) as

$$\hat{\Sigma}_{ik} = \frac{N_i - 1}{N_i - 2}\hat{\Sigma}_i - \frac{N_i}{(N_i - 1)(N_i - 2)}(X_k - \hat{M}_i)(X_k - \hat{M}_i)^T \quad \text{(A5.1-1)}$$

The inverse matrix of $\hat{\Sigma}_{ik}$ is

$$\hat{\Sigma}_{ik}^{-1} = \left(\frac{N_i - 2}{N_i - 1}\right)\left[\hat{\Sigma}_i^{-1} + \frac{N_i\hat{\Sigma}_i^{-1}(X_k - \hat{M}_i)(X_k - \hat{M}_i)^T\hat{\Sigma}_i^{-1}}{(N_i - 1)^2 - N_i\hat{d}_i^2(X_k)}\right] \quad \text{(A5.1-2)}$$

where $\hat{d}_i^2(X_k)$ is given in (5-177). Then, using (5-169), the quadratic term is given by

$$\begin{aligned}(X_k - \hat{M}_{ik})^T\hat{\Sigma}_{ik}^{-1}(X_k - \hat{M}_{ik}) &= \left(\frac{N_i}{N_i - 1}\right)^2(X_k - \hat{M}_i)^T\hat{\Sigma}_{ik}^{-1}(X_k - \hat{M}_i)\\ &= \left(\frac{N_i}{N_i - 1}\right)^2\left(\frac{N_i - 2}{N_i - 1}\right)\left[\hat{d}_i^2(X_k) + \frac{N_i\hat{d}_i^4(X_k)}{(N_i - 1)^2 - N_i\hat{d}_i^2(X_k)}\right]\\ &= \hat{d}_i^2(X_k) + \frac{(N_i^2 - 3N_i + 1)\hat{d}_i^2(X_k)/(N_i - 1) + N_i\hat{d}_i^4(X_k)}{(N_i - 1)^2 - N_i\hat{d}_i^2(X_k)} \quad \text{(A5.1-3)}\end{aligned}$$

(2) *Determinant Terms*

Using (A5.1-1), the determinant of $\hat{\Sigma}_{ik}$ can be calculated as follows:

$$|\hat{\Sigma}_{ik}| = \left(\frac{N_i - 1}{N_i - 2}\right)^n |\hat{\Sigma}_i| \left| I - \frac{N_i}{(N_i - 1)^2}\hat{\Sigma}_i^{-1}(X_k - \hat{M}_i)(X_k - \hat{M}_i)^T \right| \quad \text{(A5.1-4)}$$

Let $\hat{\lambda}_1, \hat{\lambda}_2, \ldots, \hat{\lambda}_n$ be the eigenvalues of the matrix $\hat{\Sigma}_i^{-1}(X_k - \hat{M}_i)(X_k - \hat{M}_i)^T$. Then the last determinant of (A5.1-4) is

$$\left| I - \frac{N_i}{(N_i - 1)^2} \hat{\Sigma}_i^{-1}(X_k - \hat{M}_i)(X_k - \hat{M}_i)^T \right| = \prod_{i=1}^{n} \left(1 - \frac{N_i}{(N_i - 1)^2} \hat{\lambda}_i\right) \tag{A5.1-5}$$

The rank of the matrix $(X_k - \hat{M}_i)(X_k - \hat{M}_i)^T$ is one. Consequently, the rank of the matrix $\hat{\Sigma}_i^{-1}(X_k - \hat{M}_i)(X_k - \hat{M}_i)^T$ is also one. Therefore, the $\hat{\lambda}$'s should satisfy the following conditions:

$$\hat{\lambda}_1 \neq 0, \ \hat{\lambda}_2 = \hat{\lambda}_3 = \cdots = \hat{\lambda}_n = 0, \tag{A5.1-6}$$

and

$$\begin{aligned} \sum_{i=1}^{n} \hat{\lambda}_i = \hat{\lambda}_1 &= \operatorname{tr}[\hat{\Sigma}_i^{-1}(X_k - \hat{M}_i)(X_k - \hat{M}_i)^T] = (X_k - \hat{M}_i)^T \hat{\Sigma}_i^{-1}(X_k - \hat{M}_i) \\ &= \hat{d}_i^2(X_k) \end{aligned} \tag{A5.1-7}$$

Using these results, (A5.1-5) becomes

$$\left| I - \frac{N_i}{(N_i - 1)^2} \hat{\Sigma}_i^{-1}(X_k - \hat{M}_i)(X_k - \hat{M}_i)^T \right| = 1 - \frac{N_i}{(N_i - 1)^2} \hat{d}_i^2(X_k) \tag{A5.1-8}$$

From (A5.1-4),

$$\ln |\hat{\Sigma}_{ik}| = \ln |\hat{\Sigma}_i| + n \ln \frac{N_i - 1}{N_i - 2} + \ln\left(1 - \frac{N_i}{(N_i - 1)^2} \hat{d}_i^2(X_k)\right) \tag{A5.1-9}$$

(3) *A priori Probabilities*

If we assume $X_k \in \omega_i$, from (5-172) and (5-173)

$$\begin{aligned} \hat{P}_k(\omega_i) &= \frac{N_i - 1}{N - 1} = \frac{N_i}{N} \frac{N}{N - 1} \frac{N_i - 1}{N_i} \\ &= \hat{P}(\omega_i) \frac{N}{N - 1} \frac{N_i - 1}{N_i} \end{aligned} \tag{A5.1-10}$$

Also

$$\hat{P}_k(\omega_j) = \frac{N_j}{N - 1} = \frac{N_j}{N} \frac{N}{N - 1} = \hat{P}(\omega_j) \frac{N}{N - 1} \qquad (j \neq i) \tag{A5.1-11}$$

Therefore,

$$\frac{\hat{P}_k(\omega_i)}{\hat{P}_k(\omega_j)} = \frac{\hat{P}(\omega_i)}{\hat{P}(\omega_j)} \frac{N_i - 1}{N_i} \tag{A5.1-12}$$

The equations (A5.1-3), (A5.1-9), and (A5.1-12) give all terms of (5-175) and (5-176). Thus the proof is completed.

(4) *Proof of* $g(\cdot) > 0$ *of* (5-176)

Assuming $N_i > 2$, $|\hat{\Sigma}_{ik}|$ of (A5.1-4) should be positive because $\hat{\Sigma}_{ik}$ is a sample covariance matrix and should be a positive definite matrix. Therefore, the determinant of (A5.1-8) should also be positive. That is,

$$1 - [N_i/(N_i - 1)^2]\, \hat{d}_i^2(X_k) > 0 \tag{A5.1-13}$$

On the other hand, from (5-176)

$$\begin{aligned}\frac{\partial g}{\partial \hat{d}_i^2} &= \frac{1}{2}\,\frac{[(N_i^2 - 3N_i + 1)/(N_i - 1)] + 2N_i\hat{d}_i^2}{(N_i - 1)^2 - N_i\hat{d}_i^2} \\ &\quad + \frac{1}{2}\,\frac{[\{(N_i^2 - 3N_i + 1)/(N_i - 1)\}\,\hat{d}_i^2 + N_i\hat{d}_i^4]N_i}{[(N_i - 1)^2 - N_i\hat{d}_i^2]^2} \\ &\quad + \frac{1}{2}\,\frac{-N_i/(N_i - 1)^2}{1 - [N_i/(N_i - 1)^2]\hat{d}_i^2} \\ &= \frac{1}{2}\,\frac{-N_i^2\hat{d}_i^4 + N_i(2N_i^2 - 3N_i + 2)\hat{d}_i^2 - (N_i - 1)(2N_i - 1)}{[(N_i - 1)^2 - N_i\hat{d}_i^2]^2}\end{aligned} \tag{A5.1-14}$$

The term $\partial g/\partial \hat{d}_i^2$ is equal to zero when

$$\hat{d}_i^2 = 1/N_i \qquad \text{or} \qquad (3N_i^3 - 3N_i^2 + N_i)/N_i^2 \tag{A5.1-15}$$

The second solution of (A5.1-15) does not satisfy the condition of (A5.1-13). Since g and $\partial g/\partial \hat{d}_i^2$ for $\hat{d}_i^2 = 0$ are positive and negative, respectively, the first solution of (A5.1-15) gives the minimum g, which is

$$\begin{aligned}&\frac{1}{2}\,\frac{[(N_i^2 - 3N_i + 1)/(N_i - 1)] + 1}{N_i[(N_i - 1)^2 - 1]} + \frac{1}{2}\ln\left(1 - \frac{1}{(N_i - 1)^2}\right) \\ &\quad + \ln\frac{N_i}{N_i - 1} + \frac{n}{2}\ln\frac{N_i - 1}{N_i - 2} \\ &= \frac{1}{2}\,\frac{1}{N_i(N_i - 1)} + \ln\frac{N_i(N_i^2 - 2N_i)^{1/2}}{(N_i - 1)^2} + \frac{n}{2}\ln\frac{N_i - 1}{N_i - 2} > 0\end{aligned} \tag{A5.1-16}$$

for $N_i > 2$. The inequality of (A5.1-16) holds since the numerators of the second and third terms are larger than the corresponding denominators.

Computer Projects

Write the following programs:

5-1 Generate M sets of N samples. Calculate M sample mean vectors and covariance matrices. Study the relation of the dispersion of these vectors and matrices to N and M.

Data: Standard Data $i = 1$.

5-2 Calculate the confidence region for the expected values and variances of individual variables for a normal distribution. Study the relation of N, a, b, and γ of (5-89) and (5-93).

Data: Standard Data $i = 1$.

5-3 The probability of error is given by $\varepsilon_i = \int_t^\infty p(h/\omega_i)\,dh$. Calculate the confidence region of t for a given ε_i by using order statistics. Generate M sets of N samples and confirm the above result experimentally.

Data: Standard Data $i = 1$.

5-4 Tabulate and discuss the relation of a tolerance limit $(\mathbf{y}_i, \mathbf{y}_j)$ to N, p, and γ of (5-117). Generate M sets of N samples and confirm the above result experimentally.

Data: Standard Data $i = 1$.

5-5 Generate N samples from each of two distributions. Use $s \times N$ samples to calculate the sample mean vectors and covariance matrices and set up the Bayes classifier based on these estimates. Then test $(1 - s)N$ samples to estimate the probability of error. Repeat the same experiment for different sets of N samples, and study the relation between s and the dispersion of the error estimate.

Data: Standard Data $i = 1, 2$.

5-6 Estimate the probability of error by the C method and leaving-one-out method.

Data: Standard Data $i = 1, 2$.

Problems

5-1 Assuming that we draw N samples from a distribution, find the maximum likelihood estimate of p for

$$\Pr\{\mathbf{x} = 1\} = p \qquad \text{and} \qquad \Pr\{\mathbf{x} = 0\} = 1 - p$$

5-2 Based on N samples from a one-dimensional normal distribution, find the maximum likelihood estimate of the variance.

5-3 Let $\hat{\boldsymbol{\sigma}}^2$ be the sample variance of N samples. Find the lowest bound (Cramèr–Rao bound) for the variance of $\hat{\boldsymbol{\sigma}}^2$.

5-4 A fixed signal s is sent through a channel which has an amplification factor k and an additive normal noise with zero mean and variance σ^2. The received signal is $\mathbf{x} = ks + \mathbf{n}$. Based on N observed $\mathbf{x}$,

(a) find the maximum likelihood estimate of k, assuming that k is a fixed value;

(b) find the maximum *a posteriori* estimate of $\mathbf{k}$, assuming that $\mathbf{k}$ is normally distributed with mean k_0 and variance σ_0^2.

5-5 For the same problem as 5-4b, find the minimum mean-square estimate of $\mathbf{k}$. (Hint: $p(x_1, \ldots, x_N/k)p(k)$ is a normal distribution with respect to k, and its expected value is the minimum mean-square estimate of $\mathbf{k}$.)

5-6 For the same problem as 5-5, find the lowest bound of the mean-square error.

5-7 Suppose that we draw two sets of samples $\mathbf{x}_1, \ldots, \mathbf{x}_{N_1}$ and $\mathbf{y}_1, \ldots, \mathbf{y}_{N_2}$ from two independent distributions whose variances are known to be equal. Find the equation for the confidence interval of $m_1 - m_2$, where m_i's are the expected values of class i $(i = 1, 2)$.

5-8 Find the smallest N to give the confidence region $\Pr\{\mathbf{y}_1 \leq \xi < \mathbf{y}_N\} = 0.99$ for the quantile ξ of order p, where $\mathbf{y}_1$ and $\mathbf{y}_N$ are the smallest and largest samples among N samples drawn from a distribution.

5-9 Find the smallest N to give a tolerance limit $\Pr\{P(\mathbf{y}_N) - P(\mathbf{y}_1) \geq p\} = 0.95$, where $\mathbf{y}_1$ and $\mathbf{y}_N$ are the smallest and largest samples among N samples drawn from a distribution.

5-10 Assume that the density function of $\hat{\boldsymbol{\varepsilon}}$ of (5-121) can be approximated by a normal distribution with unknown expected value ε and known variance $\hat{\boldsymbol{\varepsilon}}(1 - \hat{\boldsymbol{\varepsilon}})/N$. When $N = 250$ and $\hat{\boldsymbol{\varepsilon}} = 0.2$, find the confidence interval of ε for $\gamma = 0.95$ and compare the result with the one from Fig. 5-2.

5-11 Derive (5-175) from (5-174) for one-dimensional samples.

5-12 For two normal univariate distributions with expected values m_1 and m_2 and equal variance σ^2, find the error-reject rule and give a geometrical interpretation of the rule. Find the error and reject rates as a function of the threshold t.

Chapter 6

ESTIMATION OF DENSITY FUNCTIONS

So far we have been discussing the estimation of parameters. Thus, if we can assume we have a density function that can be characterized by a set of parameters, we can design a classifier using estimates of the parameters. Unfortunately, we often cannot assume a parametric form for the density function, and in order to apply the likelihood ratio test we have to somehow estimate the density functions, using an unstructured approach. This type of approach is called *nonparametric estimation*, while the former is called *parametric estimation*. Since the number of parameters in parametric estimation is usually far less than the number of samples, a nonparametric approach is more complex than a parametric one.

Nonparametric estimation of a density function is basically the estimation of a function of several variables. It can be used even when no *a priori* knowledge of the density is available. However, when sufficient knowledge is available, it is advisable to try to fit a density function of prescribed form to the data. For example, if it is somehow determined that the data are clustered about several modes, then the density can be postulated as a weighted sum of normal densities. Thus, the nonparametric techniques presented in this chapter work best in situations where little information about the density is available.

Another aspect of nonparametric estimation is the design of a classifier without an attempt to estimate the respective densities. In this case, we parameterize the classifier by assuming a functional form for the decision rule. The estimation of these parameters from the samples was discussed in Chapter 4 and will be discussed again in relation to successive estimation in Chapter 7.

6.1 Parzen Estimate

A Class of Estimates of a Density Function

For simplicity's sake, let us begin by discussing the estimation of a one dimensional density function [Parzen, 1962]. The multivariate case can be discussed in a similar manner and will be presented later.

Let $\mathbf{x}_1, \ldots, \mathbf{x}_N$ be independent and identically distributed observations of a random variable. An estimate of the distribution function is easily obtained as

$$\hat{\mathbf{P}}_N(x) = \{\text{No. of observations} \leq x \text{ among } \mathbf{x}_1, \ldots, \mathbf{x}_N\}/N \tag{6-1}$$

The term $\hat{\mathbf{P}}_N(x)$ is a discrete random variable and binomially distributed as

$$\Pr\{\hat{\mathbf{P}}_N(x) = k/N\} = \binom{N}{k} P(x)^k \{1 - P(x)\}^{N-k} \tag{6-2}$$

where $P(x)$ is the true distribution function of $\mathbf{x}$. As we discussed in (5-121), (6-1) is the maximum likelihood estimate of $P(x)$.

The expected value and the variance of $\hat{\mathbf{P}}_N(x)$ are given by

$$E\{\hat{\mathbf{P}}_N(x)\} = \sum_{k=0}^{N} (k/N) \binom{N}{k} P(x)^k \{1 - P(x)\}^{N-k} = P(x) \tag{6-3}$$

$$\begin{aligned} \operatorname{Var}\{\hat{\mathbf{P}}_N(x)\} &= \sum_{k=0}^{N} \{(k/N) - P(x)\}^2 \binom{N}{k} P(x)^k \{1 - P(x)\}^{N-k} \\ &= [P(x)\{1 - P(x)\}]/N \end{aligned} \tag{6-4}$$

Therefore, $\hat{\mathbf{P}}_N(x)$ is an unbiased estimate.

The estimate of a density function cannot be defined as easily. Since a density function is generally defined as the derivative of the distribution function, we may write an estimate of a density function as

$$\hat{\mathbf{p}}_N(x) = [\hat{\mathbf{P}}_N(x+h) - \hat{\mathbf{P}}_N(x-h)]/(2h) \tag{6-5}$$

where h is a properly selected positive number. However, it is not apparent how h should be chosen. It is clear that h should be chosen as a function of N which tends toward 0 as N tends to ∞. But how fast should h tend toward 0. In order to answer this question we have to study the statistical properties of the estimate defined by (6-5).

Equation (6-5) can be rewritten as

$$\begin{aligned}\hat{\mathbf{p}}_N(x) &= (2h)^{-1}\int_{x-h}^{x+h} d\hat{\mathbf{P}}_N(\xi) = \int_{-\infty}^{+\infty} (1/h)k[(x-\xi)/h]\, d\hat{\mathbf{P}}_N(\xi) \\ &= (1/N)\sum_{i=1}^{N} (1/h)k[(x-\mathbf{x}_i)/h]\end{aligned} \tag{6-6}$$

where

$$k(y/h) = \begin{cases} 1/2 & \text{for } |y/h| \le 1 \\ 0 & \text{for } |y/h| > 1 \end{cases} \tag{6-7}$$

We notice here that (6-5) is a special case of (6-6) with $k(y/h)$ defined by (6-7) and we could select other $k(y/h)$'s to relate $\hat{\mathbf{P}}_N(x)$ to $\hat{\mathbf{p}}_N(x)$. Thus, our problem is generalized to the selection of both $k(y/h)$ and h. The term $(1/h)k(y/h)$ will be called the *kernel of the estimate*.

If $k(y/h)$ and h satisfy the following conditions, then the estimate of (6-6) is asymptotically unbiased and consistent. The proof will be given later.

(1) The conditions for $k(y/h)$ are

$$\int_{-\infty}^{+\infty} k(y/h)\, dy/h = \int_{-\infty}^{+\infty} k(z)\, dz = 1 \tag{6-8}$$

$$\int_{-\infty}^{+\infty} |k(y/h)|\, dy/h = \int_{-\infty}^{+\infty} |k(z)|\, dz < \infty \tag{6-9}$$

$$\sup_{-\infty < y/h < +\infty} |k(y/h)| = \sup_{-\infty < z < +\infty} |k(z)| < \infty \tag{6-10}$$

$$\lim_{y/h \to \infty} |(y/h)k(y/h)| = \lim_{z \to \infty} |zk(z)| = 0 \tag{6-11}$$

(2) The conditions for $h(N)$ are

$$\lim_{N \to \infty} h(N) = 0 \qquad \text{for asymptotic unbiasedness} \tag{6-12}$$

$$\lim_{N \to \infty} Nh(N) = \infty \qquad \text{for asymptotic consistency} \tag{6-13}$$

TABLE 6-1

TYPICAL KERNELS[a]

$\frac{1}{h} k\left(\frac{y}{h}\right)$		$K(h\omega) = \int_{-\infty}^{+\infty} e^{j\omega y} k\left(\frac{y}{h}\right) \frac{dy}{h}$	$\int_{-\infty}^{+\infty} k^2(z)\, dz = \frac{1}{2\pi} \int_{-\infty}^{+\infty} K^2(\omega)\, d\omega$
$\frac{1}{2h}$ for $\left\|\frac{y}{h}\right\| \le 1$ 0 for $\left\|\frac{y}{h}\right\| > 1$	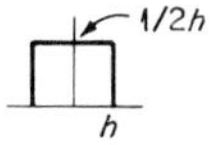	$\frac{\sin h\omega}{h\omega}$	$\frac{1}{2}$
$\frac{1}{h}\left\{1 - \left\|\frac{y}{h}\right\|\right\}$ for $\left\|\frac{y}{h}\right\| \le 1$ 0 for $\left\|\frac{y}{h}\right\| > 1$	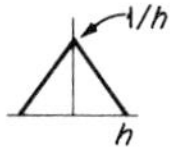	$\left(\frac{\sin h\omega/2}{h\omega/2}\right)^2$	$\frac{2}{3}$
$\frac{1}{\sqrt{2\pi}\, h} \exp\left(-\frac{y^2}{2h^2}\right)$	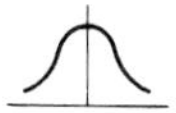	$\exp(-h^2\omega^2/2)$	$\frac{1}{2\sqrt{\pi}}$
$\frac{1}{2h} \exp\left(-\left\|\frac{y}{h}\right\|\right)$	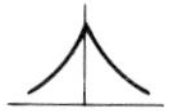	$\frac{1}{1 + h^2\omega^2}$	$\frac{1}{2}$
$\frac{1}{\pi h} \frac{1}{1 + (y/h)^2}$	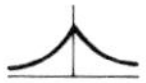	$\exp(-\|h\omega\|)$	$\frac{1}{\pi}$
$\frac{1}{2\pi h}\left(\frac{\sin y/2h}{y/2h}\right)^2$	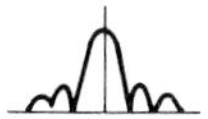	$1 - \|h\omega\|$ for $\|h\omega\| \le 1$ 0 for $\|h\omega\| > 1$	$\frac{1}{3\pi}$

[a] [Parzen, 1962].

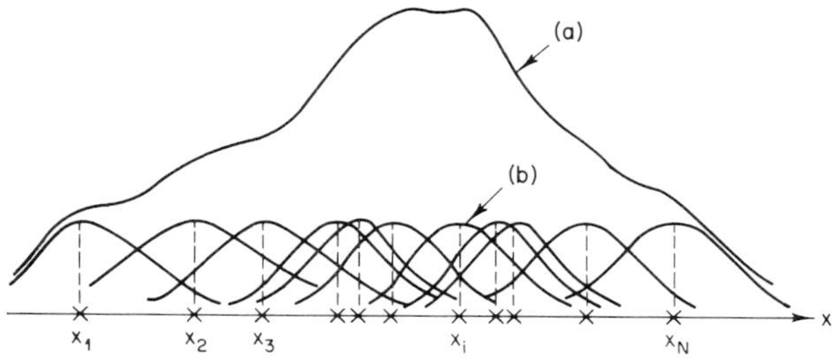

Fig. 6-1 Approximation of a density function by the sum of normal kernels: (a) $p(x)$; (b) $(Nh)^{-1}k[(x-x_i)/h]$.

There are many kernels which satisfy (6-8) through (6-11). Typical examples are shown in Table 6-1. Figure 6-1 shows the result of estimating a density function using a normal kernel.

Proof of Asymptotic Unbiasedness and Consistency

Now we will show that the estimate of (6-6) $\hat{\mathbf{p}}_N(x)$ is asymptotically unbiased and consistent, provided that (6-8) through (6-13) are satisfied. First, let us calculate the expected value of (6-6) as

$$E\{\hat{\mathbf{p}}_N(x)\} = E\{(1/h)k[(x-\mathbf{x})/h]\} = \int_{-\infty}^{+\infty} (1/h)k[(x-\xi)/h]p(\xi)\,d\xi$$
$$= \int_{-\infty}^{+\infty} (1/h)k(y/h)p(x-y)\,dy \tag{6-14}$$

In order to prove asymptotic unbiasedness, we would like to show

$$\lim_{N\to\infty} \int_{-\infty}^{+\infty} (1/h)k(y/h)p(x-y)\,dy = p(x)\int_{-\infty}^{+\infty} k(y/h)\,dy/h \tag{6-15}$$

for any $k(y/h)$ which satisfies (6-9) through (6-11). Then, because of (6-8), we can obtain

$$\lim_{N\to\infty} E\{\hat{\mathbf{p}}_N(x)\} = p(x) \tag{6-16}$$

Equation (6-15) is proved for the continuous points of $p(x)$ as follows. Let δ be a properly chosen positive constant, and let us separate the integral region into two parts $|y| \leq \delta$ and $|y| > \delta$. Then

$$\left| \int_{-\infty}^{+\infty} \{p(x-y) - p(x)\}(1/h)k(y/h)\,dy \right|$$
$$\leq \max_{|y|\leq\delta} |p(x-y) - p(x)| \int_{|z|\leq\delta/h} |k(z)|\,dz$$
$$+ \int_{|y|>\delta} \{|p(x-y)|/|y|\}\{|y|/h\}|k(y/h)|\,dy$$
$$+ |p(x)| \int_{|y|>\delta} (1/h)|k(y/h)|\,dy$$
$$\leq \max_{|y|\leq\delta} |p(x-y) - p(x)| \int_{-\infty}^{+\infty} |k(z)|\,dz$$
$$+ (1/\delta) \sup_{|z|>\delta/h} |zk(z)| \int_{-\infty}^{+\infty} |p(y)|\,dy + |p(x)| \int_{|z|>\delta/h} |k(z)|\,dz \tag{6-17}$$

When N tends toward ∞, $h(N)$ tends toward zero from (6-12), which leads the second and third terms of (6-17) toward zero with the conditions of (6-9) through (6-11). Then, by making δ tend toward zero, the first term of (6-17) tends toward zero. Thus, the proof of (6-15) is complete.

Asymptotic unbiasedness also can be seen in frequency analysis. Since (6-14) is a convolution integral of $p(x)$ and $(1/h)k(x/h)$, the characteristic functions of $p(x)$, $(1/h)k(x/h)$ and $E\{\hat{\mathbf{p}}_N(x)\}$ are related by

$$\varphi[E\{\hat{\mathbf{p}}_N(x)\}] = \varphi[(1/h)k(x/h)]\varphi[p(x)] \tag{6-18}$$

Therefore, in order for

$$\lim_{N\to\infty} \varphi[E\{\hat{\mathbf{p}}_N(x)\}]$$

to be equal to $\varphi[p(x)]$, $\varphi[(1/h)k(x/h)] = K(h\omega)$ should tend toward 1, as N tends toward ∞. The term $K(\omega)$ is the characteristic function of $k(z)$. This can be seen in Table 6-1, where every $K(h\omega)$ tends toward 1 as $h(N)$ tends toward 0.

Next, let us calculate the variance of the estimate.

$$\mathrm{Var}[\hat{\mathbf{p}}_N(x)] = E\{\hat{\mathbf{p}}_N^2(x)\} - E^2\{\hat{\mathbf{p}}_N(x)\} \tag{6-19}$$

Substituting (6-6) into (6-19) and using the condition of independence among the $\mathbf{x}_i$'s, (6-19) can be rewritten as

$$\mathrm{Var}[\hat{\mathbf{p}}_N(x)] = (1/N)[E\{(1/h^2)k^2[(x-\mathbf{x})/h]\} - E^2\{(1/h)k[(x-\mathbf{x})/h]\}] \tag{6-20}$$

From (6-15), we have

$$\lim_{N\to\infty} E\{(1/h)k[(x - \mathbf{x})/h]\} = p(x) \int_{-\infty}^{+\infty} k(z)\,dz = p(x) \tag{6-21}$$

$$\lim_{N\to\infty} E\{(1/h)k^2[(x - \mathbf{x})/h]\} = p(x) \int_{-\infty}^{+\infty} k^2(z)\,dz \tag{6-22}$$

because k^2 satisfies (6-9) through (6-11), if k satisfies these conditions. Substituting (6-21) and (6-22) into (6-20), we obtain

$$\begin{aligned}\lim_{N\to\infty} \mathrm{Var}[\hat{\mathbf{p}}_N(x)] &= \lim_{N\to\infty} (Nh)^{-1}p(x) \int_{-\infty}^{+\infty} k^2(z)\,dz - \lim_{N\to\infty} (1/N)p^2(x) \\ &= \lim_{N\to\infty} (Nh)^{-1}p(x) \int_{-\infty}^{+\infty} k^2(z)\,dz \end{aligned} \tag{6-23}$$

Since $\int k^2(z)\,dz$ is a finite number from (6-9) through (6-11), (6-23) can be made zero if

$$\lim_{N\to\infty} Nh(N) = \infty \tag{6-24}$$

This is the condition for asymptotic consistency. As a measure of the variance, $\int k^2(z)\,dz$ is listed in Table 6-1.

As we see in (6-6), $\hat{\mathbf{p}}_N(x)$ is the summation of N random variables $(1/h)k[(x - \mathbf{x}_i)/h]$. Therefore, under certain conditions, $\hat{\mathbf{p}}_N(x)$ tends toward a normal distribution as N tends toward ∞, although the detailed discussion is omitted here [Parzen, 1962].

Uniform Consistency and Estimation of the Mode

In this subsection, we would like to determine the conditions under which the estimated density function tends toward the true density function in probability (uniformly). Under the same conditions, we can also obtain consistent estimates of the mode.

The conditions for uniform consistency are stated as follows:

Theorem If $h(N)$, in addition to (6-12), satisfies

$$\lim_{N\to\infty} Nh^2(N) = \infty \tag{6-25}$$

and the characteristic function

$$K(h\omega) = \int_{-\infty}^{+\infty} \exp(j\omega y)k(y/h)(1/h)\,dy \tag{6-26}$$

of $(1/h)k(y/h)$ is absolutely integrable, (hence $p(x)$ is uniformly continuous), then, for every $\varepsilon > 0$,

$$\lim_{N\to\infty} \Pr\left\{ \sup_{-\infty<x<+\infty} | \hat{\mathbf{p}}_N(x) - p(x) | > \varepsilon \right\} = 0 \tag{6-27}$$

The term $K(\omega)$ is the characteristic function of $k(z)$.

PROOF Let us express the sample characteristic function of (6-6) as

$$\boldsymbol{\varphi}_N(\omega) = \int_{-\infty}^{+\infty} \exp(j\omega x)\, d\hat{\mathbf{P}}_N(x) = (1/N) \sum_{i=1}^{N} \exp(j\omega \mathbf{x}_i) \tag{6-28}$$

Then the characteristic function of $\hat{\mathbf{p}}_N(x)$ should be the product of $\boldsymbol{\varphi}_N(\omega)$ and $K(h\omega)$. Therefore, applying the inverse operation,

$$\begin{aligned} \hat{\mathbf{p}}_N(x) &= (1/N) \sum_{i=1}^{N} (1/h)k[(x - \mathbf{x})/h] \\ &= (2\pi)^{-1} \int_{-\infty}^{+\infty} \exp(-j\omega x)\boldsymbol{\varphi}_N(\omega)K(h\omega)\, d\omega \end{aligned} \tag{6-29}$$

Hence,

$$\begin{aligned} &E\left[\sup_{-\infty<x<+\infty} | \hat{\mathbf{p}}_N(x) - E\{\hat{\mathbf{p}}_N\} | \right] \\ &\quad \leq (2\pi)^{-1} \int_{-\infty}^{+\infty} | K(h\omega) |\, E[| \boldsymbol{\varphi}_N(\omega) - E\{\boldsymbol{\varphi}_N(\omega)\} |]\, d\omega \\ &\quad \leq (2\pi)^{-1} \int_{-\infty}^{+\infty} | K(h\omega) |\, [\mathrm{Var}\{\boldsymbol{\varphi}_N(\omega)\}]^{1/2}\, d\omega \qquad \text{(Jensen's inequality)} \\ &\quad = (2\pi)^{-1} \int_{-\infty}^{+\infty} | K(h\omega) | \\ &\qquad \times [(1/N)\,\mathrm{Var}\{\exp(j\omega\mathbf{x}_i)\}]^{1/2}\, d\omega \qquad \text{(independent } \mathbf{x}_i\text{)} \\ &\quad \leq (2\pi)^{-1} \int_{-\infty}^{+\infty} | K(h\omega) |\, [(1/N)E\{\exp(j\omega\mathbf{x}_i)\exp(-j\omega\mathbf{x}_i)\}]^{1/2}\, d\omega \\ &\quad = (2\pi)^{-1} \int_{-\infty}^{+\infty} | K(h\omega) |\, (1/N)^{1/2}\, d\omega \\ &\quad = (2\pi)^{-1}h^{-1}N^{-1/2} \int_{-\infty}^{+\infty} | K(u) |\, du \end{aligned} \tag{6-30}$$

which tends toward zero under the condition of (6-25). Equation (6-30) implies

$$E^{1/2}\left[\sup_{-\infty<x<+\infty} | \hat{\mathbf{p}}_N(x) - E\{\hat{\mathbf{p}}_N(x)\} | \right] \to 0 \qquad \text{for} \quad N \to \infty \tag{6-31}$$

On the other hand, considering the uniform continuity of $p(x)$, we can modify (6-17) to prove

$$\lim_{N\to\infty}\Big[\sup_{-\infty<x<+\infty}|\,E\{\hat{\mathbf{p}}_N(x)\}-p(x)\,|\Big]=0 \tag{6-32}$$

Therefore, combining (6-31) and (6-32), we can obtain

$$\lim_{N\to\infty} E^{1/2}\Big[\sup_{-\infty<x<+\infty}|\,\hat{\mathbf{p}}_N(x)-p(x)\,|\Big]=0 \tag{6-33}$$

which is equivalent to (6-27). Thus the proof is complete.

Now we can show that under the same conditions the estimate of the mode or the peak of the density function is consistent. The peak of a density function is sought when we want to use the maximum likelihood or the *a posteriori* estimate. For a uniformly continuous $p(x)$, we can obtain an estimate $\hat{\mathbf{p}}_N(x)$ and find the peak of $\hat{\mathbf{p}}_N(x)$ at $x=\hat{\mathbf{x}}_0$, while the true peak of $p(x)$ occurs at $x=x_0$. Then

$$|\,\hat{\mathbf{p}}_N(\hat{\mathbf{x}}_0)-p(x_0)\,|=\Big|\sup_x \hat{\mathbf{p}}_N(x)-\sup_x p(x)\Big|\le\sup_x|\,\hat{\mathbf{p}}_N(x)-p(x)\,| \tag{6-34}$$

Combinating (6-33) and (6-34) gives

$$\lim_{N\to\infty}\Pr\{|\,\hat{\mathbf{x}}_0-x_0\,|<\varepsilon\}=1 \tag{6-35}$$

Thus, (6-25) is the condition of $h(N)$ to guarantee the uniform consistency of $\hat{\mathbf{p}}_N(x)$ as well as the uniform consistency of $\hat{\mathbf{x}}_0$.

Extension to Multivariate Densities

The above discussion can be easily extended to the multivariate case, although a detailed discussion is omitted [Cacoullos, 1964]. The only difference is that h^n is used instead of h. The estimate of $\hat{\mathbf{p}}_N(X)$ is given by

$$\hat{\mathbf{p}}_N(X)=(1/N)\sum_{i=1}^{N}(1/h^n)k[(X-\mathbf{X}_i)/h]=\int_{\mathscr{S}}(1/h^n)k[(X-\Xi)/h]\,d\hat{\mathbf{P}}_N(\Xi) \tag{6-36}$$

More generally, $\hat{\mathbf{p}}_N(X)$ could be constructed as

$$\hat{\mathbf{p}}_N(X)=(1/N)\sum_{i=1}^{N}\Big(\prod_{j=1}^{n}h_j\Big)^{-1}k[(x_1-\mathbf{x}_{1i})/h_1,\,\ldots,\,(x_n-\mathbf{x}_{ni})/h_n] \tag{6-37}$$

Without losing too much generality, $h_1 = h_2 = \cdots = h_n$ is assumed in order to obtain (6-36).

The conditions for $k(Y/h)$ and h, which correspond to (6-8) through (6-13), are

$$\int_{\mathscr{S}} k(Y/h)\, dY/h^n = \int_{\mathscr{S}} k(Z)\, dZ = 1 \tag{6-38}$$

$$\int_{\mathscr{S}} | k(Y/h) |\, dY/h^n = \int_{\mathscr{S}} | k(Z) |\, dZ < \infty \tag{6-39}$$

$$\sup_{Y \in \mathscr{S}} | k(Y/h) | = \sup_{Z \in \mathscr{S}} | k(Z) | < \infty \tag{6-40}$$

$$\lim_{Y/h \to \infty} | (Y/h) k(Y/h) | = \lim_{Z \to \infty} | Z k(Z) | = 0 \tag{6-41}$$

$$\lim_{N \to \infty} h^n(N) = 0 \qquad \text{for asymptotic unbiasedness} \tag{6-42}$$

$$\lim_{N \to \infty} N h^n(N) = \infty \qquad \text{for asymptotic consistency} \tag{6-43}$$

$$\lim_{N \to \infty} N h^{2n}(N) = \infty \qquad \text{for uniform consistency} \tag{6-44}$$

If these conditions are satisfied, $\hat{\mathbf{p}}_N(X)$ becomes an asymptotically unbiased and consistent estimate for the continuous points of $p(X)$.

Although we can consider the multivariate kernels which correspond to those in Table 6-1, we will choose a normal distribution as a typical kernel for further study. The normal kernel is given by

$$\begin{aligned}(1/h^n) k[(X - \mathbf{X}_i)/h] \\ = (2\pi)^{-n/2} h^{-n} | \Sigma |^{-1/2} \exp[-\tfrac{1}{2} h^{-2} (X - \mathbf{X}_i)^T \Sigma^{-1} (X - \mathbf{X}_i)]\end{aligned} \tag{6-45}$$

Since $\mathbf{X}_i$ are the given samples, the parameters which we have to determine for this kernel are Σ and $h(N)$. The term $h(N)$ could be any function of N. But, for simplicity's sake, let us select the following functional form for $h(N)$.

$$h(N) = N^{-k/n} \tag{6-46}$$

If (6-42), (6-43), and (6-44) are to be satisfied, then k should be bounded as follows:

$$1 > k > 0 \qquad \text{for asymptotic consistency} \tag{6-47}$$

$$\tfrac{1}{2} > k > 0 \qquad \text{for uniform consistency} \tag{6-48}$$

The selection of Σ does not affect the asymptotic properties. But for a finite number of samples, Σ is an important parameter to determine the goodness of the approximation. Some criteria, such as minimizing the bias or variance for a finite N, could be set up to find the optimum Σ. However, because of complexity involved, it is not known how to select Σ for a given set of samples. An intuitive answer for this problem is to use the sample covariance matrix of the given data as Σ. By choosing Σ, the covariance matrix of this Parzen estimate Σ_p is proportional to the sample covariance matrix as

$$\Sigma_p = (1/N) \sum_{i=1}^{N} (X_i X_i^T + h^2 \Sigma) = (1 + h^2)\Sigma \tag{6-49}$$

Therefore, we can maintain the statistical properties similar to those of the sample distribution up to the second moment, even when h is not very small with a relatively small N. Or, after whitening the data, we use a unit matrix as Σ. Mathematically, both procedures are identical, but the computation load could be significantly reduced by the latter method when the estimated densities are used for some other purposes, such as a classifier design, etc. Figure 6-2 shows a two-dimensional example.

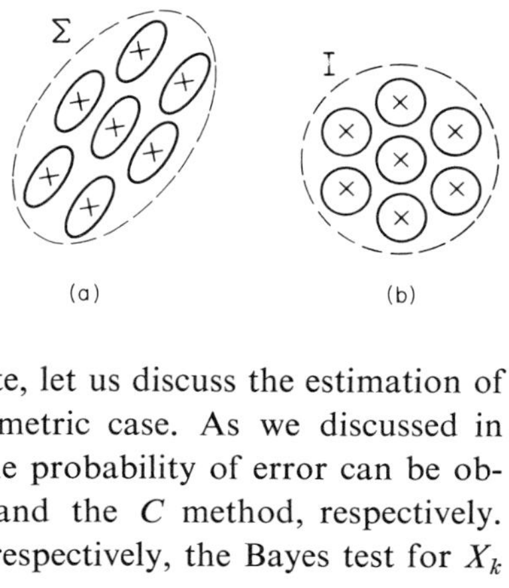

Fig. 6-2 Selection of a kernel: (a) original distribution; (b) whitened distribution.

As an application of the Parzen estimate, let us discuss the estimation of the probability of error for the nonparametric case. As we discussed in Chapter 5, upper and lower bounds of the probability of error can be obtained by the leaving-one-out method and the C method, respectively. With N_1 and N_2 samples for ω_1 and ω_2, respectively, the Bayes test for X_k can be stated as

$$\frac{N_1}{N_1 + N_2} \hat{p}_{N_1}(X_k/\omega_1) \gtrless \frac{N_2}{N_1 + N_2} \hat{p}_{N_2}(X_k/\omega_2) \rightarrow X_k \in \begin{cases} \omega_1 \\ \omega_2 \end{cases} \tag{6-50}$$

This test is repeated for all N_1 and N_2 samples, and the number of misclassified samples is counted to estimate the probability of error. The parzen estimate is used for the density estimates $\hat{\mathbf{p}}_{N_i}(X_k/\omega_i)$ $i = 1, 2$.

In the C method, all N_1 and N_2 samples are used to estimate $\hat{\mathbf{p}}_{N_1}(X_k/\omega_1)$ and $\hat{\mathbf{p}}_{N_2}(X_k/\omega_2)$, respectively. Using a normal kernel of (6-45) with Σ_1 and Σ_2 for ω_1 and ω_2, (6-50) becomes

$$N_1^k(2\pi)^{-n/2}|\Sigma_1|^{-1/2}\sum_{j=1}^{N_1}\exp[-\tfrac{1}{2}N_1^{2k/n}(X_k - X_j^{(1)})^T\Sigma_1^{-1}(X_k - X_j^{(1)})]$$
$$\gtrless N_2^k(2\pi)^{-n/2}|\Sigma_2|^{-1/2}\sum_{l=1}^{N_2}\exp[-\tfrac{1}{2}N_2^{2k/n}(X_k - X_l^{(2)})^T\Sigma_2^{-1}(X_k - X_l^{(2)})] \tag{6-51}$$

where $X_j^{(1)}$ and $X_l^{(2)}$ are samples from ω_1 and ω_2.

On the other hand, in the leaving-one-out method, for testing $X_k(\in \omega_1)$ $N_1 - 1$ samples, excluding X_k, are used to estimate $\hat{\mathbf{p}}_{N_1}(X/\omega_1)$. Therefore, the left-hand side of (6-51) is replaced by

$$(N_1 - 1)^k(2\pi)^{-n/2}|\Sigma_1|^{-1/2}$$
$$\times\left[\left\{\sum_{j=1}^{N_1}\exp[-\tfrac{1}{2}(N_1 - 1)^{2k/n}(X_k - X_j^{(1)})^T\Sigma_1^{-1}(X_k - X_j^{(1)})]\right\} - 1\right] \tag{6-52}$$

When $X_k \in \omega_2$, the right-hand side of (6-51) should be modified as (6-52).

The calculation of error for the nonparametric case is laborious mainly because we have to calculate all pairs of distances $(X_k - X_j^{(i)})^T\Sigma_i^{-1}(X_k - X_j^{(i)})$. However, there is no difference between the computation times of the C method and the leaving-one-out method, because in the leaving-one-out method the distances are multiplied by $(N_1 - 1)^{2k/n}$ rather than by $N_1^{2k/n}$, as in the C method, before the exponential function is computed.

EXAMPLE 6-1 The above method is applied to the samples which are generated according to Standard Data $i = 1, 2$.

TABLE 6-2

EFFECT OF k ($N_1 = N_2 = 100$)[a]

k	The probability of error	
	C method (%)	Leaving-one-out method (%)
$\frac{1}{3}$	0.1	2.9
$\frac{1}{5}$	0.2	2.6
$\frac{1}{7}$	0.4	2.5

[a] [Fukunaga, 1971c].

First, in order to see the effect of k on the estimation of the probability of error, an experiment is conducted with 100 samples per class, with $k = \frac{1}{3}, \frac{1}{5}$, and $\frac{1}{7}$ to satisfy (6-48). The results are shown in Table 6-2. Although there is some variation in the performance, it does not appear as though the choice of k is of critical importance.

Based on the above information, k is fixed as $\frac{1}{3}$. Twenty sets of samples are generated for each of $N_1 = N_2 = 100$, 200, and 400. The probabilities of errors are counted and summarized as Table 6-3. It should be pointed out that the theoretical true error is 1.9% from Table 3-3.

TABLE 6-3

EFFECT OF N_1 AND N_2 ($k = \frac{1}{3}$)[a]

	C method		Leaving-one-out method	
$N_1 = N_2$	Mean (%)	Standard deviation (%)	Mean (%)	Standard deviation (%)
100	0.1	0.2	2.9	0.7
200	0.45	0.2	2.35	0.7
400	0.65	0.2	2.2	0.5

[a] [Fukunaga, 1971c].

6.2 k-Nearest Neighbor Approach

As we saw in the previous section, the Parzen estimate can give an estimate of a density function. However, the calculation of the kernel for each sample requires considerable computation time. In this section, we discuss a modification of the Parzen estimate which is more practical. Particularly, when our concern is not the estimation of a density function but the classification of two density functions, we can concentrate upon the question of whether one density function is larger or smaller than the other at each point.

Asymptotic Unbiasedness and Consistency

In the Parzen estimate, we generated a fixed kernel around each sample. A similar estimate can be obtained from a different point of view as follows.

Using N samples from a distribution, find the distance r between X and the kth-nearest neighbor of X. "Nearenss" is measured by any convenient metric. Then let

$$\hat{\mathbf{p}}_N(X) = \frac{k-1}{N} \frac{1}{\mathbf{A}(k, N, X)} \tag{6-53}$$

where $A(k, N, X)$ is the volume of the set of all points whose distance from X is less than r. When a Euclidean distance is used, $A(k, N, X)$ becomes a hypersphere with radius r and is given by

$$A(k, N, X) = \frac{2r^n \pi^{n/2}}{n\Gamma(n/2)} \tag{6-54}$$

The term $\mathbf{A}$ is a random variable, depending on the selected set of N samples.

If $k(N)$ of (6-53) satisfies

$$\lim_{N \to \infty} k(N) = \infty \tag{6-55}$$

and

$$\lim_{N \to \infty} k(N)/N = 0 \tag{6-56}$$

then it has been proved that $\hat{\mathbf{p}}_N(X)$ is an asymptotically unbiased and consistent estimate of $p(X)$ [Loftsgaarden, 1965]. The proof is omitted.

The k-nearest neighbor estimation provides a very simple estimate of a density. However, since r should be small enough to keep the density function relatively constant within the hypersphere, we are often forced to select a small k and to sacrifice accuracy, unless N is very large. This disadvantage might be serious in estimation but is not serious when the estimates are used for classification purposes.

k-Nearest Neighbor Decision Rule

The estimate of (6-53) can be used for classification as follows. When an unknown sample X is to be classified, the k-nearest neighbors of X are found among N samples, which consist of N_1 samples from ω_1 and N_2 from ω_2 and which are stored in a memory. Let k_1 and k_2 be the number of samples from ω_1 and ω_2, respectively, among these k-nearest neighbors. Then the estimate of (6-53) becomes

$$\hat{p}_{N_i}(X/\omega_i) = \frac{k_i - 1}{N_i} \frac{1}{A} \qquad (i = 1, 2) \tag{6-57}$$

Since both k_1 and k_2 samples drawn from the same hypersphere, A is common for both ω_1 and ω_2. Hence the Bayes test for minimum error becomes

$$(N_1/N)\hat{p}_{N_1}(X/\omega_1) \gtrless (N_2/N)\hat{p}_{N_2}(X/\omega_2) \rightarrow X \in \begin{cases} \omega_1 \\ \omega_2 \end{cases} \tag{6-58}$$

Or, substituting (6-57) into (6-58),

$$k_1 \gtrless k_2 \rightarrow X \in \begin{cases} \omega_1 \\ \omega_2 \end{cases} \tag{6-59}$$

We can decide the class of X simply by comparing k_1 and k_2 after choosing the k-nearest neighbors.

The k-nearest neighbor decision rule is very simple and knowledge about the density functions is not required. Its disadvantage lies in the necessity to store all samples and compare each with an unknown sample. Let us consider here the performance of this algorithm [Cover, 1967]. For simplicity's sake, we first look at the simplest case with $k = 1$. This case is termed the *nearest neighbor decision rule.*

Probability of Error for the Nearest Neighbor Decision Rule

Let us consider the case where X is classified into ω_i because the nearest neighbor X_k is found to belong to ω_i. Assuming $X \in \omega_j$, then, if ω_j is not equal to ω_i, an error occurs. Therefore, the conditional error given X and X_k is given by

$$r(X, X_k) = \Pr\{\omega_i \neq \omega_j/X_k, X\} = P(\omega_1/X_k)P(\omega_2/X) + P(\omega_2/X_k)P(\omega_1/X) \tag{6-60}$$

If we assume a large N, such that X and its nearest neighbor X_k are very closely located, we have the following approximation:

$$P(\omega_i/X_k) \cong P(\omega_i/X) \tag{6-61}$$

Then (6-60) becomes

$$\begin{aligned} r(X) &\cong 2P(\omega_1/X)P(\omega_2/X) = 2P(\omega_1/X)[1 - P(\omega_1/X)] \\ &= 2P(\omega_2/X)[1 - P(\omega_2/X)] \end{aligned} \tag{6-62}$$

which is a function of X alone because of the approximation in (6-61). It can be proved easily that (6-60) converges to (6-62) with probability 1, as N tends toward ∞.

On the other hand, from (3-1) the conditional Bayes error $r^*(X)$, given X, is given by

$$r^*(X) = \min[P(\omega_1/X), P(\omega_2/X)] = \min[P(\omega_1/X), 1 - P(\omega_1/X)] \quad (6\text{-}63)$$

Thus $r(X)$ and $r^*(X)$ are related by

$$r(X) = 2r^*(X)[1 - r^*(X)] \quad (6\text{-}64)$$

Since the probability of error ε is the expected value of the conditional error $r(X)$,

$$\begin{aligned}\varepsilon &= E\{r(\mathbf{X})\} = \int_{\mathscr{S}} r(X)p(X)\,dX = 2E\{r^*(\mathbf{X})[1 - r^*(\mathbf{X})]\} \\ &= 2\varepsilon^*(1 - \varepsilon^*) - 2\operatorname{Var}[r^*(\mathbf{X})] \leq 2\varepsilon^*(1 - \varepsilon^*)\end{aligned} \quad (6\text{-}65)$$

where ε^* is the Bayes error, given by the expectation

$$\varepsilon^* = E\{r^*(\mathbf{X})\} \quad (6\text{-}66)$$

Thus, we conclude from (6-65) that the probability of error due to the nearest neighbor decision rule is less than twice the Bayes error, assuming that N is large enough for (6-61) to hold. In Table 3-4, we showed that the Chernoff bound gave a value of 4.6% for a true error of 1.9% (a factor of 2.4) for an example of normal distributions. Considering the fact that the nearest neighbor decision rule does not require any knowledge of distributions, the performance indicated by (6-65) is very good.

A lower bound on the probability of error due to the nearest neighbor decision rule can be derived as

$$\varepsilon = E[r^*(X) + r^*(X)\{1 - 2r^*(X)\}] = \varepsilon^* + E[r^*(X)\{1 - 2r^*(X)\}] \geq \varepsilon^* \quad (6\text{-}67)$$

The last inequality is true because (6-63) implies that $0.5 \geq r^*(X) \geq 0$. Thus, ε is bounded below by the Bayes error and the equality holds when $r^*(X)\{1 - 2r^*(X)\} = 0$ almost everywhere, that is $r^*(X) = 0$ or 0.5 almost everywhere.

Probability of Error for the k-Nearest Neighbor Decision Rule

The discussion of the performance of the nearest neighbor decision rule can be easily extended to the k-nearest neighbor decision rule. The conditional error, given X, is given by

$$r_k(X) = P(\omega_1/X) \sum_{j=0}^{(k-1)/2} \binom{k}{j} P(\omega_1/X)^j P(\omega_2/X)^{k-j}$$
$$+P(\omega_2/X) \sum_{j=0}^{(k-1)/2} \binom{k}{j} P(\omega_2/X)^j P(\omega_1/X)^{k-j} \qquad (6\text{-}68)$$

where the first and second terms are the conditional error for $X \in \omega_1$ and $X \in \omega_2$, respectively. In order to obtain a decision, k should be an odd number. Equation (6-68) can be rewritten as

$$r_k(X) = P(\omega_i/X) \sum_{j=0}^{(k-1)/2} \binom{k}{j} P(\omega_i/X)^j [1 - P(\omega_i/X)]^{k-j}$$
$$+[1 - P(\omega_i/X)] \sum_{j=(k+1)/2}^{k} \binom{k}{j} P(\omega_i/X)^j [1 - P(\omega_i/X)]^{k-j} \quad (i = 1, 2) \qquad (6\text{-}69)$$

Since the Bayes conditional error is given by (6-63), (6-69) becomes, in terms of $r^*(X)$,

$$r_k(X) = r^*(X) \sum_{j=0}^{(k-1)/2} \binom{k}{j} r^*(X)^j [1 - r^*(X)]^{k-j}$$
$$+[1 - r^*(X)] \sum_{j=(k+1)/2}^{k} \binom{k}{j} r^*(X)^j [1 - r^*(X)]^{k-j} \qquad (6\text{-}70)$$

To obtain the unconditional error ε_k, we would take the expectation of (6-70) over all X's. This, however, requires knowledge of the density function of r^* (X), or, equivalently $P(\omega_1/X)$ and $P(\omega_2/X)$, for all X's. This information is, by assumption, not available.

To obtain a bound on ε_k in terms of the Bayes error ε^* define $\varphi_k(r^*(X))$ to be the least concave function greater than $r_k(X)$. Now

$$r_k(X) \leq \varphi_k(r^*(X)) \qquad (6\text{-}71)$$

for all X's, and by Jensen's inequality

$$\varepsilon_k = E\{r_k(X)\} \leq E\{\varphi_k(r^*(X))\} \leq \varphi_k(E\{r^*(X)\}) = \varphi_k(\varepsilon^*) \qquad (6\text{-}72)$$

Since the $r_k(X)$'s, given in (6-69), are monotonically decreasing in k, it follows that the least concave functions φ_k are also monotonically decreasing in k. Therefore,

$$\varepsilon^* \leq \varepsilon_k \leq \varphi_k(\varepsilon^*) \leq \varphi_{k-1}(\varepsilon^*) \cdots \leq \varphi_1(\varepsilon^*) = 2\varepsilon^*(1 - \varepsilon^*) \qquad (6\text{-}73)$$

Equation (6-73) yields an asymptotic bound on the performance of the k-nearest neighbor as $N \to \infty$ in terms of the minimum error ε^* of the Bayes classifier.

It should be emphasized that ε^* is very rarely known. In fact, given $\varepsilon^* \leq \varepsilon_k \leq \varphi_k(\varepsilon^*)$, from (6-73), we may take the inverse of φ to get

$$\varphi_k^{-1}(\varepsilon_k) \leq \varepsilon^* \leq \varepsilon_k \tag{6-74}$$

Thus, we have a bound on ε^* in terms of ε_k which may be experimentally estimated.

EXAMPLE 6-2 For the nearest neighbor decision rule

$$r_1(X) = 2r^*(X)[1 - r^*(X)] \tag{6-75}$$

Now $r_1(X)$ is a concave function and is therefore equal to the $\varphi_1(r^*(X))$ of (6-71). Applying (6-72) gives

$$\varepsilon^* \leq \varepsilon_1 \leq 2\varepsilon^*(1 - \varepsilon^*) \tag{6-76}$$

Taking the inverse of this relationship gives

$$[1 - (1 - 2\varepsilon_1)^{1/2}]/2 \leq \varepsilon^* \leq \varepsilon_1 \tag{6-77}$$

Thus, (6-77) yields the bounds on the Bayes error in terms of the nearest neighbor asymptotic error.

Extension to Multiclass Problem

The k-nearest neighbor decision rule can be easily extended to the multiclass problem. Selecting k nearest neighbors of X, we count the number of samples from each class. Let $k_1, k_2, \ldots, k_M$ be the number of samples from $\omega_1, \ldots, \omega_M$, respectively. Then, according to the multiclass Bayes test, the decision rule is

$$k_i = \max\{k_1, \ldots, k_M\} \to X \in \omega_i \tag{6-78}$$

For simplicity's sake, let us study the performance of this decision rule for the nearest neighbor case [Cover, 1967]. As for the two-class case, better performance is obtained for larger k.

The conditional error, given X, can be expressed as

$$r(X) = P(\omega_1/X) \sum_{\substack{j=1 \\ j\neq 1}}^{M} P(\omega_j/X) + \cdots + P(\omega_M/X) \sum_{\substack{j=1 \\ j\neq M}}^{M} P(\omega_j/X) \tag{6-79}$$

The first term of (6-79) shows the conditional error for $X \in \omega_1$, and so on. Using $P(\omega_1) + \cdots + P(\omega_M) = 1$, (6-79) is rewritten as

$$r(X) = 1 - \sum_{j=1}^{M} P^2(\omega_j/X) \tag{6-80}$$

On the other hand, the Bayes conditional error, given X, is

$$r^*(X) = 1 - \max_j\{P(\omega_j/X)\} = 1 - P(\omega_l/X) \tag{6-81}$$

where $P(\omega_l/X)$ is assumed to be $\max_j \{P(\omega_j/X)\}$. Using the Schwarz inequality

$$(M-1)\sum_{\substack{j=1\\ j\neq l}}^{M} P^2(\omega_j/X) \geq \left\{\sum_{\substack{j=1\\ j\neq l}}^{M} P(\omega_j/X)\right\}^2 = \{1 - P(\omega_l/X)\}^2 = r^{*^2}(X) \tag{6-82}$$

Adding $(M-1)P^2(\omega_l/X)$ to each side,

$$(M-1)\sum_{j=1}^{M} P^2(\omega_j/X) \geq r^{*^2}(X) + (M-1)[1 - r^*(X)]^2 \tag{6-83}$$

Combining (6-83) and (6-80), we can bound $r(X)$ by a function of $r^*(X)$ as

$$r(X) \leq 2r^*(X) - [M/(M-1)]r^{*^2}(X) \tag{6-84}$$

Taking the expectation of (6-84), we obtain

$$\varepsilon \leq 2\varepsilon^* - [M/(M-1)]\varepsilon^{*^2} \tag{6-85}$$

Again, ε is less than twice the Bayes error. Substituting $M = 2$ into (6-85), we obtain (6-65).

The Condensed k-Nearest Neighbor Decision Rule

The disadvantage of the k-nearest neighbor decision rule lies in the necessity to store all samples and compare an unknown sample with all of these samples. In order to overcome this disadvantage, we would like to eliminate some of the samples, leaving a smaller number of representatives. The samples near the Bayes decision boundary are crucial to the k-nearest neighbor decision, but the samples far from the boundary do not affect the decision. Therefore, a systematic removal of these ineffective samples helps to reduce both computation time and storage requirement. The procedure is called the *condensed k-nearest neighbor decision rule* [Hart, 1968].

For simplicity's sake, we show a method of condensing samples for the nearest neighbor decision rule. The method can be easily modified for the k-nearest neighbor decision rule. The method is described as follows, where STORE and GRABBAG are storage identifications.

(1) The first sample is placed STORE.

(2) The second sample is classified by the nearest neighbor decision rule, using only samples in STORE as the reference. If the classification is correct, throw the sample to GRABBAG. If the sample is misclassified the sample is placed in STORE as a new reference.

(3) Repeat the same process until all N samples are used.

(4) After one pass, apply the above operation to the samples in GRABBAG again. Repeat this procedure until there are no transfers of samples from GRABBAG to STORE in testing all samples of GRABBAG.

Hart reports two examples showing the effectiveness of the above method. His results are:

(1) 482 two-dimensional samples from two classes, which are generated artificially, are reduced to 40 representatives, after four iterations through all samples. All 40 representatives are located along the boundary of two classes.

(2) 6295 uppercase typewritten characters, which come from 25 classes in a 96-dimensional space, are represented by 197 samples after four iterations.

6.3 Histogram Approach

Considering both k and A of (6-53) as variables, we may have various estimates of a density function, which are known as *histograms*. In this section, two typical histograms will be discussed.

Fixed Cells

We can partition the space into mutually disjoint cells $\Gamma_1, \ldots, \Gamma_M$, whose volumes are equal. The density function is approximated by the number of samples which fall in each cell. Figure 6-3 shows an example for one dimension.

The histogram approach is distribution-free and, if we use regular meshes for the Γ's, the selection of cells is straightforward. However, the major

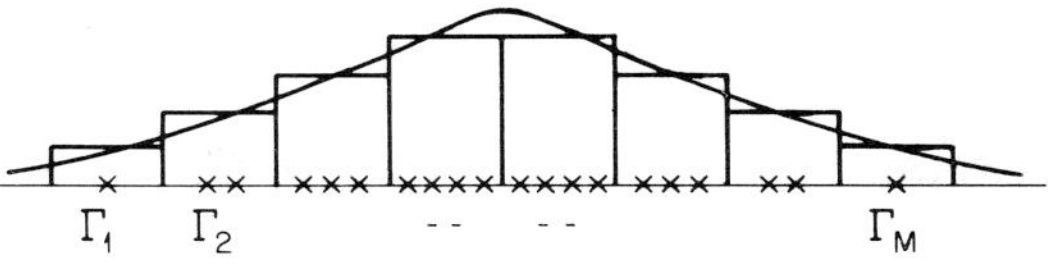

Fig. 6-3 A histogram with fixed cells.

disadvantage of this method is that it requires too much storage; for example M^n cells for n variables with M sections for each variable. Therefore, most modifications which have been proposed are designed to reduce the number of cells.

Variable Cells

The number of cells could be reduced by using variable cell sizes. Figure 6-4 shows an example for the one dimensional case.

If we know the number of samples in each cell, the cell volume, and the cell's location, we can still use (6-53) as a density estimate. In order to apply this concept in practice, we must have a method to determine the number of samples and the volume for each cell.

Here we show one of many possible solutions [Sebestyen, 1966].

(1) Suppose that we have m cells $\Gamma_1, \ldots, \Gamma_m$, each characterized by the coordinate of the center X_i, the variances of the n variables $(\sigma_{i1}^2, \ldots, \sigma_{in}^2)$, and the number of samples within the cell k_i. Given a new sample X, the distance of X from each cell center is calculated by

$$d(X, X_i) = \sum_{j=1}^{n} (x_j - x_{ij})^2/\sigma_{ij}^2 \qquad (i = 1, 2, \ldots, m) \tag{6-86}$$

The nearest cell is found by selecting X_k, such that $d(X, X_k) = \min_i d(X, X_i)$. Then X is classified as one of the following:

$$\begin{aligned} &d(X, X_k) \leq \tau \rightarrow X \text{ is assigned to } \Gamma_k \\ &d(X, X_k) \geq \theta\tau \rightarrow X \text{ creates a new cell} \qquad (\theta > 1) \\ &\text{Otherwise} \rightarrow X \text{ is assigned to an undecided cell} \end{aligned} \tag{6-87}$$

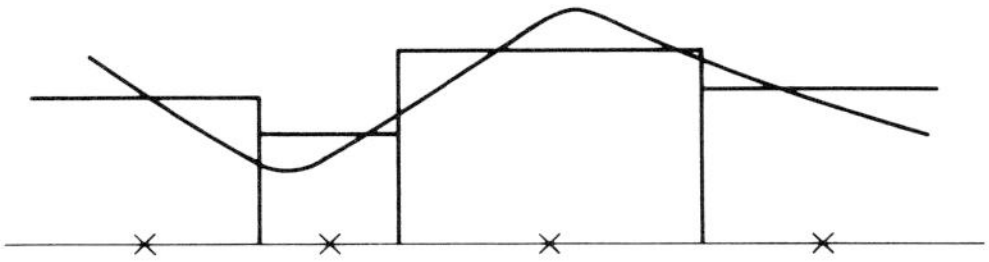

Fig. 6-4 A histogram with variable cells.

where τ and θ are control parameters that adjust the number of cells and the accuracy of the approximation, and so forth.

(2) When a new sample is classified to the ith cell, the parameters of the cell are adjusted by the following method.

(a) Increase the number of samples in the cell by 1. Let k_i be the new number of samples.

(b) Calculate the new expected vector $M_i(k_i)$ from k_i samples.

$$M_i(k_i) = (1/k_i) \sum_{l=1}^{ki} X_i(l) \tag{6-88}$$

(c) Determine the new variances by

$$\sigma_{ij}^2(k_i) = \max[\sigma_{ij}^2(0), s_{ij}^2(k_i)] \tag{6-89}$$

and

$$s_{ij}^2(k_i) = (1/k_i) \sum_{l=1}^{k_i} [x_{ij}(l) - m_{ij}(k_i)]^2 \tag{6-90}$$

The term $s_{ij}^2(k_i)$ of (6-90) is the variance of the jth variable in the ith cell, based on k_i samples. The term $\sigma_{ij}^2(0)$ is the initial assignment of σ_{ij}^2. Only when $s_{ij}^2(k_i)$ exceeds $\sigma_{ij}^2(0)$, we replace $\sigma_{ij}^2(0)$ by $s_{ij}^2(k_i)$.

(3) The first sample always creates a new cell. The second sample is tested and classified by (1), and so on. After all samples are classified, or the average number of samples in the cells reaches a certain level, the undecided samples are forced into the nearest cells and the parameters of these cells are modified by (2).

The control parameters τ, θ, and $\sigma_{ij}^2(0)$ may be properly chosen by repeating the above process for the same set of samples.

6.4 Expansion by Basis Functions

Expansion of Density Functions

Another approach to approximating a density function is to find an expansion in a set of *basis functions* $\varphi_i(X)$ as

$$p(X) = \sum_{i=1}^{\infty} c_i \varphi_i(X) \tag{6-91}$$

If the basis functions satisfy

$$\int_{\mathscr{S}} k(X)\varphi_i(X)\varphi_j^*(X)\,dX = \lambda_i\delta_{ij} \tag{6-92}$$

we say that the $\varphi_i(X)$'s are orthogonal with respect to the *kernel* $k(X)$. The term $\varphi_i^*(X)$ is the complex conjugate of $\varphi_i(X)$ and equals $\varphi_i(X)$ when $\varphi_i(X)$ is a real function. If the basis functions are orthogonal with respect to $k(X)$, the coefficients of (6-91) are given by

$$\lambda_i c_i = \int_{\mathscr{S}} k(X)p(X)\varphi_i^*(X)\,dX \tag{6-93}$$

When we terminate the expansion of (6-91) for $i = m$, the squared error is given by

$$\begin{aligned}\varepsilon^2 &= \int_{\mathscr{S}} k(X)\Big\{p(X) - \sum_{i=1}^{m} c_i\varphi_i(X)\Big\}\Big\{p(X) - \sum_{i=1}^{m} c_i\varphi_i(X)\Big\}^* dX \\ &= \int_{\mathscr{S}} k(X)\Big\{\sum_{i=m+1}^{\infty} c_i\varphi_i(X)\Big\}\Big\{\sum_{i=m+1}^{\infty} c_i\varphi_i(X)\Big\}^* dX \\ &= \sum_{i=m+1}^{\infty} \lambda_i \,|\, c_i \,|^2 \end{aligned} \tag{6-94}$$

Thus $\lambda_i \,|\, c_i \,|^2$ represents the error due to the elimination of the ith term in the expansion. This means that, if we can find a set of basis functions such that $\lambda_i \,|\, c_i \,|^2$ decreases quickly as i increases, the set of basis functions forms an economical representation of the density function.

There is no known procedure for choosing a set of basis functions in the general multivariate case. Therefore, we will only consider special cases where the basis functions are well defined.

Both the Fourier series and the Fourier transform are examples of expanding a function in a set of basis functions. The characteristic function of a density function is a Fourier transform and is thus one kind of expansion of a density function. Here we seek a simpler kind of expansion.

One-Dimensional Case

When a density function is one dimensional, we may try many well-known basis functions, such as Fourier series, Legendre, Gegenbauer, Jacobi, Hermite and Leguerre polynomials, etc. [Deutsch, 1969]. Most of them have been developed for approximating a waveform, but obviously we can look at a one-dimensional density function as a waveform.

As a typical example of the expansion, let us study the Hermite polynomial which is used to approximate a density function distorted from a normal distribution. That is,

$$p(x) = (2\pi)^{-1/2}\sigma^{-1} \exp(-\tfrac{1}{2}x^2/\sigma^2)\Big[\sum_{i=0}^{\infty} c_i\varphi_i(x)\Big] \tag{6-95}$$

$$k(x) = (2\pi)^{-1/2}\sigma^{-1} \exp(-\tfrac{1}{2}x^2/\sigma^2) \tag{6-96}$$

$$\begin{aligned}\varphi_i(x) &= (-\sigma)^i \exp(\tfrac{1}{2}x^2/\sigma^2)\,\frac{d^i \exp(-\frac{1}{2}\,x^2/\sigma^2)}{dx^i} \\ &= \left(\frac{x}{\sigma}\right)^i - \binom{i}{2}\left(\frac{x}{\sigma}\right)^{i-2} + 1\cdot 3\binom{i}{4}\left(\frac{x}{\sigma}\right)^{i-4} - \cdots\end{aligned} \tag{6-97}$$

The orthogonal condition is given by

$$\int_{-\infty}^{+\infty} (2\pi)^{-1/2}\sigma^{-1} \exp(-\tfrac{1}{2}x^2/\sigma^2)\varphi_i(x)\varphi_j(x)\,dx = (i!)\delta_{ij} \tag{6-98}$$

The coefficients c_i can be obtained by

$$\begin{aligned} i!c! &= \int_{-\infty}^{+\infty} k(x)\,\frac{p(x)}{(2\pi)^{-1/2}\sigma^{-1}\exp(-\frac{1}{2}x^2/\sigma^2)}\,\varphi_i(x)\,dx \\ &= \int_{-\infty}^{+\infty} p(x)\varphi_i(x)\,dx \\ &= \frac{m_i}{\sigma^i} - \binom{i}{2}\frac{m_{i-2}}{\sigma^{i-2}} + 1\cdot 3\binom{i}{4}\frac{m_{i-4}}{\sigma^{i-4}} - \cdots \end{aligned} \tag{6-99}$$

where m_i is the ith moment of $p(x)$ as

$$m_i = \int_{-\infty}^{+\infty} x^i p(x)\,dx \tag{6-100}$$

For example, if $p(x)$ has zero-mean and has σ^2 as the variance, then

$$c_0 = m_0/\sigma^0 = 1 \tag{6-101}$$

$$c_1 = m_1/\sigma = 0 \tag{6-102}$$

$$2!c_2 = \frac{m_2}{\sigma^2} - \binom{2}{2}\frac{m_0}{\sigma^0} = 0 \tag{6-103}$$

$$3!c_3 = \frac{m_3}{\sigma^3} - \binom{3}{2}\frac{m_1}{\sigma} = \frac{m_3}{\sigma^3} \tag{6-104}$$

$$4!c_4 = \frac{m_4}{\sigma^4} - \binom{4}{2}\frac{m_2}{\sigma^2} + 1\cdot 3\binom{4}{4}\frac{m_0}{\sigma^0} = \frac{m_4}{\sigma^4} - 3 \tag{6-105}$$

Therefore, terminating at $i = 4$, we have an approximation of a density function $p(x)$ in terms of the moments of $p(x)$ and $\varphi_i(X)$ as

$$p(x) \cong \frac{1}{(2\pi)^{1/2}\sigma} \exp\left(-\frac{x^2}{2\sigma^2}\right)\left[1 + \frac{m_3}{3!\sigma^3}\varphi_3(x) + \frac{1}{4!}\left(\frac{m_4}{\sigma^4} - 3\right)\varphi_4(x)\right]$$
$$= \frac{1}{(2\pi)^{1/2}\sigma} \exp\left(-\frac{x^2}{2\sigma^2}\right)\left[1 + \frac{m_3}{3!\sigma^3}\left\{\left(\frac{x}{\sigma}\right)^3 - \binom{3}{2}\left(\frac{x}{\sigma}\right)\right\}\right.$$
$$\left. + \frac{1}{4!}\left(\frac{m_4}{\sigma^4} - 3\right)\left\{\left(\frac{x}{\sigma}\right)^4 - \binom{4}{2}\left(\frac{x}{\sigma}\right)^2 + 1 \cdot 3\binom{4}{4}\right\}\right] \tag{6-106}$$

Multidimensional Case

Because of the complexity involved in the multivariate case, it is not as easy to find general basis functions or to calculate the coefficients.

A successive approximation method for determining the coefficients has been developed and is known as *the method of potential functions.* This method will be discussed in Chapter 7 with other successive approaches.

Density Function of Binary Inputs

When the n inputs are binary numbers $+1$ or -1, it is known that a linear combination of 2^n independent basis functions can yield any density function without error.

$$p(X) = \sum_{i=0}^{2^n-1} c_i\varphi_i(X) \tag{6-107}$$

Table 6-4 shows the truth table that specifies $p(X)$.

TABLE 6-4

SPECIFICATION OF A DENSITY FUNCTION OF BINARY VARIABLES

X	$\mathbf{x}_1$	$\mathbf{x}_2$	$\cdots$	$\mathbf{x}_n$	$p(X)$
X_0	-1	-1	$\cdots$	-1	$p(X_0)$
X_1	$+1$	-1	$\cdots$	-1	$p(X_1)$
.	.	.	.	.	.
.	.	.	.	.	.
.	.	.	.	.	.
X_{2^n-1}	$+1$	$+1$	$\cdots$	$+1$	$p(X_{2^n-1})$

Again, it is hard to say how we should select the 2^n basis functions. However, a typical set of basis functions is given as follows [Ito, 1968]:

$$
\begin{aligned}
\varphi_0(X) &= 1 \\
\varphi_1(X) &= [(x_1 - a_1)/(1 - a_1^2)^{1/2}] \\
&\vdots \\
\varphi_n(X) &= [(x_n - a_n)/(1 - a_n^2)^{1/2}] \\
\varphi_{n+1}(X) &= [(x_1 - a_1)/(1 - a_1^2)^{1/2}]\,[(x_2 - a_2)/(1 - a_2^2)^{1/2}] \\
&\vdots \\
\varphi_{2^n-1}(X) &= [(x_1 - a_1)/(1 - a_1^2)^{1/2}] \cdots [(x_n - a_n)/(1 - a_n^2)^{1/2}]
\end{aligned}
\tag{6-108}
$$

which is a complete orthonormal set with the kernel

$$k(X) = (1/2^n) \prod_{i=1}^{n} (1 + a_i)^{(1+x_i)/2}(1 - a_i)^{(1-x_i)/2} \tag{6-109}$$

That is,

$$\sum_{l=0}^{2^n-1} k(X_l)\varphi_i(X_l)\varphi_j(X_l) = \delta_{ij} \tag{6-110}$$

The a_i's are control parameters and must be in the range $0 < a_i < 1$. The c_i's can be calculated by

$$c_i = \sum_{l=0}^{2^n-1} k(X_l)p(X_l)\varphi_i(X_l) \tag{6-111}$$

Two special cases of the above expansion are well known.

The Walsh Function

Selecting $a_i = 0$ $(i = 1, \ldots, n)$, the basis functions become

$$
\begin{aligned}
&\varphi_0(X) = 1, \qquad \varphi_1(X) = x_1, \quad \ldots, \quad \varphi_n(X) = x_n \\
&\varphi_{n+1}(X) = x_1x_2, \quad \ldots, \quad \varphi_{2^n-1} = x_1x_2 \cdots x_n
\end{aligned}
\tag{6-112}
$$

with the kernel

$$k(X) = 1/2^n \tag{6-113}$$

This set of basis functions is known as the Walsh functions and is used often for the expansions of binary functions.

The Bahadur Expansion

Let us introduce the following transformation:

$$\mathbf{y}_i = (\mathbf{x}_i + 1)/2 \qquad \text{or} \qquad \mathbf{x}_i = 2\mathbf{y}_i - 1 \tag{6-114}$$

That is, $\mathbf{x}_i = +1$ and -1 correspond to $\mathbf{y}_i = 1$ and 0. Also, let P_i be the marginal probability of $\mathbf{y}_i = 1$,

$$P_i = \Pr\{\mathbf{y}_i = +1\} \tag{6-115}$$

Then the expected value and variance of $\mathbf{y}_i$ are given by

$$E\{\mathbf{y}_i\} = 1 \times P_i + 0 \times (1 - P_i) = P_i \tag{6-116}$$

$$\text{Var}\{\mathbf{y}_i\} = (1 - P_i)^2 P_i + (0 - P_i)^2(1 - P_i) = P_i(1 - P_i) \tag{6-117}$$

If we select a_i as

$$a_i = 2P_i - 1 \qquad \text{or} \qquad P_i = (a_i + 1)/2 \tag{6-118}$$

then the basis function of (6-108) becomes

$$\begin{gathered} \varphi_0(Y) = 1, \qquad \varphi_1(Y) = s_1, \ \ldots, \ \varphi_n(Y) = s_n \\ \varphi_{n+1}(Y) = s_1 s_2, \ \ldots, \ \varphi_{2^n-1}(Y) = s_1 s_2 \ \cdots \ s_n \end{gathered} \tag{6-119}$$

where

$$s_i = \frac{y_i - P_i}{P_i(1 - P_j)} = \frac{y_i - E\{\mathbf{y}_i\}}{(\text{Var}\{\mathbf{y}_i\})^{1/2}} \tag{6-120}$$

which is the normalized y_i.

On the other hand, the kernel of (6-109) becomes

$$k(Y) = \prod_{i=1}^{n} P_i^{y_i}(1 - P_i)^{1-y_i} \tag{6-121}$$

If the $\mathbf{y}_i$'s are mutually independent, $p(Y)$ becomes equal to $k(Y)$.

Thus, we can find the expansion of $p(Y)$ as

$$p(Y) = k(Y)\left[\sum_{i=0}^{2^n-1} c_i \varphi_i(Y)\right] \tag{6-122}$$

where the first term $k(Y)$ equals $p(Y)$ under the independence assumption and all other terms $[\cdot]$ are the correction terms. The c_i's are calculated by

$$c_i = \sum_{l=0}^{2^n-1} k(Y_l)[p(Y_l)/k(Y_l)]\varphi_i(Y_l) = \sum_{l=0}^{2^n-1} p(Y_l)\varphi_i(Y_l) = E\{\varphi_i(\mathbf{Y})\} \quad (6\text{-}123)$$

Thus, (6-122) becomes

$$p(Y) = \left\{\prod_{i=1}^{n} P_i^{y_i}(1-P_i)^{1-y_i}\right\}\left[1 + \sum_{i<j}\sum \gamma_{ij}s_is_j + \sum_{i<j<k}\sum\sum \gamma_{ijk}s_is_js_k + \cdots\right] \quad (6\text{-}124)$$

where γ's are the correlation coefficients of the associated variables.

$$\gamma_{ij} = E\{\mathbf{s}_i\mathbf{s}_j\} = E\left[\frac{\mathbf{y}_i - E\{\mathbf{y}_i\}}{(\mathrm{Var}\{\mathbf{y}_i\})^{1/2}} \frac{\mathbf{y}_j - E\{\mathbf{y}_j\}}{(\mathrm{Var}\{\mathbf{y}_j\})^{1/2}}\right] \quad (6\text{-}125)$$

$$\gamma_{ijk} = E\{\mathbf{s}_i\mathbf{s}_j\mathbf{s}_k\} = E\left[\frac{\mathbf{y}_i - E\{\mathbf{y}_i\}}{(\mathrm{Var}\{\mathbf{y}_i\})^{1/2}} \frac{\mathbf{y}_j - E\{\mathbf{y}_j\}}{(\mathrm{Var}\{\mathbf{y}_j\})^{1/2}} \frac{\mathbf{y}_k - E\{\mathbf{y}_k\}}{(\mathrm{Var}\{\mathbf{y}_k\})^{1/2}}\right] \quad (6\text{-}126)$$

This expansion is called the *Bahadur expansion* [Bahadur, 1967]. In this expansion, we can see the effects of the correlations on the approximation of a density function. In general, since the higher-order correlations are usually smaller than lower-order correlations, we may terminate the expansion with a reasonable number of terms and reasonable accuracy.

Example 6-3 Let us calculate the Bahadur expansion for the data given in Figure 6-5.
We obtain the same basis functions and the same kernels for both $p_1(Y)$ and $p_2(Y)$ as

$$P_1 = \tfrac{1}{2} \quad \text{and} \quad P_2 = \tfrac{1}{2} \quad (6\text{-}127)$$

$$s_i = (y_i - \tfrac{1}{2})/\tfrac{1}{2} = 2y_i - 1 \qquad (i = 1, 2) \quad (6\text{-}128)$$

$$k(Y) = (\tfrac{1}{2})^{y_1}(\tfrac{1}{2})^{1-y_1}(\tfrac{1}{2})^{y_2}(\tfrac{1}{2})^{1-y_2} = \tfrac{1}{4} \quad (6\text{-}129)$$

	y_1	y_2	$P_1(Y)$	$P_2(Y)$
Y_0	0	0	1/4	1/6
Y_1	1	0	1/4	1/3
Y_2	0	1	1/4	1/3
Y_3	1	1	1/4	1/6

(a)

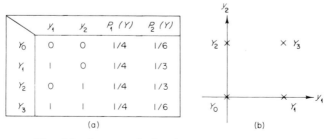

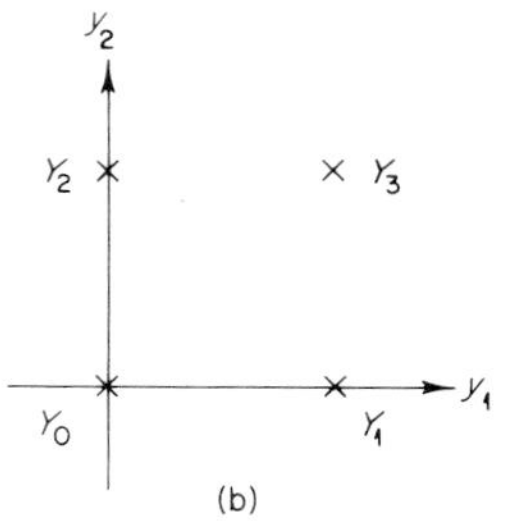

(b)

Fig. 6-5 An example for the Bahadur expansion.

The sample correlation coefficients of $\mathbf{y}_1$ and $\mathbf{y}_2$ for $p_1(Y)$ and $p_2(Y)$, $\gamma_{12}^{(1)}$ and $\gamma_{12}^{(2)}$, are different and are calculated by

$$\gamma_{12}^{(1)} = \tfrac{1}{4}\{(2 \times 0 - 1)(2 \times 0 - 1) + (2 \times 1 - 1)(2 \times 0 - 1) + (2 \times 0 - 1)(2 \times 1 - 1) + (2 \times 1 - 1)(2 \times 1 - 1)\} = 0 \tag{6-130}$$

$$\gamma_{12}^{(2)} = \tfrac{1}{6}(2 \times 0 - 1)(2 \times 0 - 1) + \tfrac{1}{3}(2 \times 1 - 1)(2 \times 0 - 1) + \tfrac{1}{3}(2 \times 0 - 1)(2 \times 1 - 1) + \tfrac{1}{6}(2 \times 1 - 1)(2 \times 1 - 1) = -\tfrac{1}{3} \tag{6-131}$$

Therefore, substituting these results into (6-124), we obtain

$$p_1(Y) = \tfrac{1}{4} \tag{6-132}$$

$$p_2(Y) = \tfrac{1}{4}[1 - \tfrac{1}{3}(2y_1 - 1)(2y_2 - 1)] \tag{6-133}$$

Computer Projects

Write the following programs:

6-1 The Parzen approximation for multivariate densities, with a normal kernel. Study the effect of N, k, and Σ to the degree of approximation.

Data: Standard Data $i = 1$.

6-2 Calculate the upper and lower bounds of the probability of error using the Parzen approximation with the C method and leaving-one-out method.

Data: Standard Data $i = 1, 2$.

$$N_1 = N_2 = 100, \quad k = \tfrac{1}{3}, \quad \text{and} \quad \Sigma_1 \quad \text{and} \quad \Sigma_2.$$

6-3 Decide the class of an unknown sample X by the k-nearest neighbor decision rule.

Data: Standard Data $i = 1, 2$.

$$N_1 = N_2 = 100$$

6-4 Condense $N_1 = N_2 = 100$ of 6-3 to less representatives for the nearest neighbor decision rule.

6-5 Provide the program to construct variable cells. Study the effects of the control parameters, $\sigma_{ij}^2(0)$, τ, and θ to the number of representatives.

Data: Standard Data $i = 1, 2, 3, 4.$

$$N_1 = N_2 = N_3 = N_4 = 100$$

6-6 Calculate the Hermite expansion of a given density function.
Data: a χ^2 distribution

6-7 Calculate the Bahadur expansion of a given distribution up to the second-order correlations.
Data: Generate data with five binary inputs.

Problems

6-1 Suppose that a set of samples $\{x = -7, -5, -4, -3, -2, 0\ 2, 3, 4, 5, 7\}$ is given. Find the Parzen approximation by using a rectangular kernel. Use $h(N) = N^{-k}$ and discuss the effect of k to the approximation where $1 > k > 0$.

6-2 Repeat 6-1 by using a triangular kernel.

6-3 Prove asymptotic unbiasedness and consistency of the Parzen estimate for multivariable case. (Hint: Follow the same procedure as the one for one variable.)

6-4 Show that, when we use the k-nearest neighbor decision rule, the decision boundary becomes piecewise linear.

6-5 We would like to estimate the probability of error by using the k-nearest neighbor decision rule. We discussed the C method and leaving-one-out method in Chapter 5; combine these and propose a method to find the upper and lower bounds of the probability of error.

6-6 Extend the condensed nearest neighbor decision rule to the k-nearest neighbor for multiclass problem.

6-7 Show a histogram for the data of 6-1 with fixed cells.

6-8 Repeat 6-7 with variable cells. Let us use $\sigma_i(0) = 1$, $\tau = 2$, and $\theta = 2$.

6-9 Find the continuous version of the expansion (6-91), and show that the Fourier transform is a special case. Also show λ_i, the kernel, and basis functions.

6-10 A density function is given in the figure. Find the Hermite expansion up to the fourth term and show how closely the expansion approximates the density function.

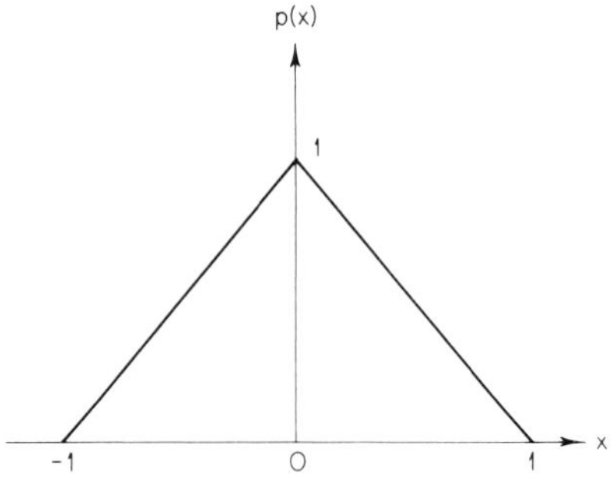

6-11 A density function of three binary inputs is given in the table. (a) Show the Walsh expansion. (b) Show the Bahadur expansion.

x_1	x_2	x_3	$p(X)$
-1	-1	-1	1/4
$+1$	-1	-1	1/40
-1	$+1$	-1	1/40
$+1$	$+1$	-1	1/5
-1	-1	$+1$	1/5
$+1$	-1	$+1$	1/40
-1	$+1$	$+1$	1/40
$+1$	$+1$	$+1$	1/4

Chapter 7

SUCCESSIVE PARAMETER ESTIMATION

In the approaches to parameter estimation presented so far, estimates have been determined from all of the observable data in a single calculation. Sometimes it is more practical to use a procedure based on a sequence of calculations. In this case, the parameters are first approximated by an initial "guess." Then each observation vector is used in turn to update the estimate. Hopefully, as the number of observations increases, the estimate will converge in some sense toward the true parameters. A major advantage of this successive approach is the fact that an infinite number of observations can be accounted for, using a finite amount of storage.

7.1 Successive Adjustment of a Linear Classifier

When each of the conditional density functions corresponding to the classes to be separated belongs to a known parametric family, the classifier design is fairly straightforward. After the estimates of the unknown parameters have been obtained, the Bayes decision rule is determined. Quite often, however, even the functional form of the conditional densities cannot be assumed. The densities could be approximated by the techniques described in Chapter 6, but, on the other hand, it may be possible to avoid the calculation of the densities completely. Suppose it is decided *a priori* that the decision rule belongs to a parameteric family of decision rules. The problem then reduces to that of estimating the parameters of the decision rule. By this approach we sacrifice, perhaps, a certain amount of insight into the nature of the classifier problem, however, this sacrifice is often more than justified by savings in computation.

Suppose, for a two-class problem, we decide to use a linear classifier of the form

$$V^T X + v_0 \gtrless 0 \rightarrow X \in \begin{cases} \omega_1 \\ \omega_2 \end{cases} \tag{7-1}$$

Then our problem is that of estimating the parameters V and v_0. The linear classifier is chosen because of its simplicity, but it should be recalled from Chapter 4 that (7-1) can include a broad range of nonlinear functions. This is the case if X is considered a vector in a functional space instead of being thought of as the original variable space.

In Chapter 4, we discussed the design of V and v_0 from a given set of observations, provided these are all simultaneously available. In the present case, however, we would rather not store all of the observation vectors simultaneously. Instead, we store only the current parameter estimate and update this estimate each time a single observation vector is presented to the estimation system. This type of system was first developed as a simplified model of learning and decision-making in early pattern recognition research, and has since been called a *perceptron*. In this model, we have to have an algorithm which modifies the parameters on the basis of the present observation vector and the present values of these parameters.

Linear Classifier for Two-Class Problems

Let us rewrite (7-1) as

$$h(Y) = W^T Y = \sum_{i=0}^{n} w_i y_i \gtrless 0 \rightarrow Y \in \begin{cases} \omega_1 \\ \omega_2 \end{cases} \tag{7-2}$$

where $y_0 = 1$ and $y_i = x_i$ $(i = 1, 2, \ldots, n)$. Then the current value of W

is updated to the new value to W', as follows [Nilsson, 1965].

$$\text{(1)} \quad W' = W \quad \text{if} \quad Y \in \omega_1 \quad \text{and} \quad W^T Y > 0$$
$$\text{or} \quad \text{if} \quad Y \in \omega_2 \quad \text{and} \quad W^T Y < 0 \tag{7-3}$$

$$\text{(2)} \quad W' = W + cY \quad \text{if} \quad Y \in \omega_1 \quad \text{and} \quad W^T Y \leq 0 \tag{7-4}$$

$$\text{(3)} \quad W' = W - cY \quad \text{if} \quad Y \in \omega_2 \quad \text{and} \quad W^T Y \geq 0 \quad (c > 0) \tag{7-5}$$

Since W of (7-3) correctly classifies the sample, we have no reason to change W. In (7-4), W should be modified to increase $W^T Y$. W' of (7-4) satisfies this condition because

$$W'^T Y = W^T Y + cY^T Y > W^T Y \tag{7-6}$$

Likewise, W' of (7-5) decreases $W^T Y$. Since we have limited ourselves to the use of only one sample and the present parameter values to adjust W, the above procedure is fairly general, and we need only to choose a value for c.

There are three common ways to choose c. These are as follows:

(1) *Fixed increment rule*: $c =$ constant

(2) *Absolute correction rule*: Select c large enough to obtain $W'^T Y > 0$ for $Y \in \omega_1$ and $W'^T Y < 0$ for $Y \in \omega_2$. That is,

$$W'^T Y = (W + cY)^T Y > 0 \quad \text{for} \quad Y \in \omega_1 \quad \text{and} \quad W^T Y \leq 0 \tag{7-7}$$

$$W'^T Y = (W - cY)^T Y < 0 \quad \text{for} \quad Y \in \omega_2 \quad \text{and} \quad W^T Y \geq 0 \tag{7-8}$$

In order to satisfy (7-7) and (7-8), c should satisfy

$$c > | W^T Y | / (Y^T Y) \tag{7-9}$$

(3) *Gradient correction rule*: When we maximize or minimize a criterion such as the mean-square error between the desired and actual outputs, we can determine c depending on both Y and W from the gradient of the criterion. For example, by analogy with (4-76) we can minimize the mean-square error between $\gamma(\mathbf{Z})$ and $W^T \mathbf{Z}$ of (4-44) by selecting

$$c = \varrho[\gamma(Z) - W^T Z] \tag{7-10}$$

where $Z = Y$ for $Y \in \omega_1$ and $Z = -Y$ for $Y \in \omega_2$. Obviously, c depends on the criterion we select and ϱ should be a positive constant properly chosen.

EXAMPLE 7-1 Let us design a classifier which separates the four samples of Fig. 7-1. The samples are presented to the machine in the order Y_0, Y_1, Y_2, Y_3, Y_0, ... The fixed increment rule is used with $c = 1$. The sequence of W in the training period is shown in Table 7-1. The term W converges to

$$\begin{aligned} 2y_1 - 1 &> 0 \qquad Y \in \omega_1 \\ &< 0 \qquad Y \in \omega_2 \end{aligned} \tag{7-11}$$

As is seen in Fig. 7-1, this classifier separates the given four samples correctly.

Input sample	y_0	y_1	y_2	Class
Y_0	1	0	0	ω_2
Y_1	1	1	0	ω_1
Y_2	1	0	1	ω_2
Y_2	1	1	1	ω_1

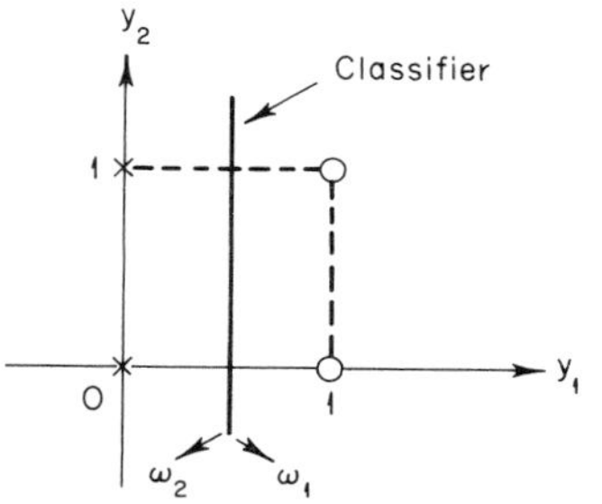

Fig. 7-1 Samples of the example.

TABLE 7-1

SEQUENCE OF W

	Input	Present W w_0	w_1	w_2	W^TY	True class	Adjustment	New W w_0	w_1	w_2
Iteration 1	Y_0	0	0	0	0	ω_2	$W - Y_0$	−1	0	0
	Y_1	−1	0	0	−1	ω_1	$W + Y_1$	0	1	0
	Y_2	0	1	0	0	ω_2	$W - Y_2$	−1	1	−1
	Y_3	−1	1	−1	−1	ω_1	$W + Y_3$	0	2	0
Iteration 2	Y_0	0	2	0	0	ω_2	$W - Y_0$	−1	2	0
	Y_1	−1	2	0	1	ω_1	No	−1	2	0
	Y_2	−1	2	0	−1	ω_2	No	−1	2	0
	Y_3	−1	2	0	1	ω_1	No	−1	2	0
	Y_0	−1	2	0	−1	ω_2	No	−1	2	0

Example 7-2 An example of a linearly nonseparable case is given here. Six samples are given in Fig. 7-2, and they are fed into the machine in the order $Y_0, Y_1, \ldots, Y_5, Y_0, \ldots, Y_5, Y_0, \ldots$. The fixed increment rule is used again, with $c = 1$. The sequence of W in the training period is shown in Table 7-2. We have a cyclic sequence of W without convergence, although

Input sample	y_0	y_1	y_2	Class
Y_0	1	0	2	ω_1
Y_1	1	1	1	ω_2
Y_2	1	2	0	ω_1
Y_3	1	0	−2	ω_2
Y_4	1	−1	−1	ω_1
Y_5	1	−2	0	ω_2

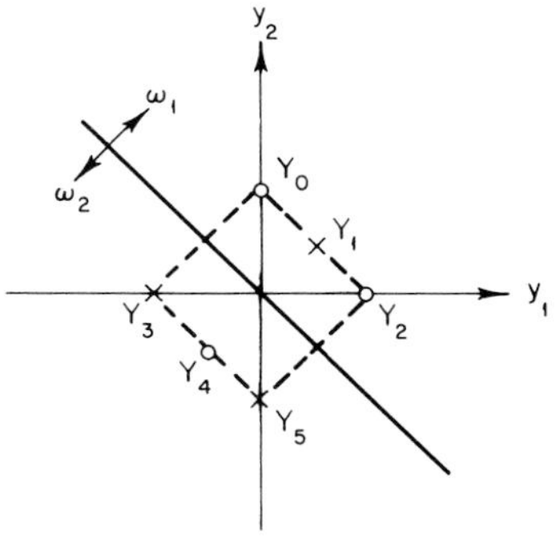

Fig. 7-2 Linearly nonseparable example.

TABLE 7-2

Sequence of W for a Linearly Nonseparable Case

	Input	Present W w_0	w_1	w_2	W^TY	True class	Adjustment	New W w_0	w_1	w_2
Iteration 1	Y_0	0	0	0	0	ω_1	No	0	0	0
	Y_1	0	0	0	0	ω_2	$W - Y_1$	−1	−1	−1
	Y_2	−1	−1	−1	−3	ω_1	$W + Y_2$	0	1	−1
	Y_3	0	1	−1	2	ω_2	$W - Y_3$	−1	1	1
	Y_4	−1	1	1	−3	ω_1	$W + Y_4$	0	0	0
	Y_5	0	0	0	0	ω_2	$W - Y_5$	−1	2	0
Iteration 2	Y_0	−1	2	0	−1	ω_1	$W + Y_0$	0	2	2
	Y_1	0	2	2	4	ω_2	$W - Y_1$	−1	1	1
	Y_2	−1	1	1	1	ω_1	No	−1	1	1
	Y_3	−1	1	1	−3	ω_2	No	−1	1	1
	Y_4	−1	1	1	−3	ω_1	$W + Y_4$	0	0	0
	Y_5	0	0	0	0	ω_2	$W - Y_5$	−1	2	0
	Y_0	−1	2	0						

the best linear classifier $[w_0 \quad w_1 \quad w_2] = [0 \quad 2 \quad 2]$ is included in the sequence of W.

Whenever we have an iterative process like this, there is a question of whether the convergence of the process is guaranteed. When two distributions are *linearly separable*, the convergence of the above process for the fixed increment rule, the absolute correction rule, and the gradient correction rule with a proper range of ϱ has been proved.

Convergence Proof for the Linearly Separable Case

The convergence proof of the above algorithm is as follows [Nilsson, 1965].

Let us introduce a new vector Z defined by

$$\begin{aligned} Z &= Y \qquad \text{for} \quad Y \in \omega_1 \\ Z &= -Y \qquad \text{for} \quad Y \in \omega_2 \end{aligned} \tag{7-12}$$

Then (7-2) becomes

$$W^T Z > 0 \qquad \text{for both} \quad Z \in \omega_1 \quad \text{and} \quad Z \in \omega_2 \tag{7-13}$$

Also the modification of W by (7-4) and (7-5) becomes

$$W' = W + cZ \qquad \text{if} \qquad W^T Z \leq 0 \qquad c > 0 \tag{7-14}$$

Let us eliminate, from a training sequence $Z_1, Z_2, \ldots, Z_k, \ldots$, the Z's which do not change W, and call it the reduced training sequence $Z_1{}^*$, $Z_2{}^*, \ldots$. Since the eliminated Z's do not affect W, they have no influence on the proof of convergence.

Also, let us assume $c = 1$. This assumption does not reduce the generality of the proof for the following reasons:

(1) For the fixed increment rule, a change of c corresponds to a change of the coordinate scale. The scale of the coordinate does not affect the structure of the data and the linear classifier.

(2) The absolute and gradient correction rules become equivalent to the fixed increment rule, if we generate a sequence of artificial samples $Z_k = Z_{k+1} = \cdots = Z_{k+u}$ whenever we have $W^T Z_k \leq 0$. The term u is determined by (7-9) and (7-10).

A reduced sequence of samples generates the corresponding sequence of W^* given by

$$W_{k+1}^* = W_k{}^* + Z_k{}^* \tag{7-15}$$

where

$$W_k^{*T} Z^* \leq 0 \tag{7-16}$$

Let W_s be any final classifier satisfying (7-13). Since we assume that the two distributions are linearly separable, the following inequality must hold for all samples

$$W_s^T Z_k > 0 \tag{7-17}$$

Selecting

$$a = \max_k Z_k^T Z_k \quad \text{and} \quad b > 0 \tag{7-18}$$

we can select the scale of W so that

$$W_s^T Z_k > (a + b)/2 > 0 \tag{7-19}$$

The change of scale of W does not change the decision rule of (7-13) or (7-2).

Now we calculate the distance between W_s and W_k^* as

$$\| W_s - W_k^* \|^2 = \| W_s \|^2 + \| W_k^* \|^2 - 2W_s^T W_k^* \tag{7-20}$$

Hence, using (7-15),

$$\begin{aligned} \| W_s - W_k^* \|^2 - \| W_s - W_{k+1}^* \|^2 &= \| W_k^* \|^2 - \| W_{k+1}^* \|^2 \\ -2W_s^T(W_k^* - W_{k+1}^*) &= -2W_k^{*T} Z_k^* - Z_k^{*T} Z_k^* + 2W_s^T Z_k^* \end{aligned} \tag{7-21}$$

Recalling $W_k^{*T} Z_k^* \leq 0$ from (7-16) and the inequalities of (7-18) and (7-19), (7-21) becomes

$$\| W_s - W_k^* \|^2 - \| W_s - W_{k+1}^* \|^2 > -a + 2(a + b)/2 = b > 0 \tag{7-22}$$

Equation (7-22) shows that, whenever a new Z_k^* is applied, $\| W_s - W_k^* \|^2$ decreases by more than b. Therefore, after a finite number of samples, W_k^* should be equal to W_s.

Linear Classifier for Multiclass Problems

The algorithm of designing a linear classifier for the two-class problem can be extended to linear classifiers for the multiclass problem.

For M classes, we set up M linear discriminant functions W_i. The decision rule then becomes

$$W_i^T Y > W_j^T Y \qquad (j = 1, 2, \ldots, M\colon\ j \neq i) \rightarrow Y \in \omega_i \tag{7-23}$$

When all $Y \in \omega_i$ ($i = 1, 2, \ldots, M$) satisfy (7-23), we call *these M classes linearly separable*. An algorithm to adjust these W's is given as follows:

(1) If $W_i^T Y > W_j^T Y$ ($j = 1, 2, \ldots, M$: $j \neq i$) for $Y \in \omega_i$, then
$$W_k' = W_k \quad (k = 1, 2, \ldots, M) \tag{7-24}$$

(2) If $W_l^T Y > W_i^T Y$ and $W_i^T Y > W_j^T Y$ for $Y \in \omega_i$, then
$$W_l' = W_l - cY, \qquad W_i' = W_i + cY, \qquad W_j' = W_j \qquad (j \neq i, l) \tag{7-25}$$

This multiclass problem can be reformulated as a two-class problem, if we extend our dimension to $n \times M$ as

$$W = [W_1^T : \cdots \; W_{i-1}^T W_i^T W_{i+1}^T \; \cdots \; W_{l-1}^T \; W_l^T W_{l+1}^T \; \cdots \; W_M^T]^T \tag{7-26}$$

$$Z = [0^T \; \cdots \; 0^T \quad Y^T \; 0^T \; \cdots \; 0^T \; -Y^T 0^T \; \cdots \; 0^T]^T \tag{7-27}$$

for the Y of (7-25).

Then, for the reduced sequence of samples, $Z_1^*, Z_2^*, \ldots$, we can obtain a corresponding sequence of W, $W_1^*, W_2^*, \ldots$. The terms W_k^*'s are related by

$$W_{k+1}^* = W_k^* + cZ_k^* \tag{7-28}$$

Equation (7-28) is equivalent to (7-25). Since (7-28) is the same as (7-15), the convergence of (7-28) and, consequently, the convergence of (7-25) is guaranteed by the proof presented in the previous subsection.

As discussed in Chapter 4, a piecewise linear classifier is often used for separating many classes. Unfortunately, the convergence proof for a piecewise linear classifier is not known. However, similar algorithms to adjust the W's can be found in some references [Nilsson, 1965; Duda, 1966].

7.2 Stochastic Approximation

The successive estimation algorithm of the last section does not always converge when the observation vectors are not linearly separable (Example 7-2). This fact leads us to consider an estimation algorithm for which convergence is guaranteed. Stochastic approximation is a technique that has been developed as an optimization technique for random environments [Wilde, 1964; Mendel, 1970]. Stochastic approximation can be used for parameter estimation in pattern recognition, and convergence is guaranteed under very general circumstances. It is usually difficult, however, to discuss the rate of convergence.

Before, we begin a detailed discussion, let us examine a simple example. Suppose we want to estimate the expected vector from a finite number of observation vectors. Suppose, further, that we want to use a successive estimate. Now the nonsuccessive estimate $\hat{\mathbf{M}}_N$ of the expected vector, based on N observation vectors, $\mathbf{X}_1, \ldots, \mathbf{X}_N$, is given by

$$\hat{\mathbf{M}}_N = (1/N) \sum_{i=1}^{N} \mathbf{X}_i \tag{7-29}$$

The equation can be modified to

$$\begin{aligned} \hat{\mathbf{M}}_N &= [(N-1)/N)]\left\{[1/(N-1)] \sum_{i=1}^{N-1} \mathbf{X}_i\right\} + (1/N)\mathbf{X}_N \\ &= [(N-1)/N]\hat{\mathbf{M}}_{N-1} + (1/N)\mathbf{X}_N \end{aligned} \tag{7-30}$$

That is, $\hat{\mathbf{M}}_N$ can be calculated with a new sample $\mathbf{X}_N$ if we store only $\hat{\mathbf{M}}_{N-1}$ and N. Also, the effect of the new sample on the sample mean vector should decrease, with an increase in N, as follows:

$$\mathbf{X}_1, \tfrac{1}{2}\mathbf{X}_2, \tfrac{1}{3}\mathbf{X}_3, \ldots, \tfrac{1}{N}X_N \tag{7-31}$$

The sequence of coefficients $1, \frac{1}{2}\ \frac{1}{3}, \ldots, \frac{1}{N}, \ldots$ is known as a *harmonic sequence*.

The above simple example suggests the following basic approach to successive estimation.

(1) When the mathematical expression for an estimate is available, we may obtain the successive expression of the estimate by separating the estimate calculated from $N-1$ samples and the contribution of the Nth sample.

(2) Even when we have to use a search process, in order to minimize or maximize a certain criterion, we may diminish the effect of the Nth sample by using a coefficient which is a decreasing function of N.

Root-Finding Problem

The simplest form of stochastic approximation is seen in finding a root of a regression function. This process is also called the *Robbins–Monro method*. Let $\boldsymbol{\theta}$ and $\mathbf{z}$ be two random variables with some correlation, as shown in Fig. 7-3. Our problem is to find the root of the regression function

$f(\theta)$, which is given by

$$f(\theta) = E\{\mathbf{z}/\theta\} \tag{7-32}$$

If we can collect all samples for a fixed θ and estimate $E\{\mathbf{z}/\theta\}$, then finding the root of $f(\theta)$ can be carried out by a root-finding technique for a deterministic function, such as the Newton method. However, when it is predetermined that only one sample is observed for a given θ and we try to change θ accordingly, then the observation of $f(\theta)$ is very noisy and may introduce an erroneous adjustment of θ, particularly around the root.

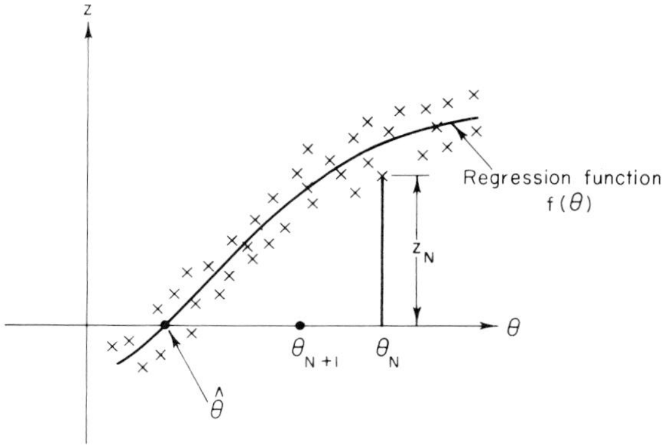

Fig. 7-3 Root-finding problem.

In the Robbins–Monro method, the new successive estimate $\boldsymbol{\theta}_{N+1}$ based on the present estimate $\boldsymbol{\theta}_N$ and the new observation $\mathbf{z}_N$ is given by

$$\boldsymbol{\theta}_{N+1} = \boldsymbol{\theta}_N - a_N \mathbf{z}_N \tag{7-33}$$

where we assume, without losing any generality, that θ approaches $\hat{\theta}$, the root of (7-32), from the larger side; that is, $f(\hat{\theta}) > 0$ for $\theta > \hat{\theta}$ and $f(\theta) < 0$ for $\theta < \hat{\theta}$, as is shown in Fig. 7-3. Then a_N is a sequence of positive numbers which satisfy the following conditions:

(1) $$\lim_{N\to\infty} a_N = 0 \tag{7-34}$$

(2) $$\sum_{N=1}^{\infty} a_N = \infty \tag{7-35}$$

(3) $$\sum_{N=1}^{\infty} a_N^2 < \infty \tag{7-36}$$

Although we will see later how these conditions for a_N are used for the convergence proof, the physical meaning of these equations can be described as follows. Equation (7-34) is similar to the $\frac{1}{N}$ term discussed earlier and allows the process to settle down in the limit. On the other hand, (7-35) insures that there is enough corrective action to avoid stopping short of the root. Equation (7-36) guarantees the variance of the accumulated noise to be finite so that we can correct for the effect of noise.

With a sequence of a_N satisfying (7-34) through (7-36), $\boldsymbol{\theta}_N$ of (7-33) converges toward $\hat{\theta}$ in the mean-square sense and with probability 1, that is,

$$\lim_{N\to\infty} E\{(\boldsymbol{\theta}_N - \hat{\theta})^2\} = 0 \tag{7-37}$$

$$\lim_{N\to\infty} \Pr\{\boldsymbol{\theta}_N = \hat{\theta}\} = 1 \tag{7-38}$$

The harmonic sequence of (7-31) is a suitable candidate for $\{a_N\}$. More generally, a sequence of the form

$$a_N = 1/N^k \quad 1 \geq k > \tfrac{1}{2} \tag{7-39}$$

satisfies (7-34) through (7-36), altough (7-39) is not the only possible sequence.

Before discussing convergence of the Robbins–Monro method, let us consider a feedback system analogy with this process.

Figure 7-4 shows an equivalent feedback circuit, where $\gamma(t)$ is a noise process. Instead of a fixed feedback gain, we have a time-decreasing feedback gain $a(t)$. From the conventional design concept of a feedback circuit, one can notice that the decreasing $a(t)$ could guarantee the stability of the circuit but could also result in a slow response.

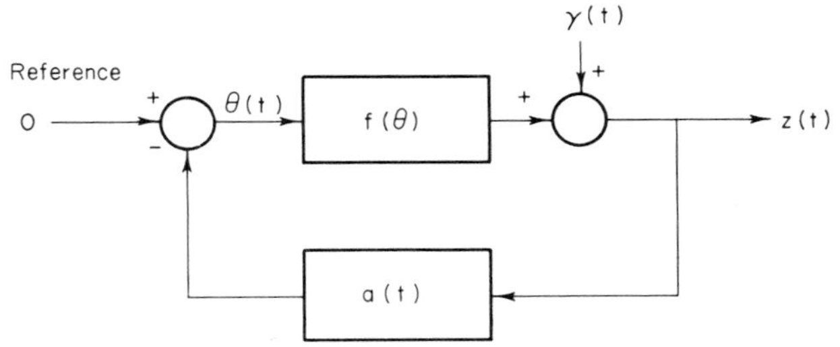

Fig. 7-4 Equivalent feedback circuit.

Convergence Proof of the Robbins–Monro Method

The convergence of the Robbins–Monro method is proved as follows. First let us divide $\mathbf{z}_N$ into two parts: regression function $f(\boldsymbol{\theta}_N)$ and noise $\boldsymbol{\gamma}_N$. Then (7-33) is rewritten as

$$\boldsymbol{\theta}_{N+1} = \boldsymbol{\theta}_N - a_N f(\boldsymbol{\theta}_N) - a_N \boldsymbol{\gamma}_N \tag{7-40}$$

where

$$\boldsymbol{\gamma}_N = \mathbf{z}_N - f(\boldsymbol{\theta}_N) \tag{7-41}$$

Then, from the definition of the regression function $f(\theta)$ in (7-32), $\boldsymbol{\gamma}_N$ is a random variable with zero mean as

$$E\{\boldsymbol{\gamma}_N/\theta_N\} = E\{\mathbf{z}_N/\theta_N\} - f(\theta_N) = 0 \tag{7-42}$$

Also, it is reasonable to assume that the variance of $\boldsymbol{\gamma}_N$ is bounded, that is,

$$E\{\boldsymbol{\gamma}_N^2\} \leq \sigma^2 \tag{7-43}$$

and that $\boldsymbol{\gamma}_N$ and $\boldsymbol{\theta}_N$ are statistically independent.

Next, let us study the difference between $\hat{\theta}$ and $\boldsymbol{\theta}_N$. From (7-40), we have

$$(\boldsymbol{\theta}_{N+1} - \hat{\theta}) = (\boldsymbol{\theta}_N - \hat{\theta}) - a_N f(\boldsymbol{\theta}_N) - a_N \boldsymbol{\gamma}_N \tag{7-44}$$

Taking the expectation of the square of (7-44).

$$\begin{aligned} &E\{(\boldsymbol{\theta}_{N+1} - \hat{\theta})^2\} - E\{(\boldsymbol{\theta}_N - \hat{\theta})^2\} \\ &\quad = a_N^2 E\{f(\boldsymbol{\theta}_N)^2\} + a_N^2 E\{\boldsymbol{\gamma}_N^2\} - 2a_N E\{(\boldsymbol{\theta}_N - \hat{\theta}) f(\boldsymbol{\theta}_N)\} \end{aligned} \tag{7-45}$$

Therefore, repeating (7-45), we obtain

$$\begin{aligned} &E\{(\boldsymbol{\theta}_N - \hat{\theta})^2\} - E\{(\boldsymbol{\theta}_1 - \hat{\theta})^2\} \\ &\quad = \sum_{i=1}^{N-1} a_i^2 [E\{f(\boldsymbol{\theta}_i)^2\} + E\{\boldsymbol{\gamma}_i^2\}] - 2 \sum_{i=1}^{N-1} a_i E\{(\boldsymbol{\theta}_i - \hat{\theta}) f(\boldsymbol{\theta}_i)\} \end{aligned} \tag{7-46}$$

We assume that the regression function is also bounded in the region of our interest as

$$E\{f(\boldsymbol{\theta}_N)^2\} \leq M \tag{7-47}$$

Then (7-46) is bounded by

$$\begin{aligned} &E\{(\boldsymbol{\theta}_N - \hat{\theta})^2\} - E\{(\boldsymbol{\theta}_1 - \hat{\theta})^2\} \\ &\quad \leq (M + \sigma^2) \sum_{i=1}^{N-1} a_i^2 - 2 \sum_{i=1}^{N-1} a_i E\{(\boldsymbol{\theta}_i - \hat{\theta}) f(\boldsymbol{\theta}_i)\} \end{aligned} \tag{7-48}$$

Let us examine (7-48) term by term. First, since $E\{(\hat{\boldsymbol{\theta}}_N - \hat{\theta})^2\}$ is positive and assuming $\boldsymbol{\theta}_1$ is selected so that $E\{(\boldsymbol{\theta}_1 - \hat{\theta})^2\}$ is finite, the left-hand side of (7-48) is bounded from below. The first term on the right-hand side of (7-48) is finite because of (7-36).

Recall from Fig. 7-3 that the regression function satisfies:

$$\begin{aligned} f(\theta) &> 0 \quad \text{if} \quad (\theta - \hat{\theta}) > 0 \\ f(\theta) &= 0 \quad \text{if} \quad (\theta - \hat{\theta}) = 0 \\ f(\theta) &< 0 \quad \text{if} \quad (\theta - \hat{\theta}) < 0 \end{aligned} \tag{7-49}$$

Therefore,

$$(\theta - \hat{\theta})f(\theta) \geq 0 \tag{7-50}$$

and

$$E\{(\boldsymbol{\theta} - \hat{\theta})f(\boldsymbol{\theta})\} \geq 0 \tag{7-51}$$

Now consider the following proposition:

$$\lim_{i\to\infty} E\{(\boldsymbol{\theta}_i - \hat{\theta})f(\boldsymbol{\theta}_i)\} = 0 \tag{7-52}$$

If (7-52) does not hold, then, because of (7-35), the last term of (7-48) tends toward $-\infty$. But this contradicts the fact that the left-hand side of (7-48) is bounded from below. Hence, (7-52) must hold. Since (7-50) holds for all θ's, (7-52) is equivalent to

$$\lim_{i\to\infty} \Pr\{\boldsymbol{\theta}_i = \hat{\theta}\} = 1 \tag{7-53}$$

Thus, the convergence with probability 1 is proved. The convergence in mean-square sense has also been proved but this proof is omitted here.

Peak-Seeking Problem

The Robbins–Monro method can be easily modified so as to seek the peak of a regression function instead of the root. As is well known, the peak or the optimum point of a function $f(\theta)$ is a root of $df(\theta)/d\theta = 0$. Therefore, if we can measure $df(\theta)/d\theta$, then we can apply the Robbins–Monro method directly. Unfortunately, in most applications, the measurement of $df(\theta)/d\theta$ is not available. Therefore, we measure the derivative experimentally and modify $\boldsymbol{\theta}_N$ as

$$\boldsymbol{\theta}_{N+1} = \boldsymbol{\theta}_N - a_N[\mathbf{z}(\boldsymbol{\theta}_N + c_N) - \mathbf{z}(\boldsymbol{\theta}_N - c_N)]/(2c_N) \tag{7-54}$$

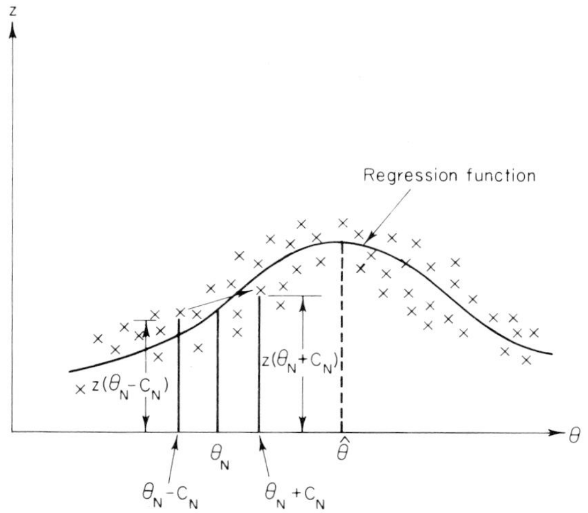

Fig. 7-5 The Kiefer–Wolfowitz method.

This successive equation is called the *Kiefer–Wolfowitz method.* Figure 7-5 illustrates the Kiefer–Wolfowitz method.

Both a_N and c_N are sequences of positive numbers. They must vanish in the limit, that is,

$$\lim_{N\to\infty} a_N = 0 \tag{7-55}$$

$$\lim_{N\to\infty} c_N = 0 \tag{7-56}$$

so that the process eventually converges. In order to make sure that we have enough corrective action to avoid stopping short of the peak, a_N should satisfy

$$\sum_{N=1}^{\infty} a_N = \infty \tag{7-57}$$

Also, to cancel the accumulated noise effects we must have

$$\sum_{N=1}^{\infty} (a_N/c_N)^2 < \infty \tag{7-58}$$

With a_N and c_N satisfying these conditions, it has been proven that $\boldsymbol{\theta}_N$ of (7-54) converges to $\hat{\theta}$ both in the mean-square sense and with probability 1, provided that we have a bounded variance for the noise and a bounded slope for the regression function. The proof is similar to the one for root-finding and is omitted here.

Multidimensional Extension

So far, we have discussed stochastic approximation for a single variable. This has been done mainly for simplicity's sake. The conclusions and the criterion for the selection of a_N are all valid for the multivariate case and the previous discussion, including the convergence proof, can be repeated simply by replacing x^2 by $\| X \|^2$.

Thus, for the Robbins–Monro method, (7-33) can be rewritten as

$$\mathbf{\Theta}_{N+1} = \mathbf{\Theta}_N - a_N \mathbf{Z}_N \tag{7-59}$$

with a_N satisfying (7-34) through (7-36). The convergence in the mean-square sense and with probability 1 is guaranteed, provided that both the variances of the noise and the regression function are bounded.

For the Kiefer–Wolfowitz method, the partial derivatives should be approximated by

$$\partial z(\Theta_N)/\partial\theta_i \cong [z(\Theta_N + c_N E_i) - z(\Theta_N)]/c_N \tag{7-60}$$

or

$$\partial z(\Theta_N)/\partial\theta_i \cong [z(\Theta_N + c_N E_i) - z(\Theta_N - c_N E_i)]/(2c_N) \tag{7-61}$$

where E_i is the ith unit coordinate vector $[0 \quad 0 \cdots 0 \quad 1 \quad 0 \cdots 0]^T$. Then (7-54) can be extended to

$$\mathbf{\Theta}_{N+1} = \mathbf{\Theta}_N - a_N \begin{bmatrix} \partial \mathbf{z}(\mathbf{\Theta}_N)/\partial\theta_1 \\ \vdots \\ \partial \mathbf{z}(\mathbf{\Theta}_N)/\partial\theta_n \end{bmatrix} \tag{7-62}$$

Figure 7-6 shows how the partial derivatives are measured; $n + 1$ observations for (7-60) and $2n$ observations for (7-61) are needed. Again the convergence in the mean-square sense and with probability 1 is guaranteed, provided that both the noise variances and the slope of the regression function are bounded.

Now we can relate stochastic approximation to the design of a classifier. Let us design a classifier which minimizes the mean-square error between the desired output $\gamma(Z_j)$ and the actual output $W^T Z_j$ as in (4-45), where $Z_j = Y_j$ for $Y_j \in \omega_1$ and $Z_j = -Y_i$ for $Y \in \omega_2$. Although we discuss only one criterion, the same discussion can be applied to other criteria. The successive adjustment of W of (4-48) can be rewritten as

$$W(l+1) = W(l) - \varrho(\partial\bar{\varepsilon}^2/\partial W) = W(l) - 2\varrho(1/N) \sum_{i=1}^{N} \{W(l)^T Z_i - \gamma(Z_i)\} Z_i \tag{7-63}$$

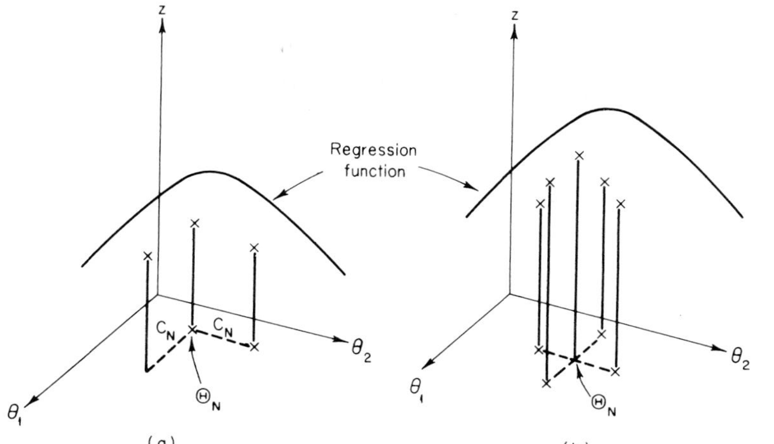

Fig. 7-6 The Kiefer–Wolfowitz method for multivariate case.

That is, $W(l)$ is modified by the sample mean vector of $\{W(l)^T\mathbf{Z} - \gamma(\mathbf{Z})\}\mathbf{Z}$. Therefore, when we can use all N samples to calculate the sample mean vector for a given W, the successive adjustment becomes a simple optimization process for the regression function. When we can use only one sample at a time to modify $W(l)$, (7-63) is converted to

$$W(l+1) = W(l) - 2\varrho\{W(l)^T Z_l - \gamma(Z_l)\}Z_l \tag{7-64}$$

This is identical to (7-59), the Robbins–Monro method for the multivariate case, where $2\{W(l)^T Z_l - r(Z_l)\}Z_l$ corresponds to Z_N of (7-59). Thus, although this is a peak-seeking problem, we can calculate the partial derivatives from $W(l)$ and Z_l and, therefore, we can apply the simpler Robbins–Monro method rather than the Kiefer–Wolfowitz method.

EXAMPLE 7-3 Let us apply the Robbins–Monro method to the six samples, given in Example 7-2, which are not linearly separable and for which the method of the previous section could not make the sequence of W converge. The result is shown in Table 7-3, where the starting W is $[0 \quad 0 \quad 0]^T$, $\gamma(Z_j) = 3$ for $j = 0, 1, \ldots, 5$, and ϱ is sequenced from $\frac{1}{10}$ as $\frac{1}{10}, \frac{1}{11}, \ldots$. This sequence is selected mainly because we felt that all six samples should contribute to the design of the classifier equally, at least at the initial stage, and that the sequence $1, \frac{1}{2}, \frac{1}{3}, \ldots$ places too much weight on Z_0. The sequence $\frac{1}{10}, \frac{1}{11}, \ldots$ does not violate the conditions (7-34) through (7-36). We can easily find that $0.5x_1 + 0.5x_2 = 0$ minimizes the mean-square error, and Table 7-3 shows that the sequence of W approaches the optimum classifier.

EXAMPLE 7-4 For comparison, let us find the sequence of W by using (7-63) instead of (7-64) for the same six samples. This time, W is changed after six samples are received. Table 7-4 shows the result. Starting with $W = [0 \quad 0 \quad 0]^T$, $\gamma(Z_j) = 3$ $(j = 0, 1, \ldots, 5)$, and the sequence of ϱ, 1, $\frac{1}{2}$, ..., the optimum classifier is obtained in two iterations.

TABLE 7-3

AN EXAMPLE OF CLASSIFIER DESIGN BY USING INDIVIDUAL SAMPLES

	Input sample	z_0	z_1	z_2	Present W w_0	w_1	w_2	$\gamma - W^TZ$	ϱ	ΔW $2\varrho(\gamma - W^TZ)Z$		
Iteration 1	Z_0	1	0	2	0	0	0	3.0	1/10	0.6	0	1.2
	Z_1	−1	−1	−1	0.6	0	1.2	4.8	1/11	−0.9	−0.9	−0.9
	Z_2	1	2	0	−0.3	−0.9	0.3	5.1	1/12	0.9	1.8	0
	Z_3	−1	0	2	0.6	0.9	0.3	3.0	1/13	−0.5	0	1.0
	Z_4	1	−1	−1	0.1	0.9	1.3	5.1	1/14	0.7	−0.7	−0.7
	Z_5	−1	2	0	0.8	0.2	0.6	3.4	1/15	−0.5	1.0	0
Iteration 2	Z_0	1	0	2	0.3	1.2	0.6	1.5	1/16	0.2	0	0.4
	Z_1	−1	−1	−1	0.5	1.2	1.0	5.7	1/17	−0.7	−0.7	−0.7
	Z_2	1	2	0	−0.2	0.5	0.3	2.2	1/18	0.2	0.4	0
	Z_3	−1	0	2	0	0.9	0.3	2.4	1/19	−0.3	0	0.6
	Z_4	1	−1	−1	−0.3	0.9	0.9	5.1	1/20	0.5	−0.5	−0.5
	Z_5	−1	2	0	0.2	0.4	0.4	2.4	1/21	−0.2	0.4	0
	Z_0	1	0	2	0	0.8	0.4	2.2	1/22	0.2	0	0.4
	Z_1	−1	−1	−1	0.2	0.8	0.8					

The Method of Potential Functions

In stochastic approximation, successive approximation is applied to estimate a set of parameters which gives either the root or the extremal point of the regression function. The results can be extended to the estimation of the regression function itself.

Let us express a regression function $f(X)$ by an expansion of a given set

TABLE 7-4

AN EXAMPLE OF CLASSIFIER DESIGN BY USING THE REGRESSION FUNCTION

	Input samples	z_0	z_1	z_2	Present W: w_0	w_2	w_2	$\gamma - W^TZ$	ϱ	$2\varrho(\gamma - W^TZ)Z$			$\frac{1}{6}\sum_{i=1}^{6} 2\varrho(\gamma - W^TZ_i)Z_i$		
Iteration 1	Z_0	1	0	2	0	0	0	3	1	6	0	12			
	Z_1	−1	−1	−1	0	0	0	3	1	−6	−6	−6			
	Z_2	1	2	0	0	0	0	3	1	6	12	0			
	Z_3	−1	0	2	0	0	0	3	1	−6	0	12			
	Z_4	1	−1	−1	0	0	0	3	1	6	−6	−6			
	Z_5	−1	2	0	0	0	0	3	1	−6	12	0	0	2	2
Iteration 2	Z_0	1	0	2	0	2	2	−1	1/2	−0.5	0	−1			
	Z_1	−1	−1	−1	0	2	2	7	1/2	−3.5	−3.5	−3.5			
	Z_2	1	2	0	0	2	2	−1	1/2	−0.5	−1	0			
	Z_3	−1	0	2	0	2	2	−1	1/2	0.5	0	−1			
	Z_4	1	−1	−1	0	2	2	7	1/2	3.5	−3.5	−3.5			
	Z_5	−1	2	0	0	2	2	−1	1/2	0.5	−1	0	0	−1.5	−1.5
Iteration 3	Z_0	1	0	2	0	0.5	0.5	2	1/3	4/3	0	8/3			
	Z_1	−1	−1	−1	0	0.5	0.5	4	1/3	−8/3	−8/3	−8/3			
	Z_2	1	2	0	0	0.5	0.5	2	1/3	4/3	8/3	0			
	Z_3	−1	0	2	0	0.5	0.5	2	1/3	−4/3	0	8/3			
	Z_4	1	−1	−1	0	0.5	0.5	4	1/3	8/3	−8/3	−8/3			
	Z_5	−1	2	0	0	0.5	0.5	2	1/3	−4/3	8/3	0	0	0	0
	Z_0				0	0.5	0.5		1/4						

of basis functions as

$$f(\mathbf{X}) = \sum_{i=1}^{\infty} \theta_i \varphi_i(\mathbf{X}) \tag{7-65}$$

where $\{\theta_i\}$ should satisfy

$$\sum_{i=1}^{\infty} \theta_i^2 < \infty \tag{7-66}$$

Assuming that the φ_i's are known and given, the regression function $f(\mathbf{X})$ is characterized by a set of parameters Θ. This is somewhat the same as designing a linear classifier in which $\mathbf{x}_i$ is used for $\varphi_i(\mathbf{X})$. The selection of the basis functions is very much problem-oriented and depends on the functional form of $f(\mathbf{X})$. In general, we have to look for φ_i so that θ_i decreases quickly as i increases. Also, it is common practice to select an orthonormal set of φ_i for theoretical convenience.

$$E\{\varphi_i(\mathbf{X})\varphi_j(\mathbf{X})\} = \int_{\mathscr{S}} \varphi_i(X)\varphi_j(X)p(X)\,dX = \delta_{ij} \tag{7-67}$$

In a noisy environment, for a given X, our observation is a random variable $\mathbf{z}(X)$ whose expected value is $f(X)$. Therefore, if we want to determine the θ_i's to minimize the mean-square error between $\mathbf{z}(\mathbf{X})$ and $\sum \theta_i \varphi_i(\mathbf{X})$, then we solve

$$\begin{aligned} \frac{\partial}{\partial \theta_i} E\left[\left\{\mathbf{z}(\mathbf{X}) - \sum_{j=1}^{\infty} \theta_j \varphi_j(\mathbf{X})\right\}^2\right] &= -2E\left[\left\{\mathbf{z}(\mathbf{X}) - \sum_{j=1}^{\infty} \theta_j \varphi_j(\mathbf{X})\right\}\varphi_i(\mathbf{X})\right] \\ &= -2[E\{\mathbf{z}(\mathbf{X})\varphi_i(\mathbf{X})\} - \theta_i] = 0 \end{aligned} \tag{7-68}$$

where the φ_i's are assumed to be orthonormal. Therefore, θ_i is determined by

$$\begin{aligned} \theta_i = E\{\mathbf{z}(\mathbf{X})\varphi_i(\mathbf{X})\} &= \int_{\mathscr{S}} \int_{-\infty}^{+\infty} z(X)\varphi_i(X)p(z/X)p(X)\,dz\,dX \\ &= \int_{\mathscr{S}} f(X)\varphi_i(X)p(X)\,dX = E\{f(\mathbf{X})\varphi_i(\mathbf{X})\} \end{aligned} \tag{7-69}$$

When a successive approximation is required, θ_i can be estimated by the sequence

$$\begin{aligned} \theta_i(l+1) &= \theta_i(l) - a_l\, \partial \bar{\varepsilon}^2/\partial \theta_i \\ &= \theta_i(l) - 2a_l\left\{\sum_{j=1}^{\infty} \theta_j(l)\varphi_j(X_l) - z(X_l)\right\}\varphi_i(X_l) \qquad (i = 1, 2, \ldots) \end{aligned} \tag{7-70}$$

Or, in vector form,

$$\Theta(l+1) = \Theta(l) - 2a_l\{\Theta^T(l)\Phi(X_l) - z(X_l)\}\Phi(X_l) \tag{7-71}$$

where $\Theta = [\theta_1 \cdots \theta_\infty]^T$ and $\Phi = [\varphi_1 \cdots \varphi_\infty]^T$. This equation suggests the use of the Robbins–Monro method with the sequence a_l satisfying (7-34) through (7-36).

A successive approximation of a functional form $f(\mathbf{X})$, rather than Θ, is also obtained by multiplying (7-71) by $\Phi(X)$. That is,

$$\begin{aligned} f_{l+1}(X) &= \Theta^T(l+1)\Phi(X) \\ &= \Theta^T(l)\Phi(X) - 2a_l\{\Theta^T(l)\Phi(X_l) - z(X_l)\}\Phi^T(X_l)\Phi(X) \\ &= f_l(X) - \gamma_l k(X_l, X) \end{aligned} \tag{7-72}$$

where

$$\gamma_l = 2a_l\{f_l(X_l) - z(X_l)\} \tag{7-73}$$

$$k(X_l, X) = \Phi^T(X_l)\Phi(X) \tag{7-74}$$

$k(Y, X)$ is called the *potential function*, and the successive approximation of (7-72) is called the *method of potential functions*.

Although we have derived the method of the potential functions from a stochastic approximation point of view, the method can be stated in a more general form as follows.

A function $f(X)$ which is either deterministic or stochastic can be successively approximated by

$$f_{l+1}(X) = f_l(X) - \gamma_l k(X_l, X) \tag{7-75}$$

where $f(X)$, its observation $z(X)$, and $k(Y, X)$ are all bounded. The potential function satisfies

$$k(Y, X) = k(X, Y) \tag{7-76}$$

and

$$k(Y, X) = \sum_{i=1}^{\infty} \lambda_i^2 \varphi_i(Y)\varphi_i(X) \tag{7-77}$$

where

$$\lambda_i < \infty \tag{7-78}$$

Selecting γ_l as

$$\gamma_l = a_l\{f_l(X_l) - z(X_l)\} \tag{7-79}$$

where a_l satisfies (7-34) through (7-36), the successive approximation of (7-75) converges in probability. The proof is omitted [Braverman, 1965].

Although we may select a broad range of potential functions which satisfy the above conditions, we can be a little more specific by using the fact that the potential functions are symmetric with respect to two vectors X and Y. It has been suggested that the distance between X and Y be used as a symmetric function, that is,

$$k(Y, X) = g(\| Y - X \|) \tag{7-80}$$

Two typical examples of $g(\cdot)$ are

$$k(Y, X) = \exp\{-c \| Y - X \|^2\}$$

and

$$k(Y, X) = (1 + \| Y - X \|^2)^{-1} \quad \text{for} \quad \| Y - X \| < 1 \tag{7-81}$$

Acceleration of Convergence

As we stated previously, a stochastic approximation converges very slowly, particularly in the steady-state region. This is the price for guaranteed convergence. There have been many proposals to improve this disadvantage. In this subsection, we show two typical ones.

(1) *Flatter Sequence of* a_N

Since the primary cause of slow convergence is the choice of the decreasing sequence a_N, we can make the sequence decrease more slowly and still guarantees convergence. One way to do this is to change a_N to the next value only when a sign change of z_N is observed in root-finding. As long as the sign of z_N remains the same, we are not close to the root and convergence speed is more important than guaranteed convergence. When a sign change of z_N is observed, we have to start worrying about convergence. The same argument holds for the peak-seeking problem, where the sign of slope should be observed instead of the sign of z_N. Table 7-5 shows this altered sequence a_N.

(2) *More Observations for a Given* θ

If we can take many observations for a given θ and calculate the mean, then we can obtain the regression function. Therefore, the problem becomes that of the convergence of a deterministic function. As a compromise

TABLE 7-5

ACCELERATED SEQUENCE OF a_N

Trial N:	1	2	3	4	5	6	7	8
Sign of z_N:	+	+	+	−	−	+	+	−
Conventional a_N:	1	1/2	1/3	1/4	1/5	1/6	1/7	1/8
Accelerated a_N:	1	1	1	1/2	1/2	1/3	1/3	1/4

between this deterministic approach and stochastic approximation we may select a few observations for a given θ rather than one, take the average of these observations, and use it as z_N. An analogy can be found in a conventional feedback circuit where a filter is used to eliminate noise from the observation signal. Determining how many observations should be averaged to obtain a reasonable response corresponds to the design of the filter.

7.3 Successive Bayes Estimation

Since the estimates of parameters are random vectors, complete knowledge of the statistical properties of the estimates is obtained from their joint density, distribution, or characteristic functions. In this section, we show how the density function of the estimate can be calculated by a successive process.

Supervised Estimation

Let $\mathbf{X}_1, \ldots, \mathbf{X}_N$ be N samples which are used to estimate the density function of a parameter vector Θ. The terms $\mathbf{X}_i$ are given successively one by one. Thus, using the Bayes theorem, we can obtain a recursive expression for the conditional density function of $\mathbf{\Theta}$, given $X_1, \ldots, X_N$, as

$$p(\Theta/ X_1, \ldots, X_N) = \frac{p(X_N/ X_1, \ldots, X_{N-1}, \Theta)p(\Theta/ X_1, \ldots, X_{N-1})}{p(X_N/ X_1, \ldots, X_{N-1})} \tag{7-82}$$

where the *a priori* density function of $\mathbf{X}_N$, $p(X_N/X_1, \ldots, X_{N-1}, \Theta)$, is assumed to be known. If the numerator of (7-82) is available, the denominator can be calculated by integrating the numerator as follows:

$$p(X_N/X_1, \ldots, X_{N-1}) = \int_{\mathscr{S}} p(X_N/X_1, \ldots, X_{N-1}, \Theta)p(\Theta/X_1, \ldots, X_{N-1})\, d\Theta \tag{7-83}$$

Thus (7-82) shows that if $p(\Theta/X_1, \ldots, X_{N-1})$ is available, $p(\Theta/X_1, \ldots, X_N)$ may be calculated. Repeating the same operation until N becomes one shows that we need only $p(\Theta)$ to start this sequence of calculations. The term $p(\Theta)$ is the *a priori* density function of $\mathbf{\Theta}$ and reflects our initial knowledge about $\mathbf{\Theta}$.

Estimation of an Expected Vector with Known Covariance Matrix

Let us estimate the expected vector M of a normal distribution with a known covariance matrix Σ. The density function $p(M)$ is assumed to be normal with the expected vector M_0 and covariance matrix Σ_0. Then, after observing the first sample X_1,

$$\begin{aligned} p(M/X_1) &= \frac{p(X_1/M)p(M)}{\int_{\mathscr{S}} p(X_1/M)p(M)\, dM} \\ &= c_1 \exp[-\tfrac{1}{2}(X_1 - M)^T\Sigma^{-1}(X_1 - M) \\ &\quad - \tfrac{1}{2}(M - M_0)^T\Sigma_0^{-1}(M - M_0)] \\ &= c_2 \exp[-\tfrac{1}{2}(M - M_1)^T\Sigma_1^{-1}(M - M_1)] \end{aligned} \tag{7-84}$$

where

$$M_1 = \Sigma_0(\Sigma_0 + \Sigma)^{-1}X_1 + \Sigma(\Sigma_0 + \Sigma)^{-1}M_0 \tag{7-85}$$

$$\Sigma_1 = \Sigma_0(\Sigma_0 + \Sigma)^{-1}\Sigma \tag{7-86}$$

That is, $p(M/X_1)$ is also a normal distribution and its expected vector and covariance matrix are given by (7-85) and (7-86). Since $\int p(X_1/M) \times p(M)\, dM$ of (7-84) is independent of M, c_1, and c_2 are independent of M and are constants such that $\int p(M/X_1)\, dM = 1$.

We repeat the same process, replacing M_0 and Σ_0 of $p(M)$ by M_1 and Σ_1 of $p(M/X_1)$. The term $p(M/X_1, X_2)$ is also normal, and M_2 and Σ_2 are calculated by (7-85) and (7-86) with M_1 and Σ_1 instead of M_0 and Σ_0. Thus, after N iterations,

$$p(M/X_1, \ldots, X_N) = N(M_N, \Sigma_N) \tag{7-87}$$

where $N(M_N, \Sigma_N)$ denotes a normal distribution with expected vector M_N

and covariance matrix Σ_N. The terms M_N and Σ_N are given by

$$M_N = (\Sigma/N)[\Sigma_0 + (\Sigma/N)]^{-1}M_0 + \Sigma_0[\Sigma_0 + (\Sigma/N)]^{-1}\left[(1/N)\sum_{i=1}^{N} X_i\right] \quad (7\text{-}88)$$

$$\Sigma_N = \Sigma_0[\Sigma_0 + (\Sigma/N)]^{-1}(\Sigma/N) \quad (7\text{-}89)$$

As N increases, the effect of the initial knowledge of M, M_0, and Σ_0, decreases and finally

$$\lim_{N\to\infty} M_N = (1/N)\sum_{i=1}^{N} X_i \quad (7\text{-}90)$$

$$\lim_{N\to\infty} \Sigma_N = 0 \quad (7\text{-}91)$$

Thus, M_N for large N is estimated by the sample mean vector, and the dispersion is Σ/N.

Throughout this process, we notice that both *a priori* and *a posteriori* density functions are always normal. Because of this fact, we calculated only M_N and Σ_N recursively instead of calculating the density function. In general, when the *a posteriori* density function after each iteration is a member of the same family as the *a priori* density function and only the parameters of the density function change, we call the density functions a *conjugate or reproducing pair.*

In addition to its simplicity of computation, it has been shown that the reproducing density function of $\mathbf{\Theta}$ becomes more concentrated and converges toward the true parameter vector Θ in some appropriate sense as $N \to \infty$ [Spragins, 1963, 1965].

Many well-known density functions which are reproducing pairs are listed in a reference [Spragins, 1965].

Estimation of a Covariance Matrix with Zero Expected Vector

The successive estimation of a covariance matrix for a normally distributed random vector $\mathbf{X}$ can be discussed in the same manner as that of the expected vector. Here we assume that the expected vector is known and, without further loss of generality, that it is equal to zero. As we assumed, the *a priori* density function of $p(X/\Sigma)$ is normal. On the other hand, it is known that the sample covariance matrix has a Wishart distribution. Therefore, we start from the distribution of a sample covariance matrix $p(\Sigma/\Sigma_0, N_0)$ with N_0 as the number of samples and Σ_0 as the initial guess of the true covariance matrix. The term N_0 is the number of samples for the initial sample covariance matrix and may be considered as a confidence constant about the initial estimate of Σ_0. Furthermore, instead of calculating $p(\Sigma/\Sigma_0, N_0)$ let us compute $p(K/\Sigma_0, N,)$, where $K = \Sigma^{-1}$. The reason for doing this is that the covariance matrix is always used in the inverse form for a normal distribution. Then $p(K/\Sigma_0, N_0)$ is given by

$$p(K/\Sigma_0, N_0) = c(n, N_0) \,|\, \tfrac{1}{2}N_0\Sigma_0 \,|^{(N_0-1)/2} \,|\, K \,|^{(N_0-n-2)/2} \exp[-\tfrac{1}{2}\operatorname{tr}(N_0 \Sigma_0 K)] \tag{7-92}$$

where

$$c(n, N_0) = \left\{\pi^{n(n-1)/4} \prod_{i=1}^{n} \Gamma[(N_0 - i)/2]\right\}^{-1} \tag{7-93}$$

Using (7-92) as $p(\Theta)$ and applying (7-82) repeatedly, $p(K/X_1, \ldots, X_N)$ also becomes the Wishart distribution and the parameters of the Wishart distribution Σ_0 and N_0 are updated as follows [Keehn, 1965]:

$$\Sigma_N = \frac{\left[(1/N) \sum_{i=1}^{N} X_i X_i^T\right] + (N_0/N)\Sigma_0}{1 + (N_0/N)} \tag{7-94}$$

$$N_N = N_0 + N \tag{7-95}$$

Thus, as N increases, Σ_N approaches the sample covariance matrix $(1/N)\Sigma X_i X_i^T$ with zero-mean.

Estimation of a Expected Vector and Covariance Matrix

When both expected vector and covariance matrix are to be estimated successively, we have to calculate the joint *a posteriori* density function $p(M, \Sigma/X_1, \ldots, X_N)$. When M and Σ are estimated by the sample mean vector and sample covariance matrix and $\mathbf{X}$ is normally distributed, $p(M, K/M_0, \Sigma_0, \mu_0, N_0)$ $(K = \Sigma^{-1})$ is known to be the Gaussian–Wishart distribution as

$$\begin{aligned} p(M, K/M_0, \Sigma_0, \mu_0, N_0) &\\ = (2\pi)^{-n/2} \,|\, \mu_0 K \,|^{1/2} &\exp[-\tfrac{1}{2}\mu_0(M - M_0)^T K(M - M_0)] \\ &\times c(n, N_0) \,|\, \tfrac{1}{2}N_0\Sigma_0 \,|^{(N_0-1)/2} \,|\, K \,|^{(N_0-n-2)/2} \exp[-\tfrac{1}{2}\operatorname{tr}(N_0\Sigma_0 K)] \end{aligned} \tag{7-96}$$

where $c(n, N_0)$ is given in (7-93). The term μ_0 is the confidence constant about the initial estimate of M_0 as N_0 for Σ_0. Again, using (7-96) as $p(\Theta)$ and applying (7-82) repeatedly, $p(M, K/X_1, \ldots, X_N)$ becomes the Gaussian–Wishart distribution and the parameters of the distribution $M_0, \Sigma_0, \mu_0,$

and N_0 are updated as follows [Keehn, 1965]:

$$M_N = \frac{\left((1/N)\sum_{i=1}^{N} X_i\right) + (\mu_0/N)M_0}{1 + (\mu_0/N)} \tag{7-97}$$

$$\Sigma_N = \frac{1}{1 + (N_0/N)} \left\{\left[(1/N)\sum_{i=1}^{N} X_i X_i^T\right] - [1 + (\mu_0/N)]M_N M_N^T \right.$$
$$\left. + [(N_0/N)\Sigma_0 + (\mu_0/N)M_0 M_0^T]\right\} \tag{7-98}$$

$$\mu_N = \mu_0 + N \tag{7-99}$$

$$N_N = N_0 + N \tag{7-100}$$

Unsupervised Estimation

Suppose that we have two distributions characterized by Θ_1 and Θ_2. In successive unsupervised estimation, our task is to estimate Θ_1 and Θ_2 successively, assuming that we do not know the true distributions from which the incoming samples are taken. This is also termed *learning without a teacher*. Because of the additional ambiguity we impose, the computation of unsupervised estimation becomes more complex. However, the development of this kind of technique is motivated by the hope that the machine may improve the performance without any outside supervision after initial learning in a supervised mode.

Since we do not know the class of $\mathbf{X}_N$, our best guess is that $\mathbf{X}_N$ may belong to ω_i with probability $P(\omega_i)$ $(i = 1, 2)$, provided that we know $P(\omega_i)$. Therefore, the *a priori* density function of (7-82) becomes

$$\begin{aligned} p(X_N/ X_1, \ldots, X_{N-1}, \Theta_1, \Theta_2) &= \sum_{i=1}^{2} p(X_N/ X_1, \ldots, X_{N-1}, \Theta_1, \Theta_2, \omega_i)P(\omega_i) \\ &= \sum_{i=1}^{2} p(X_N/ X_1, \ldots, X_{N-1}, \Theta_i, \omega_i)P(\omega_i) \end{aligned} \tag{7-101}$$

Hence, if we know the *a priori* density function of each class $p(X_N/X_1, \ldots, X_{N-1}, \Theta_i, \omega_i)$ and the *a priori* class probability $P(\omega_i)$,$p(X_N/X_1, \ldots, X_{N-1}, \Theta_1, \Theta_2)$ can be computed by (7-101) and subsequently $p(X_N/X_1, \ldots, X_{N-1})$ by (7-83).

Thus we obtain a recursive expression for the *a posteriori* density function as

$$p(\Theta_1, \Theta_2/\ X_1, \ldots, X_N) = \frac{\sum_{i=1}^{2} p(X_N/\ X_1, \ldots, X_{N-1}, \Theta_i, \omega_i)P(\omega_i)}{p(X_N/\ X_1, \ldots, X_{N-1})} p(\Theta_1, \Theta_2/\ X_1, \ldots, X_{N-1}) \tag{7-102}$$

Therefore, as a concept, successive unsupervised estimation of (7-102) is the same as successive supervised estimation of (7-82). But because of the summation involved in the calculation of *a priori* density function, the reproducing property is lost for all density functions listed previously, including the normal distribution. This means that we cannot easily estimate a set of parameters so that we have to deal with the recursive estimation of multivariate functions.

Using all available samples at a time, there are more practical techniques available for unsupervised estimation and classification. The problem is stated as the method of finding the *clusters* of given samples and finding the natural boundaries of these clusters without knowing the classes of the samples. This problem will be discussed in Chapter 11.

Computer Projects

Write the following programs:

7-1 Generate samples one by one, according to Standard Data $i = 1, 2$ with $P(\omega_1) = P(\omega_2) = 0.5$. Find the linear classifier, by three successive adjustments. Find a way to detect the oscillation of the classifier around the steady state and show what kind of samples make this oscillation.

7-2 Repeat 7-1 for a linear classifier for the multiclass problem.
Data: Standard Data $i = 1, 2, 3, 4.$

$$P(\omega_1) = P(\omega_2) = P(\omega_3) = P(\omega_4) = 0.25$$

7-3 Repeat 7-1 by using the Robbins–Monro method.

7-4 Repeat 7-1 by using the Kiefer–Wolfowitz method.

7-5 Attach two acceleration programs to 7-3.

7-6 Attach two acceleration programs to 7-4.

Problems

7-1 Repeat Example 7-2 and 7-3 by using

(a) the absolute correction rule of (7-9);
(b) the gradient correction rule of (7-10).

7-2 Suppose that we have six samples from three classes as $(+1, 0)$, $(0, +1)$ for ω_1, $(-1, +1)$, $(-1, 0)$ for ω_2 and $(0, -1)$, $(+1, -1)$ for ω_3. Find a linear classifier to separate these three classes by a successive method.

7-3 In Chapter 4, we discussed a piecewise linear classifier. Propose an algorithm of successive adjustment for a piecewise linear classifier in a multiclass problem.

7-4 A regression function is given by $f = \theta^3$. Find the root of the regression function by the Robbins–Monro method starting from $\theta = 2$. Assume that the lth observation is $z_l = \theta_l^3 + (-0.3)^l$, where $(-0.3)^l$ is an additive noise.

7-5 A regression function is given by $f = -\theta^2$. Find the maximum point of the regression function by the Kiefer–Wolfowitz method. Assume that the observation is $\mathbf{z} = -\theta^2 + 0.3\mathbf{a}$, where $\mathbf{a}$ is either $+1$ or -1 depending on the face of a tossed coin.

7-6 Repeat the convergence proof of the Robbins–Monro method for the multivariate case.

7-7 Repeat Example 7-4 by using (4-74) so as to maximize (4-70). If the linear classifier does not converge to $a(x_1 + x_2) = 0$ (a is a positive constant), point out the problem of this procedure.

7-8 The term $\mathbf{x}$ is a random variable $+1$ or 0 with probability P or $(1 - P)$, respectively. Let $\mathbf{y}$ be the number of 1's out of N observations of $\mathbf{x}$. Then the *a priori* density function of $\mathbf{y}$, given P and N, is given by

$$\Pr\{\mathbf{y} = y / P, N\} = \binom{N}{y} P^y (1 - P)^{N-y},$$

which is a binomial distribution. Find the successive Bayes estimate of P. Also show that the binomial distribution is a reproducing pair. (Hint: Start from

$$p(P / y_0, N_0) = \binom{N_0}{y_0} P^{y_0} (1 - P)^{N_0 - y_0})$$

7-9 Let $\mathbf{x}$ be normally distributed with zero-mean and variance σ^2. Find the successive Bayes estimate of σ^2, assuming $\sigma_0{}^2$ as the initial estimate of σ^2 with the confidence constant N_0. (Hint: The sample variance with zero mean has the χ^2 distributions.)

7-10 Let $\mathbf{x}_i$ be a sample from the mixture of two normal distributions whose means and variances are given by 0 and σ^2 for ω_1 and m and σ^2 for ω_2. Assuming $P(\omega_1) = P(\omega_2) = 0.5$ find the successive unsupervised estimate of m when the first sample $\mathbf{x}_1$ is received. Is $p(m/x_1)$ normal? The mean of ω_1, 0, and both variances σ^2 are assumed to be known.

Chapter 8

FEATURE SELECTION AND LINEAR MAPPING FOR ONE DISTRIBUTION

Up to now we have discussed how to design a classifier to separate samples into two or more classes, assuming that the variables of these samples are already selected and given. Obviously, the selection of these variables is important and strongly affects classifier design. That is, if the variables show significant differences from one class to another, the classifier can be designed more easily with better performance. Therefore, the selection of variables is a key problem in pattern recognition and is termed *feature selection* or *feature extraction.*

Feature selection is generally considered a process of mapping the original measurements into more effective features. If the mapping is linear, the mapping function is well defined and our task is simply to find the coefficients of the linear function so as to maximize or minimize a criterion. Therefore, if we have the proper criterion for evaluating the effectiveness of features, we can use the well-developed techniques of linear algebra for simple criteria, or, in the case of a complex criterion, we can apply optimizing techniques to determine these mapping coefficients. Unfortunately, in many applications of pattern recognition, there are important features which are not linear functions of original measurements, but are highly nonlinear functions. Then, the basic problem is to find a proper nonlinear mapping function for the given data. Since we do not have any general theory to generate mapping functions systematically and to find the optimum one, the selection of features becomes very much problem oriented. Some of these problems will be discussed in Chapter 10.

In this and in the next chapter, we will discuss criteria for measuring feature effectiveness. Since linear mappings are based on these criteria, we discuss linear mappings as well as the criteria. In this chapter, we deal with features of one distribution. Since the evaluation of eigenvalues and eigenvectors is the central problem for one distribution, we will discuss their estimation in this chapter. In the next chapter we will extend the discussion to two or more classes, and features will be evaluated by their effectiveness on class separability.

8.1 The Discrete Karhunen–Loève Expansion

First, let us discuss feature selection for one distribution. With only one distribution, we cannot discuss class separability, which actually is the problem in pattern recognition. Instead, we discuss how closely we can represent samples of a distribution with a set of features. If a small set of features are found to represent the samples accurately, we may say that these features are effective. Although this problem is not directly related to pattern classification, knowledge of the characteristics of individual distributions

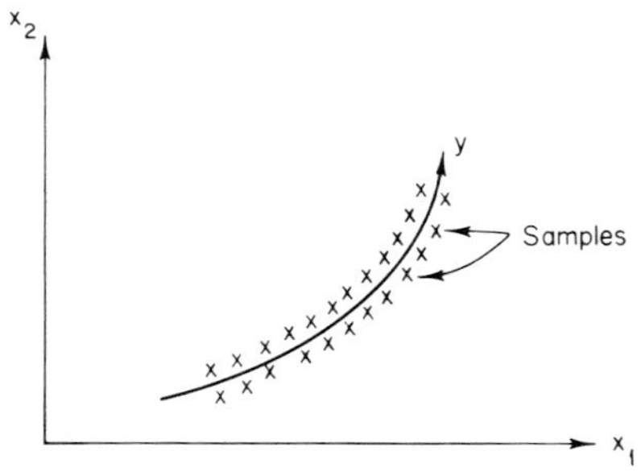

Fig. 8-1 Nonlinear mapping.

should help to separate one distribution from others. Also, feature selection for one distribution has wide applications in other areas, such as signal representation and data compression in communication systems.

Another limitation stems from the fact that we seek only features which can be obtained by a linear transformation of the original variables. Figure 8-1 shows that a new feature $\mathbf{y}$ is very effective in representing the given samples, but that $\mathbf{y}$ is a nonlinear function of $\mathbf{x}_1$ and $\mathbf{x}_2$.

Minimum Mean-Square Error

Let $\mathbf{X}$ be an n-dimensional random vector. Then $\mathbf{X}$ can be represented without error by an expansion of the form

$$\mathbf{X} = \sum_{i=1}^{n} \mathbf{y}_i \Phi_i = \Phi \mathbf{Y} \tag{8-1}$$

where

$$\Phi = [\Phi_1 \cdots \Phi_n] \tag{8-2}$$

and

$$\mathbf{Y} = [\mathbf{y}_1 \cdots \mathbf{y}_n]^T \tag{8-3}$$

The matrix Φ is deterministic and is made up of n linearly independent column vectors, that is,

$$|\Phi| \neq 0 \tag{8-4}$$

Thus, the columns of Φ span the n-dimensional space containing $\mathbf{X}$ and are called *basis vectors*. Furthermore, we may assume that the columns of Φ form an orthonormal set, that is,

$$\Phi_i^T \Phi_j = \begin{cases} 1 & (i = j) \\ 0 & (i \neq j) \end{cases} \tag{8-5}$$

If the orthonormality condition is satisfied, then the components of $\mathbf{Y}$ are given by

$$\mathbf{y}_i = \Phi_i^T \mathbf{X} \qquad (i = 1, \ldots, n) \tag{8-6}$$

Therefore, $\mathbf{Y}$ is simply an orthonormal transformation of the random vector $\mathbf{X}$, and is itself a random vector. Each component of $\mathbf{Y}$ is a feature which contributes to representing the observed vector $\mathbf{X}$.

Suppose that we determine only $m(<n)$ components of $\mathbf{Y}$ and that we still want to, at least, estimate $\mathbf{X}$. We can do this by replacing those compo-

nents of **Y** which we do not calculate with preselected constants and form the following estimate:

$$\hat{\mathbf{X}}(m) = \sum_{i=1}^{m} \mathbf{y}_i \Phi_i + \sum_{i=m+1}^{n} b_i \Phi_i \tag{8-7}$$

We lose no generality by assuming that only the first m **y**'s are calculated. If we do not use all of our features, then we introduce a representation error which is given by

$$\Delta\mathbf{X}(m) = \mathbf{X} - \hat{\mathbf{X}}(m) = \mathbf{X} - \sum_{i=1}^{m} \mathbf{y}_i \Phi_i - \sum_{i=m+1}^{n} b_i \Phi_i = \sum_{i=m+1}^{n} (\mathbf{y}_i - b_i)\Phi_i \tag{8-8}$$

Note that both $\hat{\mathbf{X}}$ and $\Delta\mathbf{X}$ are random vectors. We will use the mean-square magnitude of $\Delta\mathbf{X}$ as a criterion to measure the effectiveness of the subset of m features. We have

$$\begin{aligned} \bar{\varepsilon}^2(m) &= E\{\| \Delta\mathbf{X}(m) \|^2\} \\ &= E\left\{ \sum_{i=m+1}^{n} \sum_{j=m+1}^{n} (\mathbf{y}_i - b_i)(\mathbf{y}_j - b_j)\Phi_i^T\Phi_j \right\} \\ &= \sum_{i=m+1}^{n} E\{(\mathbf{y}_i - b_i)^2\} \end{aligned} \tag{8-9}$$

For every choice of basis vectors and constant terms, we obtain a value for $\bar{\varepsilon}^2(m)$. We would like to make the choice which minimizes $\bar{\varepsilon}^2(m)$.

The optimum choice for b_i is given by

$$b_i = E\{\mathbf{y}_i\} = \Phi_i^T E\{\mathbf{X}\} \tag{8-10}$$

That is, we should replace those $\mathbf{y}_i$'s which we do not measure by their expected values. This is easily shown by minimizing $\bar{\varepsilon}^2(m)$ with respect to b_i as follows:

$$\frac{\partial}{\partial b_i} E\{(\mathbf{y}_i - b_i)^2\} = -2[E\{\mathbf{y}_i\} - b_i] = 0 \tag{8-11}$$

Now, the mean-square error can be written as

$$\begin{aligned} \bar{\varepsilon}^2(m) &= \sum_{i=m+1}^{n} E[(\mathbf{y}_i - E\{\mathbf{y}_i\})^2] \\ &= \sum_{i=m+1}^{n} \Phi_i^T E[(\mathbf{X} - E\{\mathbf{X}\})(\mathbf{X} - E\{\mathbf{X}\})^T]\Phi_i \\ &= \sum_{i=m+1}^{n} \Phi_i^T \Sigma_{\mathbf{X}} \Phi_i \end{aligned} \tag{8-12}$$

where $\Sigma_{\mathbf{X}}$ is, by definition, the covariance matrix of **X**. We shall presently show that the optimum choice for the Φ's is those which satisfy

$$\Sigma_{\mathbf{X}}\Phi_i = \lambda_i\Phi_i \tag{8-13}$$

that is, the eigenvectors of $\Sigma_{\mathbf{X}}$. Thus, the minimum mean-square error is

$$\bar{\varepsilon}^2(m)_{\text{opt}} = \sum_{i=m+1}^{n} \lambda_i \tag{8-14}$$

The expansion of a random vector in the eigenvectors of the covariance matrix is the discrete version of *the Karhunen–Loève expansion.*

In the context of pattern recognition, the coefficients $\mathbf{y}_1, \ldots \mathbf{y}_n$, in the expansion are viewed as features representing the observed vector **X**. These features have several attractive properties which we can list.

(1) The effectiveness of each feature, in terms of representing **X**, is determined by its corresponding eigenvalue. If a feature, say $\mathbf{y}_i$ is deleted, then the mean-square error increases by λ_i. Therefore, the feature with the smallest eigenvalue should be deleted first, and so on. If the eigenvalues are indexed such that

$$\lambda_1 > \lambda_2 > \cdots > \lambda_n > 0 \tag{8-15}$$

then the features should be ordered in the same manner.

(2) The features are mutually uncorrelated, that is, the covariance matrix of **Y** is diagonal. This follows since

$$\Sigma_{\mathbf{y}} = \Phi^T\Sigma_{\mathbf{X}}\Phi = \begin{bmatrix} \lambda_1 & & & 0 \\ & \lambda_2 & & \\ & & \ddots & \\ 0 & & & \lambda_n \end{bmatrix} = \Lambda \tag{8-16}$$

In the special case where **X** is normally distributed, the $\mathbf{y}_i$'s are mutually independent.

(3) The eivenvectors of $\Sigma_{\mathbf{X}}$ minimize $\bar{\varepsilon}^2(m)$ over all choices of orthonormal basis vectors. Linear transformations which are not orthonormal are not considered in this chapter. In the case of representing a single distribution, we are concerned only with transformations which preserve the structure of the distribution.

PROOF OF (3) Suppose we expand $\mathbf{X}$ in the columns of another orthonormal matrix Ψ. Consider the matrix

$$H = \Psi^T \Sigma_{\mathbf{X}} \Psi \tag{8-17}$$

The ith diagonal element of H is given by

$$h_{ii} = \Psi_i^T \Sigma_{\mathbf{X}} \Psi_i \tag{8-18}$$

Suppose we partition H as

$$H = \begin{bmatrix} \overbrace{H_{11}}^{m} & \overbrace{H_{12}}^{n-m} \\ H_{12}^T & H_{22} \end{bmatrix} \begin{matrix} \}\, m \\ \}\, n-m \end{matrix} \tag{8-19}$$

Then, the mean-square error committed when we measure only m components of $\mathbf{Y}$ is given by

$$\bar{\varepsilon}^2(m) = \text{tr}\, H_{22} \tag{8-20}$$

because of (8-12) which was derived using only the orthonormal condition of Φ_i. The object of this proof is to show that $\bar{\varepsilon}^2(m)$ of (8-20) is bounded from below by $\bar{\varepsilon}^2(m)_{\text{opt}}$ of (8-14). Let Φ and Λ be the eigenvector and eigenvalue matrices, respectively, of $\Sigma_{\mathbf{X}}$. Then we can write

$$H = (\Psi^T \Phi) \Lambda (\Phi^T \Psi) \tag{8-21}$$

Since both Ψ and Φ are orthonormal, then so is $\Psi^T \Phi$ because

$$(\Psi^T \Phi)^T (\Psi^T \Phi) = (\Psi^T \Phi)(\Psi^T \Phi)^T = I \tag{8-22}$$

We can again partition H of (8-21) so that

$$H = \begin{matrix} m\, \{ \\ n-m\, \{ \end{matrix} \begin{bmatrix} \overbrace{K_1}^{m} & \overbrace{K_2}^{n-m} \\ K_3 & K_4 \end{bmatrix} \begin{bmatrix} \overbrace{\Lambda_1}^{m} & \overbrace{0}^{n-m} \\ 0 & \Lambda_2 \end{bmatrix} \begin{bmatrix} K_1^T & K_3^T \\ K_2^T & K_4^T \end{bmatrix} \tag{8-23}$$

and it follows that

$$\bar{\varepsilon}^2(m) = \text{tr}\, H_{22} = \text{tr}(K_3 \Lambda_1 K_3^T + K_4 \Lambda_2 K_4^T) \tag{8-24}$$

Then the essence of our proof is to show that

$$\text{tr}\, \Lambda_2 \leq \text{tr}(K_3 \Lambda_1 K_3^T + K_4 \Lambda_2 K_4^T) \tag{8-25}$$

From the orthonormality of $K = \Psi^T\Phi$, we have the following identities:

$$K_1K_1^T + K_2K_2^T = I \tag{8-26}$$

$$K_1^TK_1 + K_3^TK_3 = I \tag{8-27}$$

$$K_2^TK_2 + K_4^TK_4 = I \tag{8-28}$$

The proof proceeds as

$$\begin{aligned}
\mathrm{tr}(K_3\Lambda_1K_3^T + K_4\Lambda_2K_4^T) &= \mathrm{tr}(\Lambda_1K_3^TK_3 + \Lambda_2K_4^TK_4) \\
&= \mathrm{tr}\,\Lambda_2 + \mathrm{tr}(\Lambda_1K_3^TK_3 - \Lambda_2K_2^TK_2) \\
&\geq \mathrm{tr}\,\Lambda_2 + \{\lambda_m\,\mathrm{tr}(K_3^TK_3) - \lambda_{m+1}\,\mathrm{tr}(K_2^TK_2)\} \\
&= \mathrm{tr}\,\Lambda_2 + \{\lambda_m\,\mathrm{tr}(I - K_1^TK_1) - \lambda_{m+1}\,\mathrm{tr}(I - K_1K_1^T)] \\
&= \mathrm{tr}\,\Lambda_2 + (\lambda_m - \lambda_{m+1})\,\mathrm{tr}(I - K_1^TK_1) = \mathrm{tr}\,\Lambda_2 + (\lambda_m - \lambda_{m+1})\,\mathrm{tr}\,K_3^TK_3 \\
&\geq \mathrm{tr}\,\Lambda_2
\end{aligned} \tag{8-29}$$

The first inequality follows from the fact that λ_m is the smallest eigenvalue of Λ_1 and λ_{m+1} is the largest eigenvalue of Λ_2. We have made extensive use of the matrix identity $\mathrm{tr}(AB) = \mathrm{tr}(BA)$ and the identities (8-26) through (8-28). Detailed confirmation of (8-29) is left as an exercise. When $\Psi = \Phi$, we have $K_1 = K_4 = I$ and $K_2 = K_3 = 0$, so that the equality holds. Thus, the proof is completed.

In order to give some feeling for the Karhunen–Loève expansion, two simple examples are given here.

Example 8-1 Let us examine two sets of data as shown in Fig. 8-2a and b. The expected vectors are zero in both cases. First, we calculate the

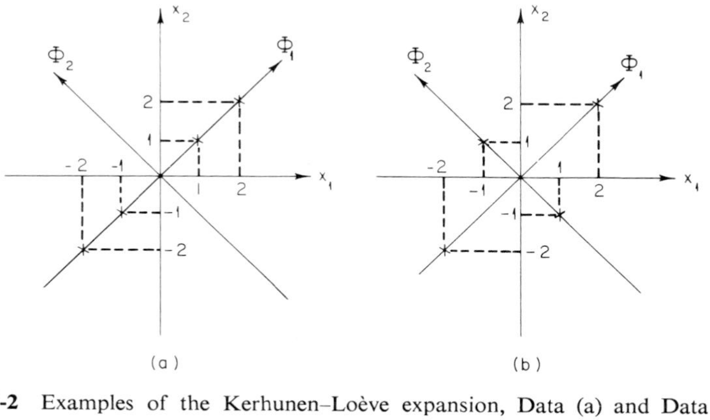

Fig. 8-2 Examples of the Kerhunen–Loève expansion, Data (a) and Data (b).

sample covariance matrix $\Sigma_{\mathbf{X}}$.

$$\Sigma_{\mathbf{X}a} = \tfrac{1}{4}\sum_{i=1}^{4} X_i X_i^T = \frac{1}{4}\left\{\begin{bmatrix}1\\1\end{bmatrix}[1 \quad 1] + \begin{bmatrix}2\\2\end{bmatrix}[2 \quad 2] + \begin{bmatrix}-1\\-1\end{bmatrix}[-1 \quad -1] + \begin{bmatrix}-2\\-2\end{bmatrix}[-2 \quad -2]\right\}$$

$$= \begin{bmatrix}\frac{10}{4} & \frac{10}{4}\\ \frac{10}{4} & \frac{10}{4}\end{bmatrix} \quad \text{[for Data (a)]} \tag{8-30}$$

$$\Sigma_{\mathbf{X}b} = \tfrac{1}{4}\sum_{i=1}^{4} X_i X_i^T = \frac{1}{4}\left\{\begin{bmatrix}-1\\+1\end{bmatrix}[-1 \quad +1] + \begin{bmatrix}2\\2\end{bmatrix}[2 \quad 2] + \begin{bmatrix}+1\\-1\end{bmatrix}[+1 \quad -1] + \begin{bmatrix}-2\\-2\end{bmatrix}[-2 \quad -2]\right\}$$

$$= \begin{bmatrix}\frac{10}{4} & \frac{6}{4}\\ \frac{6}{4} & \frac{10}{4}\end{bmatrix} \quad \text{[for Data (b)]} \tag{8-31}$$

Secondly, we calculate the eigenvalues and eigenvectors of $\Sigma_{\mathbf{X}}$.

$$\lambda_{1a} = 5, \qquad \lambda_{2a} = 0$$

$$\Phi_{1a} = \begin{bmatrix}1/\sqrt{2}\\1/\sqrt{2}\end{bmatrix}, \qquad \Phi_{2a} = \begin{bmatrix}-1/\sqrt{2}\\1/\sqrt{2}\end{bmatrix} \quad \text{[for Data (a)]} \tag{8-32}$$

$$\lambda_{1b} = 4, \qquad \lambda_{2b} = 1$$

$$\Phi_{1b} = \begin{bmatrix}1/\sqrt{2}\\1/\sqrt{2}\end{bmatrix}, \qquad \Phi_{2b} = \begin{bmatrix}-1/\sqrt{2}\\1/\sqrt{2}\end{bmatrix} \quad \text{[for Data (b)]} \tag{8-33}$$

Thus, for both cases, the basis vectors become 45° lines, as shown in Fig. 8-2.

Finally, let us consider the effect of eliminating one of these basis vectors. For Data (a), $\lambda_{2a} = 0$. Therefore, even if we eliminate Φ_2 in the Karhunen–Loève expansion, the mean-square error should be zero. Figure 8-2a shows that all four points can be expressed by the first basis vector Φ_1 without error. On the other hand, for Data (b), $\lambda_{2b} = 1$. Therefore, we expect a mean-square error of 1 in eliminating Φ_2 in the expansion. From Fig. 8-2b, we see that $X_2 = [2 \quad 2]^T$ and $X_4 = [-2 \quad -2]^T$ can be expressed by Φ_1 only without error, but $X_1 = [-1 \quad 1]^T$ and $X_3 = [1 \quad -1]^T$ have errors of $\sqrt{2}$. Therefore, the mean-square error is $(0^2 + 0^2 + \sqrt{2}^2 + \sqrt{2}^2)/4 = 1$, which equals λ_{2b}.

Normalization Problem

In the Karhunen–Loève expansion, we decide whether we select an eigenvector or not by observing the corresponding eigenvalue. However, the absolute value of the eigenvalue does not give adequate information for selection. The ratio of the eigenvalue to the summation of the eigenvalues expresses what the percentage of the mean-square error introduced by eliminating the corresponding eigenvector. Thus, we may use

$$\mu_i = \lambda_i \Big/ \Big(\sum_{j=1}^{n} \lambda_j\Big) = \lambda_i/(\operatorname{tr} \Sigma_{\mathbf{X}}) \tag{8-34}$$

as a criterion for retaining or deleting the ith eigenvector.
Note that

$$\sum_{i=1}^{n} \mu_i = 1 \tag{8-35}$$

Sometimes the samples are normalized prior to application of the Karhunen–Loève expansion. The magnitude-normalized vector $\mathbf{Z}$ is given by

$$\mathbf{Z} = (\mathbf{X} - M)/\| \mathbf{X} - M \| \tag{8-36}$$

so that

$$\| \mathbf{Z} \| = 1 \tag{8-37}$$

Let $\Sigma_{\mathbf{Z}}$ and λ_i' be the covariance matrix of $\mathbf{Z}$ and its eigenvalues. Then the summation of λ_i' is

$$\sum_{i=1}^{n} \lambda_i' = \operatorname{tr} \Sigma_{\mathbf{Z}} = E\{\mathbf{Z}^T\mathbf{Z}\} = 1 \tag{8-38}$$

That is, the λ_i''s are the normalized eigenvalues. However, the transformation of (8-36) must be justified by some physical aspect of the problem. The statistical properties of $\mathbf{Z}$, including the covariance matrix, are entirely different from those of $\mathbf{X}$. Thus, application of the Karhunen–Loève expansion to $\mathbf{Z}$ produce completely different eigenvectors and, therefore, completely different features, than for $\mathbf{X}$.

8.2 Other Criteria for One Distribution

In addition to the mean-square error of approximation, there are some other criteria for evaluating features for one distribution. In this section, we will discuss two typical criteria: scatter measure and entropy [Tou, 1967].

Scatter Measure

One measure of scatter is the expected value of squared between-sample distances, which is given by

$$\bar{d}_{\mathbf{X}}^2 = E\{\| \mathbf{X}_i - \mathbf{X}_j \|^2\} = E\{\mathbf{X}_i^T\mathbf{X}_i + \mathbf{X}_j^T\mathbf{X}_j\} - E\{\mathbf{X}_i^T X_j + \mathbf{X}_j^T\mathbf{X}_i\} \quad (8\text{-}39)$$

where $\mathbf{X}_i$ and $\mathbf{X}_j$ are mutually independent sample vectors taken from a single distribution. By virtue of the independence property, (8-39) becomes

$$\begin{aligned} \bar{d}_{\mathbf{X}}^2 &= 2E\{\mathbf{X}^T\mathbf{X}\} - 2E\{\mathbf{X}^T\}E\{\mathbf{X}\} = 2 \operatorname{tr}[E\{\mathbf{X}\mathbf{X}^T\} - MM^T] \\ &= 2 \operatorname{tr}(S - MM^T) = 2 \operatorname{tr} \Sigma_{\mathbf{X}} \end{aligned} \quad (8\text{-}40)$$

where S and $\Sigma_{\mathbf{X}}$ are the autocorrelation and covariance matrices and M is the expected vector of the distribution.

Let $\mathbf{Y}$ be related to $\mathbf{X}$ by an orthonormal transformation matrix Ψ, that is,

$$\mathbf{Y} = \Psi^T\mathbf{X} \quad (8\text{-}41)$$

The random vector $\mathbf{Y}$ has the same scatter as $\mathbf{X}$ since

$$\bar{d}_{\mathbf{Y}}^2 = 2 \operatorname{tr} \Sigma_{\mathbf{Y}} = 2 \operatorname{tr} \Psi^T\Sigma_{\mathbf{X}}\Psi = 2 \operatorname{tr} \Sigma_{\mathbf{X}} \quad (8\text{-}42)$$

Equation (8-42) follows from the orthonormality of Ψ. We restrict ourselves to orthonormal transformations because of their distance preserving property. Scatter, which from (8-39) is based on distances, can be made arbitrarily large or small by general linear transformations and, thereby, lose its meaning.

We can also write $\bar{d}_{\mathbf{Y}}^2$ as a summation of the contributions of each component of $\mathbf{Y}$:

$$\bar{d}_{\mathbf{Y}}^2 = 2 \sum_{i=1}^{n} \Psi_i^T\Sigma_{\mathbf{X}}\Psi_i \quad (8\text{-}43)$$

where Ψ_i is the ith column of Ψ (using (8-41)). (The reader can verify that the ith term of (8-43) is the scatter of $\mathbf{y}_i$). If only $m(m < n)$ components of $\mathbf{Y}$ are considered, their scatter is given by

$$\bar{d}_{\mathbf{Y}}^2(m) = 2 \sum_{i=1}^{m} \Psi_i\Sigma_{\mathbf{X}}\Psi_i \quad (8\text{-}44)$$

Now the feature selection problem may be stated in terms of choosing orthonormal vectors $\Psi_1, \ldots, \Psi_m$ so as to maximize $\bar{d}_{\mathbf{Y}}^2(m)$. But from (8-12) and the proof of the optimality of the Karhunen–Loève expansion,

$\Psi_1, \ldots, \Psi_m$ should again be the dominant eigenvectors of $\Sigma_{\mathbf{X}}$. Thus we can conclude:

(1) The dominant eigenvectors of $\Sigma_{\mathbf{X}}$ are the optimum features among all orthonormal transformations with respect to the scatter criterion $\bar{d}^2$.

(2) From (8-43) or (8-44), the contribution of each feature to the total scatter is twice the value of the corresponding eigenvalue.

Population Entropy

The population entropy can be used as a measure of diversity of a distribution, and is defined by

$$h = -E\{\ln p(\mathbf{X})\} \tag{8-45}$$

When the components of **X** are independent, h can be expressed as the summation of the entropies of individual variables.

$$h = -\sum_{i=1}^{n} E\{\ln p(\mathbf{x}_i)\} \tag{8-46}$$

The entropy is a far more complex criterion than the previous two criteria because the density function of **X** is involved.

Again, feature selection consists of finding features so as to maximize h for a given $m (m < n)$. As with the scatter measure, we should limit ourselves to structure-preserving transformations.

Some special cases are given as examples:

EXAMPLE 8-2 When the distribution of **X** is normal, h of (8-45) becomes

$$\begin{aligned} h &= -\int_{\mathscr{S}} (2\pi)^{-n/2} |\Sigma|^{-1/2} \exp\{-\tfrac{1}{2}(X-M)^T\Sigma^{-1}(X-M)\} \\ &\quad \times \{-\tfrac{1}{2}(X-M)^T\Sigma^{-1}(X-M) - \tfrac{1}{2}\ln|\Sigma| - \tfrac{1}{2}n\ln(2\pi)\}\, dX \\ &= \tfrac{1}{2}n + \tfrac{1}{2}\ln|\Sigma| + \tfrac{1}{2}n\ln(2\pi) \end{aligned} \tag{8-47}$$

which is simply a function of $|\Sigma|$. If we select the eigenvectors of Σ as features, (8-47) becomes

$$h = \tfrac{1}{2}\sum_{i=1}^{n} \{1 + \ln\lambda_i + \ln(2\pi)\} \tag{8-48}$$

Thus the effect of individual features on h can be evaluated by $\frac{1}{2}\{1 + \ln(\lambda_i) + \ln(2\pi)\}$ independently.

EXAMPLE 8-3 When components of $\mathbf{X}$ are binary and independent, h of (8-46) becomes

$$h = -\sum_{i=1}^{n} \{P_i \ln P_i + (1 - P_i) \ln(1 - P_i)\} \tag{8-49}$$

where P_i is the probability of $\mathbf{x}_i = +1$. Thus, individual variables $\mathbf{x}_i$ are evaluated by $-\{P_i \ln P_i + (1 - P_i) \ln(1 - P_i)\}$. When the inputs are not independent, we may use the Bahadur expansion of Chapter 6 as the approximation of $p(X)$ of (8-45). Obviously, h becomes much more complex.

General Remarks Regarding Feature Selection for One Distribution

In the foregoing discussion, we have dealt exclusively with orthonormal linear transformations. This is necessary in order to maintain the structure of the distribution. It is easy to show that, for a given distribution, we can cause one eigenvalue to dominate the others by an arbitrary amount simply by changing the scales. But unless we are given some physical reason to introduce such distortion, we would only be performing a mathematical maneuver, and the results would be highly questionable.

Let us also consider the type of criteria we have used. Both the mean-square error and scatter measure were the expected values of some quadratic functions of the variables. For this reason, our features are all given in terms of the second-order statistics of the distribution. The only second-order statistics are the covariance and autocorrelation matrices. The eigenvalues of these matrices are invariant under linear orthonormal transformations.

In the statistical literature, the above is generally called *factor analysis* or *principle components analysis.*

On the other hand, when we discuss feature selection for classifying two or more distributions, we will allow a more general class of transformations. This is because the class separability, for example the probability of error due to the Bayes classifier, is invariant under any nonsingular transformations. These transformations preserve the structure of these distributions as far as classification is concerned.

In this section, we concluded that the optimum basis vectors of the Karhunen–Loève expansion are the eigenvectors of the covariance matrix of a given distribution. However, it should be pointed out that even if we select the eigenvectors of the autocorrelation matrix as the basis vectors of the expansion for some reason, the discussion is exactly the same as for the covariance matrix. The eigenvalue of the autocorrelation matrix represents the mean-square error due to the elimination of the corresponding eigenvector from the expansion.

8.3 The Karhunen–Loève Expansion for Random Processes

Random Processes and Their Expansion

Since the Karhunen–Loève expansion originally was developed and discussed to represent a random process, in this section we relate our previous discussion to the case of random processes and also add some specific properties of the expansion for random processes.

A random process $\mathbf{x}(t)$, defined in a time domain $(0, T)$, can be expressed in a linear combination of basis functions.

$$\mathbf{x}(t) = \sum_{i=1}^{\infty} \mathbf{y}_i \varphi_i(t) \qquad (0 \leq t \leq T) \tag{8-50}$$

where the *basis functions* $\varphi_i(t)$ are deterministic time functions and the coefficients $\mathbf{y}_i$ are random variables. An infinite number of $\varphi_i(t)$ are required in order to form *a complete set*. Therefore, the summation is taken to ∞. The orthonormal condition of $\varphi_i(t)$ is given by

$$\int_0^T \varphi_i(t)\varphi_j^*(t)\,dt = \delta_{ij} \tag{8-51}$$

where $\varphi_j^*(t)$ is the complex conjugate of $\varphi_j(t)$. If $\varphi_j(t)$ is a real function, $\varphi_j^*(t)$ becomes $\varphi_j(t)$. The inverse operation to calculate $\mathbf{y}_i$ from $\mathbf{x}(t)$ is

$$\int_0^T \mathbf{x}(t)\varphi_i^*(t)\,dt = \mathbf{y}_i \tag{8-52}$$

The expected value, autocorrelation, and covariance functions of $\mathbf{x}(t)$ are defined by

$$m(t) = E\{\mathbf{x}(t)\} \tag{8-53}$$

$$R(t, \tau) = E\{\mathbf{x}(t)\mathbf{x}^*(\tau)\} \tag{8-54}$$

$$C(t, \tau) = E[\{\mathbf{x}(t) - m(t)\}\{\mathbf{x}(\tau) - m(\tau)\}^*] \tag{8-55}$$

For simplicity's sake let us assume $m(t) = 0$, $0 \leq t \leq T$. If $\varphi_i(t)$ are the *eigenfunctions* of $R(t, \tau)$, then they must satisfy the following integral equation:

$$\int_0^T R(t, \tau)\varphi_i(\tau)\,d\tau = \lambda_i\varphi_i(t) \qquad (i = 1, 2, \ldots) \tag{8-56}$$

where the λ_i's are the *eigenvalues* of $R(t, \tau)$.

These equations are exactly the same as the ones for random vectors. Suppose we take n time-sampled values of these time functions and convert them to vectors as

$$\mathbf{X} = [\mathbf{x}(t_1)\ \mathbf{x}(t_2)\ \cdots\ \mathbf{x}(t_n)]^T \tag{8-57}$$

$$\Phi_i = [\varphi_i(t_1)\ \varphi_i(t_2)\ \cdots\ \varphi_i(t_n)]^T \tag{8-58}$$

where each time-sampled value of $\mathbf{x}(t)$, $\mathbf{x}(t_i)$, is a random variable. Then, for example, (8-51) and (8-56) can be rewritten as follows:

$$\sum_{k=1}^{n} \varphi_i(t_k)\varphi_j^*(t_k) = \Phi_i^T\Phi_j^* = \delta_{ij} \tag{8-59}$$

and

$$\sum_{k=1}^{n} R(t_l, t_k)\varphi_i(t_k) = \lambda_i\varphi_i(t_l) \qquad (i, l = 1, 2, \ldots, n) \tag{8-60}$$

Equation (8-60) can be rewritten in matrix form to define the eigenvalues and eigenvectors as

$$S\Phi_i = \lambda_i\Phi_i \qquad (i = 1, 2, \ldots, n) \tag{8-61}$$

where S is

$$S = \begin{bmatrix} R(t_1, t_1) & \cdots & R(t_1, t_n) \\ \vdots & & \vdots \\ R(t_n, t_1) & \cdots & R(t_n, t_n) \end{bmatrix}$$

$$= \begin{bmatrix} E\{\mathbf{x}(t_1)\mathbf{x}^*(t_1)\} & \cdots & E\{\mathbf{x}(t_1)\mathbf{x}^*(t_n)\} \\ \vdots & & \vdots \\ E\{\mathbf{x}(t_n)\mathbf{x}^*(t_1)\} & \cdots & E\{\mathbf{x}(t_n)\mathbf{x}^*(t_n)\} \end{bmatrix} \tag{8-62}$$

Since S is an $n \times n$ matrix, we can obtain only n eigenvalues and eigenvectors instead of an infinite number.

In order to minimize the mean-square error in the continuous version, we can follow a procedure similar to the one for the discrete case. For orthonormal $\varphi_i(t)$'s,

$$\bar{\varepsilon}^2 = E\left[\int_0^T \left\{\mathbf{x}(t) - \sum_{i=1}^{m} \mathbf{y}_i\varphi_i(t)\right\}\left\{\mathbf{x}(t) - \sum_{i=1}^{m} \mathbf{y}_i\varphi_i(t)\right\}^* dt\right]$$

$$= E\left[\int_0^T \left\{\sum_{i=m+1}^{\infty} \mathbf{y}_i\varphi_i(t)\right\}\left\{\sum_{i=m+1}^{\infty} \mathbf{y}_i\varphi_i(t)\right\}^* dt\right]$$

$$= \sum_{i=m+1}^{\infty} E\{\mathbf{y}_i\mathbf{y}_i^*\} \tag{8-63}$$

From (8-52), $E\{\mathbf{y}_i\mathbf{y}_i^*\}$ can be calculated by

$$E\{\mathbf{y}_i\mathbf{y}_i^*\} = \int_0^T \int_0^T E\{\mathbf{x}(t)\mathbf{x}^*(\tau)\}\varphi_i^*(t)\varphi_i(\tau)\,dt\,d\tau$$

$$= \int_0^T \int_0^T R(t, \tau)\varphi_i(\tau)\varphi_i^*(t)\,d\tau\,dt \tag{8-64}$$

Therefore, if the $\varphi_i(t)$'s are the eigenfunctions of $R(t, \tau)$,

$$E\{\mathbf{y}_i\mathbf{y}_i^*\} = \int_0^T \lambda_i\varphi_i(t)\varphi_i^*(t)\,dt = \lambda_i \tag{8-65}$$

Hence

$$\bar{\varepsilon}^2 = \sum_{i=m+1}^{\infty} \lambda_i \tag{8-66}$$

Recalling our assumption that $E\{\mathbf{x}(t)\} = 0$ and therefore $E\{\mathbf{y}_i\} = 0$, the result is the same as the one for the discrete version of the Karhunen–Loève expansion.

The difficulty in the continuous Karhunen–Loève expansion is that we have to solve the integral equation of (8-56) in order to obtain eigenvalues and eigenvectors. Except in very special cases, explicit solutions are hard to obtain. Therefore, in order to get the solution numerically, we have to go to the discrete version; that is, take time-samples values, calculate the autocorrelation matrix, and find the eigenvalues and eigenvectors.

Stationary Process

For simplicity's sake, the stationary condition is imposed for many cases of discussing random processes. A random process is called *stationary in the strict sense*, if $\mathbf{x}(t)$ and $\mathbf{x}(t + \varepsilon)$ have the same statistics for any ε. However, since this condition is too strict, we introduce a weaker condition which can be satisfied by a wider range of random processes. That is, a random process is called *stationary in the wide sense*, if the following two conditions are satisfied:

$$m(t) = m \qquad \text{(constant)} \tag{8-67}$$

$$R(t, \tau) = R(t - \tau) \tag{8-68}$$

Unless otherwise stated, we will use "stationary" for "stationary in the wide sense". Also, we will continue to assume $m = 0$. Since our discussion is quite specific, the reader should consult more general texts on random processes for background.

For stationary processes, the integral equation of (8-56) becomes

$$\int_{-T/2}^{T/2} R(t-\tau)\varphi_i(\tau)\,d\tau = \lambda_i \varphi_i(t) \qquad (-T/2 \leq t \leq T/2) \tag{8-69}$$

where the time region is shifted from [0, T] to [$-T/2$, $T/2$]. Let us extend T to ∞. Then (8-69) becomes

$$\int_{-\infty}^{+\infty} R(t-\tau)\varphi_i(\tau)\,d\tau = \lambda_i \varphi_i(t) \qquad (-\infty \leq t \leq +\infty) \tag{8-70}$$

Since (8-70) is the convolution integral of $R(t)$ and $\varphi_i(t)$, the Fourier transform of this equation becomes

$$\mathscr{S}(\omega)\mathbf{\Phi}_i(j\omega) = \lambda_i \mathbf{\Phi}_i(j\omega) \tag{8-71}$$

where $\mathscr{S}(\omega)$ and $\mathbf{\Phi}_i(j\omega)$ are the Fourier transform of $R(t)$ and $\varphi_i(t)$. Particularly, $\mathscr{S}(\omega)$, the Fourier transform of the autocorrelation function of a random process, is known as the *power spectrum* of the random process $\mathbf{x}(t)$. In order to satisfy (8-71), $\mathbf{\Phi}_i(j\omega)$ should be an impulse function

$$\mathbf{\Phi}_i(j\omega) = \delta(\omega - \omega_i) \tag{8-72}$$

which corresponds to, in the time domain,

$$\varphi_i(t) = \exp(j\omega_i t) \tag{8-73}$$

Then (8-71) becomes

$$\mathscr{S}(\omega_i) = \lambda_i \tag{8-74}$$

Thus, we conclude that the eigenfunctions are complex sinusoidals and the eigenvalues are the power spectrum, if the random process is stationary and the time domain is extended to [$-\infty$, $+\infty$].

When the time domain is limited to [$-T/2$, $T/2$], the above conclusion is no longer true but is still approximately true for any reasonably large T. When T is finite, the lowest frequency is determined by

$$f_0 = 1/T \qquad \text{or} \qquad \omega_0 = 2\pi/T \tag{8-75}$$

Subsequently, the eigenvalues and eigenfunctions are

$$\lambda_k \cong \mathscr{S}(k\omega_0), \qquad \varphi_k(t) \cong \exp(jk\omega_0 t) \qquad (k = 1, 2, \ldots) \tag{8-76}$$

Assuming $\exp(jk\omega_0 t)$ as the eigenfunctions for finite T and expressing

$R(t - \tau)$ by the inverse Fourier transform of $\mathscr{S}(\omega)$ as

$$R(t - \tau) = (2\pi)^{-1} \int_{-\infty}^{+\infty} \mathscr{S}(\omega) \exp[j\omega(t - \tau)]\, d\omega \tag{8-77}$$

(8-69) becomes

$$\begin{aligned} \lambda_k \varphi_k(t) &= (2\pi)^{-1} \int_{-\infty}^{+\infty} \mathscr{S}(\omega) \int_{-T/2}^{T/2} \exp[j\omega(t - \tau)] \exp(jk\omega_0\tau)\, d\tau\, d\omega \\ &= (2\pi)^{-1} \int_{-\infty}^{+\infty} \mathscr{S}(\omega) \exp(j\omega t) T \left\{ \frac{\sin\{[(k\omega_0 - \omega)/2]T\}}{[(k\omega_0 - \omega)/2]T} \right\} d\omega \end{aligned} \tag{8-78}$$

The function in the bracket is known as the *band limited sampling function* and is shown in Fig. 8-3 with the power spectrum. Assuming that $\mathscr{S}(\omega) \times \exp(j\omega t)$ does not change much between the adjacent sampling points in ω, the integration of (8-78) can be approximated by

$$\begin{aligned} \lambda_k \varphi_k(t) &\cong \mathscr{S}(k\omega_0) \exp(jk\omega_0 t)(2\pi)^{-1} \int_{-\infty}^{+\infty} T \left\{ \frac{\sin\{[(k\omega_0 - \omega)/2]T\}}{[(k\omega_0 - \omega)/2]T} \right\} d\omega \\ &= \mathscr{S}(k\omega_0) \exp(jk\omega_0 t) \end{aligned} \tag{8-79}$$

Therefore, with the degree of approximation between (8-78) and (8-79),

$$\lambda_k \cong \mathscr{S}(k\omega_0) \tag{8-80}$$

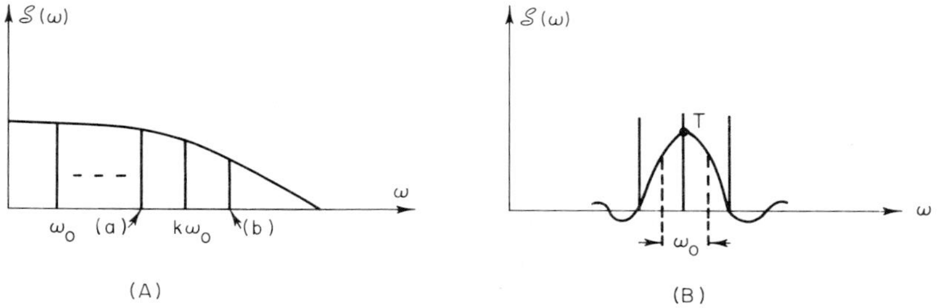

Fig. 8-3 (A) Power spectrum and (B) sampling function: (a) $(k - 1)\omega_0$; (b) $(k + 1)\omega_0$.

8.4 Estimation of Eigenvalues and Eigenvectors

From the previous discussion, we realize that selecting features for one distribution by linear transformations requires a considerable amount of eigenvalue and eigenvector calculation. Theoretically, this is the end of this subject. However, there are many problems to be solved in order to apply the technique to real-life data. Some of the problems, which will be discussed in this section, are the following [Fukunaga, 1970b].

(1) *The number of sampling points for random processes*: In some applications of pattern recognition, the number of variables n is very much predetermined and cannot be controlled. However, in some other areas, particularly in waveform analysis, we have to determine the number of sampling points n. Furthermore, in waveform analysis, n becomes fairly large, say in the hundreds, and computer time grows rapidly with n. Therefore, proper procedures should be provided to select the minimum possible number of sampling points, while maintaining sufficient accuracy for reppresenting the random process.

(2) *The number of samples*: We always have to know how many samples are needed to insure the accuracy of estimation of eigenvalues and eigenvectors.

(3) *Dominant eigenvalues and eigenvectors*: In many cases it has been found that the number of dominant eigenvalues are small, although the original dimension n is very large. Therefore, it is convenient to have procedures to calculate only dominant eigenvalues and corresponding eigenvectors without going through an $n \times n$ matrix.

Determining the Dimensionality

In this subsection, we will develop a procedure for determining n, the number of time samples taken from a random process $\mathbf{x}(t)$.

Let us begin our discussion with a simple example. Let $\mathbf{x}(t)$ be sampled at four instants, t_2, t_4, t_6, and t_8, as shown by the solid vertical lines in Fig. 8-4a. Then the autocorrelation matrix S has four eigenvalues whose magnitudes are indicated by the solid lines in Fig. 8-4b. Let the number of sampling points be doubled to include t_1, t_3, t_5, and t_7. Now S has eight eigenvalues, as shown by the dashed lines in Fig. 8-4b. The features corresponding to

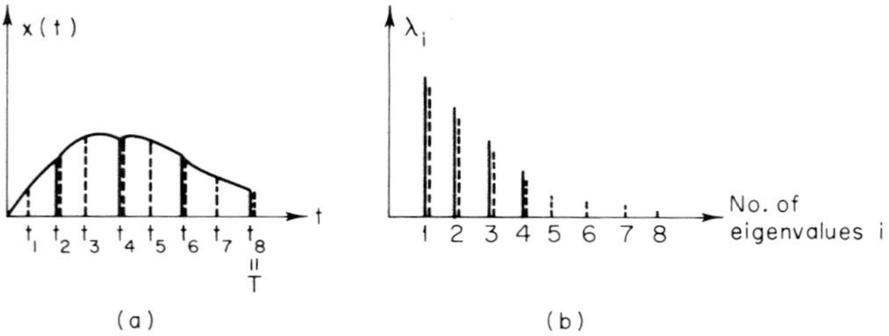

Fig. 8-4 A typical (a) waveform and (b) its eigenvalues.

the first four eigenvalues are essentially the same features derived in the four-sample case. The remaining four features are those which result from doubling the sampling rate. If the eigenvalues corresponding to the new features are small, then the error committed by deleting these features is also small. If the new features are unimportant, then the features derived in the four-sample case adequately represent $\mathbf{x}(t)$.

In general, suppose the dimension is $2n$. Then we would have a $2n \times 2n$ autocorrelation matrix, S^{2n}. If the summation of some n of the $2n$ eigenvalues of S^{2n} is small compared to the summation of all $2n$ eigenvalues, then n is sufficiently large. However, the computation of eigenvalues is time-consuming. Let us instead use the perturbation result of Chapter 2 to obtain a simpler test for n.

Let the elements of the $2n$-dimensional feature vector X^{2n} be ordered so that

$$\mathbf{X}^{2n} = \begin{bmatrix} \mathbf{x}(t_2) \\ \mathbf{x}(t_4) \\ \vdots \\ \mathbf{x}(t_{2n}) \\ \mathbf{x}(t_1) \\ \mathbf{x}(t_3) \\ \vdots \\ \mathbf{x}(t_{2n-1}) \end{bmatrix} = \begin{bmatrix} \mathbf{X}_{\mathrm{e}}^{n} \\ \mathbf{X}_{\mathrm{d}}^{n} \end{bmatrix} \tag{8-81}$$

Then S^{2n} is given by

$$S^{2n} = E\{\mathbf{X}^{2n}\mathbf{X}^{2nT}\} = \begin{bmatrix} E\{\mathbf{X}_{\mathrm{e}}^{n}\mathbf{X}_{\mathrm{e}}^{nT}\} & E\{\mathbf{X}_{\mathrm{e}}^{n}\mathbf{X}_{\mathrm{d}}^{nT}\} \\ E\{\mathbf{X}_{\mathrm{d}}^{n}\mathbf{X}_{\mathrm{e}}^{nT}\} & E\{\mathbf{X}_{\mathrm{d}}^{n}\mathbf{X}_{\mathrm{d}}^{nT}\} \end{bmatrix} = \begin{bmatrix} S_{11}^{n} & S_{12}^{n} \\ S_{12}^{nT} & S_{22}^{n} \end{bmatrix} \tag{8-82}$$

For large n, S_{11}^{n}, S_{12}^{n}, and S_{22}^{n} are nearly equal. We write S^{2n} as

$$S^{2n} = \begin{bmatrix} S_{11}^{n} & S_{11}^{n} \\ S_{11}^{n} & S_{11}^{n} \end{bmatrix} + \begin{bmatrix} 0 & S_{12}^{n} - S_{11}^{n} \\ S_{12}^{nT} - S_{11}^{n} & S_{22}^{n} - S_{11}^{n} \end{bmatrix} = S_{0}^{2n} + \varDelta S^{2n} \tag{8-83}$$

Now if

$$\varPhi^{n} = [\varPhi_1^{n}\varPhi_2^{n} \cdots \varPhi_n^{n}] \tag{8-84}$$

is the eigenvector matrix of S_{11}^{n}, then

$$\varPhi_0^{2n} = \frac{1}{\sqrt{2}} \begin{bmatrix} \varPhi^{n} & \varPhi^{n} \\ \varPhi^{n} & -\varPhi^{n} \end{bmatrix} \tag{8-85}$$

is the eigenvector matrix of S_0^{2n}. Since ΔS^{2n} is small for large n, then by (2-205) the eigenvalues of S^{2n} are given approximately by the diagonal elements of

$$G^{2n} = \Phi_0^{2nT} S^{2n} \Phi_0^{2n} = \begin{bmatrix} G_{11}^n & G_{12}^n \\ G_{12}^{nT} & G_{22}^n \end{bmatrix} \tag{8-86}$$

where

$$G_{11}^n = \tfrac{1}{2}\Phi^{nT}(S_{11}^n + S_{12}^n + S_{12}^{nT} + S_{22}^n)\Phi^n \tag{8-87}$$

$$G_{12}^n = \tfrac{1}{2}\Phi^{nT}(S_{11}^n - S_{12}^n + S_{12}^{nT} - S_{22}^n)\Phi^n \tag{8-88}$$

and

$$G_{22}^n = \tfrac{1}{2}\Phi^{nT}(S_{11}^n - S_{12}^n - S_{12}^{nT} + S_{22}^n)\Phi^n \tag{8-89}$$

We define a criterion J_n as

$$J_n = (\operatorname{tr} G_{22}^n)/\operatorname{tr}(G_{11}^n + G_{22}^n) \tag{8-90}$$

Then J_n is approximately the ratio of the sum of n smaller eigenvalues of S^{2n} to the sum of all $2n$ eigenvalues. If $J_n \ll 1$, then n samples are sufficient, and the assumption concerning the smallness of ΔS^{2n} is reinforced. Using (8-87), (8-89), and the orthogonality of Φ^n, we can rewrite J_n as

$$J_n = \operatorname{tr}(S_{11}^n - S_{12}^n - S_{12}^{nT} + S_{22}^n)/[2 \operatorname{tr}(S_{11}^n + S_{22}^n)] \tag{8-91}$$

Or, recalling (8-81) and (8-82), we can write J_n in terms of the autocorrelation function, $R(t, \tau)$, of $\mathbf{x}(t)$ as

$$J_n = \frac{1}{2} \frac{\sum_{i=1}^{n} \{R(t_{2i}, t_{2i}) - R(t_{2i}, t_{2i-1}) - R(t_{2i-1}, t_{2i}) + R(t_{2i-1}, t_{2i-1})\}}{\sum_{i=1}^{n} \{R(t_{2i}, t_{2i}) + R(t_{2i-1}, t_{2i-1})\}} \tag{8-92}$$

Special Case: Stationary Process

In stationary processes, $R(t_{2i}, t_{2i}) = R(t_{2i-1}, t_{2i-1}) = R(0)$, and $R(t_{2i-1}, t_{2i}) = R(t_{2i}, t_{2i-1}) = R(t_{2i} - t_{2i-1}) = R(\frac{1}{2}T/n)$. Therefore,

$$J_n = \tfrac{1}{2}\{R(0) - R(\tfrac{1}{2}T/n)\}/R(0) \tag{8-93}$$

EXAMPLE 8-4 Let us calculate J_n of (8-93) for $R(\tau) = \exp(-|\tau|)$, and $T = 1$. In this example

$$J_n = \tfrac{1}{2}\left[1 - \exp\left(-\frac{1}{2n}\right)\right] \tag{8-94}$$

If $2n = 6$, we have $J_n \cong 0.04$ which indicates that three eigenvalues of S are very small compared to the other three. Thus, we would expect to gain little additional characterization of $\mathbf{x}(t)$ by increasing n further.

EXAMPLE 8-5 $R(\tau)$ triangular
For this example

$$R(\tau) = \begin{cases} R(0)(1 - |\tau|/T_0) & (|\tau| \leq T_0) \\ 0 & (|\tau| > T_0) \end{cases} \tag{8-95}$$

If $T \leq T_0$, J_n is given by

$$J_n = T/(4nT_0) \tag{8-96}$$

The result of this example is useful in problems where stationarity may be assumed, but $R(\tau)$ is unknown. We assume the triangular form and use a minimum value estimate of T.

Estimation of Eigenvalues and Eigenvectors

Having chosen n, our next task is to estimate the eigenvalues and eigenvectors λ_i and Φ_j $(j = 1, \ldots, n)$ of the autocorrelation matrix S. To do this, we calculate the sample autocorrelation matrix $\hat{\mathbf{S}}$ by

$$\hat{\mathbf{S}} = (1/N) \sum_{i=1}^{N} \mathbf{X}_i \mathbf{X}_i^T \tag{8-97}$$

and then calculate the eigenvalues and eigenvectors $\hat{\boldsymbol{\lambda}}_j$ and $\hat{\boldsymbol{\Phi}}_j$ $(j = 1, \ldots, n)$ of $\hat{\mathbf{S}}$.

It is important to note that $\hat{\boldsymbol{\lambda}}_j$ and $\hat{\boldsymbol{\Phi}}_j$ are estimates of λ_j and Φ_j and that they are random variables and vectors. They are functions of $\mathbf{X}_1, \ldots, \mathbf{X}_N$, the sample vectors. In this subsection, we shall show approximate formulas for the expected values and variances of these estimates. Using these formulas, we can determine a value of N, such that the estimates are sufficiently accurate.

The statistics of the eigenvectors and eigenvalues of a matrix of random variables have been studied previously [Wilkinson, 1965; Anderson, 1958]. The general approach is to calculate the distribution of $\hat{\mathbf{S}}$ and from this find the distribution of the eigenvectors and eigenvalues.

However, since $\hat{\mathbf{S}} \cong S$ for N sufficiently large, we may use the approximations (2-205) and (2-206) to express $\hat{\boldsymbol{\Phi}}_i$ and $\hat{\boldsymbol{\lambda}}_i$, that is,

$$\hat{\boldsymbol{\Phi}}_i \cong \Phi_i + \sum_{\substack{j=1 \\ j \neq i}}^{n} [\Phi_i^T \hat{\mathbf{S}} \Phi_j / (\lambda_i - \lambda_j)] \Phi_j \tag{8-98}$$

and

$$\hat{\boldsymbol{\lambda}}_i \cong \Phi_i^T \hat{\mathbf{S}} \Phi_i \qquad (i = 1, \ldots, n) \tag{8-99}$$

First, we consider the expected value of the estimate. Since $S = E\{\mathbf{X}\mathbf{X}^T\}$, the expected value of $\hat{\mathbf{S}}$ of (8-97) becomes

$$E\{\hat{\mathbf{S}}\} = (1/N) \sum_{i=1}^{N} E\{\mathbf{X}\mathbf{X}^T\} = S \tag{8-100}$$

Therefore,

$$E\{\Phi_i^T \hat{\mathbf{S}} \Phi_j\} = \Phi_i^T E\{\hat{\mathbf{S}}\} \Phi_j = \Phi_i^T S \Phi_j = \lambda_i \delta_{ij} \tag{8-101}$$

It follows from (8-98) and (8-99) that

$$E\{\hat{\boldsymbol{\Phi}}_i\} \cong \Phi_i \tag{8-102}$$

and

$$E\{\hat{\boldsymbol{\lambda}}_i\} \cong \lambda_i \tag{8-103}$$

Thus, the estimates are seen to be approximately unbiased. The variances of $\hat{\boldsymbol{\lambda}}_i$ and $\hat{\boldsymbol{\Phi}}_i$ are given by

$$\mathrm{Var}[\hat{\boldsymbol{\lambda}}_i] = E\{(\hat{\boldsymbol{\lambda}}_i - \lambda_i)^2\} = E\{\hat{\boldsymbol{\lambda}}_i^2\} - \lambda_i^2 \cong E\{(\Phi_i^T \hat{\mathbf{S}} \Phi_i)^2\} - \lambda_i^2 \tag{8-104}$$

$$\mathrm{Var}[\hat{\boldsymbol{\Phi}}_i] = E\{\| \hat{\boldsymbol{\Phi}}_i - \Phi_i \|^2\} \cong \sum_{\substack{j=1 \\ j \neq i}}^{n} E\{(\Phi_i^T \hat{\mathbf{S}} \Phi_j)^2\} / (\lambda_i - \lambda_j)^2 \tag{8-105}$$

The expectations of (8-104) and (8-105) can be fulfilled by the moment-generating functions of the samples, as shown in Appendix 8-1.

Normal process

For the special case where the $\mathbf{X}_k$'s come from a normal distribution with the expected vector M and autocorrelation matrix S, (8-104) and (8-105) become, from (A8.1-10) of Appendix 8-1,

$$\mathrm{Var}[\hat{\boldsymbol{\lambda}}_i] \cong (2/N)(\lambda_i^2 - d_i^4) \tag{8-106}$$

$$\mathrm{Var}[\hat{\boldsymbol{\Phi}}_i] \cong (1/N) \sum_{\substack{j=1 \\ j \neq i}}^{n} (\lambda_i \lambda_j - 2 d_i^2 d_j^2) / (\lambda_i - \lambda_j)^2 \tag{8-107}$$

where

$$d_i = \Phi_i^T M \qquad (i = 1, 2, \ldots, n) \tag{8-108}$$

Equations (8-106) and (8-107) indicate that variances are the product of $1/N$ and some coefficient which is independent of N. These coefficients are determined by S and M.

Much simpler expressions may be obtained as upper bounds of $\mathrm{Var}[\hat{\boldsymbol{\lambda}}_i]$ and $\mathrm{Var}[\hat{\boldsymbol{\Phi}}_i]$ by dropping out the d terms as follows:

$$\mathrm{Var}[\hat{\boldsymbol{\lambda}}_i] \leq (2/N)\lambda_i^2 \quad \text{or} \quad \mathrm{Var}[\hat{\boldsymbol{\lambda}}_i]/\lambda_i^2 \leq 2/N \tag{8-109}$$

$$\mathrm{Var}[\hat{\boldsymbol{\Phi}}_i] \leq \frac{1}{N} \sum_{\substack{j=1 \\ j\neq i}}^{n} \frac{\lambda_i \lambda_j}{(\lambda_i - \lambda_j)^2} = \frac{1}{N} \sum_{\substack{j=1 \\ j\neq i}}^{n} \frac{\lambda_j/\lambda_i}{(1 - \lambda_j/\lambda_i)^2} \triangleq \frac{1}{N}\gamma_i \tag{8-110}$$

The equalities hold when the expected vectors are known to be zero.

Equation (8-109) gives us a bound on $\mathrm{Var}[\hat{\boldsymbol{\lambda}}_i]/\lambda_i^2$ which depends only on N. Equation (8-110) gives a bound on $\mathrm{Var}[\hat{\boldsymbol{\Phi}}_i]$ which depends on N and the ratios of the eigenvalues of S. Thus, we can choose N to estimate the eigenvalues to the desired accuracy and then determine N, which gives accurate eigenvector estimation.

Example 8-6 We now present a numerical example that illustrates some interesting points.

Let $\mathbf{x}(t)$, $t \in [0, T]$, be a stationary, normal random process with

$$R(\tau) = E\{\mathbf{x}(t)\mathbf{x}(t-\tau)\} = \exp(-a\mid\tau\mid) \tag{8-111}$$

If $\mathbf{x}(t)$ is time-sampled at $t = lT/n$ $(l = 1, \ldots, n)$, then S becomes a matrix whose element s_{lm} is

$$s_{lm} = \exp(-a\mid l - m \mid T/n) = \varrho^{|l-m|/n} \qquad (l, m = 1, \ldots, n) \tag{8-112}$$

where

$$\varrho = \exp(-aT) \tag{8-113}$$

The error coefficients of (8-110) are fixed by the eigenvalues of S. By varying ϱ and n of (8-112), we have a family of S matrices. Let us then examine the error coefficients of various matrices in the family.

A. Fixed ϱ. For each value of n, we have n error coefficients, $\gamma_1, \ldots, \gamma_n$. We order γ_i according to decreasing magnitude of λ_i.

Figure 8-5 is a plot for $\varrho = 0.1$ of the variation of each γ_i with n for $i \leq n$. The most important observation is the following: The range of the error coefficients is on the order of 100. Thus, the number of samples needed to estimate only the dominant eigenvectors is much less than the number needed to estimate all of the eigenvectors.

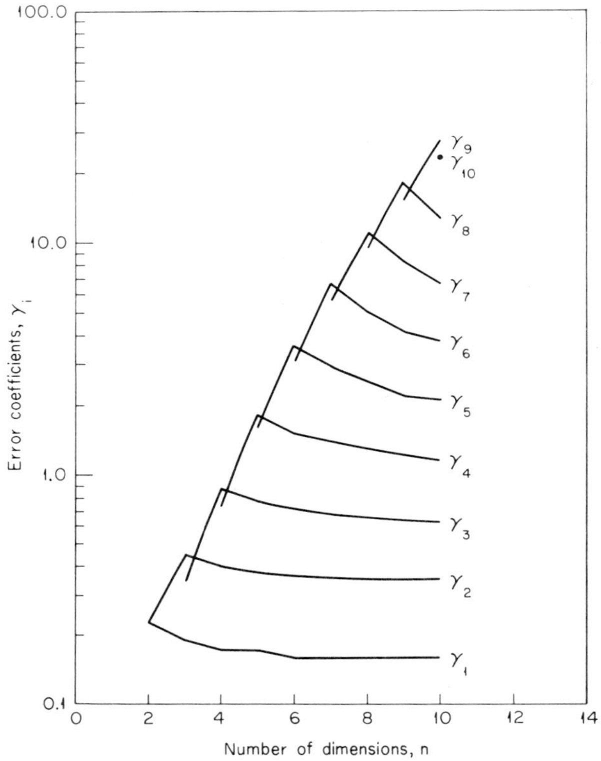

Fig. 8-5 Error coefficients for $\varrho = 0.1$ [Fukunaga, 1970b].

B. Variation of the Largest Coefficient. Suppose we must measure all of the eigenvectors with a certain accuracy. Then when the dimension is n, $\gamma_{\max} = \max\{\gamma_1, \ldots, \gamma_n\}$ is the constraining factor. Thus, the variation of $\gamma_{\max}$ with n indicates how the sample size must grow with n to maintain a fixed accuracy.

Figure 8-6 shows the variation of $\gamma_{\max}$ with n for various values of ϱ. We see that $\gamma_{\max}$ grows roughly as n^2.

Nonnormal Processes

The results for the normal case should be useful for most problems with a unimodal probability structure. When the structure is very complex or unknown, evaluation of (8-104) and (8-105) becomes very difficult. However, in this case the utility of the Karhunen–Loève expansion, itself, becomes questionable. Thus, we feel that this limitation is a natural one.

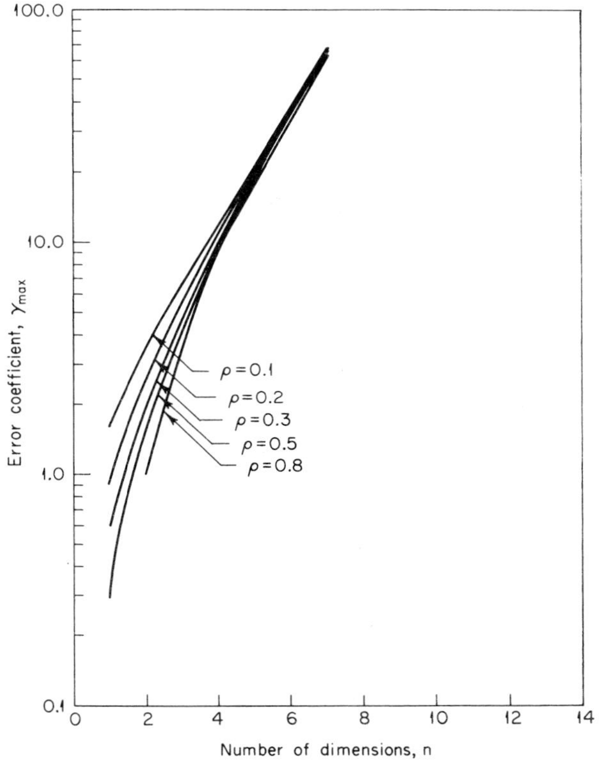

Fig. 8-6 Value of the maximum error coefficient [Fukunaga, 1970b].

Dominant Eigenvalues

In this subsection, we are concerned with the estimation of dominant eigenvalues and eigenvectors. Calculating only dominant eigenvalues and eigenvectors is very effective, since the number of dominant ones is so small in comparison with the original dimensionality in many problems of pattern recognition. Although this problem was discussed in the subsection on the determination of the dimensionality, a different approach is offered in this subsection.

Suppose we somehow know that the number of dominant eigenvalues is m or less ($m \ll n$). We can divide the N sample vectors into N/m groups of m vectors $\{X_1^{(i)}, X_2^{(i)}, \ldots, X_m^{(i)}\}$ ($i = 1, 2, \ldots, N/m$). For the ith group, we can form an $n \times m$ data matrix, $W^{(i)}$, (see Example 2-20), and calculate the m eigenvectors and eigenvalues of the $m \times m$ matrix $(W^{(i)T}W^{(i)})/m$.

If the eigenvector and eigenvalue matrices are $\Phi^{(i)}_{m\times m}$ and $\Lambda^{(i)}_{m\times m}$, respectively, then, from (2-169) through (2-175), the dominant n-dimensional eigenvector and eigenvalue matrices can be estimated by $(W^{(i)}\Phi^{(i)})_{n\times m}$ and $\Lambda^{(i)}_{m\times m}$. More accurate estimates, $(\widehat{W\Phi})_{n\times m}$ and $\hat{\Lambda}_{m\times m}$, are given by the arithmetic mean of these estimates.

$$(\widehat{W\Phi})_{n\times m} = (m/N) \sum_{i=1}^{N/m} (W^{(i)}\Phi^{(i)})_{n\times m} \tag{8-114}$$

$$\hat{\Lambda}_{m\times m} = (m/N) \sum_{i=1}^{N/m} \Lambda^{(i)}_{m\times m} \tag{8-115}$$

In order to make sure that the dominant eigenvalues are all included in these m eigenvalues of $\hat{\Lambda}_{m\times m}$, we show that

$$\operatorname{tr} \hat{\Lambda}_{m\times m} = \operatorname{tr} S_{n\times n} \tag{8-116}$$

where $S_{n\times n}$ is the sample autocorrelation matrix of N samples, and $\operatorname{tr} S_{n\times n}$ is equal to the sum of all eigenvalues of $S_{n\times n}$. From (8-114) and (2-172)

$$\begin{aligned}
\operatorname{tr} \hat{\Lambda}_{m\times m} &= (m/N) \sum_{i=1}^{N/m} \operatorname{tr} \Lambda^{(i)}_{m\times m} \\
&= (m/N) \sum_{i=1}^{N/m} (1/m) \operatorname{tr}[\Phi^{(i)T}_{m\times m}(W^{(i)T}W^{(i)})_{m\times m}\Phi^{(i)}_{m\times m}] \\
&= \operatorname{tr}\left[(1/N) \sum_{i=1}^{N/m} (W^{(i)}W^{(i)T})_{n\times n}\right] \\
&= \operatorname{tr}\left[(1/N) \sum_{j=1}^{N} X_j X_j^T\right] \\
&= \operatorname{tr} S_{n\times n}
\end{aligned} \tag{8-117}$$

Appendix 8-1 Calculation of $E\{\Phi_i^T \hat{\mathbf{S}} \Phi_j)^2\}$

Recall that $\hat{\mathbf{S}}$ is given by

$$\hat{\mathbf{S}} = (1/N) \sum_{k=1}^{N} \mathbf{X}_k \mathbf{X}_k^T \tag{A8.1-1}$$

thus, we have

$$\Phi_i^T \hat{\mathbf{S}} \Phi_j = (1/N) \sum_{k=1}^{N} \mathbf{y}_{ik} \mathbf{y}_{jk} \tag{A8.1-2}$$

where

$$\mathbf{y}_{ik} = \Phi_i{}^T\mathbf{X}_k \tag{A8.1-3}$$

If both sides of (A8.1-2) are squared and expectation is taken, the result is

$$\begin{aligned} E\{(\Phi_i{}^T\hat{\mathbf{S}}\Phi_j)^2\} &= (1/N^2)\sum_{k=1}^{N}\sum_{l=1}^{N} E\{\mathbf{y}_{ik}\mathbf{y}_{jk}\mathbf{y}_{il}\mathbf{y}_{jl}\} \\ &= (1/N^2)\sum_{\substack{k=1\\k\neq l}}^{N}\sum_{l=1}^{N} E\{\mathbf{y}_{ik}\mathbf{y}_{jk}\}E\{\mathbf{y}_{il}\mathbf{y}_{jl}\} + (1/N^2)\sum_{k=1}^{N} E\{\mathbf{y}_{ik}^2\mathbf{y}_{jk}^2\} \end{aligned} \tag{A8.1-4}$$

since the $\mathbf{X}_k$'s are independent.
Now

$$E\{\mathbf{y}_{ik}\mathbf{y}_{jk}\} = \Phi_i{}^T E\{(\mathbf{X}_k\mathbf{X}_k{}^T)\}\Phi_j = \lambda_i\,\delta_{ij} \qquad (k = 1, \ldots, N) \tag{A8.1-5}$$

and (A8.1-4) may be rewritten as

$$E\{(\Phi_i{}^T\hat{\mathbf{S}}\Phi_j)^2\} = [(N-1)/N]\lambda_i{}^2\,\delta_{ij} + (1/N)E\{\mathbf{y}_i{}^2\mathbf{y}_j{}^2\} \tag{A8.1-6}$$

The second subscript on $\mathbf{y}$ is dropped since the $\mathbf{X}_k$'s are identically distributed. The last term in (A8.1-6) may be calculated if the moment-generating function of $\mathbf{X}$ is known. The joint moment-generating function of $\mathbf{y}_i$ and $\mathbf{y}_j$ is

$$\begin{aligned} M_{ij}(t_1, t_2) &= E\{\exp(t_1\Phi_i{}^T\mathbf{X} + t_2\Phi_j{}^T\mathbf{X})\} = E\{\exp[(t_1\Phi_i{}^T + t_2\Phi_j{}^T)\mathbf{X}]\} \\ &= M_{\mathbf{X}}(t_1\Phi_i + t_2\Phi_j) \end{aligned} \tag{A8.1-7}$$

where $M_{\mathbf{X}}(\cdot)$ is the moment-generating function of $\mathbf{X}$. It follows then that

$$E\{\mathbf{y}_i{}^2\mathbf{y}_j{}^2\} = \begin{cases} \partial^4 M_{ij}(t_1, t_2)/(\partial t_1{}^2\,\partial t_2{}^2)\,|_{t_1=t_2=0} & (i \neq j) \\ \partial^4 M_{ij}(t_1, t_2)/\partial t_1{}^4\,|_{t_1=t_2=0} & (i = j) \end{cases} \tag{A8.1-8}$$

If $\mathbf{X}$ comes from a multivariate normal distribution with mean vector M and autocorrelation matrix S, then

$$E\{\mathbf{y}_i{}^2\mathbf{y}_j{}^2\} = 2\lambda_i{}^2\,\delta_{ij} + \lambda_i\lambda_j - 2d_i{}^2\,d_j{}^2 \tag{A8.1-9}$$

Combining (A8.1-9) and (A8.1-6), we have

$$E\{(\Phi_i{}^T\hat{\mathbf{S}}\Phi_j)^2\} = \lambda_i{}^2\,\delta_{ij} + (1/N)(\lambda_i{}^2\,\delta_{ij} + \lambda_i\lambda_j - 2d_i{}^2\,d_j{}^2) \tag{A8.1-10}$$

where d_i is given by (8-108).

Appendix 8-2 Rapid Eigenvalue–Eigenvector Calculation

In this Appendix, we present a rapid algorithm for calculating the eigenvalues and eigenvectors of an autocorrelation matrix, S [Fukunaga, 1970b]. This method is a correlary of the results of Section 8-4.

Many existing algorithms to calculate eigenvalues and eigenvectors are iterative. We start with an orthogonal matrix $\Phi^{(1)}$ and form a sequence $\{\Phi^{(N)}\}$, such that

$$\Phi = \lim_{N\to\infty} \Phi^{(N)} \tag{A8.2-1}$$

where

$$\Phi^T S \Phi = \Lambda \tag{A8.2-2}$$

and

$$\Phi^T \Phi = I \tag{A8.2-3}$$

Λ being diagonal and I being the identity. Most of these algorithms start with $\Phi^{(1)} = I$.

However, suppose the $2n \times 2n$ matrix S^{2n} is partitioned as in (8-82) and that we know Φ^n of (8-84) already. Then we can use Φ_0^{2n} of (8-85) as the initial guess in an iterative algorithm. If we double n, the dimension of the autocorrelation matrix goes to $4n \times 4n$ and we denote it by S^{4n}. Thus, we can define S^2, S^4, S^8, . . .

The algorithm is simply the following:

(1) Start with eigenvector of S^1, which is the scalar 1.

(2) Having calculated the eigenvectors of S^n, use Φ_0^{2n} as an initial guess in an iteration to calculate the eigenvectors of S^{2n}.

(3) Repeat step 2, until n reaches the desired value.

We call this the *fast eigen algorithm*, because the basic approach is borrowed from the fast Fourier transform.

The computation time for this algorithm depends on the iterative method used. The threshold Jacobi method [Greenstadt, 1962] is a widely used iterative method. The computation time for this method is given roughly as

$$T_J \cong K_J n^3 \tag{A8.2-4}$$

To incorporate an initial guess into Jacobi's method, we must transform S^{2n} to Q^{2n} as

$$Q^{2n} = \Phi_0^{2nT} S^{2n} \Phi_0^{2n} \tag{A8.2-5}$$

and apply successive Jacobi transformations to diagonalize Q^{2n}. Substituting (8-82) and (8-85) into (A8.2-5) we have

$$Q^{2n} = \begin{bmatrix} (\Lambda + B_{12} + B_{12}^T + B_{22}) & (\Lambda - B_{12} + B_{12}^T - B_{22}) \\ (\Lambda + B_{12} - B_{12}^T - B_{22}) & (\Lambda - B_{12} - B_{12}^T + B_{22}) \end{bmatrix} \tag{A8.2-6}$$

where

$$B_{12} = \Phi^{n^T} S_{12}^n \Phi^n \tag{A8.2-7}$$

and

$$B_{22} = \Phi^{n^T} S_{22}^n \Phi^n \tag{A8.2-8}$$

Hence, we need only calculate B_{12} and B_{22}. The total number of multiplications required to do this is about $0.5n^3$. This time must be added to T_J. However, since $K_J \cong 10$, the additional time is not significant.

In the algorithm, we apply Jacobi's method for $n = 2, 4, \ldots, 2^m$. The computation time for the lth step is reduced by a factor of θ_l, because of the better starting point. For simplicity's sake, let us assume that θ_l is constant, θ. Then the total time T_{FE} is given by

$$T_{\text{FE}} \cong \sum_{l=1}^{m} K_J\theta(2^l)^3 = 2^{3m}K_J\theta \sum_{l=1}^{m} 2^{-3(m-l)} \leq 2^{3m}K_J\theta/(1 - 2^{-3}) = \tfrac{8}{7}\theta T_J \tag{A8.2-9}$$

Hence, the computation time is less by a factor of $\frac{8}{7}\theta$ than that of the Jacobi method.

For Jacobi's method, θ is determined experimentally. The computation time is essentially proportional to the number of Jacobi iterations required to achieve convergence to the desired accuracy. Thus, θ is given by

$$\theta = I_n/I_J \tag{A8.2-10}$$

where I_n is the number of iterations required to obtain Φ^{2n} from Φ^n, and I_J is the number of iterations required conventionally.

Figure A8.2-1. shows curves of I_n and I_J for a matrix S whose i, j element is

$$s_{ij} = \nu^{|i-j|} \tag{A8.2-11}$$

versus the matrix dimension for various values of ν. The spacing between the fast eigen and conventional curves on the semilog plot is nearly constant for fixed ν, and θ varies between about 0.25 and 0.35.

Thus, computation time can be reduced by the fast eigen approach. The significance of the timesaving, of course, depends on the details of the application.

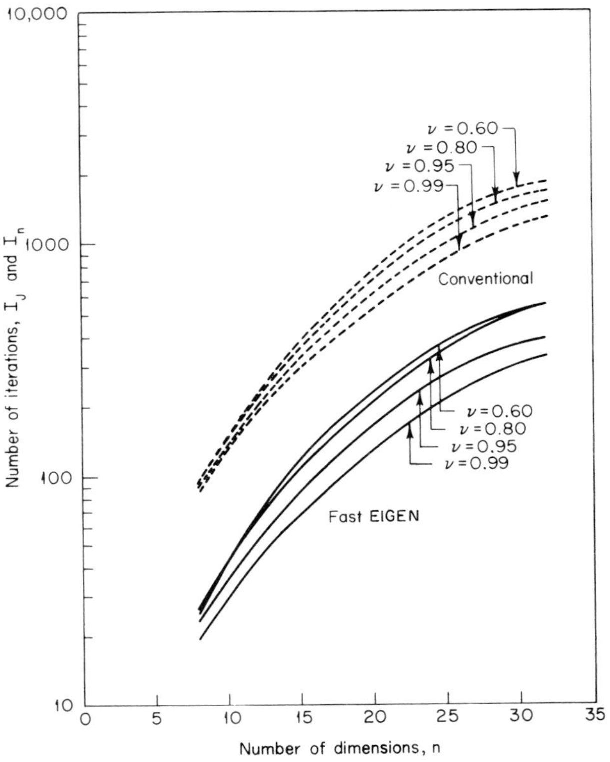

Fig. A.8.2-1. Experimental curves for determining the convergence ratio [Fukunaga, 1970b].

Computer Projects

Write the following programs:

8-1 The Karhunen–Loève expansion for covariance and autocorrelation matrices. (a) Calculate the eigenvalues and the ratio of the eigenvalues to the total sum, and order them from the largest to smallest; (b) Print out the eigenvectors.

Data: (a) Standard Data $i = 1, 2$

(b) The mixture of Standard Data $i = 1, 2$.

8-2 A feature selection program to maximize the population entropy for normal distributions.

Data: (a) Standard Data $i = 1, 2$;
(b) The mixture of Standard Data $i = 1, 2$.

8-3 Calculate the eigenvalues for the covariance matrix of a stationary process $\mathbf{x}(t)$ for $[-T/2, T/2]$, whose covariance function is given by $\exp(-a \times | t - \tau |)$. Compare the results for various sampling rates with the power spectrum of the process.

8-4 Add the following capabilities to the program in 8-1: (a) automatic sampling rate selection; (b) fast EIGEN program.

8-5 Calculate the eigenvalues by using m $(m < n)$ samples and repeat this for k sets of m samples. Compare the sample mean of these eigenvalues with the eigenvalues calculated from $m \times k$ samples.

Data: A generated data according to a proper distribution of eigenvalues.

Problems

8-1 Suppose we have three samples as shown in the figure. (a) Find the Karhunen–Loève expansion of the sample autocorrelation matrix, and calculate the mean-square error when only one feature is selected. (b) Do the same problem for the sample covariance matrix.

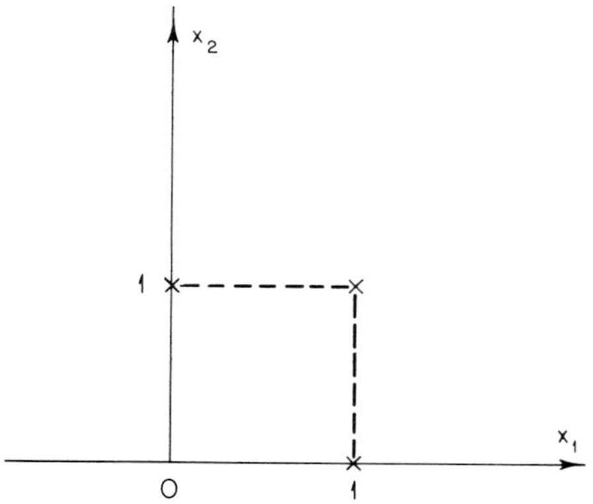

8-2 Show for 8-1b that λ_1 is the largest among $E\{\mathbf{y}_1^2\}$'s, where $\mathbf{y}_1$'s and $\mathbf{y}_2$'s are obtained from $\mathbf{x}_1$ and $\mathbf{x}_2$ by various orthonormal transformations. (Do not use the proof of (8-25), but confirm the simplest case of (8-25) by some other method.)

8-3 Let us express two sets of samples by $\mathbf{X}^{(1)} \in \omega_1$ and $\mathbf{X}^{(2)} \in \omega_2$. They are mutually independent. The between-class scatter matrix is defined by

$$S_b = E\{(\mathbf{X}^{(1)} - \mathbf{X}^{(2)})(\mathbf{X}^{(1)} - \mathbf{X}^{(2)})^T\}$$

Find S_b in terms of the covariance matrices and expected vectors of these samples.

8-4 Calculate

$$\int_{\mathscr{S}} p(X/\omega_1) \ln p(X/\omega_2)\, dX$$

where $p(X/\omega_i)$ are normal distributions with M_i and Σ_i.

8-5 The autocorrelation function and expected value of a stationary process $\mathbf{x}(t)$ for $[-\frac{1}{2}, +\frac{1}{2}]$ are given by $\exp(-4 \mid t - \tau \mid)$ and zero. Find the approximate eigenvalues using the power spectrum.

8-6 The covariance function of a stationary process $\mathbf{x}(t)$ for $[-T/2, +T/2]$ is given by $\exp(-a \mid t - \tau \mid)$. Let ϱ be $\exp(-a\, \Delta T)$ where ΔT is the sampling interval of the random process. Find the corresponding covariance matrix and calculate $(M_1 - M_2)^T \Sigma^{-1} (M_1 - M_2)$.

8-7 The figure shows a block diagram of a linear filter problem, where $s(t)$ is the original signal, $\mathbf{x}(t)$ is the observed signal with $s(t)$ and the noise $\mathbf{n}(t)$ added, and $\hat{\mathbf{s}}(t)$ is the estimate of $s(t)$. The impulse response $h(t, \tau)$ of the optimum linear filter is found by minimizing

$$E\left[(1/T) \int_0^T \{s(t) - \hat{\mathbf{s}}(t)\}^2\, dt\right] = E\left[(1/T) \int_0^T \left\{s(t) - \int_0^T h(t, \tau)\mathbf{x}(\tau)\, d\tau\right\}^2 dt\right]$$

with respect to $h(t, \tau)$. Find the optimum $h(t, \tau)$ by using the vector-matrix approach.

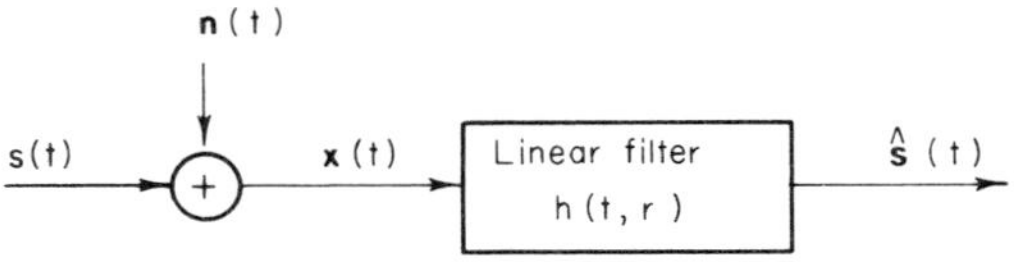

8-8 A stationary process is normally distributed in $[-T/2, +T/2]$ with the covariance function $\exp(-a \mid t - \tau \mid)$. Find the upper bound of $\mathrm{Var}[\hat{\mathbf{\Phi}}_i]$.

8-9 The autocorrelation function of a Poisson process is given by $\lambda t + \lambda^2 t\tau$ $(\tau \geq t)$ and $\lambda\tau + \lambda^2 t\tau$ $(t \geq \tau)$.

Assuming $0 \leq t, \tau \leq T$, find the sampling interval or the number of sampling points to assure that, even if we double the sampling rate, the summation of the newly generated eigenvalues is less than $\varepsilon\%$ of the summation of total eigenvalues.

8-10 We can calculate the autocorrelation matrix of the truncated coefficients of the Fourier series of a stationary random process. Prove that the eivengalues of the above matrix are approximately equal to the eigenvalues of the autocorrelation function of the process. (Hint: The calculation of the Fourier coefficients is an orthonormal transformation in a continuous form.)

Chapter 9

FEATURE SELECTION AND LINEAR MAPPING FOR MULTIDISTRIBUTIONS

When we have two or more classes, feature selection becomes the choosing of those features which are most effective for showing class separability. Class separability is essentially independent of coordinate systems, and this property is different from the criteria for one distribution. Furthermore, class separability depends not only on the class distributions but also on the classifier to be used. For example, the optimum feature set for a linear classifier may not be the optimum set for other classifiers for the same distributions. In order to avoid this complexity, let us assume that we seek the optimum feature set with reference to the Bayes classifier; this will result in minimum error. Then class separability becomes equivalent to the probability of error due to the Bayes classifier, which is the best we can expect.

Therefore, theoretically speaking, the probability of error is the optimum measure of feature effectiveness. Also, in practice, the probability of error calculated experimentally is one of the most popular criteria. That is, having selected a set of features intuitively from given data, construct the Bayes classifier and count the number of classification errors experimentally. The procedure is flexible, distribution free and, theoretically optimum. Furthermore, its computer time can be competitive to many other criteria which are given by explicit mathematical expressions but require complex calculations.

A major disadvantage of the probability of error as a criterion is the fact that an explicit mathematical expression is not available except for a very few special cases and, therefore, we cannot expect a great deal of theoretical development. In Chapter 3, we showed that, even for normal distributions, the calculation of error requires a numerical integration, except for the equal covariance case.

In this chapter, several criteria, which have explicit mathematical expressions, will be discussed. These expressions are derived from some physical notions. However, the reader should be reminded that, whenever a criterion is proposed, the performance of the criterion has to be discussed in relation to the probability of error. When the criterion is not related to the probability of error directly, upper and lower bounds of the error are discussed instead.

9.1 General Properties of Class Separability

Let us express criteria which measure the separability of two classes by

$$c(\omega_i, \omega_j\colon \quad \mathbf{y}_1, \ldots, \mathbf{y}_l) = c(\omega_i, \omega_j\colon \quad \mathbf{Y}_l) \tag{9-1}$$

where l random variables $\mathbf{y}_1, \ldots, \mathbf{y}_l$ are used as the features. Also, we assume that the criteria increase as better class separability is obtained. It is desirable that the criteria satisfy the following conditions.

(1) Monotonic relationship with the probability of error: This condition is usually hard to satisfy.

(2) Monotonic relationship with the upper and lower bounds of the probability of error: The performance of criteria can be evaluated by how close these bounds are to the probability of error.

(3) Invariant property under one-to-one mappings: The probability of error due to the Bayes classifier is invariant under any transformation which holds one-to-one correspondence. Therefore, any criterion which varies under a nonsingular transformation has a serious disadvantage that the criterion is valid only for the given coordinate (and a family of coordinates in which the criterion is invariant).

(4) Additive independent features: If $\mathbf{y}_i$ are mutually independent,

$$c(\omega_i, \omega_j: \mathbf{Y}_l) = \sum_{k=1}^{l} c(\omega_i, \omega_j: \mathbf{y}_k) \tag{9-2}$$

(5) Metric properties:

$$\text{(i)} \quad c(\omega_i, \omega_j: \mathbf{Y}_l) > 0 \quad \text{for} \quad i \neq j \tag{9-3}$$

$$\text{(ii)} \quad c(\omega_i, \omega_i: \mathbf{Y}_l) = 0 \tag{9-4}$$

$$\text{(iii)} \quad c(\omega_i, \omega_j: \mathbf{Y}_l) = c(\omega_j, \omega_i: \mathbf{Y}_l) \tag{9-5}$$

$$\text{(iv)} \quad c(\omega_i, \omega_j: \mathbf{Y}_l) \leq c(\omega_i, \omega_j: \mathbf{Y}_{l+1}) \tag{9-6}$$

It should be noted here that all these conditions are not "must" but "preferred." For example, the probability of error does not satisfy (9-2).

9.2 Discriminant Analysis

Scatter Matrices and Separability Criteria

In *discriminant analysis* of statistics, *within-class* and *between-class scatter matrices* are used to formulate criteria of class separability.

A within-class scatter matrix shows the scatter of samples around their class expected vector, and is expressed by

$$S_w = \sum_{i=1}^{2} P(\omega_i) E\{(\mathbf{X} - M_i)(\mathbf{X} - M_i)^T/\omega_i\} = \sum_{i=1}^{2} P(\omega_i)\Sigma_i \tag{9-7}$$

On the other hand, a between-class scatter matrix can be defined in several ways. For example,

$$S_{b1} = \sum_{i=1}^{2} P(\omega_i)(M_i - M_0)(M_i - M_0)^T \tag{9-8}$$

$$S_{b2} = (M_1 - M_2)(M_1 - M_2)^T \tag{9-9}$$

$$\begin{aligned} S_{b3} &= E\{(\mathbf{X}^{(1)} - \mathbf{X}^{(2)})(\mathbf{X}^{(1)} - \mathbf{X}^{(2)})^T\} \\ &= E\{\mathbf{X}^{(1)}\mathbf{X}^{(1)T}\} + E\{\mathbf{X}^{(2)}\mathbf{X}^{(2)T}\} - 2E\{\mathbf{X}^{(1)}\mathbf{X}^{(2)T}\} \\ &= \Sigma_1 + \Sigma_2 + (M_1 - M_2)(M_1 - M_2)^T \end{aligned} \tag{9-10}$$

where $\mathbf{X}^{(i)}$'s are the samples from class i ($i = 1, 2$), and $\mathbf{X}^{(1)}$ and $\mathbf{X}^{(2)}$ are assumed to be independent. The term M_0 represents the expected vector of the mixture and is given by

$$M_0 = E\{\mathbf{X}\} = P(\omega_1)M_1 + P(\omega_2)M_2 \tag{9-11}$$

The scatter matrix of the mixture is defined by

$$S_m = E\{(\mathbf{X} - M_0)(\mathbf{X} - M_0)^T\} = S_w + S_{b1} \tag{9-12}$$

All these scatter matrices are designed to be invariant under coordinate shifts. In this section, primarily S_w and S_{b1} are used in the discussion, but modification to others is very easy.

In order to formulate criteria for class separability, we have to derive a number from these matrices. The number should be larger when the between-class scatter is larger or the within-class scatter is smaller. There are several ways to do this, and typical criteria are the following:

$$(1) \quad J_1 = \operatorname{tr}(S_2^{-1}S_1) \tag{9-13}$$

$$(2) \quad J_2 = \ln| S_2^{-1}S_1 | = \ln\{| S_1 | / | S_2 |\} \tag{9-14}$$

$$(3) \quad J_3 = \operatorname{tr} S_1 - \mu(\operatorname{tr} S_2 - c) \tag{9-15}$$

$$(4) \quad J_4 = \operatorname{tr} S_1/\operatorname{tr} S_2 \tag{9-16}$$

The following remarks pertain to these criteria:

(1) Usually S_{bi} is used for S_1, and either S_w or $S_w + S_b$ is used for S_2. However, for J_2, $S_w + S_{bi}$ and S_w are used for S_1 and S_2, respectively, because $| S_{b1} | = 0$ and $| S_{b2} | = 0$.

(2) The term J_2 is given by $| S_1 | / | S_2 |$ in many references [Friedman, 1967]. The logarithm is taken in this book in order to obtain the additive property of independent features.

(3) When J_3 is used, we maximize $\operatorname{tr} S_1$, subject to the constraint $\operatorname{tr} S_2 = c$. Therefore, μ is the Lagrange multiplier and c is a constant.

(4) The terms J_1 and J_2 are invariant under any nonsingular linear transformation, while J_3 and J_4 are dependent on the coordinate system.

Feature Selection to Maximize J_1

Suppose that we select m $(m < n)$ features $\mathbf{Y} = [\mathbf{y}_1 \cdots \mathbf{y}_m]^T$, which are obtained by applying an $m \times n$ transformation matrix A to the original n-dimensional vector $\mathbf{X} = [\mathbf{x}_1 \cdots \mathbf{x}_n]^T$ as

$$\mathbf{Y} = A\mathbf{X} \tag{9-17}$$

The scatter matrices of $\mathbf{Y}$, which correspond to S_1 and S_2 in the X space, are

$$S_{1m} = AS_1A^T \qquad \text{and} \qquad S_{2m} = AS_2A^T \tag{9-18}$$

Let λ_i, Φ_i ($i = 1, 2, \ldots, n$) and μ_j, Ψ_j ($j = 1, 2, \ldots, m$) be the eigenvalues and eigenvectors of $S_2^{-1}S_1$ and $S_{2m}^{-1}S_{1m}$, respectively. Although $S_2^{-1}S_1$ is not a symmetric matrix, the eigenvalues and eigenvectors of $S_2^{-1}S_1$ are calculated by diagonalizing S_1 and S_2 simultaneously, as $AS_1A^T = \Lambda$ and $AS_2A^T = I$ [see (2-123) and (2-124)].

Then the J_1's for n and m features are

$$J_1(n) = \operatorname{tr} S_2^{-1}S_1 = \sum_{i=1}^{n} \lambda_i \tag{9-19}$$

$$J_1(m) = \operatorname{tr} S_{2m}^{-1}S_{1m} = \sum_{j=1}^{m} \mu_j \tag{9-20}$$

Once an m-dimensional subspace is determined by A of (9-17), $J_1(m)$ is invariant for any nonsingular $m \times m$ transformation matrix B since

$$\begin{aligned}\operatorname{tr}\{(BS_{2m}B^T)^{-1}(BS_{1m}B^T)\} &= \operatorname{tr}(B^{T^{-1}}S_{2m}^{-1}B^{-1}BS_{1m}B^T) = \operatorname{tr}(B^{T^{-1}}S_{2m}^{-1}S_{1m}B^T)\\ &= \operatorname{tr}(S_{2m}^{-1}S_{1m}B^TB^{T^{-1}}) = \operatorname{tr}(S_{2m}^{-1}S_{1m})\end{aligned} \tag{9-21}$$

Therefore, feature selection for maximizing J_1 means finding a subspace for a given m, such that the eigenvalues of $S_{2m}^{-1}S_{1m}$ in the subspace are larger than those of other m-dimensional subspaces. Once the subspace is fixed, linear transformations within the subspace neither improve nor harm the value of $J_1(m)$.

The term $J_1(m)$ of (9-20) can be maximized with respect to A by finding A, such that

$$\begin{aligned}\Delta J_1(m) = {} & \operatorname{tr}[\{(A + \Delta A)S_2(A^T + \Delta A^T)\}^{-1}\{(A + \Delta A)S_1(A^T + \Delta A^T)\}]\\ & -\operatorname{tr}\{(AS_2A^T)^{-1}(AS_1A^T)\} = 0\end{aligned} \tag{9-22}$$

regardless of ΔA. Using $(I + \Delta)^{-1} \cong I - \Delta$ and ignoring the second or higher-order terms of ΔA,

$$\begin{aligned}\Delta J_1(m) \cong {} & \operatorname{tr}[-(AS_2A^T)^{-1}(\Delta AS_2A^T + AS_2\,\Delta A^T)(AS_2A^T)^{-1}(AS_1A^T)\\ & + (AS_2A^T)^{-1}(\Delta AS_1A^T + AS_1\,\Delta A^T)]\\ = {} & -\operatorname{tr}[(AS_2A^T)^{-1}\,\Delta AS_2\{A^T(AS_2A^T)^{-1}(AS_1A^T) - S_2^{-1}S_1A^T\}]\\ & -\operatorname{tr}[\{(AS_1A^T)(AS_2A^T)^{-1}A - AS_1S_2^{-1}\}S_2\,\Delta A^T(AS_2A^T)^{-1}]\end{aligned} \tag{9-23}$$

Since S_1, S_2, $AS_1A^T(= S_{1m})$, and $AS_2A^T(= S_{2m})$ are all scatter matrices and symmetric, (9-23) has the form of $\Delta J_1(m) = -\mathrm{tr}[\cdot] - \mathrm{tr}[\cdot]^T$. Since $\mathrm{tr}[\cdot] = \mathrm{tr}[\cdot]^T$, (9-23) becomes

$$\Delta J_1(m) \cong -2\,\mathrm{tr}[(AS_2A^T)^{-1}\,\Delta AS_2\{A^T(AS_2A^T)^{-1}(AS_1A^T) - S_2^{-1}S_1A^T\}] = 0 \tag{9-24}$$

In order to satisfy (9-24) regardless of ΔA, $\{\cdot\}$ of (9-24) should be a zero matrix, that is,

$$A^T(AS_2A^T)^{-1}(AS_1A^T) = S_2^{-1}S_1A^T \tag{9-25}$$

Since the matrix $(AS_2A^T)^{-1}(AS_1A^T)$ is $S_{2m}^{-1}S_{1m}$, it can be expressed by using its eigenvalue and eigenvector matrices $\mathscr{M}$ and Ψ as

$$(AS_2A^T)^{-1}(AS_1A^T) = S_{2m}^{-1}S_{1m} = \Psi\mathscr{M}\Psi^T \tag{9-26}$$

Therefore, (9-25) becomes

$$(A^T\Psi)\mathscr{M} = S_2^{-1}S_1(A^T\Psi) \tag{9-27}$$

or,

$$\mu_i(A^T\Psi)_i = S_2^{-1}S_1(A^T\Psi)_i \qquad (i = 1, 2, \ldots, m) \tag{9-28}$$

where $(A^T\Psi)_i$ is the ith column vector of the $n \times m$ matrix $(A^T\Psi)$. Equation (9-28) shows that μ_i and $(A\Psi)_i$ $(i = 1, 2, \ldots, m)$ are also the eigenvalues and eigenvectors of $S_2^{-1}S_1$.

We already know from (9-21) that, after we select an m-dimensional subspace by an $m \times n$ transformation matrix A, a further $m \times m$ transformation matrix Ψ^T does not change $J_1(m)$. Therefore, we can conclude from (9-28) that the optimum transformation A is to select an m-dimensional subspace, such that the eigenvalues of $S_{2m}^{-1}S_{1m}$ in the subspace are

$$\mu_i = \lambda_i \qquad (i = 1, 2, \ldots, m) \tag{9-29}$$

where λ_i are ordered as

$$\lambda_1 > \lambda_2 > \cdots > \lambda_n \tag{9-30}$$

This can be achieved by selecting the first m eigenvectors Φ_i $(i = 1, 2, \ldots, m)$ for A^T.

$$A^T = [\Phi_1\,\Phi_2 \cdots \Phi_m] \tag{9-31}$$

Actually $A^T = [\Phi_1 \cdots \Phi_m]B$ gives the same $J_1(m)$ for any $m \times m$ nonsingular matrix B.

The value of $J_1(m)$ is

$$J_1(m) = \operatorname{tr} \mathscr{M} = \sum_{i=1}^{m} \lambda_i \tag{9-32}$$

Equation (9-32) shows that the effect of an individual feature is independent, and the additive property of (9-2) is satisfied.

EXAMPLE 9-1 Let us use S_{b1} of (9-8) and S_w of (9-7) for S_1 and S_2, respectively. Since the rank of S_{b1} is two, $S_w^{-1}S_{b1}$ has only two nonzero eigenvalues. That is,

$$\begin{aligned} J_1 &= \lambda_1 + \lambda_2 = \operatorname{tr}(S_w^{-1}S_{b1}) \\ &= \sum_{i=1}^{2} P(\omega_i)(M_i - M_0)^T[P(\omega_1)\Sigma_1 + P(\omega_2)\Sigma_2]^{-1}(M_i - M_0) \end{aligned} \tag{9-33}$$

$$\lambda_3 = \lambda_4 = \cdots = \lambda_n = 0 \tag{9-34}$$

Therefore, we can select only two features without reducing J_1.

EXAMPLE 9-2 Let us use S_{b2} of (9-9) and S_w of (9-7) for S_1 and S_2, respectively. Since the rank of S_{b2} is one, $S_w^{-1}S_{b2}$ has only one nonzero eigenvalue. That is,

$$\begin{aligned} J_1 &= \lambda_1 = \operatorname{tr}(S_w^{-1}S_{b2}) \\ &= (M_1 - M_2)^T\{P(\omega_1)\Sigma_1 + P(\omega_2)\Sigma_2\}^{-1}(M_1 - M_2) \end{aligned} \tag{9-35}$$

$$\lambda_2 = \lambda_3 = \cdots = \lambda_n = 0 \tag{9-36}$$

We can select only one feature without reducing J_1. Referring to (3-104), (9-35) is the Chernoff bound for normal distributions when the two distributions have equal covariance matrices $P(\omega_1)\Sigma_1 + P(\omega_2)\Sigma_2$.

Feature Selection to Maximize J_2

The term J_2 can be maximized with respect to A by a procedure similar to the one for J_1.

$$\begin{aligned} \Delta J_2(m) &= \ln \frac{|(A + \Delta A)S_1(A^T + \Delta A^T)|}{|(A + \Delta A)S_2(A^T + \Delta A^T)|} - \ln \frac{|AS_1A^T|}{|AS_2A^T|} \\ &\cong \ln \frac{|I + (\Delta AS_1A^T + AS_1\,\Delta A^T)(AS_1A^T)^{-1}|}{|I + (\Delta AS_2A^T + AS_2\,\Delta A^T)(AS_2A^T)^{-1}|} \\ &\cong \operatorname{tr}\{(\Delta AS_1A^T + AS_1\,\Delta A^T)(AS_1A^T)^{-1}\} \\ &\quad - \operatorname{tr}\{(\Delta AS_2A^T + AS_2\,\Delta A^T)(AS_2A^T)^{-1}\} \\ &= 2\operatorname{tr}[\Delta AS_2\{S_2^{-1}S_1A^T(AS_1A^T)^{-1} - A^T(AS_2A^T)^{-1}\}] = 0 \end{aligned} \tag{9-37}$$

Again, in order to satisfy (9-37) regardless of ΔA, $\{\cdot\}$ of (9-37) should be a zero matrix. Therefore,

$$S_2^{-1}S_1A^T = A^T(AS_2A^T)^{-1}(AS_1A^T) \tag{9-38}$$

Equation (9-38) is the same as (9-25). Also, it can be proved that $J_2(m)$ is invariant under any nonsingular $m \times m$ transformation matrix B, since

$$\ln \frac{|BS_{1m}B^T|}{|BS_{2m}B^T|} = \ln \frac{|B||S_{1m}||B^T|}{|B||S_{2m}||B^T|} = \ln \frac{|S_{1m}|}{|S_{2m}|} \tag{9-39}$$

Thus, for maximizing $J_2(m)$, the first m eivenvectors of $S_2^{-1}S_1$ are selected as the features, and $J_2(m)$ becomes

$$J_2(m) = \sum_{i=1}^{m} \ln \lambda_i \tag{9-40}$$

Also, the additive property (9-2) is satisfied for the orthogonal features.

Feature Selection to Maximize J_3

The terms J_3 and J_4 are coordinate dependent criteria. For example, an $n \times n$ matrix B changes J_3 and J_4 as

$$\begin{aligned} J_3 &= \operatorname{tr}(BS_1B^T) - \mu\{\operatorname{tr}(BS_2B^T) - c\} = \operatorname{tr}(S_1B^TB) - \mu\{\operatorname{tr}(S_2B^TB) - c\} \\ &\neq \operatorname{tr} S_1 - \mu(\operatorname{tr} S_2 - c) \end{aligned} \tag{9-41}$$

$$J_4 = \operatorname{tr}(BS_1B^T)/\operatorname{tr}(BS_2B^T) = \operatorname{tr}(S_1B^TB)/\operatorname{tr}(S_2B^TB) \neq \operatorname{tr} S_1/\operatorname{tr} S_2 \tag{9-42}$$

unless $B^TB = I$, which is an orthonormal transformation.

The optimum features for this case are found by maximizing $J_3(m)$ with respect to A [Sebestyen, 1962].

$$\begin{aligned} \Delta J_3(m) &= \operatorname{tr}\{(A + \Delta A)S_1(A^T + \Delta A^T)\} - \mu[\operatorname{tr}\{(A + \Delta A)S_2(A^T + \Delta A^T)\} - c] \\ &\quad - \operatorname{tr}(AS_1A^T) + \mu\{\operatorname{tr}(AS_2A^T) - c\} \\ &\cong \operatorname{tr}[\{\Delta AS_1A^T - \mu\,\Delta AS_2A^T\} + \{AS_1\,\Delta A^T - \mu AS_2\,\Delta A^T\}] \\ &= 2\operatorname{tr}\{\Delta A(S_1A^T - \mu S_2A^T)\} = 0 \end{aligned} \tag{9-43}$$

In order to satisfy (9-43) regardless of ΔA, $(\cdot)$ of the last line of (9-43) should be a zero matrix. That is,

$$S_2^{-1}S_1A^T = \mu A^T \tag{9-44}$$

Since we have to determine only one μ, A^T becomes a singular matrix, consisting of m identical column vectors. From (9-44), the column vector should be the eigenvector of $S_2^{-1}S_1$, Φ_1, whose corresponding eigenvalue is the largest.

$$A^T = [\overbrace{\Phi_1 \Phi_1 \cdots \Phi_1}^{m}] \tag{9-45}$$

From (9-15) and (9-44), $J_3(m)$ becomes

$$J_3(m) = \operatorname{tr}(AS_1A^T) = \lambda_1 \operatorname{tr}(AS_2A^T) = \lambda_1 c \tag{9-46}$$

Equations (9-44) through (9-46) show that, in order to maximize $J_3(m)$, only one feature is selected, no matter which S_1 is used, and the addition of other features does not help to improve $J_3(m)$. The feature is the eigenvector of $S_2^{-1}S_1$.

Feature Selection to Maximize J_4

Although J_4 is one of the most well-known criteria [Wilks, 1960] it is not easy to find A to maximize J_4 by the procedure which we have used for the other J's. However, if we do not seek absolute optimality, we may choose the eigenvectors of $S_2^{-1}S_1$ again as the features. Normalizing the eigenvectors with respect to S_2, we obtain A which diagonalizes both S_1 and S_2 simultaneously as

$$AS_2A^T = I \qquad AS_1A^T = \Lambda \tag{9-47}$$

Then $J_4(m)$ becomes

$$J_4(m) = \left(\sum_{i=1}^{m} \lambda_i\right) \Big/ \left(\sum_{i=1}^{m} 1\right) = (1/m) \sum_{i=1}^{m} \lambda_i \tag{9-48}$$

Although there is no guarantee that this set of features maximizes $J_4(m)$, they generally give a near optimum $J_4(m)$. Also, the effect of the individual features is independent and additive.

Extension to Multiclass Problems

One of the significant advantages of J_1 through J_4 is the fact that these criteria can be used for multiclass problems. The only modification needed is that we must extend the definitions of scatter matrices, (9-7) through

(9-10). It is difficult to extend (9-9) and (9-10) to multiclass problems. However, (9-7) and (9-8) can be extended easily as

$$S_w = \sum_{i=1}^{M} P(\omega_i)E\{(\mathbf{X} - M_i)(\mathbf{X} - M_i)^T/\omega_i\} = \sum_{i=1}^{M} P(\omega_i)\Sigma_i \tag{9-49}$$

$$S_b = \sum_{i=1}^{M} P(\omega_i)(M_i - M_0)(M_i - M_0)^T \tag{9-50}$$

while the mixture scatter is

$$S_m = E\{(\mathbf{X} - M_0)(\mathbf{X} - M_0)^T\} = S_w + S_b \tag{9-51}$$

The same criteria and the same feature selection procedures used for two-class problems are applicable here.

It should be pointed out that the rank of S_b is M. Therefore, when J_1 is used with S_b for S_1, $S_2^{-1}S_1$ has only M nonzero eigenvalues. The other $n - M$ features do not contribute to J_1.

Obviously, as the number of classes increases, the criteria become more and more inaccurate as indications of class separability. However, this is true for all other criteria as well. One way of overcoming this difficulty is to consider the classes in pairs.

9.3 The Chernoff Bound and the Bhattacharyya Distance

The criteria discussed in the previous section are simple, and selection of the optimum features is straightforward. Furthermore, the criteria can be extended to multiclass problems without major revision. However, one disadvantage is the fact that these criteria do not have a direct relationship to the probability of error for the Bayes classifier. In this section, we will discuss a criterion which is more complicated than the previous ones, but which is related to the upper and lower bounds of the probability of error.

The Chernoff Bound and the Bhattacharyya Distance

As we discussed in Chapter 3, the probability of error is bounded by the Chernoff bound. Recalling (3-100),

$$\begin{aligned} \varepsilon &\le P(\omega_1)^{1-s}P(\omega_2)^s \exp[-\mu(s)] \\ &= P(\omega_1)^{1-s}P(\omega_2)^s \int_{\mathscr{S}} p(X/\omega_1)^{1-s}p(X/\omega_2)^s \, dX \end{aligned} \tag{9-52}$$

This inequality holds for all s between 0 and 1. However, as we saw in (3-101), the optimum s, which gives the lowest bound, satisfies

$$-d\mu(s)/ds = \ln\{P(\omega_1)/P(\omega_2)\} \tag{9-53}$$

where

$$\mu(s) = -\ln \int_{\mathscr{S}} p(X/\omega_1)^{1-s} p(X/\omega_2)^s \, dX \tag{9-54}$$

Thus, (9-52) or $\mu(s)$ of (9-54) can serve as a criterion for class separability.

In general, the evaluation of $\mu(s)$ is difficult. But when both densities are normal, as they are in (3-104), $\mu(s)$ becomes

$$\mu(s) = \tfrac{1}{2}s(1-s)(M_1 - M_2)^T\{(1-s)\Sigma_1 + s\Sigma_2\}^{-1}(M_1 - M_2) + \tfrac{1}{2}\ln\frac{|(1-s)\Sigma_1 + s\Sigma_2|}{|\Sigma_1|^{1-s}\,|\Sigma_2|^s} \tag{9-55}$$

Because of the difficulty of finding the optimum s as well as the relative insensitivity of s around the optimum value, we select 0.5 for s, which still gives the upper bound of ε even though it is not the lowest one. Then

$$\begin{aligned}\varepsilon &\le [P(\omega_1)P(\omega_2)]^{1/2}\exp[-\mu(\tfrac{1}{2})] \\ &= [P(\omega_1)P(\omega_2)]^{1/2}\int_{\mathscr{S}} [p(X/\omega_1)p(X/\omega_2)]^{1/2}\, dX\end{aligned} \tag{9-56}$$

where

$$\mu(\tfrac{1}{2}) = -\ln\int_{\mathscr{S}} [p(X/\omega_1)p(X/\omega_2)]^{1/2}\, dX \tag{9-57}$$

This $\mu(\frac{1}{2})$ is called the *Bhattacharyya distance*, and will be used as a criterion for class separability. In particular, the Bhattacharyya distance for normal distributions is

$$\mu(\tfrac{1}{2}) = \tfrac{1}{8}(M_1 - M_2)^T\left(\frac{\Sigma_1 + \Sigma_2}{2}\right)^{-1}(M_1 - M_2) + \tfrac{1}{2}\ln\frac{|\frac{1}{2}(\Sigma_1 + \Sigma_2)|}{|\Sigma_1|^{1/2}\,|\Sigma_2|^{1/2}} \tag{9-58}$$

The Bhattacharyya distance also gives the lower bound of the probability of error, which is shown as follows [Kailath, 1967]. The probability of error can be expressed as

$$2\varepsilon = 1 - \int_{\mathscr{S}} |P(\omega_1)p(X/\omega_1) - P(\omega_2)p(X/\omega_2)|\, dX \tag{9-59}$$

Figure 9-1 shows a one-dimensional illustration. The summation of areas

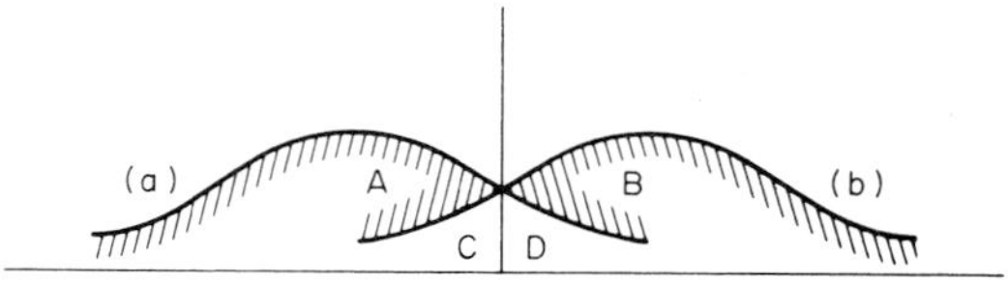

Fig. 9-1 Calculation of ε: (a) $P(\omega_1)p(X/\omega_1)$; (b) $P(\omega_2)p(X/\omega_2)$.

A, D and C yields $P(\omega_1)$ and the summation of areas B, D, and C gives $P(\omega_2)$. On the other hand, the integral of (9-59) gives the summation of areas A and B. Therefore, $1 - (A + B)$ should be equal to $2(C + D)$, which is 2ε. The integral of (9-59) is known as the *variational distance of Kolmogorov*. Using Schwarz's inequality, the Kolmogorov distance is bounded by

$$\begin{aligned}
\left[\int_{\mathscr{S}} | P(\omega_1)p(X/\omega_1) - P(\omega_2)p(X/\omega_2) | \, dX\right]^2 \\
&\leq \int_{\mathscr{S}} | [P(\omega_1)p(X/\omega_1)]^{1/2} - [P(\omega_2)p(X/\omega_2)]^{1/2} |^2 \, dX \\
&\quad \times \int_{\mathscr{S}} | [P(\omega_1)p(X/\omega_1)]^{1/2} + [P(\omega_2)p(X/\omega_2)]^{1/2} |^2 \, dX \\
&= \{1 - 2[P(\omega_1)P(\omega_2)]^{1/2} \exp[-\mu(\tfrac{1}{2})]\}\{1 + 2[P(\omega_1)P(\omega_2)]^{1/2} \exp[-\mu(\tfrac{1}{2})]\} \\
&= 1 - 4P(\omega_1)P(\omega_2) \exp[-2\mu(\tfrac{1}{2})] \qquad (9\text{-}60)
\end{aligned}$$

Combining (9-59) and (9-60), the lower bound of ε is given by

$$\varepsilon \geq \tfrac{1}{2} - \tfrac{1}{2}\{1 - 4P(\omega_1)P(\omega_2) \exp[-2\mu(\tfrac{1}{2})]\}^{1/2} = \tfrac{1}{2} - \tfrac{1}{2}(1 - 4\varepsilon_u{}^2)^{1/2} \qquad (9\text{-}61)$$

where ε_u is the upper bound of ε, from (9-56). When ε_u is very small, the lower bound of ε, ε_l, can be expressed approximately as

$$\varepsilon_l \cong \tfrac{1}{2} - \tfrac{1}{2}(1 - 2\varepsilon_u{}^2) = \varepsilon_u{}^2 \qquad (9\text{-}62)$$

That is, when $\varepsilon_u = 0.3$, 0.1, 0.05, ε_l becomes 0.09, 0.01, and 0.0025.

EXAMPLE 9-3 Let us calculate the lower bound of ε for the data of Example 3-4. Since $\varepsilon_u = 0.048$, the lower bound of (9-61) becomes 0.0023. The true error $\varepsilon = 0.019$ is closer as a ratio to the upper bound than to the lower bound.

In addition to being the upper bound of the probability of error, the Chernoff bound and, subsequently the Bhattacharyya distance, satisfy all preferred properties of class separability which are listed in Section 9-1.

(1) Invariant property by one-to-one mappings:
According to (2-75), for a one-to-one mapping

$$\mathbf{Y} = G(\mathbf{X}) \tag{9-63}$$

the density functions $p(X/\omega_i)$ and $p(Y/\omega_i)$ and the corresponding domains dX and dY are related by

$$p(Y/\omega_i) = p(X/\omega_i)/|\,J\,| \tag{9-64}$$

$$dY = |\,J\,|\,dX \tag{9-65}$$

where $|\,J\,|$ is the Jacobian of this mapping. Therefore,

$$\int_{\mathscr{S}} p(Y/\omega_i)^{1-s} p(Y/\omega_2)^s \, dY = \int_{\mathscr{S}} p(X/\omega_1)^{1-s} p(X/\omega_2)^s \, dX \tag{9-66}$$

Thus $\mu(s)$ is invariant under any one-to-one mapping.

(2) Additive independent features:
When all variables $\mathbf{x}_1, \ldots, \mathbf{x}_n$ are mutually independent for both $p(X/\omega_1)$ and $p(X/\omega_2)$,

$$\int_{\mathscr{S}} p(X/\omega_1)^{1-s} p(X/\omega_2)^s \, dX = \prod_{i=1}^{n} \int_{-\infty}^{+\infty} p(x_i/\omega_1)^{1-s} p(x_i/\omega_2)^s \, dx_i \tag{9-67}$$

Therefore, $\mu(s)$ can be expressed by the summation of the functions of individual variables as

$$\mu(s) = -\sum_{i=1}^{n} \ln \int_{-\infty}^{+\infty} p(x_i/\omega_1)^{1-s} p(x_i/\omega_2)^s \, dx_i \tag{9-68}$$

(3) Metric properties:
The term $\mu(s)$ satisfies (9-3) through (9-6) as follows:

(i)

$$\begin{aligned}\mu(s) &= -\ln \int_{\mathscr{S}} p(X/\omega_1)^{1-s} p(X/\omega_2)^s \, dX \\ &\geq -\ln \int_{\mathscr{S}} \{(1-s)p(X/\omega_1) + sp(X/\omega_2)\} \, dX \\ &= -\ln\{(1-s)+s\} = 0\end{aligned} \tag{9-69}$$

The inequality of (9-69) can be restated as

$$f(s, X) = (1-s)p(X/\omega_1) + sp(X/\omega_2) - p(X/\omega_1)^{1-s} p(X/\omega_2)^s \geq 0 \qquad (0 \leq s \leq 1) \tag{9-70}$$

This can be proved by

$$f(0, X) = 0 \qquad \text{and} \qquad f(1, X) = 0$$

$$\frac{\partial^2 f(s, X)}{\partial s^2} = -p(X/\omega_1)\left\{\frac{p(X/\omega_2)}{p(X/\omega_1)}\right\}^s \left\{\ln \frac{p(X/\omega_2)}{p(X/\omega_1)}\right\}^2 \leq 0 \qquad \text{(9-71)}$$

(ii) When $p(X/\omega_1) = p(X/\omega_2)$,

$$\mu(s) = -\ln \int_{\mathscr{S}} p(X/\omega_1)^{1-s} p(X/\omega_1)^s \, dX = -\ln \int_{\mathscr{S}} p(X/\omega_1) \, dX = -\ln 1 = 0 \qquad \text{(9-72)}$$

(iii) When $p(X/\omega_1)$ and $p(X/\omega_2)$ replace one another,

$$\mu'(s) = -\ln \int_{\mathscr{S}} p(X/\omega_2)^{1-s} p(X/\omega_1)^s \, dX \qquad \text{(9-73)}$$

is different from $\mu(s)$ of (9-54). However, the optimum s_0' which satisfies

$$-d\mu'(s')/ds' = \ln\{P(\omega_2)/P(\omega_1)\} \qquad \text{(9-74)}$$

is related to the optimum s_0 of (9-53) and (9-54) by

$$s_0 = 1 - s_0' \qquad \text{(9-75)}$$

Therefore, for the optimum s_0 and s_0',

$$\mu'(s_0') = \mu(s_0) \qquad \text{(9-76)}$$

For the Bhattacharyya distance with $s = 0.5$, (9-73) is equal to (9-54), that is,

$$\mu'(\tfrac{1}{2}) = \mu(\tfrac{1}{2}) \qquad \text{(9-77)}$$

(iv) Adding a new variable $\mathbf{x}_{n+1}$,

$$\begin{aligned}
\mu'(s) &= -\ln \int_{\mathscr{S}} \int_{-\infty}^{+\infty} p(X, x_{n+1}/\omega_1)^{1-s} p(X, x_{n+1}/\omega_2)^s \, dX \, dx_{n+1} \\
&= -\ln \int_{\mathscr{S}} p(X/\omega_1)^{1-s} p(X/\omega_2)^s \left\{ \int_{-\infty}^{+\infty} p(x_{n+1}/X, \omega_1)^{1-s} \right. \\
&\qquad \left. \times \, p(x_{n+1}/X, \omega_2)^s \, dx_{n+1} \right\} dX \\
&\geq -\ln \int_{\mathscr{S}} p(X/\omega_1)^{1-s} p(X/\omega_2)^s \\
&\qquad \times \left[\int_{-\infty}^{+\infty} \{(1-s)p(x_{n+1}/X, \omega_1) + sp(x_{n+1}/X, \omega_2)\} \, dx_{n+1} \right] dX \\
&= -\ln \int_{\mathscr{S}} p(X/\omega_1)^{1-s} p(X/\omega_2)^s \{(1-s) + s\} \, dX \\
&= \mu(s)
\end{aligned} \qquad \text{(9-78)}$$

The inequality in (9-78) is the same as the one in (9-69). Thus, the addition of a new variable always increases $\mu(s)$.

Feature Selection for Normal Distributions

Feature selection using the Chernoff bound or the Bhattacharyya distance is generally very difficult, because the integration of the product of density functions is involved. It is possible to select features based on other physical reasons and to evaluate these criteria numerically. But, since numerical multidimensional integrations are required, the criteria cannot compete with the probability of error, which has more direct physical meaning. Therefore, the applications of these criteria are limited to some well-defined density functions for which the criteria can be given by explicit mathematical expressions. Although these expressions have been obtained for several densities [Kailath, 1967], we will only discuss the criteria for normal distributions.

For normal distributions, feature selection means finding an $m \times n$ transformation matrix A for a given m to maximize

$$\mu_m(s) = \tfrac{1}{2}s(1-s)[A(M_1 - M_2)]^T[(1-s)A\Sigma_1A^T + sA\Sigma_2A^T]^{-1} \times [A(M_1 - M_2)] + \tfrac{1}{2}\ln\frac{|(1-s)A\Sigma_1A^T + sA\Sigma_2A^T|}{|A\Sigma_1A^T|^{1-s}\,|A\Sigma_2A|^s} \tag{9-79}$$

where $M_1 - M_2$, Σ_1, and Σ_2 of (9-55) are replaced by $A(M_1 - M_2)$, $A\Sigma_1A^T$, and $A\Sigma_2A^T$, respectively. The explicit solution for maximizing (9-79) with respect to A is not as easy to obtain as the one we found for discriminant analysis. However, it is possible to find the optimum A numerically by a search technique. Since $\mu(s)$ is invariant under one-to-one mappings, the search for the optimum A can start from diagonalized covariance matrices I for Σ_1 and Λ for Σ_2, and also can end at diagonalized covariance matrices I for $A\Sigma_1A^T$ and $\mathscr{M}$ for $A\Sigma_2A^T$.

When both covariance matrices are equal, $\Sigma_1 = \Sigma_2 = \Sigma$, the argument becomes very simple. For this case, $\mu_m(s)$ of (9-79) becomes

$$\begin{aligned}\mu_m(s) &= \tfrac{1}{2}s(1-s)[A(M_1 - M_2)]^T(A\Sigma A^T)^{-1}[A(M_1 - M_2)] \\ &= \tfrac{1}{2}s(1-s)\,\mathrm{tr}[(A\Sigma A^T)^{-1}\{A(M_1 - M_2)(M_1 - M_2)^TA^T\}]\end{aligned} \tag{9-80}$$

Equation (9-80) is of the form of J_1 of (9-13), with

$$S_1 = (M_1 - M_2)(M_1 - M_2)^T \qquad \text{and} \qquad S_2 = \Sigma \tag{9-81}$$

Therefore, the optimum A should be the eigenvectors of $S_2^{-1}S_1$. Furthermore, since the rank of S_1 is one, only one eigenvalue is nonzero. Thus,

$$\lambda_1 = \operatorname{tr}(S_2^{-1}S_1) = (M_1 - M_2)^T \Sigma^{-1}(M_1 - M_2) \tag{9-82}$$

$$\lambda_2 = \lambda_3 = \cdots = \lambda_n = 0 \tag{9-83}$$

Also, the first eigenvector is given by

$$\Phi_1 = \Sigma^{-1}(M_1 - M_2)/[(M_1 - M_2)^T \Sigma^{-1}(M_1 - M_2)]^{1/2} \tag{9-84}$$

where Φ_1 is normalized with respect to Σ, such that $\Phi_1{}^T \Sigma \Phi_1 = 1$. Thus, one feature can carry all information of class separability and is, therefore, a sufficient statistic, while the other features are redundant.

When $\Sigma_1 \neq \Sigma_2$, $\mu(s)$ of (9-55) consists of two parts. The first term $\mu^{(1)}(s)$ becomes $\mu(s)$ when the two covariance matrices are equal and therefore may be considered as the class separability due to the mean difference. On the other hand, the second term $\mu^{(2)}(s)$ becomes $\mu(s)$ when $M_1 = M_2$, and may be considered as the class separability due to the difference of covariance matrices. The optimum features for each part can be selected as follows:

(1) *Feature Selection for* $\mu^{(1)}(s)$

The feature selection for $\mu^{(1)}(s)$ is the same as that for the equal covariance case. Only one feature is sufficient, and is given by

$$\mu^{(1)}(s) = \tfrac{1}{2}s(1 - s)(M_1 - M_2)^T\{(1 - s)\Sigma_1 + s\Sigma_2\}^{-1}(M_1 - M_2) \tag{9-85}$$

$$\Phi_1^{(1)} = \frac{\{(1 - s)\Sigma_1 + s\Sigma_2\}^{-1}(M_1 - M_2)}{[(M_1 - M_2)^T\{(1 - s)\Sigma_1 + s\Sigma_2\}^{-1}(M_1 - M_2)]^{1/2}} \tag{9-86}$$

where the superscripts denote that $\mu^{(1)}(s)$ and $\Phi_1^{(1)}$ are for the first term. The term $\Phi_1^{(1)}$ is normalized to satisfy $\Phi_1^{(1)T}\{(1 - s)\Sigma_1 + s\Sigma_2\}\Phi_1^{(1)} = 1$.

(2) *Feature Selection for* $\mu^{(2)}(s)$

The feature selection for $\mu^{(2)}(s)$ is very similar to maximizing $J_2(m)$ of (9-14), because determinants are involved. Using the same procedure as in (9-37),

$$\begin{aligned}
\Delta\mu^{(2)}(s) &= \tfrac{1}{2}\ln\frac{|(A+\Delta A)\{(1-s)\Sigma_1+s\Sigma_2\}(A^T+\Delta A^T)|}{|(A+\Delta A)\Sigma_1(A^T+\Delta A^T)|^{1-s}\,|(A+\Delta A)\Sigma_2(A^T+\Delta A^T)|^s} \\
&\quad - \tfrac{1}{2}\ln\frac{|A\{(1-s)\Sigma_1+s\Sigma_2\}A^T|}{|A\Sigma_1A^T|^{1-s}\,|A\Sigma_2A^T|^s} \\
&\cong \operatorname{tr}[\Delta A\{(1-s)\Sigma_1+s\Sigma_2\}A^T[A\{(1-s)\Sigma_1+s\Sigma_2\}A^T]^{-1}] \\
&\quad - (1-s)\operatorname{tr}\{\Delta A\Sigma_1A^T(A\Sigma_1A^T)^{-1}\} - s\operatorname{tr}\{\Delta A\Sigma_2A^T(A\Sigma_2A^T)^{-1}\} \\
&= \operatorname{tr}\{\Delta A\Sigma_1[\{(1-s)I+s\Sigma_1^{-1}\Sigma_2\}A^T \\
&\quad - (1-s)A^T\{(1-s)I+s(A\Sigma_1A^T)^{-1}(A\Sigma_2A^T)\} \\
&\quad - s\Sigma_1^{-1}\Sigma_2A^T\{(1-s)(A\Sigma_2A^T)^{-1}(A\Sigma_1A^T)+sI\}] \\
&\quad \times [A\{(1-s)\Sigma_1+s\Sigma_2\}A^T]^{-1}\} \\
&= 0
\end{aligned} \tag{9-87}$$

In order to satisfy (9-87) regardless of ΔA, $[\cdot]$ of (9-87) should be a zero matrix. That is,

$$\begin{aligned}
&\{(1-s)I+s\Sigma_1^{-1}\Sigma_2\}A^T - (1-s)A^T\{(1-s)I+s(A\Sigma_1A^T)^{-1}(A\Sigma_2A^T)\} \\
&\qquad -s\Sigma_1^{-1}\Sigma_2A^T\{(1-s)(A\Sigma_2A^T)^{-1}(A\Sigma_1A^T)+sI\} \\
&\quad = s(1-s)[A^T+\Sigma_1^{-1}\Sigma_2A^T - A^T(A\Sigma_1A^T)^{-1}(A\Sigma_2A^T) \\
&\qquad -\Sigma_1^{-1}\Sigma_2A^T(A\Sigma_2A^T)^{-1}(A\Sigma_1A^T)] \\
&\quad = s(1-s)[\Sigma_1^{-1}\Sigma_2A^T - A^T(A\Sigma_1A^T)^{-1}(A\Sigma_2A^T)][I-(A\Sigma_2A^T)^{-1}(A\Sigma_1A^T)] \\
&\quad = 0
\end{aligned} \tag{9-88}$$

The optimum features, therefore, satisfy either

$$\Sigma_1^{-1}\Sigma_2A^T = A^T(A\Sigma_1A^T)^{-1}(A\Sigma_2A^T) \tag{9-89}$$

or

$$A\Sigma_1A^T = A\Sigma_2A^T \tag{9-90}$$

The term A of (9-90) cannot be the optimum, because this makes $\mu_m^{(2)}(s) = 0$ from (9-79). Since (9-89) is the same as (9-25) and also $\mu_m^{(2)}(s)$ is invariant under any $m \times m$ transformation matrix, A should consist of the eigenvectors of $\Sigma_1^{-1}\Sigma_2$ and the eigenvalues of $(A\Sigma_1A^T)^{-1}(A\Sigma_2A^T)$ in the m-dimensional subspace are the same as m eigenvalues of $\Sigma_1^{-1}\Sigma_2$ in the original space. Then $\mu_m^{(2)}(s)$ becomes

$$\begin{aligned}
\mu_m^{(2)}(s) &= \tfrac{1}{2}\ln\left[\prod_{i=1}^{m}\frac{(1-s)+s\lambda_i}{\lambda_i^s}\right] \\
&= \frac{1}{2}\sum_{i=1}^{m}\ln\{(1-s)\lambda_i^{-s}+s\lambda_i^{1-s}\}
\end{aligned} \tag{9-91}$$

Therefore, the first m eigenvalues $\lambda_1, \ldots, \lambda_m$ are selected to satisfy

$$(1-s)\lambda_1^{-s} + s\lambda_1^{1-s} > \cdots > (1-s)\lambda_n^{-s} + s\lambda_n^{1-s} \tag{9-92}$$

instead of $\lambda_1 > \cdots > \lambda_n$ as in a previous discussion. The selected m features are the eigenvectors which correspond to the first m eigenvalues in (9-92), and A can be given by

$$A^T = [\Phi_1^{(2)}\ \Phi_2^{(2)} \cdots \Phi_m^{(2)}] \tag{9-93}$$

where the superscripts denote the second term of $\mu(s)$.

(3) *Feature Selection for the Combination of* $\mu^{(1)}(s)$ *and* $\mu^{(2)}(s)$

When the optimum features are sought for $\mu_m(s)$, we have no analytical procedure, and must use a search technique to find A numerically. However, if we do not insist on optimum features, there are several possibilities for the selection of near-optimum features. Two examples are:

(a) We select the eigenvectors of $\Sigma_1^{-1}\Sigma_2$ and normalize the eigenvectors with respect to Σ_1. Then

$$A\Sigma_1 A^T = I \quad \text{and} \quad A\Sigma_2 A^T = \Lambda \tag{9-94}$$

Subsequently,

$$\mu_m(s) = \frac{1}{2}\sum_{j=1}^{m}\left[s(1-s)\frac{(d_{1j}-d_{2j})^2}{(1-s)+s\lambda_j} + \ln\{(1-s)\lambda_j^{-s}+s\lambda_j^{1-s}\}\right] \tag{9-95}$$

where $(d_{1j} - d_{2j})$ is the jth component of the vector

$$(D_1 - D_2) = A(M_1 - M_2) \tag{9-96}$$

Thus, we select the first m eigenvectors to satisfy [Fukunaga, 1969]

$$s(1-s)\frac{(d_{11}-d_{21})^2}{(1-s)+s\lambda_1} + \ln\{(1-s)\lambda_1^{-s} + s\lambda_1^{1-s}\}$$
$$> \cdots > s(1-s)\frac{(d_{1n}-d_{2n})^2}{(1-s)+s\lambda_n} + \ln\{(1-s)\lambda_n^{-s} + s\lambda_n^{1-s}\} \tag{9-97}$$

In this procedure we are using the features of $\mu^{(2)}(s)$, hoping that these features are also good for $\mu^{(1)}(s)$. "Good" means that $\mu^{(1)}(s)$ can be well represented by small number of features of $\mu^{(2)}(s)$. The advantage of this procedure lies in the fact that the effects of individual features are independently evaluated and are additive.

(b) When $\mu^{(1)}(s)$ is dominant in $\mu(s)$, $\Phi_1^{(1)}$ of (9-86) should be the most effective feature. Therefore, we select $\Phi_1^{(1)}$ first, and other $m - 1$ features could be selected to maximize $\mu_{m-1}^{(2)}(s)$; these are $\Phi_1^{(2)}, \ldots, \Phi_{m-1}^{(2)}$ of (9-93) [Henderson, 1969]. The disadvantage of this procedure is that $\Phi_1^{(1)}$ is not orthogonal to other features and that, therefore, the selection of individual features is no longer independent.

EXAMPLE 9-4 The Bhattacharyya distance $\mu(\frac{1}{2})$ is calculated for Standard Data $i = 1, 2$. Features are selected and ordered according to the above procedures (a) and (b), and the results are shown in Table 9-1.

TABLE 9-1

FEATURE SELECTION TO MAXIMIZE THE BHATTACHARYYA DISTANCE

Procedure (a)

i:	1	2	3	4	5	6	7	8
λ_i:	8.41	12.06	0.12	1.49	0.22	1.77	0.35	2.73
$d_{1i} - d_{2i}$:	3.86	3.10	0.84	1.64	0.84	1.08	0.26	0.01
$\mu_i(\frac{1}{2})$:	0.65	1.15	1.50	1.80	2.08	2.20	2.28	2.35
%:	27.7	48.9	64.9	76.6	88.3	93.6	96.8	100.0
Error bound								
$\frac{1}{2}\exp[-\mu_i(\frac{1}{2})]$ (%):	26.5	15.0	11.1	8.3	6.3	5.5	5.1	4.8
Actual error ε (%):	13.9	6.0	4.7	3.2	2.5	2.2	2.0	1.9

Procedure (b)

j:	1	2	3	4	5	6	7	8
Corresponding								
λ_i from (a):		λ_2	λ_1	λ_3	λ_5	λ_7	λ_8	λ_6
$(\lambda_j^{0.5} + \lambda_j^{-0.5})^2$:		14.14	10.53	10.42	6.77	5.21	5.10	4.34
$\mu_j(\frac{1}{2})$:	1.29	1.59	1.84	2.07	2.10	2.16	2.22	2.35
(%):	54.8	67.7	78.2	88.0	89.2	91.9	94.5	100.0

The Upper Bound for Nonnormal Distributions

We have stated earlier that the applications of the Chernoff bound or the Bhattacharyya distance are limited to some special distributions for which these bounds have explicit mathematical expressions. Accordingly, we discussed feature selection for normal distributions by using these bounds. However, there are some ways to find the upper bound of the probability of error for general distributions. One of these procedures is now described [Heydorn, 1968].

Let us combine the Bhattacharyya bound of (9-56) and Jensen's inequality to obtain the upper bound of error. For a concave function of square root, Jensen's inequality is stated as

$$E\{[p(X/\omega_1)p(X/\omega_2)]^{1/2}\} \leq [E\{p(X/\omega_1)p(X/\omega_2)\}]^{1/2} \tag{9-98}$$

In order to relate the left hand side of (9-98) to the Bhattacharyya bound of (9-56), we assume that we take the expectation of $[p(X/\omega_1)p(X/\omega_2)]^{1/2}$ with a uniform distribution of $\mathbf{X}$. Let A be the volume of the region Ω where $\mathbf{X}$ is distributed uniformly. Then (9-98) is converted to

$$(1/A)\int_{\Omega}[p(X/\omega_1)p(X/\omega_2)]^{1/2}\,dX \leq \left[(1/A)\int_{\Omega}p(X/\omega_1)p(X/\omega_2)\,dX\right]^{1/2} \tag{9-99}$$

or

$$\int_{\Omega}[p(X/\omega_1)p(X/\omega_2)]^{1/2}\,dX \leq \sqrt{A}\left[\int_{\Omega}p(X/\omega_1)p(X/\omega_2)\,dX\right]^{1/2} \tag{9-100}$$

The term Ω should cover the region where $p(X/\omega_1)p(X/\omega_2)$ is not negligibly small. Then the left hand side of (9-100) is almost equivalent to the Bhattacharyya bound where the integration is taken in the entire area $\mathscr{S}$. However, it should be pointed out that the bound of (9-100) is proportional to $\sqrt{A}$ and becomes ∞ for $\Omega = \mathscr{S}$. Therefore, Ω should be chosen as small as possible under the constraint mentioned above.

Thus, the probability of error is bounded by

$$\begin{aligned}\varepsilon &\leq [P(\omega_1)P(\omega_2)]^{1/2}\int_{\mathscr{S}}[p(X/\omega_1)p(X/\omega_2)]^{1/2}\,dX \\ &\leq [P(\omega_1)P(\omega_2)]^{1/2}\left[A\int_{\Omega}p(X/\omega_1)p(X/\omega_2)\,dX\right]^{1/2}\end{aligned} \tag{9-101}$$

Since we are interested in general distributions for $p(X/\omega_i)$, we will estimate the density function on the basis of the available samples. Let us take the Parzen estimate of Chapter 6 and use a normal distribution as its kernel. Then

$$\begin{aligned}p(X/\omega_i) &\cong (1/N_i)\sum_{j=1}^{N_i}(2\pi)^{-n/2}\,|\,\Sigma_i\,|^{-1/2}\,N_i^{1/k} \\ &\quad\times\exp[-\tfrac{1}{2}N_i^{2/(kn)}(X-X_j)^T\Sigma_i^{-1}(X-X_j)]\end{aligned} \tag{9-102}$$

where X_j ($j = 1, 2, \ldots, N$) are samples from class i and Σ_i is the sample covariance matrix of class i. As we discussed in (6-48), k should satisfy the conditions which guarantee the convergence of (9-102) to the true distribution with $N_i \to \infty$, that is,

$$0 < k < 0.5 \tag{9-103}$$

Therefore, the integration of the product of two density functions can be approximated by

$$\begin{aligned}
&\int_\Omega p(X/\omega_1)p(X/\omega_2)\,dX \\
&\quad\cong (N_1N_2)^{-1}\sum_{j=1}^{N_1}\sum_{l=1}^{N_2}\int_{\mathscr{S}}(2\pi)^{-n}(N_1N_2)^{1/k}\,|\,\Sigma_1\,|^{-1/2}|\,\Sigma_2\,|^{-1/2} \\
&\quad\quad\times \exp[-\tfrac{1}{2}\{N_1^{2/(kn)}(X-X_j)^T\Sigma_1^{-1}(X-X_j) \\
&\quad\quad+ N_2^{2/(kn)}(X-X_l)^T\Sigma_2^{-1}(X-X_l)\}]\,dX \\
&\quad= (N_1N_2)^{-1}\sum_{j=1}^{N_1}\sum_{l=1}^{N_2}(2\pi)^{-n/2}(N_1N_2)^{1/k}\,|\,N_2^{2/(kn)}\Sigma_2 + N_1^{2/(kn)}\Sigma_1\,|^{-1/2} \\
&\quad\quad\times \exp[-\tfrac{1}{2}(N_1N_2)^{2/(kn)}(X_j - X_l)^T\{N_2^{2/(kn)}\Sigma_2 + N_1^{2/(kn)}\Sigma_1\}^{-1}(X_j - X_l)]
\end{aligned} \tag{9-104}$$

That is, (9-104) is the sample mean of normal densities for pairwise between-class distances with a weighting function of $N_1^{-2/(kn)}\Sigma_1 + N_2^{-2/(kn)}\Sigma_2$. In practice, since large $(X_j - X_l)$'s do not greatly affect (9-104), the error-bound discussion is based on samples with small $(X_j - X_l)$, where $X_j \in \omega_1$ and $X_l \in \omega_2$. The term A should be determined for the region where samples from both classes exist.

Equation (9-104) can be extended to various kernels to form nonparametric criteria for class separability. Particularly, a hypersphere kernel with radius R leads to a simple criterion as follows.

(1) For each X_i ($X_i \in \omega_j$), count the number of sample X_k's which satisfy $\|\,X_k - X_i\,\| < R$ and $X_k \notin \omega_j$.

(2) Calculate the average of the numbers in (1).

The derivation of this criterion is similar to the derivation for criterion (9-104) and is left as an exercise. This criterion will be used for nonparametric clustering in Chapter 11 and its properties will be studied in detail.

The above discussion of the upper bound is based on Jensen's inequality. In order to check the goodness of the bound, let us examine normal distributions for which both $\int [p(X/\omega_1)p(X/\omega_2)]^{1/2}\,dX$ and $[\int p(X/\omega_1)p(X/\omega_2)\,dX]^{1/2}$

have explicit mathematical expressions:

$$\int_{\mathscr{S}} p(X/\omega_1)p(X/\omega_2)\,dX$$
$$= \int_{\mathscr{S}} (2\pi)^{-n}|\Sigma_1|^{-1/2}|\Sigma_2|^{-1/2}$$
$$\times \exp[-\tfrac{1}{2}\{(X-M_1)^T\Sigma_1^{-1}(X-M_1)+(X-M_2)^T\Sigma_2^{-1}(X-M_2)\}]\,dX$$
$$= (2\pi)^{-n/2}|\Sigma_1+\Sigma_2|^{-1/2}\exp[-\tfrac{1}{2}(M_1-M_2)^T(\Sigma_1+\Sigma_2)^{-1}(M_1-M_2)] \qquad (9\text{-}105)$$

or

$$-\ln[A\int p(X/\omega_1)p(X/\omega_2)\,dX]^{1/2}$$
$$= \tfrac{1}{8}(M_1-M_2)^T\left(\frac{\Sigma_1+\Sigma_2}{2}\right)^{-1}(M_1-M_2)+\tfrac{1}{4}\ln\frac{(4\pi)^n\,|\tfrac{1}{2}(\Sigma_1+\Sigma_2)|}{A^2} \qquad (9\text{-}106)$$

When (9-106) is compared with (9-58), the difference appears in the second term. Let us calculate A as the volume of an ellipsoid after simultaneous diagonalization from Σ_1 and Σ_2 to I and Λ. The volume of an ellipsoid with n radii $r_1, r_2, \ldots, r_n$ along the principle axes is given by

$$A = (2r_1 r_2 \cdots r_n\pi^{n/2})/[n\Gamma(n/2)] \qquad (9\text{-}107)$$

Assuming that normal densities are negligibly small outside of α times their standard deviations. The term r_i could be chosen with surplus as

$$r_i = \alpha(1+\sqrt{\lambda_i}) \qquad (9\text{-}108)$$

Figure 9-2 shows how r_i is chosen. One should remember that, after simultaneous diagonalization, 1 and $\sqrt{\lambda_i}$ are the standard deviations of class 1 and 2, respectively. Inserting (9-107) and (9-108) into (9-106), the second term

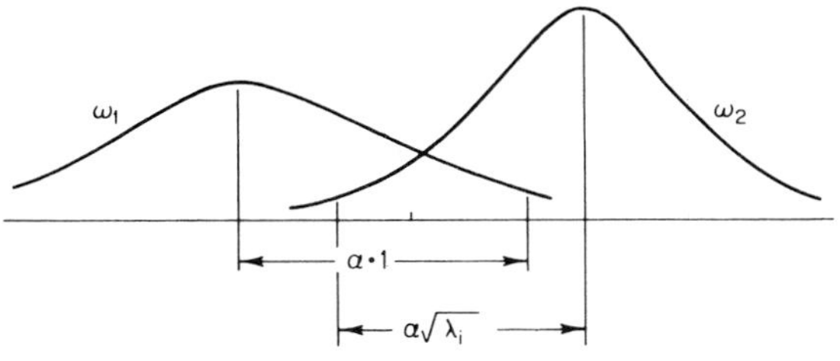

Fig. 9-2 Selection of r_i.

of (9-106) becomes

$$\frac{1}{4}\ln\frac{(4\pi)^n \prod_{i=1}^{n}(1+\lambda_i)/2}{\left[\left\{2\pi^{n/2}\prod_{i=1}^{n}\alpha(1+\sqrt{\lambda_i})\right\}\Big/\left\{n\Gamma\left(\frac{n}{2}\right)\right\}\right]^2}$$
$$=\frac{1}{4}\sum_{i=1}^{n}\ln\frac{1+\lambda_i}{1+2\sqrt{\lambda_i}+\lambda_i}+\frac{n}{4}\ln\frac{2}{\alpha^2}+\frac{1}{2}\ln\left\{\frac{n}{2}\,\Gamma\left(\frac{n}{2}\right)\right\} \tag{9-109}$$

EXAMPLE 9-5 The first and second terms of (9-58) and (9-106) are shown in Table 9-2 for Standard Data $i = 1, 2$

TABLE 9-2

GOODNESS OF JENSEN'S INEQUALITY

a:	1st term of (9-58)	1.27
b:	2nd term of (9-58)	1.08
c:	(9-109) with $\alpha = 3$	0.90
$a + b$:	(9-58)	2.35
$a + c$:	(9-106)	2.17
$e^{-(a+b)}$		0.096
$e^{-(a+c)}$		0.114

Multiclass Problem

As discussed in connection with discriminant analysis, no single criterion can be particularly indicative of multiclass separability. However, it is possible to extend the upper bound of the probability of error to multiclass problems [Lainiotis, 1969]. Let ε and ε_{ij} $(i, j = 1, 2, \ldots, M)$ be the probabilities of the total error and the pairwise error between class i and class j. Then

$$\varepsilon \leq \sum_{i>j}^{M}\sum_{j=1}^{M}\varepsilon_{ij} \tag{9-110}$$

Since the upper bound of ε_{ij} is given by the Chernoff bound or the Bhattacharyya bound, the combination of these bounds and (9-110) gives the upper bound of ε as

$$\varepsilon \leq \sum_{i>j}^{M}\sum_{j=1}^{M} P(\omega_i)^{1-s_{ij}}P(\omega_j)^{s_{ij}}\int_{\mathscr{S}} p(X/\omega_i)^{1-s_{ij}}p(X/\omega_j)^{s_{ij}}\,dX \tag{9-111}$$

where the optimum s_{ij}'s are determined by individual pairs of classes, but, for simplicity's sake, we may use $s_{ij} = 0.5$ $(i, j = 1, 2, \ldots, M)$. Furthermore, using

$$[P(\omega_i)P(\omega_j)]^{1/2} \leq \tfrac{1}{2} \tag{9-112}$$

we may set the upper bound of ε as

$$\varepsilon \leq \frac{1}{2} \sum_{i>j}^{M} \sum_{j=1}^{M} \int_{\mathscr{S}} [p(X/\omega_i)p(X/\omega_j)]^{1/2} \, dX \tag{9-113}$$

9.4 Divergence

The *divergence* is a criterion of class separability similar to the Bhattacharyya distance. Most properties of the divergence can be discussed in terms similar to those used for the Bhattacharyya distance.

In pattern recognition, the key variable is the likelihood ratio or minus-log–likelihood ratio of two density functions. Therefore, if we have some way to evaluate the density or distribution functions of the likelihood ratio for ω_1 and ω_2, it is almost equivalent to evaluating the probability of error. Unfortunately, this is not an easy task. The simplest version of this type of approach might be to use the expected values of the likelihood ratio for ω_1 and ω_2 and to evaluate the class separability by the difference of the expected values of two classes. Thus, the divergence is defined as

$$\begin{aligned} D &= E\left\{- \ln \frac{p(X/\omega_1)}{p(X/\omega_2)} \Big/ \omega_2\right\} - E\left\{- \ln \frac{p(X/\omega_1)}{p(X/\omega_2)} \Big/ \omega_1\right\} \\ &= \int_{\mathscr{S}} p(X/\omega_1) \ln \frac{p(X/\omega_1)}{p(X/\omega_2)} \, dX - \int_{\mathscr{S}} p(X/\omega_2) \ln \frac{p(X/\omega_1)}{p(X/\omega_2)} \, dX \end{aligned} \tag{9-114}$$

Figure 9-3 shows an illustration of the divergence. Since we consider only expected values in the divergence, we cannot expect a close relationship between the divergence and the probability of error. A closer relationship can be obtained by including higher-order moments, but the expressions might become very complicated.

As we discussed for the Chernoff bound in (9-63) through (9-78), D of (9-114) is coordinate independent and additive for independent variables and satisfies all metric properties.

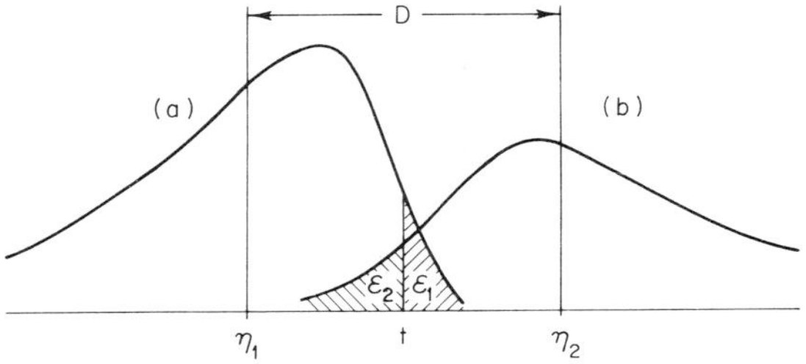

Fig. 9-3 Densities of the likelihood ratio:

(a) $p\left(-\ln \dfrac{p(X/\omega_1)}{p(X/\omega_2)} \Big/ \omega_1\right)$; (b) $p\left(-\ln \dfrac{p(X/\omega_1)}{p(X/\omega_2)} \Big/ \omega_2\right)$

When the densities $p(X/\omega_i)$ $(i = 1, 2)$ are normal, the divergence becomes

$$\begin{aligned} D = \int_{\mathscr{S}} [&- \tfrac{1}{2}\{(X - M_1)^T\Sigma_1^{-1}(X - M_1) - (X - M_2)^T\Sigma_2^{-1}(X - M_2)\} \\ &- \tfrac{1}{2}\ln\{|\Sigma_1|/|\Sigma_2|\}][(2\pi)^{-n/2}|\Sigma_1|^{-1/2}\exp\{-\tfrac{1}{2}(X - M_1)^T\Sigma_2^{-1}(X - M_1)\} \\ &- (2\pi)^{-n/2}|\Sigma_2|^{-1/2}\exp\{-\tfrac{1}{2}(X - M_2)^T\Sigma_1^{-1}(X - M_2)\}]\, dX \\ = \tfrac{1}{2}&(M_1 - M_2)^T(\Sigma_1^{-1} + \Sigma_2^{-1})(M_1 - M_2) + \tfrac{1}{2}\operatorname{tr}(\Sigma_1^{-1}\Sigma_2 + \Sigma_2^{-1}\Sigma_1 - 2I) \end{aligned} \tag{9-115}$$

When the covariance matrices are equal, $\Sigma_1 = \Sigma_2 = \Sigma$, the divergence becomes

$$D = (M_1 - M_2)^T\Sigma^{-1}(M_1 - M_2) \tag{9-116}$$

Comparing (9-116) with (9-55) and (9-58), D for equal covariance case is eight times $\mu(\frac{1}{2})$. This 8 would be used as the multiplication factor when we compare the divergence with the corresponding Bhattacharyya distance. Also, since (9-116) is equal to 2η of (3-32) through (3-34), the divergence is uniquely related to the probability of error for the equal covariance case. The same is true for both the Chernoff bound and the Bhattacharyya distance.

The upper bound of the probability of error in terms of the divergence is not known. An examination by a Monte Carlo type experiment has been reported for the multivariate normal case and yields the bounds indicated in Fig. 9-4 [Marill, 1963]. For a given value of the divergence, the probability of correct recognition (that is, one minus the probability of error) is constrained to lie between the two indicated curves. It has been noticed that the upper bound gives the relation between the probability of correct recogni-

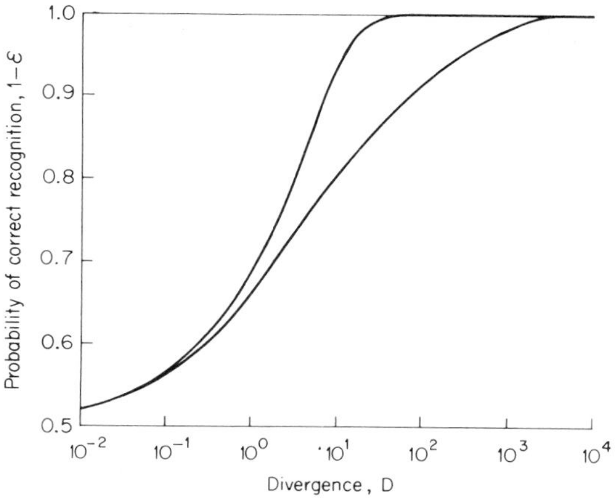

Fig. 9-4 The bounds of the probability of recognition vs the divergence [Marill, 1963].

tion and the divergence for the multivariate normal case with equal covariance matrices. The lower curve was determined from the univariate case.

Feature selection through the use of the divergence for normal distributions is very much the same as for the Bhattacharyya distance, and is stated as follows:

(1) For the first term of (9-115), the optimum feature is given by

$$\lambda_1 = (M_1 - M_2)^T(\Sigma_1^{-1} + \Sigma_2^{-2})(M_1 - M_2) \tag{9-117}$$

$$\lambda_2 = \lambda_3 = \cdots = \lambda_n = 0 \tag{9-118}$$

$$\Phi_1^{(1)} = (\Sigma_1^{-1} + \Sigma_2^{-1})(M_1 - M_2)/[(M_1 - M_2)^T(\Sigma_1^{-1} + \Sigma_2^{-1})(M_1 - M_2)]^{1/2} \tag{9-119}$$

as in (9-85) and (9-86). Only one feature is sufficient. This term is the divergence due to the mean difference.

(2) The second term is the divergence due to the difference of covariance matrices, and the optimum features are the eigenvectors of $\Sigma_1^{-1}\Sigma_2$. The most significant m features are selected by evaluating the eigenvalues in the following order:

$$\lambda_1 + 1/\lambda_1 > \lambda_2 + 1/\lambda_2 > \cdots > \lambda_n + 1/\lambda_n \tag{9-120}$$

This can be rewritten as

$$(\lambda_1^{0.5} + \lambda_1^{-0.5})^2 > (\lambda_2^{0.5} + \lambda_2^{-0.5})^2 > \cdots > (\lambda_n^{0.5} + \lambda_n^{-0.5})^2 \tag{9-121}$$

The order of (9-121) is equal to the order of (9-92) with $s = 0.5$. Therefore, both the divergence and the Bhattacharyya distance select the same features for the second term.

(3) When the optimum features are sought for D, we do not have an analytical procedure, but have to use a search technique to find the transformation matrix numerically [Tou, 1967]. However, if we do not insist on the optimum feature, we may use the following procedures.

(a) We may use the features for the second term of D, which are the eigenvectors of $\Sigma_1^{-1}\Sigma_2$, hoping that the first term of D can be expressed by a small number of these features. The selection of features is made according to the order of

$$\begin{aligned}\{(1 + 1/\lambda_1)(d_{11} - d_{21})^2 + \lambda_1 + 1/\lambda_1\} > \cdots \\ > \{(1 + 1/\lambda_n)(d_{1n} - d_{2n})^2 + \lambda_n + 1/\lambda_n\}\end{aligned} \tag{9-122}$$

where $(d_{1i} - d_{2i})$ are given in (9-96). Subsequently, the divergence with m features becomes

$$D = \frac{1}{2}\sum_{i=1}^{m} [(1 + 1/\lambda_i)(d_{1i} - d_{2i})^2 + \lambda_i + 1/\lambda_i - 2] \tag{9-123}$$

TABLE 9-3

FEATURE SELECTION TO MAXIMIZE THE DIVERGENCE

Procedure (a)

i:	1	2	3	4	5	6	7	8
λ_i:	8.41	12.06	0.12	0.22	1.49	1.77	0.35	2.73
$d_{1i} - d_{2i}$:	3.86	3.10	0.84	0.84	1.64	1.08	0.26	0.01
D:	11.6	21.9	28.2	31.4	33.8	34.8	35.6	36.1
(%):	32.1	60.7	78.1	87.0	93.6	96.4	98.7	100.0
Actual error (%):	13.9	6.0	4.7	3.8	2.5	2.2	2.0	1.9

Procedure (b)

i:	1	2	3	4	5	6	7	8
Corresponding λ_i from (a):		λ_2	λ_1	λ_3	λ_4	λ_7	λ_8	λ_6
$(\lambda_i^{0.5} + \lambda_i^{-0.5})^2$:		14.14	10.53	10.42	6.77	5.21	5.10	4.34
D:	22.5	27.2	31.0	33.5	34.8	35.4	36.0	36.1
(%):	62.2	75.2	85.9	92.6	96.3	98.1	99.6	100.0

(b) When the first term of D is dominant, $\Phi_1^{(1)}$ of (9-119) should be the most effective feature. Therefore, we select $\Phi_1^{(1)}$ first, and other $m-1$ from the features for the second term of D. The term $\Phi_1^{(1)}$ is not orthogonal to the other features.

EXAMPLE 9-6 The divergence D is calculated for Standard Data $i = 1, 2$. Features are selected and ordered according to the above procedure (a) and (b), and the results are shown in Table 9-3.

Computer Projects

Write the following programs:

9-1 Feature selection programs for J_1, J_2, J_3, and J_4 in discriminant analysis. Use S_{b1}, S_w, and S_m.

Data: (a) Standard Data $i = 1, 2, 3, 4$ for a multiclass problem;
(b) Standard Data $i = 1, 2$ for a two-class problem.

9-2 Feature selection programs to maximize the Bhattacharyya distance by using the following features:

(a) The eigenvectors of $\Sigma_1^{-1}\Sigma_2$

(b) Combination of $[\frac{1}{2}(\Sigma_1 + \Sigma_2)]^{-1}(M_1 - M_2)$ and the eigenvectors of $\Sigma_1^{-1}\Sigma_2$.

(c) The original variables.

Data: Standard Data $i = 1, 2$.

9-3 Plot the Chernoff bound vs s and find the optimum s.

9-4 A search program to find the optimum transformation matrix A to maximize the Bhattacharyya distance for a given m.

Data: Standard Data $i = 1, 2$.

9-5 Calculate the upper bound of the Bhattacharyya distance by using the Jensen's inequality and the Parzen estimate.

Data: Samples generated according to Standard Data $i = 1, 2$.

9-6 Repeat 9-2 for the divergence.

9-7 Repeat 9-4 for the divergence.

Problems

9-1 ω_1 and ω_2 consist of three samples as shown in the figure. Calculate $J_1(2)$ and $J_1(1)$ by using S_{b1} and S_w for S_1 and S_2, respectively.

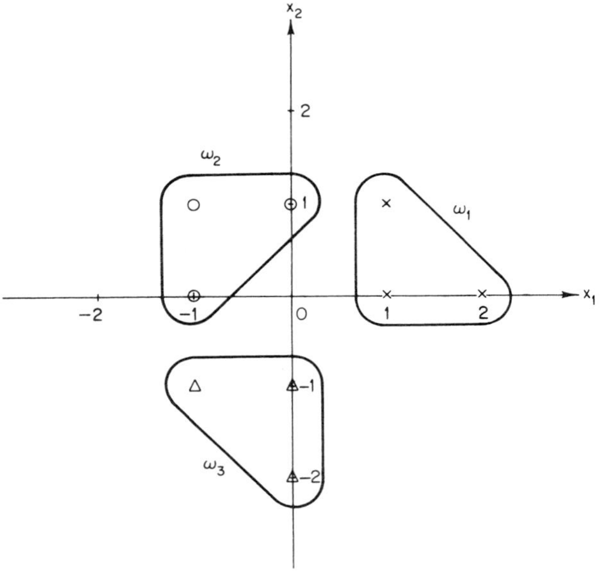

9-2 Adding ω_3 as shown in the figure, calculate $J_1(2)$ and $J_1(1)$ with S_{b1} and S_w.

9-3 Find the optimum features to maximize $\operatorname{tr} S_1$ under a constraint $AS_2A^T = I$, where A is a $m \times n$ $(m < n)$ transformation matrix.

9-4 Assume normal distributions whose expected vectors and covariance matrices are equal to those of 9-1. Calculate the Bhattacharyya distance between ω_1 and ω_2.

9-5 Two one dimensional normal distributions are characterized by their expected values and variances as

Case 1: $m_1 = 0, \quad m_2 = 2, \quad \sigma_1^2 = 4, \quad \sigma_2^2 = 0.25$

Case 2: $m_1 = 0, \quad m_2 = 2, \quad \sigma_1^2 = 1, \quad \sigma_2^2 = 1$

Find the Chernoff bound and its optimized s, and compare with the real probability of error and the Bhattacharyya bound.

9-6 Using the following vectors as the features, show the feature selection to maximize the Bhattacharyya distance.

(a) The eigenvectors of $\Sigma_1^{-1}\Sigma_2$, procedure (a); (b) combinations of $[\frac{1}{2}(\Sigma_1 + \Sigma_2)]^{-1}(M_1 - M_2)$ and the eigenvectors of $\Sigma_1^{-1}\Sigma_2$, procedure (b); (c) the original variables.

9-7 Let $\lambda_1, \ldots, \lambda_n$ be the eigenvalues of $\Sigma_1^{-1}\Sigma_2$, and $\mu_1, \ldots, \mu_m$ be the eigenvalues of $(A\Sigma_1 A^T)^{-1}(A\Sigma_2 A^T)$ where A is a $n \times m$ transformation matrix. Is it true that $\lambda_i \geq \mu_i$? (Hint: See [Kadota, 1967].)

9-8 Repeat 9-4 for the divergence.

9-9 Repeat 9-5 for the divergence.

9-10 Repeat 9-6 for the divergence.

Chapter 10

NONLINEAR MAPPING

Until now, in discussing how to find the optimum features of a given set of data, we have been limited to linear mappings. Unfortunately, a linear mapping, in general, cannot extract the minimum number of effective features. Despite this fact, nonlinear mapping has not been explored mathematically because of its complexity. In practical applications, effective features have primarily been found by the designer's intuition. The difficulty of solving a nonlinear problem is common in all engineering areas. However, this is particularly true in pattern recognition because the number of variables is large.

In this chapter, we will present several techniques available for nonlinear mapping. These are related to finding the intrinsic dimensionality of a given set of data, enhancement of class separability, and two-dimensional display of the data without loss of class separability.

10.1 Intrinsic Dimensionality of Data

Local Properties of a Distribution

Whenever we are confronted by large multidimensional data sets, it is usually advantageous for us to discover or impose some structure on the data. Therefore, we might assume that the data are governed by a certain number of underlying parameters. The minimum number n_0 of parameters required to account for the observed properties of the data is called the *intrinsic dimensionality* of the data set, or, equivalently, the data-generating process. The geometric interpretation is that the entire data set lies on a topological hypersurface of n_0 dimensions.

As we discussed in the previous chapters, linear mapping techniques calculate the principal axes of a multidimensional distribution and eliminate those axes along which the data variance is small. Although this technique is powerful for finding effective features, it is limited because it is based on a linear transformation. For example, in Fig. 10-1, a one-dimensional distribution is shown by a solid line. The principal axes are Φ_1 and Φ_2 and are the same as those for the distribution shown by the dotted line. Thus, the linear mapping fails to demonstrate the intrinsic dimensionality which is 1 for this example.

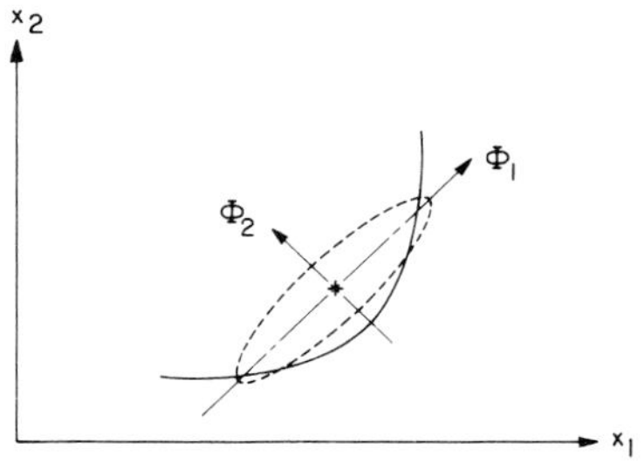

Fig. 10-1 Intrinsic dimensionality and linear mapping.

Consider the following two random processes:

$$\mathbf{x}(t) = \mathbf{a} \exp(-\mathbf{b}t) \tag{10-1}$$

$$\mathbf{x}(t) = \mathbf{a} \exp[-\tfrac{1}{2}(t - \mathbf{m})^2/\boldsymbol{\sigma}^2] \tag{10-2}$$

where **a**, **b**, **m**, and $\boldsymbol{\sigma}$ are random variables. The random processes of (10-1) and (10-2) should be characterized by two parameters **a** and **b** and three parameters **a**, **m**, and **σ**, respectively. Therefore, 2 and 3 are the intrinsic dimensionality of these processes. However, Karhunen–Loève analysis of these processes again suggests dimensionalities higher than the intrinsic value.

As we can see from Fig. 10-1, the intrinsic dimensionality is in essence a local characteristic of the distribution. Referring to Fig. 10-2, if we establish small regions around X_1, X_2, X_3, etc., then the Karhunen–Loève expansions for these local subsets of data should indicate dimensionalities which are

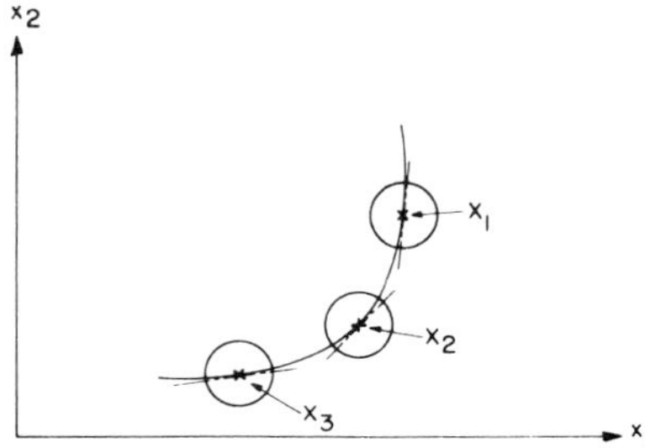

Fig. 10-2 Local subsets of data.

close to the intrinsic dimensionality. These expansions will also give the basis vectors for the local distributions. This approach is similar to local linearization of a nonlinear function. The Taylor series is a common tool for investigating local properties. In order to apply the Taylor series, let us define the *intrinsic random variables* by

$$\mathbf{Y} = [\mathbf{y}_1 \mathbf{y}_2 \cdots \mathbf{y}_{n_0}]^T \tag{10-3}$$

where n_0 is the intrinsic dimension. Then an observed random vector $\mathbf{X}$ whose dimension n is larger than n_0 is a nonlinear function of $\mathbf{Y}$ and is expressed by

$$\mathbf{X} = X(\mathbf{Y}) \tag{10-4}$$

For a random process $\mathbf{x}(t)$, we write

$$\mathbf{x}(t) = x(t, \mathbf{Y}) \tag{10-5}$$

For example, $\mathbf{y}_1 = \mathbf{a}$ and $\mathbf{y}_2 = \mathbf{b}$ for (10-1). The term $\mathbf{X}$ can be represented by a truncated Taylor series around a given vector Y, as long as $\mathbf{Y}$ is within a small region about Y.

$$\Delta\mathbf{X}(Y) = X(\mathbf{Y}) - X(Y) \cong \sum_{i=1}^{n_0} \Delta\mathbf{y}_i \Psi_i(Y) \tag{10-6}$$

where

$$\Psi_i(Y) = \partial X(Y)/\partial y_i \tag{10-7}$$

and

$$\Delta \mathbf{y}_i = \mathbf{y}_i - y_i \tag{10-8}$$

Thus, $\Delta\mathbf{X}(Y)$ can be approximated by a linear expansion of n_0 Ψ_i's. The fact that $\Delta\mathbf{X}(Y)$ is spanned by n_0 or less linearly independent vectors leads us to conclude that the covariance matrix of $\Delta\mathbf{X}(Y)$ has rank, or number of nonzero eigenvalues, equal to or less than n_0.

At this point, the following remarks are in order:

(1) Since (10-6) is an approximation, the actual covariance matrix of the observed data $\Delta\mathbf{X}(Y)$ has the rank n instead of n_0. But n_0 or fewer eigenvalues dominate in the region where the approximation of (10-6) holds.

(2) Unfortunately, the basis vectors of (10-6) Ψ_i are not mutually orthogonal, nor are $\Delta\mathbf{y}_i$, generally, uncorrelated. This means that, when we calculate the basis vectors from the observed data $\Delta\mathbf{X}(Y)$ by the Karhunen–Loève expansion, we obtain a different expansion

$$\Delta\mathbf{X}(Y) \cong \sum_{i=1}^{n_0} \Delta\mathbf{z}_i \Phi_i(Y) \tag{10-9}$$

where

$$\Sigma(Y) = E\{\Delta\mathbf{X}(Y)\,\Delta\mathbf{X}(Y)^T\} \tag{10-10}$$

$$\Sigma(Y)\Phi_i(Y) = \lambda_i(Y)\Phi_i(Y) \tag{10-11}$$

Since the $\Phi_i(Y)$'s and $\lambda_i(Y)$'s are the eigenvectors and eigenvalues of the covariance matrix $\Sigma(Y)$, the $\Phi_i(Y)$'s are mutually orthonormal and $\Delta\mathbf{z}_i$'s are uncorrelated. Both (10-6) and (10-9) are linear expressions of n_0 basis vectors with n_0 random coefficients. Therefore, the $\Delta\mathbf{y}_i$'s and Ψ_i's should be related to the $\Delta\mathbf{z}_i$'s and Φ_i's by a linear transformation, although the transformation matrix is not known. If this transformation matrix could be obtained, we could calculate the Ψ_i's from $\Sigma(Y)$ and Φ_i. Since the Ψ_i's are the partial derivatives of $X(Y)$, as shown in (10-7), this knowledge could be used to estimate the functional form of $X(\mathbf{Y})$ in terms of the intrinsic random variables.

(3) In general, there is no guarantee that the first-order terms are dominant in the Taylor series of (10-6). If the minimum local region size is limited for engineering reasons, we may have some dominant higher-order terms, or some low-order terms may be insignificant. Therefore, the pro-

cedure mentioned above is equivalent to counting the number of significant terms in the Taylor series, which we hope is close to n_0. This hope, however, is justified experimentally, in the examples.

(4) In all real situations, the data measurements are corrupted by noise. It is instructive to consider the effect of additive white noise. Since white noise is zero-mean, uncorrelated with the signal $\Delta\mathbf{X}(Y)$, and has a unit covariance matrix I, the covariance matrix of $\Delta\mathbf{X}(Y)$ plus noise is

$$\Sigma_T(Y) = E\{(\Delta\mathbf{X}(Y) + \mathbf{N})(\Delta\mathbf{X}(Y) + \mathbf{N})^T\} = \Sigma(Y) + \gamma I \qquad (10\text{-}12)$$

The term $\mathbf{N}$ is the vector representation of noise with energy density γ, and $\Sigma(Y)$ is given in (10-10). The eigenvectors of $\Sigma_T(Y)$ are identical to those of $\Sigma(Y)$, that is, the Φ_i of (10-11). The eigenvalues of $\Sigma_T(Y)$, $\mu_i(Y)$ are

$$\mu_i(Y) = \lambda_i(Y) + \gamma \qquad (10\text{-}13)$$

Thus, if the noise-free data has n_0 dominant eigenvalues and $n - n_0$ insignificant ones, the noisy data will have the same distribution of eigenvalues, each one larger by a constant γ. This means that the difference between the n_0th and $(n_0 + 1)$th eigenvalues is preserved. Detection of n_0 dominant eigenvectors means that this difference is significant and can be used to select n_0 eigenvalues in a noisy environment.

A Noniterative Algorithm

Since the intrinsic dimensionality of data is determined by local dimensionalities, with unlimited noise-free data, intrinsic dimensionality is found by reducing the size of the local regions until a limiting dimensionality is reached. In practice, however, there are several factors which complicate this procedure, such as:

(1) limited data set;
(2) noise;
(3) required computer time.

Let us examine the first two items in more detail.

Since the maximum dimensionality of a set of sample vectors is one less than the number of vectors, it is necessary to insure that there are enough data vectors in each local region. With a limited data set, it is possible that a local region with a sufficient number of vectors will be too large for the surface convolutions at that point. In these local regions, the estimated dimensionality is higher than the intrinsic dimensionality.

The most straightforward procedure to estimate a local dimensionality is to calculate the eigenvalues of the sample covariance matrix in the local region and to count the number of the dominant eigenvalues. The threshold for selecting dominant eigenvalues affects the estimation of the dimensionality. Let the threshold value D_e be $e\%$ of the largest eigenvalue.

The number of samples needed to estimate the number of dominant eigenvalues is, in general, much smaller than is required to estimate the values of the eigenvalues. Experience shows that the number of samples N should be only two or three times the number of dominant eigenvalues n_0, regardless of the number of variables n. For example, with $n_0 = 3$, $N = 6$–9 is adequate even for $n = 1000$. Since $n_0 \ll n$ for most applications, the technique of Example 2-20 should be used to determine the eigenvalues.

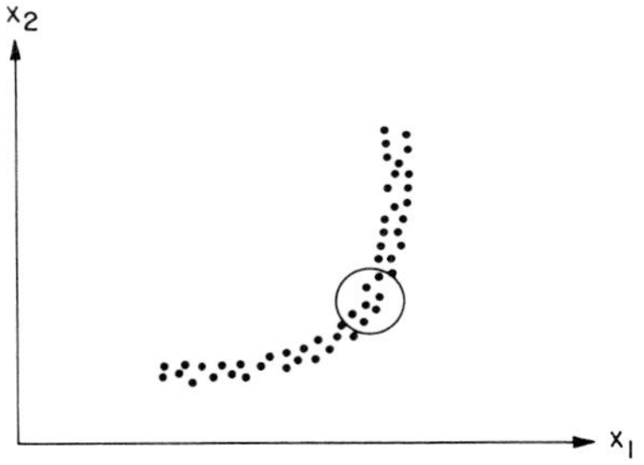

Fig. 10-3 Effect of noise.

The addition of noise has the effect of constraining the size of the local regions. This is shown in Fig. 10-3. As mentioned above, large regions may include several surface convolutions, leading to an overestimate of the intrinsic dimensionality. On the other hand, a small local region will decrease the dominant eigenvalues with respect to the noise component. Therefore, we have to make an engineering compromise on the size of local regions. Also, we have to set up a higher threshold to override the effect of noise on the estimation of the dimensionality. Since these control parameters depend on the data, it is desirable to have an iterative computer system, such that an operator has the flexibility to control these parameters from problem to problem as well as from local region to local region.

One possible algorithm is given as follows [Fukunaga, 1971a]:

(1) *Selection of the Size of Local Regions*

Although the size of local regions could be adjusted region by region, it might be more convenient to fix the size at the beginning of the program.

The proper size is chosen after studying the relationship between the size and the resulting dimensionality around the nearest sample to the sample mean vector of the entire sample set. The size is specified by either the radius of a hypersphere or the number of samples in a local region. An operator should be able to adjust the size whenever he needs to.

(2) *Selection of Local Centers*

This problem is essentially a search in a high-dimensional space and involves many compromises, such as local region size, amount of overlap, and the nature of the search. One possibility is to start by using the first sample of a sample list as a local center. The samples of the local region around the sample are used to determine the local dimensionality and then are removed from the sample list. We repeat the same procedure until the list becomes empty. Statistics of local dimensionalities are tabulated for determining the intrinsic dimensionality of data.

EXAMPLE 10-1 The Gaussian pulse is a popular function since it reasonably approximates many signals encountered in practice, and it is easily characterized by three parameters as shown in (10-2). In this example, 100, 20-dimensional samples are selected with the two parameters **a** and **m** uniformly distributed as

$$1 \leq \mathbf{a} \leq 3 \qquad 0.2 \leq \mathbf{m} \leq 0.8 \qquad \sigma = 0.1 \tag{10-14}$$

Table 10-1a and b give the results for this example. Typical values are given for the local regions as there is little difference between maximum and minimum dimensionalities. Table 10-1b is one of the summary tables produced by the algorithm. This indicates an intrinsic dimensionality of two. The global Karhunen–Loève expansion gives a dimensionality of four for D_{10} criterion and six for the D_1 criterion.

EXAMPLE 10-2 Again, a Gaussian pulse is examined with 3 random variables. A total of 125 20-dimensional samples are selected, such that the three variables are uniformly distributed in

$$1 \leq \mathbf{a} \leq 3, \qquad 0.2 \leq \mathbf{m} \leq 0.8, \qquad 0.05 \leq \boldsymbol{\sigma} \leq 0.20 \tag{10-15}$$

Only the summary table is shown in Table 10-2. The table indicates an intrinsic dimensionality of two or three, compared with the global Karhunen–Loève dimensionality of four and seven for D_{10} and D_1, respectively.

TABLE 10-1

EXAMPLE OF A GAUSSIAN PULSE WITH TWO RANDOM VARIABLES[a]

(a) Normalized Eigenvalues

Around the nearest vector to sample mean vector:

No. of samples	Hypersphere radius	Normalized eigenvalues 1	2	3	4	5	6	7 ...
5	0.84	1.00	0.15	0.02	0.00			
10	1.28	1.00	0.27	0.04	0.00			
15	1.62	1.00	0.31	0.04	0.03	0.00		
25	2.07	1.00	0.47	0.07	0.05	0.01	0.00	
100	4.60	1.00	0.56	0.19	0.13	0.05	0.01	0.00
						D_{10}		D_1

Local regions:

No. of samples	Hypersphere radius	1	2	3	4	5	
5	0.81	1.00	0.00				(Min. dim.)
5	0.83	1.00	0.67	0.03	0.00		(Max. dim.)
10	1.60	1.00	0.39	0.00			(Min. dim.)
10	2.43	1.00	0.38	0.07	0.00		(Max. dim.)
15	1.92	1.00	0.55	0.00			(Min. dim.)
15	2.15	1.00	0.56	0.05	0.01	0.00	(Max. dim.)

(b) Number of Local Regions versus Local Dimensionalities and Region Size

Criteria	Local dimension	No. of regions for region size (no. of samples) 5	10	15	100
D_1	1	15	0	0	—
	2	4	5	3	—
	3	1	15	17	—
	6	0	0	0	1
D_{10}	1	15	0	0	—
	2	5	20	20	—
	3	0	0	0	—
	4	0	0	0	1

[a] [Fukunaga, 1971a].

TABLE 10-2

THE SUMMARY TABLE OF A GAUSSIAN PULSE WITH THREE RANDOM VARIABLES[a]

Criteria	Local dimension	No. of regions for region size (no. of samples)			
		5	10	15	125
D_1	1	0	0	0	—
	2	20	0	0	—
	3	4	12	13	—
	4	0	10	4	—
	5	0	2	4	—
	6	0	0	3	—
	7	0	0	0	1
D_2	1	0	0	0	—
	2	24	13	12	—
	3	0	11	9	—
	4	0	0	3	1

[a] [Fukunaga, 1971a].

An Iterative Algorithm

A configuration of vectors in an n-dimensional space may have an intrinsic dimensionality of less than n. This is equivalent to saying that the configuration lies on an n_0 ($\ll n$) dimensional hypersurface which is imbedded in the n-dimensional space. This hypersurface may be viewed as a linear hypersurface which has been distorted in a nonlinear manner. This distortion can be removed by an iterative stretching process. Figure 10-4 shows a set of five vectors on a curve (solid line) in a two-dimensional space. These points are subsequently unfolded into a straight line (dotted line). Now the intrinsic dimensionality can be determined by Karhunen–Loève analysis.

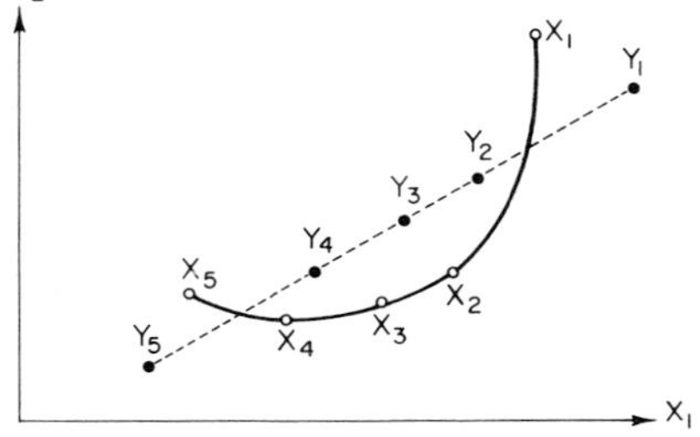

Fig. 10-4 Stretching out of data.

The stretching-out is a kind of nonlinear transformation. As the stretching process proceeds, Karhunen–Loève analysis shows that fewer and fewer variables are required to account for the observed properties of the data. But, by the definition of intrinsic dimensionality, there is some minimum number of variables required to account for properties of the original, unstretched data. Thus, the stretching process must be subject to a constraint which we will now consider.

The property of the original data which must be preserved is the rank order of the intersample distances. Let d_{ij} be the distance between the ith and jth samples, that is,

$$d_{ij} = \| X_i - X_j \| \qquad (i, j = 1, 2, \ldots, N) \tag{10-16}$$

If these distances satisfy

$$d_{15} > d_{45} > \cdots > d_{23} \tag{10-17}$$

then the rank of d_{15} is said to be 1, the rank of d_{45} is 2, and so on, that is,

$$R(d_{15}) = 1, \qquad R(d_{45}) = 2, \ \ldots, \ R(d_{23}) = \tfrac{1}{2}N(N-1) \tag{10-18}$$

After transformation from X_i to Y_i, the intersample distances of the Y's are

$$d_{ij}^* = \| Y_i - Y_j \| \qquad (i, j = 1, 2, \ldots, N) \tag{10-19}$$

The d_{ij}^*'s are in general different from d_{ij}'s, but we would like to preserve the ranks of d_{ij}^*'s to be equal to the ranks of d_{ij}'s, that is,

$$R(d_{ij}) = R(d_{ij}^*) \qquad (i, j = 1, 2, \ldots, N) \tag{10-20}$$

In order to see the relationship between the intrinsic dimensionality and the rank order, let us study the following simple examples.

EXAMPLE 10-3 For four samples, as in Fig. 10-5a, we can find a mapping to a one dimensional space, preserving the rank order as in Fig. 10-5b. But the four samples of Fig. 10-5c do not have such a mapping. The closest mapping is the one shown in Fig. 10-5d, where the ranks of d_{13}^* and d_{14}^* are different from those of d_{13} and d_{14}. It can be easily seen from this example that the more samples we have, the more difficult it is to map these samples onto a line without violating the rank order, unless the samples are located on a one-dimensional curve without heavy bend.

The distance relationship among X_2, X_3, and X_4 in Fig. 10-4 is important in the estimation of the intrinsic dimensionality. However, the ranks of

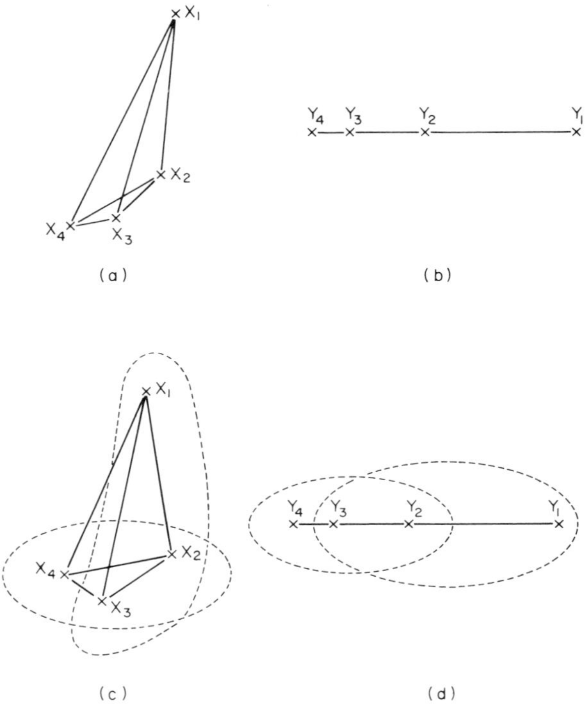

Fig. 10-5 Intrinsic dimensionality and rank order:

(a) $d_{14} > d_{13} > d_{12} > d_{24} > d_{23} > d_{34}$
(b) $d^*_{14} > d^*_{13} > d^*_{12} > d^*_{24} > d^*_{23} > d^*_{34}$
(c) $d_{13} > d_{14} > d_{12} > d_{24} > d_{23} > d_{34}$
(d) $d^*_{14} > d^*_{13} > d^*_{12} > d^*_{24} > d^*_{23} > d^*_{34}$

d_{13} and d_{35} are not as criitical to the structure of the data of Fig. 10-4. Therefore, we can relax the rank preservation to include only local intersample distances and still obtain a reasonable estimation of the intrinsic dimensionality. The size of the local regions where the rank should be preserved is a problem-dependent engineering compromise. For example, if we select two local regions in Fig. 10-5c, as shown by dotted circles, $d_{13} > d_{12} > d_{23}$ for the first region and $d_{24} > d_{23} > d_{34}$ for the second are the distance relationships which are preserved in Fig. 10-5d. Therefore, we can conclude an intrinsic dimensionality of 1 for the data of Fig. 10-5c. Whether the data of Fig. 10-5c is one or two dimensional is a very subjective question which cannot be determined uniquely, not even by a human being.

Next, we need some kind of guideline to stretch out data so as to reduce the dimensionality.

Let us consider the distribution of the intersample distance $\mathbf{d}_{ij}$, where $\mathbf{X}_i$ and $\mathbf{X}_j$ are samples uniformly distributed in a sphere of unit diameter in n dimensions. The density function of $\mathbf{d}$ has been shown to be

$$p_n(d) = \frac{2^n n\, d^{n-1}}{B[\frac{1}{2}(n+1), \frac{1}{2}]} \int_0^{1-d^2} x^{(n-1)/2}(1-x)^{-1/2}\, dx \tag{10-21}$$

where B is the beta function [Hammersley, 1950]. We are particularly interested in the variance of $\mathbf{d}$ as a function of the dimensionality n. Table 10-3 shows the expected value and variance of $\mathbf{d}$. Also, Fig. 10-6 shows the density functions of $\mathbf{d}$ for various n's.

The variance increases as n decreases. Although we do not have a uniform distribution of samples in practical applications, we can still assume an an inverse relationship between n and the variance of $\mathbf{d}$. This property suggests an iterative algorithm for reducing the dimensionality of a set of vectors. At each iteration, we calculate the average value of d_{ij} taken over all pairs of samples. This average is an estimate of $E\{\mathbf{d}\}$. If two samples are separated by more than $E\{\mathbf{d}\}$, they are moved farther apart. Otherwise, they are moved closer together. Thus, at each iteration, the variance of the intersample distances should increase and the dimensionality should de-

TABLE 10-3

EXPECTED VALUE AND VARIANCE OF $\mathbf{d}$[a]

Dimensionality, n	Expected value, $E\{\mathbf{d}\}$	Variance, $\text{Var}_n\{\mathbf{d}\}$
1	0.33	0.056
2	0.45	0.045
3	0.51	0.036
4	0.55	0.029
5	0.58	0.024
6	0.60	0.020
7	0.61	0.018
8	0.62	0.015
9	0.63	0.014
10	0.64	0.012
∞	0.71	0.000

[a] [Bennett, 1969].

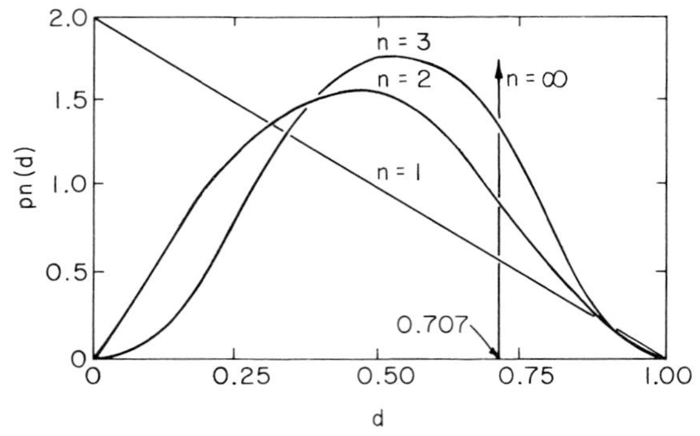

Fig. 10-6 Density function of **d** [Bennett, 1969].

crease. Note in Fig. 10-4, that if X_2, X_3, and X_4 move toward each other, the curve tends to be straightened. The lowest value to which the dimensionality can be reduced without violating the distance ranks is the intrinsic dimensionality.

There could be many ways to increase the variance of **d** without violating the rank order. One possibility is the following [Bennett, 1969].

(1) The variance of **d** is increased by displacing each X_i according to

$$X_i \leftarrow X_i + \sum_{j=1}^{N} (X_i - X_j)[\alpha(d_{ij} - E\{\mathbf{d}\})]/E\{\mathbf{d}\} \tag{10-22}$$

The total displacement of X_i consists of $N - 1$ nonzero components. If $d_{ij} > E\{\mathbf{d}\}$, then there is a component moving X_i away from X_j. If $d_{ij} < E\{\mathbf{d}\}$, there is a component moving X_i toward X_j. The denominator $E\{\mathbf{d}\}$ is a normalizing factor and α is a control parameter. The summation is taken to consider the effect of all samples on the ith sample.

(2) When the rank order is violated by the previous change of X_i, X_i should be modified to reduce the violation. This can be done by

$$X_i \leftarrow X_i - \sum_{j=1}^{N} (X_i - X_j)\gamma\{R(d_{ij}) - R(d_{ij}^*)\} \tag{10-23}$$

That is, when the new rank $R(d_{ij}^*)$ is smaller than the previous rank $R(d_{ij})$, d_{ij}^* becomes too large and is reduced in proportion to $R(d_{ij}) - R(d_{ij}^*)$. The term γ is a control parameter to adjust the degree of modification. The summation may be truncated to respond only to violations of local distance rank.

This type of analysis was originally developed for certain problems in psychology [Shepard, 1962a, b]. A collection of N samples is originally characterized by $N(N-1)/2$ pairwise similarities $S_{12}, \ldots, S_{N-1,N}$. Only the relative value or rank of each S_{ij} has physical meaning. The problem is to obtain a meaningful geometric representation for these samples.

A collection of N samples in an $(N-1)$-dimensional space can always be found, such that the intersample distance d_{ij} satisfy any rank order. Therefore, N locations of these samples are chosen so that the ranks of the d_{ij}'s correspond to those of the given S_{ij}'s. The dimension of the space is then reduced to the intrinsic level. It is remarkable that the resulting configuration and pairwise distances are very well defined. Also, in psychological applications, it is meaningful to plot the monotonic relationship between subjective similarity and geometric distance.

10.2 Separability Enhancement by Nonlinear Mapping

Nonlinear mapping has been shown to be capable of reducing the dimensionality of a configuration of points. It is an effective, off-line technique for preprocessing small sets of data (say 200–300 samples) for low dimensional display and analysis. However, if nonlinear mapping is to be useful in pattern recognition, it must be extended in two ways.

In pattern recognition the goal is to classify samples. Classification based on the observation vectors may be difficult because of the complex nature of the decision boundaries as well as high dimensionality. The observation vectors should be mapped into feature vectors which may be classified by simpler decision rules.

An equally important fact is that once a transformation is established for a finite set of classified samples, it must be made applicable in a noniterative manner to a, perhaps, infinite sequence of unclassified samples; otherwise, the transformation is merely a computational monster with limited practical value.

In this section, we will develop a nonlinear mapping algorithm for separability enhancement in pattern recognition. The object is to alter the distance structure among the samples subject to constraints imposed by the structure of the original distribution. The general tendency is to reduce distances between pairs of samples assigned to the same class (*within-class distances*), while maintaining the distances between samples assigned to different classes (*between-class distances*). Intuition tells us that such an operation will somehow render the samples more easily separable. This tendency toward separability enhancement is constrained by imposing the requirement that the distribution of the samples retain its original properties to some degree.

Separability Enhancement, Structure Preservation, and Intersample Distances

Assume that a set of N classified observation vectors, $\{X_1, \ldots, X_N\}$, is given. Let the class of the ith vector be ω_{k_i}, where k_i is a positive integer between 1 and M, the number of classes. The iterative mapping produces a set of N feature vectors, $\{Y_1, Y_2, \ldots, Y_N\}$. The functional form of the mapping is not specified. Rather, the Y's are chosen so as to optimize a criterion function of the form

$$\begin{aligned} J(Y^*; X^*, \Omega) &= J_S(Y_1, \ldots, Y_N; \omega_{k_1}, \ldots, \omega_{k_N}) + \mu J_G(Y_1, \ldots, Y_N; X_1, \ldots, X_N) \\ &= J_S(Y^*; \Omega) + \mu J_G(Y^*; X^*) \end{aligned} \tag{10-24}$$

where

$$X^* = [X_1^T \, X_2^T \cdots X_N^T]^T \tag{10-25}$$

$$Y^* = [Y_1^T \, Y_2^T \cdots Y_N^T]^T \tag{10-26}$$

and

$$\Omega = [\omega_{k_1} \, \omega_{k_2} \cdots \omega_{k_N}]^T \tag{10-27}$$

denote the entire sets of observation vectors, feature vectors, and classifications, respectively.

The term J_G measures the *goodness of fit* of the structure of the feature vectors to that of the observation vectors. The term J_S is a measure of class separability in the Y space. Finally, μ is a multiplier which governs the relative importance of J_S and J_G in determining the Y's.

The goodness of fit between Y^* and X^* is based on the intersample distances d_{ij}^* $(= \| Y_i - Y_j \|)$ and d_{ij} $(= \| X_i - X_j \|)$ in the Y and X spaces, respectively. Three types of measures are available as follows:

(1) *Monotonicity* [Shepard, 1962a, b]:

$$\sum_{j<i}^{N} \sum^{N} w_{ij} f\{R(d_{ij}^*) - R(d_{ij})\} \, d_{ij}^{*2} \tag{10-28}$$

where

$$f(\xi) \begin{cases} = 0, & \xi = 0 \\ > 0, & \xi \neq 0 \end{cases} \tag{10-29}$$

and $R(\cdot)$ is the rank of the distance as defined in (10-18).

(2) *Stress* [Kruskal, 1964a, b]:

$$\sum_{j<i}^{N}\sum^{N} w_{ij}(d_{ij}^{*} - d_{ij})^2 \tag{10-30}$$

(3) *Continuity* [Shepard, 1966]:

$$\sum_{j<i}^{N}\sum^{N} w_{ij}(d_{ij}^{*}/d_{ij})^2 \tag{10-31}$$

The summations are taken over all distinct pairs (i, j). The weights w_{ij} are usually larger for smaller d_{ij}. A typical example of w_{ij} is given by

$$w_{ij} = \frac{(1/d_{ij})^{\alpha}}{\sum_{j<i}^{N}\sum^{N} (1/d_{ij})^{\alpha}} \tag{10-32}$$

where α is a nonnegative control parameter. In some cases, many of the w's are set equal to zero, particularly for large d_{ij}'s. The monotonicity criterion tends to maintain the rank order of the intersample distances. The stress criterion imposes a stronger relation between corresponding intersample distances. The continuity criterion limits the d_{ij}^{*}'s for those d_{ij}'s which are small.

Any kind of separability criterion can conceivably be used for J_S. In Chapter 9 we presented several such criteria, including those based on scatter measure [$J_1 - J_4$ of (9-13) through (9-16)], Bhattacharyya distance, and divergence. In nonlinear mapping, computational considerations weigh more heavily in determining the utility of a criterion. Thus, although many separability criteria are available and can be used for J_S, criteria of a simple mathematical form are preferred. For example, the trace of the within-class scatter matrix may be used:

$$\begin{aligned} J_S &= \operatorname{tr} S_w \\ &= \operatorname{tr}\left\{\sum_{j=1}^{M} P(\omega_j)(1/N_j) \sum_{Y_i \in \omega_j} (Y_i - D_j)(Y_i - D_j)^T\right\} \\ &= \sum_{j=1}^{M} P(\omega_j)(1/N_j) \sum_{Y_i \in \omega_j} \| Y_i - D_j \|^2 \end{aligned} \tag{10-33}$$

where D_j is the expected vector of those Y's assigned to class j, and N_j is the population of class j. If we use S_w and S_m for S_1 and S_2 and normalize the coordinate system so as to make S_m a unity matrix, this criterion is the same as J_1 of (9-13). We may rewrite (10-33) in terms of the intersample distances.

The reader may easily verify that

$$J_S = \sum_{j=1}^{M} \tfrac{1}{2} P(\omega_j) N_j^{-2} \sum_{Y_i \in \omega_j} \sum_{Y_k \in \omega_j} \| Y_i - Y_k \|^2 \tag{10-34}$$

where the sample mean vector $\Sigma Y_i/N_j$, is used for D_j. Equation (10-34) gives J_S as a weighted summation of the squares of distances between samples in the same class. We can modify J_S slightly by altering the weights to those given by (10-32) to obtain

$$J_S = \sum_{j<i}^{N} \sum^{N} \delta(\omega_{k_i}, \omega_{k_j}) w_{ij} \, d_{ij}^{*2} \tag{10-35}$$

where

$$\delta(\omega_{k_i}, \omega_{k_j}) = \begin{cases} 1, & \omega_{k_i} = \omega_{k_j} \\ 0, & \omega_{k_i} \neq \omega_{k_j} \end{cases} \tag{10-36}$$

Once J_S, J_G, and μ are selected, the Y's can be found by a steepest-descent search technique. The recursive equations can be written in the following general form:

$$Y^*(l) = Y^*(l-1) + \varrho \, \partial J/\partial Y^* \,|_{Y^*=Y^*(l-1)} \cdot \qquad l = 1, 2, \cdots \tag{10-37}$$

where

$$Y^*(0) = X^* \tag{10-38}$$

and ϱ is a positive constant properly chosen. For example, if we use (10-30) as a measure of structure preservation, the combined criterion becomes

$$J = J_S + \mu J_G = \sum_{j<i}^{N} \sum^{N} w_{ij} [\delta(\omega_{k_i}, \omega_{k_j}) \, d_{ij}^{*2} + \mu (d_{ij}^* - d_{ij})^2] \tag{10-39}$$

and the recursive expression for $Y_i(l)$ is

$$Y_i(l) = Y_i(l-1) + \varrho \left[\sum_{\substack{j=1 \\ j \neq i}}^{N} 2 w_{ij} \{ \delta(\omega_{k_i}, \omega_{k_j}) + \mu (1 - d_{ij}/d_{ij}^*) \} \{ Y_i(l-1) - Y_j(l-1) \} \right] \tag{10-40}$$

A random search algorithm can also be used to determine the optimum Y^* [Calvert, 1969]. At each iteration $Y^*(l)$ is generated according to

$$Y^*(l) = Y^*(l-1) + V^* \tag{10-41}$$

where V^* is a random vector of the same dimension as $Y^*(l-1)$. If $Y^*(l)$ is an improvement over $Y^*(l-1)$ in terms of J, then $Y^*(l)$ is equated to it; otherwise, a new V^* is generated. The algorithm terminates when no further improvement can be obtained.

Unfortunately, the iterative nature of the algorithms presented so far limits their utility because of the comments made at the beginning of this section. We will now consider a noniterative mapping algorithm which is still based on the idea of separability enhancement and structure preservation.

A Noniterative Algorithm

The noniterative version of the mapping algorithm is derived as follows. From a finite set of classified samples, we derive a scalar *distance function* which relates distances in the original space to distances in the transformed space. The distance function "on the average" reduces within-class distances, while maintaining between-class distances. Together with a small set of "pivot points", the distance function comprises an on-line transformation which can be applied to unclassified samples. No iterative calculations are required. Further, there are no restrictions on the number of classes or the number of variables [Koontz, 1972a].

We begin by rewriting (10-39) as

$$J = \sum_{j<i}^{N} \sum^{N} [w_{ij}\{\delta(\omega_{k_i}, \omega_{k_j}) + \mu\}\{d_{ij}^* - \{\mu/[\delta(\omega_{k_i}, \omega_{k_j}) + \mu]\} d_{ij}\}^2] + b \tag{10-42}$$

where b is a constant term (that is, b does not depend on the d_{ij}^*'s). Therefore, we can use the first term of (10-42) as an equivalent criterion.

$$J' = \sum_{j<i}^{N} \sum^{N} h_{ij}(d_{ij}^* - q_{ij})^2 \tag{10-43}$$

where

$$h_{ij} = w_{ij}\{\delta(\omega_{k_i}, \omega_{k_j}) + \mu\} \tag{10-44}$$

and

$$q_{ij} = \mu\, d_{ij}/[\delta(\omega_{k_i}, \omega_{k_j}) + \mu] \tag{10-45}$$

Equation (10-43) has the same form as the simple stress of (10-30) and measures the degree of separability enhancement and structure preservation of a configuration.

Suppose that we are free to set the d_{ij}^*'s equal to any positive value. Then J' of (10-43) is clearly minimized if

$$d_{ij}^* = q_{ij} \tag{10-46}$$

for each distinct pair, (i, j). Equation (10-46) defines a discrete relationship between distances in the X configuration and distances in the Y configuration. First, we will generalize (10-46) to define a relationship between all distances in the X and Y spaces. Then we will use this distance function to map points from the X space to the Y space by a closed-form transformation.

Using the definition of q_{ij}, we can rewrite (10-46) as

$$d_{ij}^* = \begin{cases} d_{ij}, & \omega_{k_i} \neq \omega_{k_j} \\ [\mu/(1+\mu)]\, d_{ij}, & \omega_{k_i} = \omega_{k_j} \end{cases} \tag{10-47}$$

Equation (10-47) shows that points in the discrete relationship fall on one of two straight lines through the origin, as shown in Fig. 10-7.

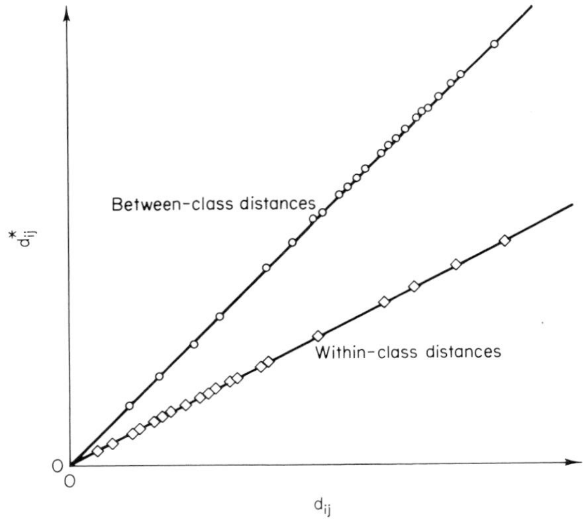

Fig. 10-7 Discrete distance function.

In Fig. 10-7, most of the small distances are shown to be within-class, while the larger ones are mostly between-class. This may not be the case for complex configurations. For example, if one class has a bimodal distribution, we may observe very small and very large within-class distances with intermediate between-class distances.

We will assume that the discrete distance function of (10-47) is sufficiently regular so that a low-order polynomial relating d_{ij}^* to d_{ij} fits most of the points. That is, we can construct a distance function f_d, such that

$$f_d(d_{ij}) \cong q_{ij} \tag{10-48}$$

for all distinct pairs, (i, j), where

$$f_d(x) = a_0 + a_1 x + \cdots + a_r x^r \tag{10-49}$$

and r is a small integer. Of course, we can specify other parametric forms for f_d, but polynomials should be adequate.

Our criterion J' can be used to uniquely specify the polynomial coefficients. We can write

$$J'(A) = \sum_{j<i}^{N} \sum^{N} h_{ij}\{f_d(d_{ij}) - q_{ij}\}^2 \tag{10-50}$$

where

$$A = [a_0 a_1 \cdots a_r]^T \tag{10-51}$$

and determine the optimum coefficients A^* according to

$$J'(A^*) = \min_A J'(A) \tag{10-52}$$

But (10-52) merely defines a standard, least-square fitting problem. The term J' can be written in matrix form.

$$J' = (DA - Q)^T H(DA - Q) \tag{10-53}$$

where

$$D = \left.\begin{bmatrix} 1 & d_{21} & \cdots & d_{21}^r \\ 1 & d_{31} & \cdots & d_{31}^r \\ \vdots & \vdots & & \vdots \\ 1 & d_{N,N-1} & \cdots & d_{N,N-1}^r \end{bmatrix}\right\} N(N-1)/2 \quad \text{(columns: } r+1\text{)} \tag{10-54}$$

$$Q = [\overbrace{q_{21} \quad q_{31} \quad \cdots \quad q_{N,N-1}}^{N(N-1)/2}]^T \tag{10-55}$$

and

$$H = \overbrace{\begin{bmatrix} h_{21} & 0 & \cdots & 0 \\ 0 & h_{31} & \cdots & 0 \\ \vdots & \vdots & & \vdots \\ 0 & 0 & \cdots & h_{N,N-1} \end{bmatrix}}^{N(N-1)/2} \Bigg\} N(N-1)/2 \tag{10-56}$$

The optimum choice for A is, therefore,

$$A^* = (D^T HD)^{-1} D^T HQ \tag{10-57}$$

Equation (10-57) is quite easy to evaluate in practice. The $(r+1)\times(r+1)$ matrix $D^T HD$ and the $r+1$ vector $D^T HQ$ can be computed directly once all of the pairwise distances d_{ij} are determined and μ is chosen. The inversion is not difficult since the polynomial order r is low. Figure 10-8 shows two

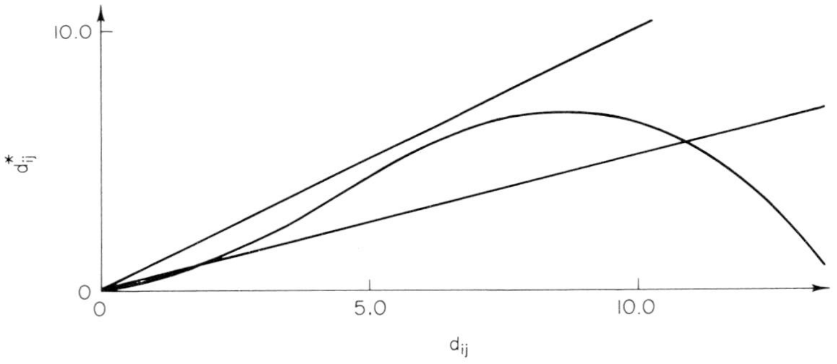

(a)

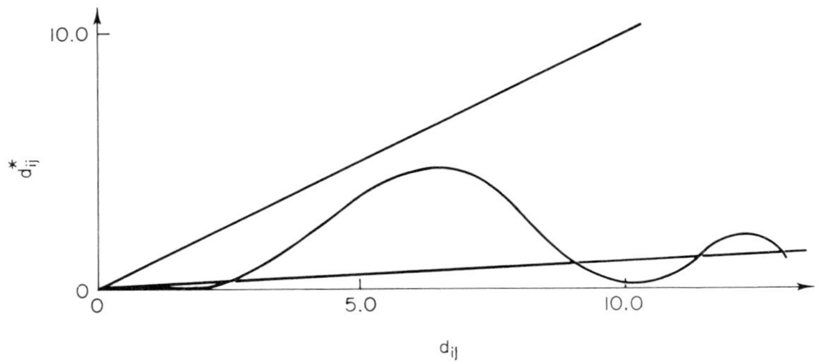

(b)

Fig. 10-8 Polynomial distance functions: (a) $\mu = 1.0$, $r = 3$; (b) $\mu = 0.1$, $r = 7$ [Koontz, 1972a].

examples of distance functions superimposed on the linear relationships of (10-47). The data from which these are derived is described toward the end of this section.

The distance function just derived serves as the key to the nonlinear mapping algorithm. Given any two points in the X space, we can determine the distance between their images in the Y space. Unfortunately, for a given configuration in the X space, there is generally no configuration in the Y space which is consistent with the distance relationships dictated by the distance function. However, we will now show how a nearly consistent configuration can sometimes be constructed.

Let d^* be a Euclidean distance in the n-dimensional Y space. Then, a given point Y can be uniquely specified in term of the distances between Y and $n+1$ suitably chosen pivot points $V_0, V_1, \cdots, V_n$. To see this, note that we can form n equations

$$\| Y - V_i \|^2 - \| Y - V_0 \|^2 = d^{*2}(i) - d^{*2}(0) \qquad (i = 1, \ldots, n) \qquad (10\text{-}58)$$

where $d^*(i)$ is the known distances between Y and V_i. But (10-58) defines a straight line, since the quadratic terms cancel leaving

$$2(V_0 - V_i)^T Y = \| V_0 \|^2 - \| V_i \|^2 + d^{*2}(i) - d^{*2}(0) \qquad (i = 1, \ldots, n) \qquad (10\text{-}59)$$

Equation (10-59) can be written in matrix form by defining

$$V = \begin{bmatrix} 2(V_0 - V_1)^T \\ 2(V_0 - V_2)^T \\ \vdots \\ 2(V_0 - V_n)^T \end{bmatrix} \qquad (10\text{-}60)$$

$$W = \begin{bmatrix} \| V_0 \|^2 - \| V_1 \|^2 \\ \| V_0 \|^2 - \| V_2 \|^2 \\ \vdots \\ \| V_0 \|^2 - \| V_n \|^2 \end{bmatrix} \qquad (10\text{-}61)$$

and

$$C = \begin{bmatrix} d^{*2}(1) - d^{*2}(0) \\ d^{*2}(2) - d^{*2}(0) \\ \vdots \\ d^{*2}(n) - d^{*2}(0) \end{bmatrix} \qquad (10\text{-}62)$$

so that we have

$$VY = W + C \tag{10-63}$$

If the V_i's are chosen so that V is nonsingular, then we can solve (10-63) for Y.

The pivot points in the X space $U_0, \ldots, U_n$ may be determined by various methods. For example, we may find a set of $n + 1$ vectors which are the expected vectors of $n + 1$ local concentrations of samples. The details of this procedure are studied in Chapter 11. Their images in the Y space $V_0, \ldots, V_1$, which make up the V matrix, may be determined by:

(1) calculating the $n(n + 1)/2$ intersample distances of the pivot points in the X space;

(2) using the distance function to find the corresponding intersample distances in the Y space; and

(3) locating the $n + 1$ points in the Y space according to the intersample distances.

Step (3) is straightforward, since the dimension of the space is only one less than the number of points.

Thus, after setting up the pivot points from the training samples in both the X and Y spaces, we can map a new sample X into the Y space by the following nonlinear mapping algorithm:

(1) Calculate the distance $d(i)$ from the point to be mapped, X, to the ith pivot point U_i for ($i = 0, 1, \ldots, n$).

(2) Calculate $d^*(i)$ from $d(i)$ using the distance function,

$$d^*(i) = f_d[d(i)] \qquad (i = 1, \ldots, n) \tag{10-64}$$

(3) Solve (10-63), that is,

$$Y = V^{-1}[W + C(X)] \tag{10-65}$$

Equation (10-65) defines Y as a linear transformation of the vector C, which is a nonlinear function of X. The form of the mapping is very simple.

A simplification of (10-65) is possible. Note that a linear classifier operating on Y can do no better than one operating on C. Therefore, the C vectors can be used as features also. By using C instead of Y, we eliminate the need for finding the V's and performing a time-consuming linear transformation. In the example which follows, we choose this simplified approach.

In deriving (10-63), we assumed that a point Y, located at the prescribed distance from each pivot point, did indeed exist. If these distances are prescribed arbitrarily, however, there is no guarantee that there is such a point. Nevertheless, (10-63) will produce a unique point. In this case, how do we interpret Y? We can circumvent this problem by arbitrarily declaring (10-65) an acceptable mapping function. Unfortunately, this reasoning may damage the arguments presented earlier concerning separability enhancement.

However, the geometrical interpretation can help us to explain what happens to Y in this case. Each equation in (10-59) or (10-63) defines a hyperplane associated with hyperspheres with centers at V_0 and V_i and radii $d^*(0)$ and $d^*(i)$, respectively. In two dimensions, this hyperplane reduces to a line associated with two circles. This line is known as the *radical axis* of two circles [Morrill, 1951] and is a standard topic in analytic geometry.

The behavior of the radical axis of two circles is illustrated in Fig. 10-9. If the two circles intersect, the radical axis is the common chord through the points of intersection. The radical axis does not exist when the two circles are concentric.

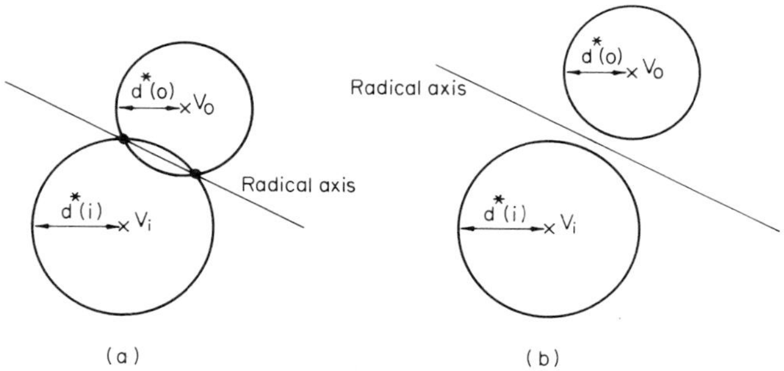

Fig. 10-9 Behavior of the radical axis of two circles: (a) intersecting circles; (b) nonintersecting circles.

The solution to (10-63) is the intersection of the radical axes of n pairs of hyperspheres. Fig. 10-10 shows two situations where there exists no Y at the proper distance from each pivot point. The solution given by (10-65) is the intersection of the radical axes as shown. This solution appears to be a reasonable compromise point. Problems arise, however, when the distances between the pivot points are small compared to the $d^*(i)$'s. In this case, the circles are nearly concentric and the radical axes are badly behaved. Thus, the pivot points should be relatively widely spaced.

EXAMPLE 10-4 The samples shown in Fig. 10-11 are not linearly separable because of the bimodal nature of the distribution for class B. However, since there is apparently little overlap, it seems that nonlinear mapping may unfold the data into a more separable configuration.

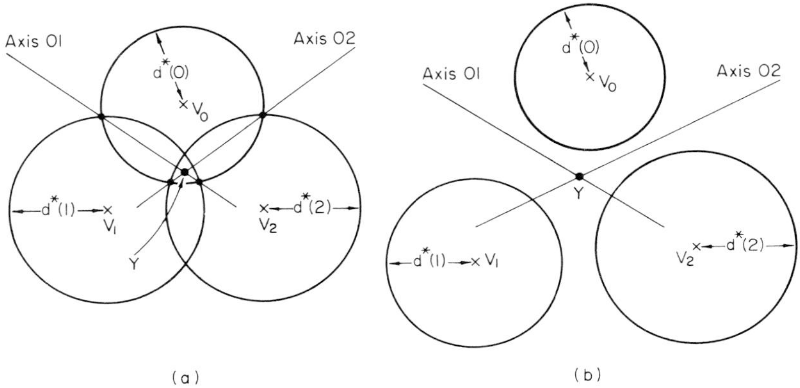

Fig. 10-10 Intersections of radical axes: (a) intersecting circles; (b) nonintersecting circles.

These samples are generated from normal distributions as follows.

Class A: 100 samples from a normal distribution with expected vector and covariance matrix

$$M_A = \begin{bmatrix} 0 \\ 0 \end{bmatrix} \quad \text{and} \quad \Sigma_A = \begin{bmatrix} 1 & 0 \\ 0 & 1 \end{bmatrix} \tag{10-66}$$

Class B: Fifty samples from each of two normal distributions with expected vectors and covariance matrices

$$M_{B1} = \begin{bmatrix} 2 \\ 5 \end{bmatrix}, \quad M_{B2} = \begin{bmatrix} 2 \\ -5 \end{bmatrix}, \quad \text{and} \quad \Sigma_{B1} = \Sigma_{B2} = \begin{bmatrix} 1 & 0 \\ 0 & 1 \end{bmatrix} \tag{10-67}$$

A training set, consisting of 25 samples from each class, is used to construct the distance function for given values of μ and r. For simplicity's sake, we use M_A, M_{B1}, and M_{B2} as pivot points. The effectiveness of the

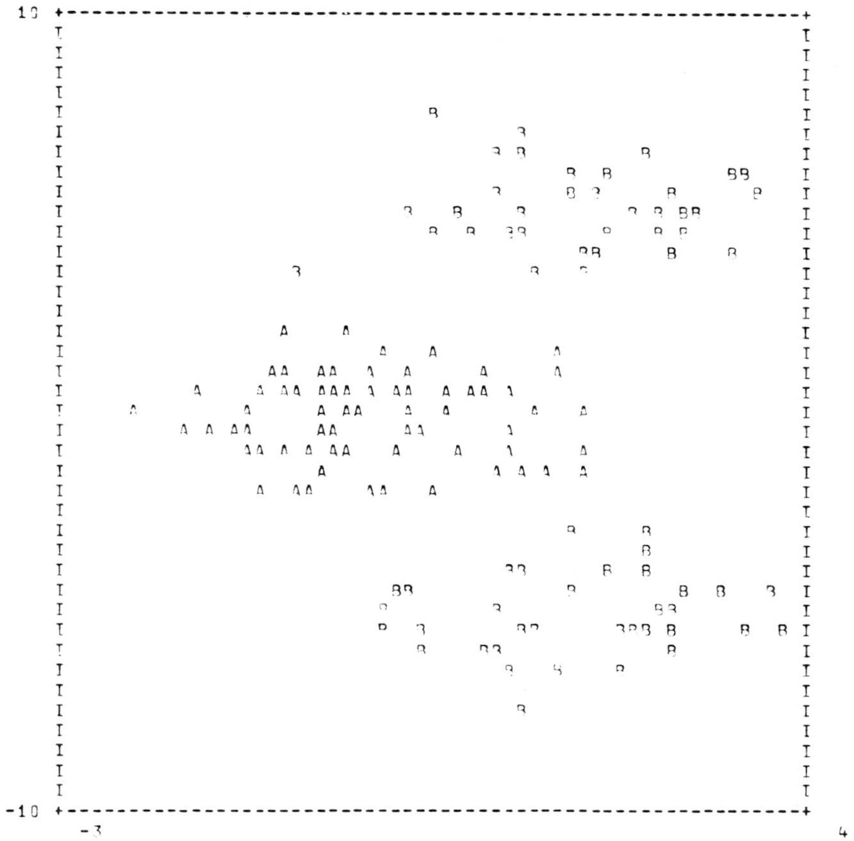

Fig. 10-11 Data for Example 10-4 [Koontz, 1972a].

mapping is determined by applying the mapping $C(X)$ of (10-62) to the balance of the generated samples. These mapped samples are classified according to a bisector linear classifier (see Chapter 4) and the percentage error is used as a measure of separability. The results for various μ's and r's are listed in Table 10-4. Figure 10-12 shows the mapped samples for $\mu = 1.0$ and $r = 3$. It would appear that smaller values of μ and larger values of r are superior. However, a kind of hard distortion becomes evident in this case. This is due to the fact that the distance function begins to exhibit a step behavior, as can be seen in Fig. 10-8. We prefer, however, a relatively smooth unfolding of the data. Therefore, a more conservative choice of μ and r seems in order.

TABLE 10-4

PERCENT CLASSIFICATION ERROR FOR VARIOUS VALUES OF THE POLYNOMIAL ORDER r AND THE CONTROL PARAMETER μ[a]

r \ μ	Polynomial order		
	3	5	7
0.01	6.7 %	2.7 %	2.0 %
0.1	6.7	3.3	2.0
1.0	7.3	4.0	2.7
10.0	10.0	8.0	7.3
100.0	30.0	30.0	29.0

[a] [Koontz, 1972a].

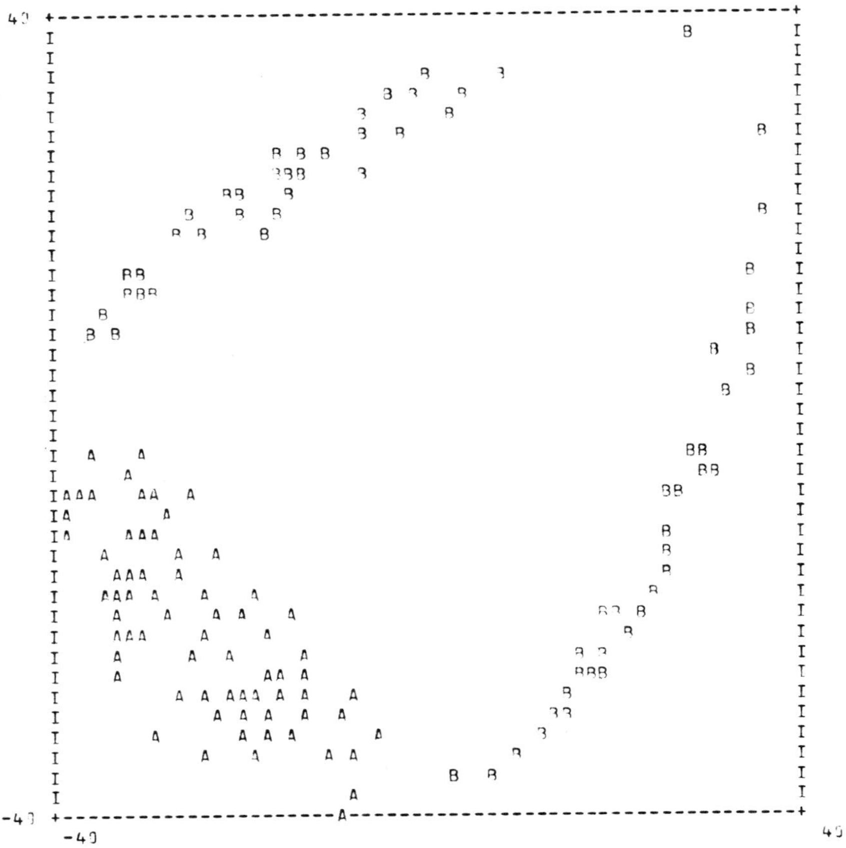

Fig. 10-12 Scatter plot of the mapped samples for $\mu = 1.0$ and $r = 3$ [Koontz, 1972a].

10.3 Two-Dimensional Displays

The aims of the nonlinear mapping algorithms presented so far have been to reduce dimensionality and to enhance separability without altering the local structure of the data. The data were allowed to unfold into as few dimensions as possible. Now we will consider the case where the number of dimensions in the feature space is constrained to be two. This constraint makes possible a display of the data. Two-dimensional display is a key element of interactive analysis.

Distance Preservation

One possibility is to preserve intersample distances as much as possible under a nonlinear mapping from an n-dimensional space to a two-dimensional space. Let d_{ij} and d_{ij}^* be the distance between the ith and jth samples for the n- and two-dimensional spaces, respectively.

$$d_{ij} = \| X_i - X_j \| = \left[\sum_{k=1}^{n} (x_{ik} - x_{jk})^2 \right]^{1/2} \tag{10-68}$$

$$d_{ij}^* = \| Y_i - Y_j \| = \left[\sum_{k=1}^{2} (y_{ik} - y_{jk})^2 \right]^{1/2} \tag{10-69}$$

where X_i and Y_j are the vectors in the n- and two-dimensional spaces, and x_{ik} and y_{jk} are their components. Then the accumulated error with a normalization factor is given by

$$\varepsilon = \left(\sum_{i<j}^{N} d_{ij} \right)^{-1} \sum_{i<j}^{N} (d_{ij} - d_{ij}^*)^2 / d_{ij} \tag{10-70}$$

In order to obtain the optimum mapping in the sense of distance preservation, we minimize ε of (10-70) by adjusting the y_{jk}'s. The steepest descent method gives the following recursive equation for the y_{jk}'s:

$$\begin{aligned} y_{ik}(l+1) &= y_{ik}(l) - \alpha\, \partial\varepsilon / \partial y_{ik} \\ &= y_{ik}(l) + \left[2\alpha \Big/ \left(\sum_{i<j}^{N} d_{ij} \right) \right] \sum_{\substack{j=1 \\ j \neq i}}^{N} [(d_{ij} - d_{ij}^*)/(d_{ij}\, d_{ij}^*)]\, [y_{ik}(l) - y_{jk}(l)] \end{aligned} \tag{10-71}$$

where α is a control parameter.

EXAMPLE 10-5 The above nonlinear mapping has been applied to the Iris data, which are taken from three species of Iris [Sammon, 1969].

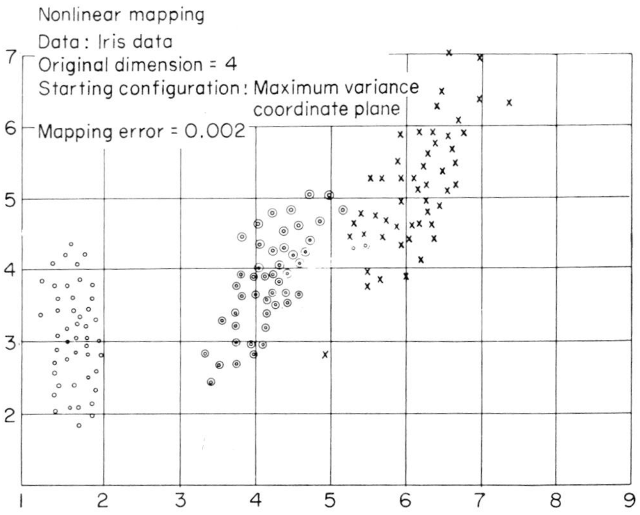

Fig. 10-13 Display of Iris data [Sammon, 1969].

The samples are four-dimensional, and 50 samples are taken from each class. Figure 10-13 shows the two-dimensional display of the data where one species is well separated, while two others overlap slightly.

Distance from Two Points

In the previous discussion, we have tried to preserve the structure of data as much as possible by maintaining the intersample distances. Therefore, it was not our concern whether the data came from more than one distribution. When we want to use a display for classification purposes, we have to choose a transformation which preserves the class separability. For two-class problems, the likelihood ratio is known to be the variable which preserves all of the information pertaining to class separability in the Bayes sense. Subsequently, two probability density functions or monotonic functions of these—usually the minus logarithm—are two such variables. Figure 10-14 shows the display using these two variables.

The Bayes classifier becomes a 45° line, regardless of the distributions. Thus, the display of Fig. 10-14 shows no information loss for classification. The only problem is that the calculation of $-\ln p(X/\omega_i)$ is complex. When the density functions can be expressed by a set of parameters, parameter estimation is involved. For example, when the density functions are

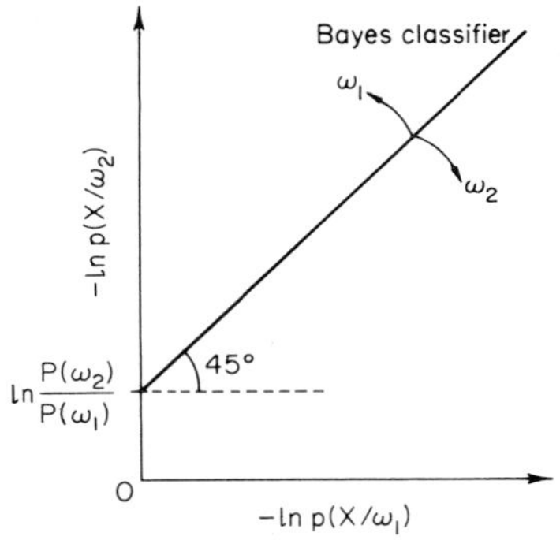

Fig. 10-14 Two-dimensional display of data.

known to be normal, $-\ln p(X/\omega_i)$ becomes

$$-\ln p(X/\omega_i) = \tfrac{1}{2}(X - \hat{M}_i)^T \hat{\Sigma}_i^{-1}(X - \hat{M}_i) + \tfrac{1}{2} \ln\{(2\pi)^n \mid \hat{\Sigma}_i \mid\} \quad (10\text{-}72)$$

where $\hat{M}_i$ and $\hat{\Sigma}_i$ are the estimates of the expected vector and covariance matrix. For the nonparametric case, the techniques of Chapter 6 (such as the Parzen estimate) can be used. Thus, the inaccuracy of display comes from estimation errors of the density functions.

Two much simpler features for display are the Euclidean distances from two points M_1 and M_2. Although there is no theoretical justification, an intuitive choice for M_1 and M_2 is the expected vectors of class 1 and class 2. Thus,

$$d_i^2(X) = (X - M_i)^T(X - M_i) \qquad (i = 1, 2) \qquad (10\text{-}73)$$

A line boundary on the d-display can be expressed by

$$d_2^2(X) = d_1^2(X) \tan\theta + c \qquad (10\text{-}74)$$

or

$$\begin{aligned}(X - M_2)^T(X - M_2) &- \tan\theta(X - M_1)^T(X - M_1) - c \\ &= (1 - \tan\theta)X^TX - 2(M_2 - \tan\theta M_1)^TX + (M_2^TM_2 - M_1^TM_1 - c) \\ &= 0 \end{aligned} \qquad (10\text{-}75)$$

where θ is the angle between the line and the d_1^2 axis, and c is the intercept of the line on the d_2^2 axis. Equation (10-75) shows that a line in the d-display corresponds to a sphere in the X space, as is shown in Fig. 10-15a and b.

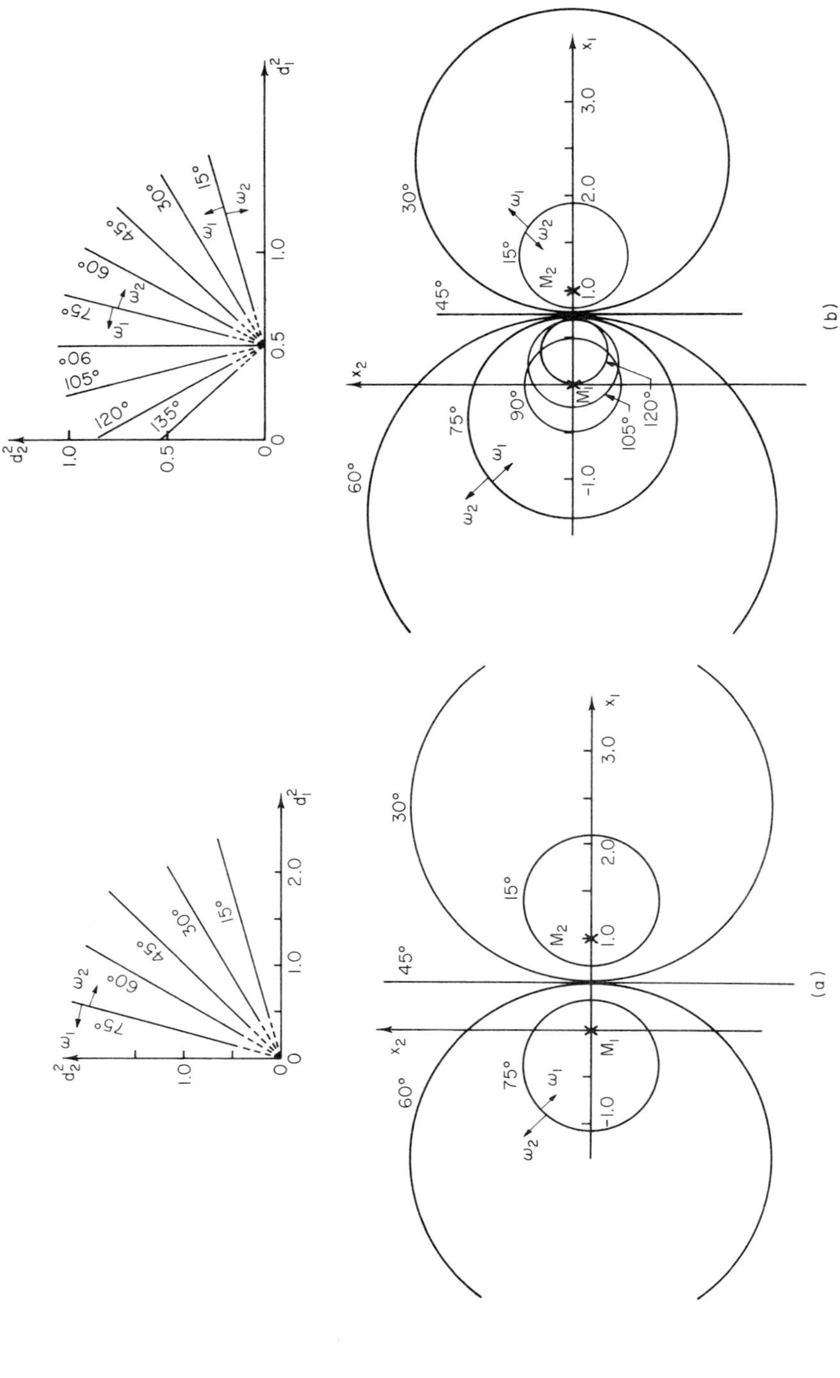

Fig. 10-15 Linear boundaries on the display.

A 45° line corresponds to a hyperplane which is perpendicular to the mean-difference vector $M_2 - M_1$.

Although lines on the display correspond to a very limited set of hypersurfaces in the X space, a combination of lines, which is a piecewise linear classifier on the display, can generate a complex surface in the X space. An example is shown in Fig. 10-16. The important idea here is that a human operator can generate a relatively complex boundary by using the display.

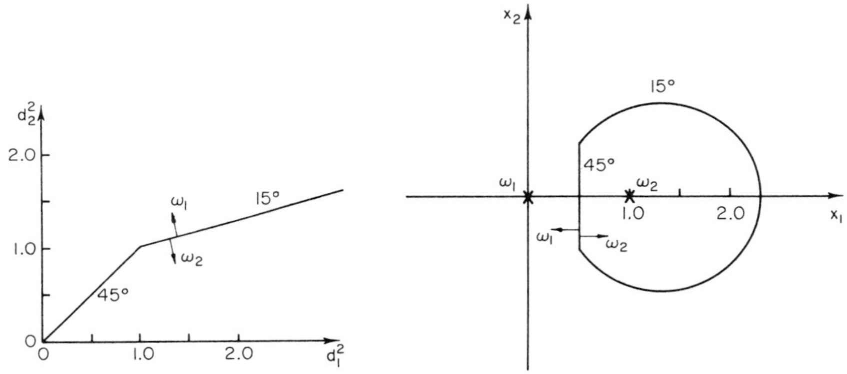

Fig. 10-16 A piecewise linear boundary on the display.

Thus, the Euclidean distances from two points are simple features for display. However, since these distances do not have a unique relationship to density functions, they cannot represent class separability exactly. The approximation is poor for some particular distributions. Therefore, we need some normalization processes in order to obtain better approximations.

(1) *Mixture Normalization*

The d-display performs poorly when the two distributions are as shown in Fig. 10-17a. In this case, both X_1 and X_2 are mapped into the same point Y in the d-display and, subsequently, the two displayed distributions overlap heavily, although they are well separated in the X space. This difficulty can be overcome by the mixture normalization of (4-53). As we discussed in Chapter 4, if two distributions are normal with equal covariance matrices, the mean-difference vector $D_2 - D_1$ becomes perpendicular to the Bayes classifier, as is shown in Fig. 10-17b. Even when the two distributions have different covariance matrices, the mean-difference vector $D_2 - D_1$ is perpendicular to the Bayes classifier for two distributions with equal averaged covariance matrices, as shown in Fig. 10-17c. Thus, the mixture normalization eliminates the difficulty mentioned above. Figure 10-18 shows the d-display of two species of Iris data which are denoted by $\times$ and ◎ in Fig. 10-13.

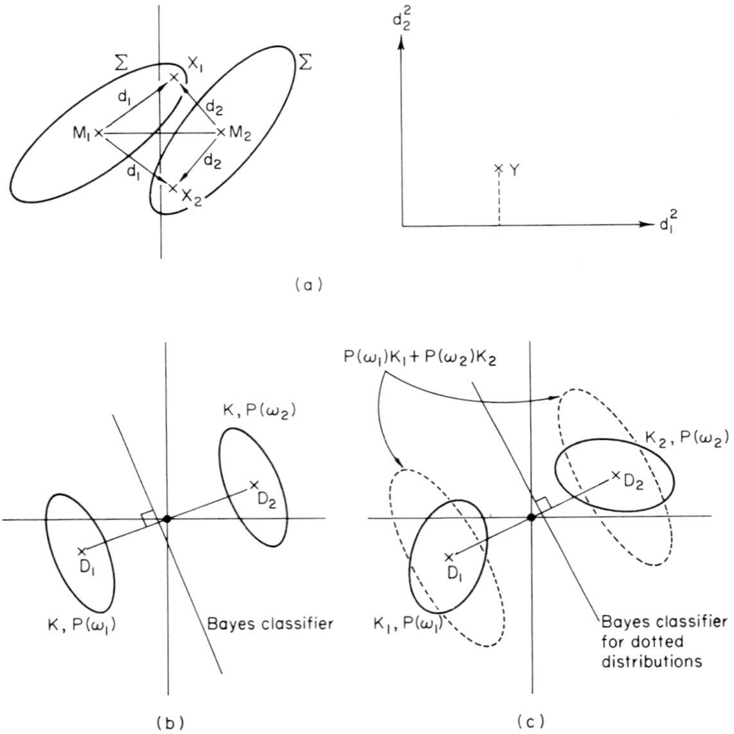

Fig. 10-17 Mixture normalization.

(2) *One-Class Normalization*

Another important normalization, which we will call a *one-class normalization*, is to transform the covariance matrix of one class to I. This normalization is particularly effective when we want to separate one class from all other classes in multiclass problems, as shown in Fig. 10-19a and b. The d-display for Fig. 10-19b is given in Fig. 10-19c, where the samples from class 1 should be located in that region where $d_1 < d_0$.

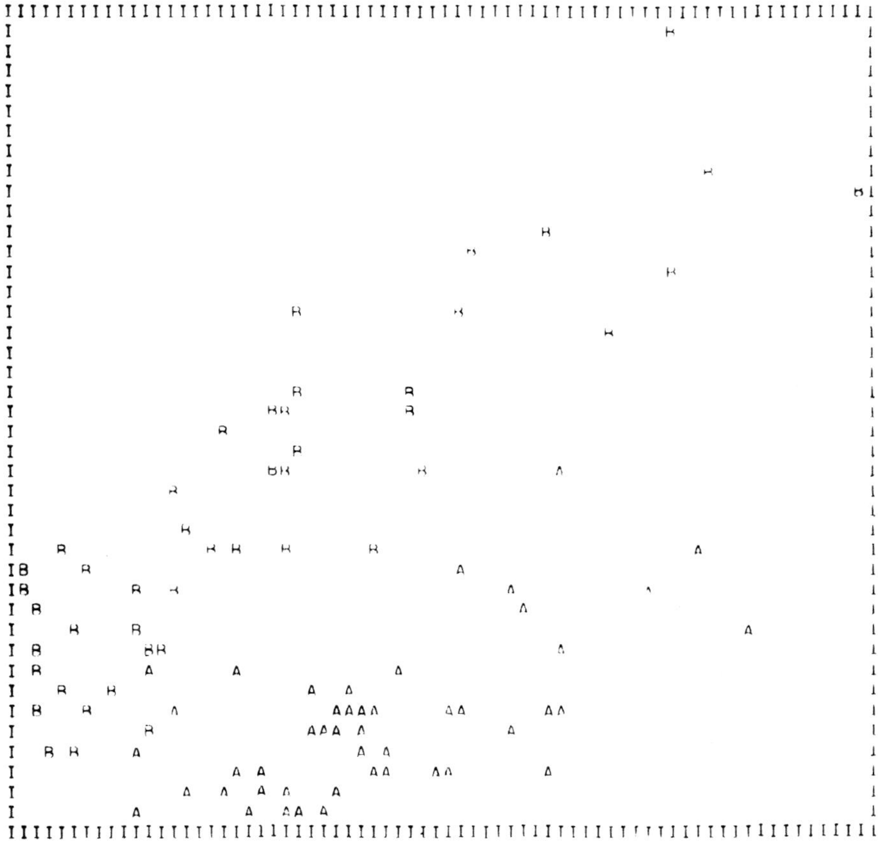

Fig. 10-18 Display of Iris data [Fukunaga, 1971b].

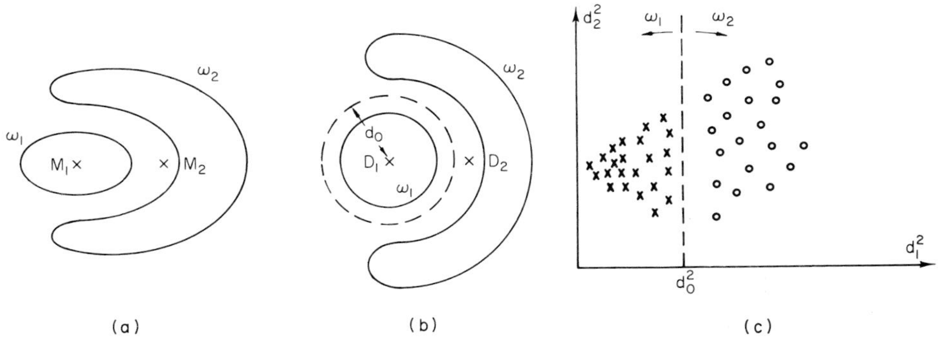

Fig. 10-19 One-class normalization: (a) original distributions; (b) after transformation; (c) the *d*-display.

Computer Projects

Write the following programs:

10-1 Generate a random process according to (10-2) with uniformly distributed parameters **a**, **m**, and **σ**. Study the dimensionalities of the local regions and determine the intrinsic dimensionality of the process.

10-2 Superimpose additive white noise to the data of 10-1. Study the effect of the noise in determining the intrinsic dimensionality.

10-3 Determine the intrinsic dimensionality of the data of 10-1 by the iterative process.

10-4 Study the effect of additive white noise on the procedure of 10-3.

10-5 Generate the coefficients of a polynomial distance function according to (10-57).

Data: μ, r and N ($N < 50$) classified, n-dimensional ($n < 5$) samples.

10-6 Extend the program of 10-5 to generate the coefficients of a generalized distance function

$$f_d(x) = \sum_{i=1}^{r} a_i \varphi_i(x),$$

where $\varphi_1(x), \varphi_2(x), \ldots, \varphi_r(x)$ are prespecified functions and $a_1, a_2, \ldots, a_r$ are the coefficients to be determined.

10-7 Plot the samples in the two dimensional space which is obtained by the "distance preservation" mapping.

Data: Ten samples from each class which are generated according to Standard Data $i = 1, 2, 3, 4$. (Use only the first four variables.)

10-8 Plot the samples in the two dimensional mapped space which is obtained by the "distances from two points" method.

Data: 50 samples from each class which are generated according to Standard Data $i = 1, 2$.

Chapter 11

CLUSTERING

In the preceding chapters, we have presented a considerable body of design theory for pattern recognition. Procedure for classifier design, parameter estimation, and density estimation have been discussed in detail. We have consistently assumed the existence of a training set of classified samples. In this chapter, we will focus our attention on the classification of samples without the aid of a training set. We will refer to this kind of classification as *clustering* or *unsupervised classification*.

There are many instances where classification must and can be performed without *a priori* knowledge. Consider, for example, the biological taxonomy problem. Over the years, all known living things have been classified according to certain observable characteristics. Of course, plants and animals have never borne labels indicating their kingdoms, phyla, and so on. Rather, they have been categorized according to their observable characteristics without outside supervision.

The clustering problem is not well defined unless the resulting classes of samples are required to exhibit certain properties. The choice of properties or, equivalently, the definition of a cluster, is the fundamental issue in the clustering problem. Given a suitable definition of a cluster, it is possible to distinguish between good and bad classifications of samples.

In our example, clusters are formed by grouping similar species and separating dissimilar ones. Similarity grouping is the most common form of clustering and the one which we will discuss in detail. However, clustering based on a more generalized relationship among samples is possible and will be discussed toward the end of this chapter.

In order to develop clustering as a mathematical procedure, we must formulate the definition of a cluster more rigorously. One way to do this is to construct a *clustering criterion*. The clustering criterion J assigns a numerical value to every possible classification of a collection of samples. The domain of J is the set of all possible classifications of the samples and the range of J consists of the real numbers. Classifications which are good in the sense of the adopted definition of a cluster are assumed to correspond to extreme values of J.

Thus, given J, we can evaluate any particular classification. However, it is generally impractical to calculate J for every possible classification. Therefore, a *clustering algorithm* is needed to efficiently determine the best classification with respect to J. In our notation, a clustering criterion and a clustering algorithm together make up a *clustering procedure*, which is the mechanism for solving the clustering problem.

In the next section, we will present a general-purpose clustering algorithm based on a generalized clustering criterion. In the following two sections, we will discuss, in detail, two major kinds of clustering criteria. In the last section, we will briefly survey some other criteria and will summarize the chapter.

11.1 An Algorithm for Clustering

Assignment of Samples to M Classes

The clustering algorithm developed in this section applies to a wide range of criteria. However, it is necessary to specify the form of the criterion as well as some other details of the clustering problem at the outset.

Assume that we want to classify N samples and that each sample is characterized by an n-dimensional vector; that is, we are given a set of vectors, $\{X_1, X_2, \ldots, X_N\}$. These vectors are not denoted as random vectors because, in the clustering problem, they are assumed to be fixed and known. Each sample is to be placed into one of M classes, $\omega_1, \ldots, \omega_M$, where M may or may not be known. The class to which the ith sample is assigned is denoted ω_{k_i} ($i = 1, \ldots, N$). For convenience, let the value of k_i be an integer between 1 and M. A *classification* Ω is a vector made up of the ω_{k_i}'s, and a *configuration* X^* is a vector made up of the X_i's, that is,

$$\Omega = [\omega_{k_1} \omega_{k_2} \cdots \omega_{k_N}]^T \tag{11-1}$$

and

$$X^* = [X_1^T X_2^T \cdots X_N^T]^T \tag{11-2}$$

The clustering criterion J is a function of Ω and X^* and can be written

$$J = J(\omega_{k_1}, \omega_{k_2}, \ldots, \omega_{k_N}; X_1, X_2, \ldots, X_N) = J(\Omega; X^*) \tag{11-3}$$

By definition, the best classification Ω_0 satisfies either

$$J(\Omega_0; X^*) = \min_{\Omega} J(\Omega; X^*) \tag{11-4}$$

or

$$J(\Omega_0; X^*) = \max_{\Omega} J(\Omega; X^*) \tag{11-5}$$

For the remainder of this section, we will discuss only (11-4), since the discussion for (11-5) is similar.

For a given clustering problem, the configuration X^* is fixed. The clustering algorithm varies only the classification Ω. Ordinary steepest-descent search techniques cannot be applied because of the discrete and unordered nature of Ω. Still, it is possible to define an iterative search algorithm based on variations in J with respect to variations in Ω.

Suppose, at the lth iteration, the classification is $\Omega(l)$, where

$$\Omega(l) = [\omega_{k_1}(l)\, \omega_{k_2}(l) \cdots \omega_{k_N}(l)]^T \tag{11-6}$$

If the ith sample is reclassified from its present class $k_i(l)$ to class j, the clustering criterion varies by an amount $\Delta J(i, j, l)$, which is given by

$$\Delta J(i, j, l) = J(\omega_{k_1}(l), \ldots, \omega_{k_{i-1}}(l), \omega_j, \omega_{k_{i+1}}(l), \ldots, \omega_{k_N}(l); X^*) - J(\Omega(l); X^*) \tag{11-7}$$

If $\Delta J(i, j, l)$ is negative, then reclassification of the ith sample to class j yields a classification that is improved in terms of J. This fact is the basis of the following algorithm:

Step 1: Choose an initial classification $\Omega(0)$.

Step 2: Given the lth classification $\Omega(l)$, calculate $\Delta J(i, j, l)$ for ($j = 1, 2, \ldots, M$) and ($i = 1, 2, \ldots, N$).

Step 3: For ($i = 1, 2, \ldots, N$), reclassify the ith sample to class t, where

$$\Delta J(i, t, l) = \min_j \Delta J(i, j, l) \tag{11-8}$$

Decide ties involving $j = k_i(l)$ in favor of the present classification. Decide other ties arbitrarily. This step forms $\Omega(l + 1)$.

Step 4: If $\Omega(l + 1) \neq \Omega(l)$ return to step 2; otherwise the algorithm is complete.

The algorithm is simply the iterative application of a classification rule based on the clustering criterion. It is important to note that at each iteration all of the samples are reclassified simultaneously. Thus, there is no guarantee of a net improvement in J and no guarantee that the algorithm converges. Even if it does converge, we cannot be certain that the absolute minimum of J has been obtained. Therefore, we must depend on empirical evidence to totally justify the algorithm.

In contrast to these potential weaknesses, the algorithm discribed above is very efficient. Like any good search algorithm, it surveys a small subset of classifications in a systematic and adaptive manner. It is easily programable for any criterion of the form of (11-3).

Determining the Number of Classes

So far, we have ignored the problem of determining the number of classes M. For the clustering procedure we would like to determine M as well as the proper classification. The algorithm described above may not be capable of doing this for many choices of J.

Let $\Omega_N{}^M$ be the set of all classifications of N samples into M classes. Our clustering algorithm searches over classifications in $\Omega_N{}^M$ only. For most choices of J, the algorithm generates M nonempty classes, regardless of the choice of M. It appears, therefore, that some external method of controlling M is necessary. Unfortunately, no unified theory for adjusting M has been fully developed and accepted. Therefore, we must content ourselves by mentioning some heuristic approaches that have been proposed.

Merging and Splitting

The basic algorithm can be generalized by introducing some mechanism for creating and destroying classes as the iteration proceeds. We may either merge two classes into a single class or split a class into two distinct classes. ISODATA is a well-known clustering procedure [Ball, 1965a, b] which employs merging and splitting. At each iteration, the classification is first altered without changing the number of classes. Then, either the merging or splitting process is applied to the present classes. If merging is called for, every pair of classes whose sample mean vectors are separated by less than a prespecified threshold is merged. In a splitting cycle, each class may or may not be split on the basis of its population and its sample covariance matrix. The procedure alternates between merging and splitting from iteration to iteration.

It goes without saying that this kind of merging and splitting is very heuristic. Its merit lies in the fact that it is efficient and requires a minimum of human interaction.

Multiple Dichotomy

It is somewhat more satisfying to adopt an approach which depends entirely on the clustering criterion J. One such approach has been suggested [Watanabe, 1969] and is outlined as follows.

Suppose that for $M = 2$ there are several distinct classifications which yield a nearly minimal value of J. If these classifications differ only in the classification of a few samples, there is no reason to suppose the existence of more than two classes. If the classifications are grossly different, however, then it is evident that several classes are actually present.

Figure 11-1 illustrates two possible dichotomies of a collection of samples apparently containing three classes A_1, A_2, and A_3. One dichotomy separates the samples into $A_1 \cup A_2$ and A_3, while the other results in the two

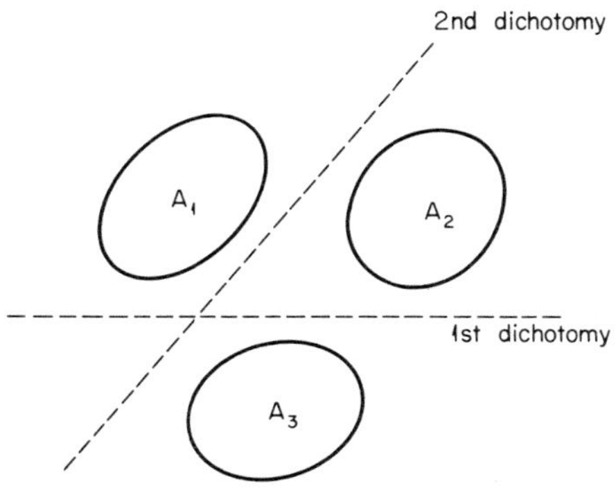

Fig. 11-1 Multiple dichotomy of three classes of samples.

classes A_1 and $A_2 \cup A_3$. Thus, A_3, A_1, and $\overline{A_1 \cup A_3} = A_2$ are seen to be distinct classes ($\bar{A}$ is the complement of the set A.)

Now let us consider the more general case where there are k dichotomies of a collection of samples containing M classes. Each dichotomy separates these samples into two groups. Let S_{ij} be the set of all samples assigned to group j by the ith dichotomy for $j = 1, 2$, $(i = 1, \ldots, k)$. Assume that the following two conditions hold.

(a) A dichotomy places each class into only one group, that is, classes are not split by dichotomies.

(b) For each pair of classes, there is at least one dichotomy which does not assign the two classes to the same group.

Select one group from each of the k dichotomies and form a subset C as the intersection of these k groups. By condition (a), if C contains one sample, then it must contain all of the samples of that class. By condition (b), for any other class, there is at least one of the k selected groups to which that class does not belong. Therefore, if C is nonempty, then C contains one and only one class. Hence, in order to construct all of the M classes, we consider the 2^k subsets of the form.

$$C(j_1, j_2, \ldots, j_k) = \bigcap_{i=1}^{k} S_{ij_i} \tag{11-9}$$

where each j equals 1 or 2. Each nonempty C is a class. In our example, we have

$$S_{11} = A_1 \cup A_2, \qquad S_{12} = A_3, \qquad S_{21} = A_1, \qquad S_{22} = A_2 \cup A_3 \tag{11-10}$$

so that

$$\begin{aligned} C(1, 1) &= S_{11} \cap S_{21} = A_1 \\ C(1, 2) &= S_{11} \cap S_{22} = A_2 \\ C(2, 1) &= S_{12} \cap S_{21} = \phi \\ C(2, 2) &= S_{12} \cap S_{22} = A_3 \end{aligned} \tag{11-11}$$

which is in agreement with our earlier argument.

The multiple dichotomy approach has a stronger theoretical basis than the merging and splitting procedure. Further, it relies on no numerical criterion other than J. However, implementation of the multiple dichotomy approach can be difficult, especially when the true number of classes is large. This difficulty may be overcome somewhat by imposing a hierarchical structure on the classes. The samples are divided into a small number of classes, each class is divided further, and so on. Under this strategy, we need not find every possible dichotomy of the entire collection of samples.

At this point, we depart from discussion of the clustering algorithm. Obviously, the discussion is incomplete. We have a basis, however, to develop and implement clustering procedures. We simply lack the degree of confidence in our approach that we enjoyed with supervised pattern recognition. Therefore, let us turn our attention to the detailed derivations of clustering criteria.

11.2 Parametric Clustering Criteria

Numerous clustering criteria have been defined in terms of parameters which arise in other areas of statistical analysis. We will first form a rational basis for these criteria and then study their properties. We will show that the algorithm of the previous section takes on a particularly simple form for one of these criteria. The idea of transformation invariance will be introduced and some interesting implications will be revealed.

Scatter Matrices and Class Separability for Clustering

Clustering can be considered as a technique to group samples so as to maximize the class separability. Then, all of the criteria which were discussed in Chapter 9 may be used as clustering criteria. In this section only functions of scatter matrices are discussed due to the following reasons:

(1) The extension to multiclass problems is straightforward.

(2) They are of simpler form than the Bhattacharyya distance or the divergence. Simplicity is necessary, since on clustering or unsupervised classification we have additional complexity due to the unknown class assignment.

Let us choose S_w, S_{b1}, and S_m as given by (9-7), (9-8), and (9-12). The multiclass extensions can be expressed by

$$S_w = \sum_{i=1}^{M} P(\omega_i)\Sigma_i \tag{11-12}$$

$$S_{b1} = \sum_{i=1}^{M} P(\omega_i)(M_i - M_0)(M_i - M_0)^T \tag{11-13}$$

and

$$S_m = S_w + S_{b1} \tag{11-14}$$

S_w, S_{b1}, and S_m are the *within-class*, *between-class*, and *mixture scatter matrices*, respectively.

When clustering is evaluated by class separability, a linear transformation invariance property should be imposed. A clustering procedure should give the same classification for a given set of samples regardless of the coordinate system of these samples.

According to the discussion of Chapter 9, (9-13) and (9-14) are coordinate independent criteria. Selecting S_1 and S_2 of (9-13) and (9-14), we have the following criteria for clustering:

$$J_1 = \mathrm{tr}(S_m^{-1} S_w) \qquad \text{(minimize)} \tag{11-15}$$

$$J_1' = \mathrm{tr}(S_w^{-1} S_{b1}) \qquad \text{(maximize)} \tag{11-16}$$

$$J_2 = \ln\{|S_m| / |S_w|\} \qquad \text{(maximize)} \tag{11-17}$$

Simpler expressions are obtained by using the mixture normalization of (4-53) which is expressed by

$$A S_m A^T = I \tag{11-18}$$

$$M_0 = 0 \tag{11-19}$$

where A is a nonsingular linear transformation. Variables, scatter matrices, and expected vectors are transformed accordingly, and they are expressed in the transformed coordinate as

$$A\mathbf{X} = \mathbf{Y} \tag{11-20}$$

$$A M_i = D_i \tag{11-21}$$

$$A S_i A^T = K_i \tag{11-22}$$

They satisfy

$$K_m = K_w + K_{b1} = \sum_{i=1}^{M} P(\omega_i)[K_i + D_i D_i^T] = I \tag{11-23}$$

$$D_0 = \sum_{i=1}^{M} P(\omega_i) D_i = 0 \tag{11-24}$$

It should be pointed out that the mixture normalization is not affected by the class assignment of each sample. The J's of (11-15), (11-16), and (11-17) can be rewritten in terms of the K's and also in terms of the eigenvalues of $K_w^{-1}K_{b1}$, $\lambda_1, \lambda_2, \ldots, \lambda_n$, (which are the same as the ones of $S_w^{-1}S_{b1}$) as

$$J_1 = \operatorname{tr} K_w = \sum_{i=1}^{n} 1/(1+\lambda_i) \qquad \text{(minimize)} \qquad (11\text{-}25)$$

$$J_1' = \operatorname{tr} K_w^{-1}K_{b1} = \sum_{i=1}^{n} \lambda_i \qquad \text{(maximize)} \qquad (11\text{-}26)$$

$$J_2 = -\ln |K_w| = \sum_{i=1}^{n} \ln(1+\lambda_i) \qquad \text{(maximize)} \qquad (11\text{-}27)$$

The above criteria give more or less similar clustering. However, for two-class problems, they become exactly the same criterion. For two classes, the rank of K_{b1} becomes 1, because

$$\begin{aligned} K_{b1} &= P(\omega_1)D_1D_1^T + P(\omega_2)D_2D_2^T \\ &= P(\omega_1)\{P(\omega_2)/P(\omega_1)\}^2 D_2D_2^T + P(\omega_2)D_2D_2^T \end{aligned} \qquad (11\text{-}28)$$

where the second line is derived by using (11-24). Therefore,

$$\lambda_1 = \operatorname{tr} K_w^{-1}K_{b1} \neq 0 \qquad (11\text{-}29)$$

$$\lambda_2 = \lambda_3 = \cdots = \lambda_n = 0 \qquad (11\text{-}30)$$

Thus

$$J_1 = 1/(1+\lambda_1) + (n-1) \qquad \text{(minimize)} \qquad (11\text{-}31)$$

$$J_1' = \lambda_1 \qquad \text{(maximize)} \qquad (11\text{-}32)$$

$$J_2 = \ln \lambda_1 \qquad \text{(maximize)} \qquad (11\text{-}33)$$

These are all optimized by maximizing λ_1. Therefore, these three criteria are exactly the same for two-class problems.

Altouhgh all three criteria can be optimized by the algorithm described in the previous section, J_1 in particular leads to a very simple clustering algorithm as follows.

Let us assume that, at the lth iteration, the number of vectors assigned to each class is large enough so that the mean vectors are negligibly altered by reclassification of a single vector. Then $\Delta J_1(i, j, l)$ (see Section 11-1) takes a particularly simple form:

$$\Delta J_1(i, j, l) = (1/N)\{\| Y_i - D_j(l) \|^2 - \| Y_i - D_{k_i}(l) \|^2\} \qquad (11\text{-}34)$$

Since the second term of (11-34) is independent of j, the decision rule at the lth iteration is

$$\| Y_i - D_t(l) \| = \min_j \| Y_i - D_j(l) \| \tag{11-35}$$

In words, the algorithm becomes:

Step 1 Choose an initial classification, $\Omega(0)$ and calculate $D_1(0), \ldots, D_M(0)$.

Step 2 Having calculated sample mean vectors $D_1(l), \ldots, D_M(l)$ at the lth iteration, reclassify each Y_i according to the nearest $D_j(l)$.

Step 3: If the classification of any Y_i is changed, calculate the new sample mean vectors $D_1(l+1), \ldots, D_M(l+1)$ for new class assignment, and repeat from step 2; otherwise, stop.

This particular realization of the basic algorithm, which we will call the *nearest-mean classification rule*, is very well known. It is the basis of the ISODATA procedure mentioned earlier, although the procedure was applied in the original coordinates. Its convergence properties for large values of N have been studied [MacQueen, 1967].

Convergence of the Nearest-Mean Classification

The results obtained so far lead us to propose the following procedure for clustering [Fukunaga, 1970d].

1. Apply the mixture normalization.
2. Classify the samples using the nearest mean classification rule.

The performance of this procedure can be determined analytically when the samples come from two normal distributions. We will establish conditions under which the separating hyperplane converges to a hyperplane perpendicular to the mean-difference vector of the given two distributions. For the equal covariance case, this is shown to be the Bayes optimum hyperplane.

Normal Distributions with Equal Covariance Matrices

When two normal distributions have the same covariance matrix $K_1 = K_2 = K$, the Bayes optimum decision surface under the mixture normalization is a hyperplane of the form

$$(D_1 - D_2)^T K^{-1} Y + \text{constant} = 0 \tag{11-36}$$

Going through the process of (4-68), (11-36) becomes

$$[P(\omega_1) - P(\omega_2)D_2{}^T D_2]^{-1} D_2{}^T Y + \text{constant} = 0 \qquad (11\text{-}37)$$

Thus, the optimum hyperplane for the equal covariance case is always in the direction of D_2, which is the same as the mean-difference vector $D_1 - D_2$ $[= -D_2/P(\omega_1) = D_1/P(\omega_2)]$. We will show that the nearest-mean classification rule sets a hyperplane perpendicular to the mean-difference vector. This property, which the original coordinate system does not have, is a significant advantage of the normalized coordinate system.

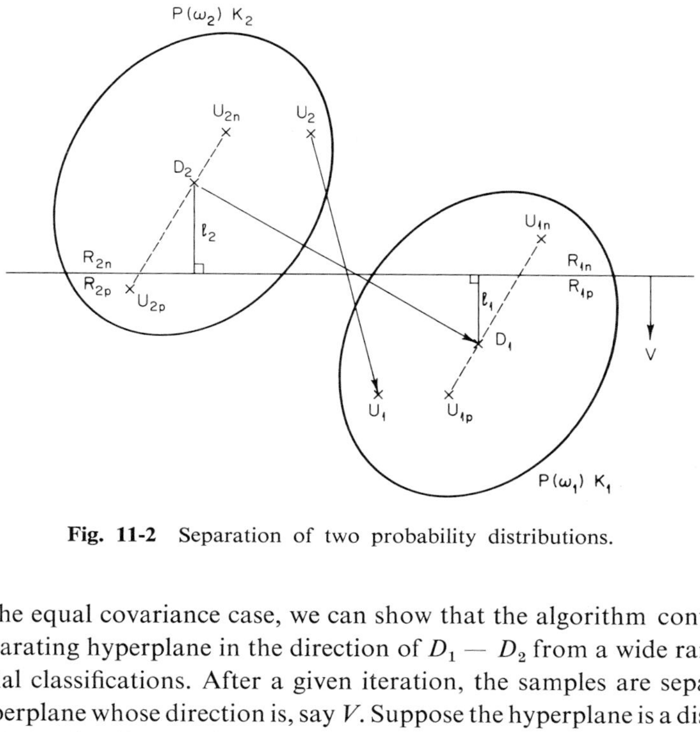

Fig. 11-2 Separation of two probability distributions.

For the equal covariance case, we can show that the algorithm converges to a separating hyperplane in the direction of $D_1 - D_2$ from a wide range of the initial classifications. After a given iteration, the samples are separated by a hyperplane whose direction is, say V. Suppose the hyperplane is a distance l_1 from D_1 and a distance l_2 from D_2, as shown in Fig. 11-2. Let U_1 and U_2 be the centers of probability mass to either side of the hyperplane. Then, following the nearest-mean classification rule, the direction of the succeeding hyperplane will be $U_1 - U_2$.

The hyperplane separates each distribution into two parts, the positive and negative side of the hyperplane. Thus, we have four probability masses R_{ij} $(i = 1, 2;\ j = p, n)$, as shown in Fig. 11-2. The centers U_{ij} and the population q_{ij} of these four masses can be obtained as follows:

$$U_{ip} = D_i + \frac{a_i}{s_i b_i} K_i V \tag{11-38}$$

$$U_{in} = D_i - \frac{a_i}{s_i(1-b_i)} K_i V \tag{11-39}$$

$$q_{ip} = P(\omega_i) b_i \tag{11-40}$$

$$q_{in} = P(\omega_i)(1-b_i) \tag{11-41}$$

where

$$a_i = (2\pi)^{-1/2} \int_{l_i/s_i}^{\infty} u \exp(-\tfrac{1}{2}u^2)\, du = (2\pi)^{-1/2} \exp(-\tfrac{1}{2}l_i^2/s_i^2) \tag{11-42}$$

$$b_i = (2\pi)^{-1/2} \int_{\pm l_i/s_i}^{+\infty} \exp(-\tfrac{1}{2}u^2)\, du = \tfrac{1}{2} - \operatorname{erf}(\pm l_i/s_i) \tag{11-43}$$

if D_i is located in R_{ip}, the positive sign is used; if D_i is located in R_{in}, the negative sign is used, and

$$s_i^2 = V^T K_i V \tag{11-44}$$

The term U_1 is the mass center of R_{1p} and R_{2p}, and U_2 is the one of R_{1n} and R_{2n}. Therefore, U_1 and U_2 are obtained as follows:

$$U_1 = (q_{1p}U_{1p} + q_{2p}U_{2p})/(q_{1p} + q_{2p}) \tag{11-45}$$

$$U_2 = (q_{1n}U_{1n} + q_{2n}U_{2n})/(q_{1n} + q_{2n}) \tag{11-46}$$

Substituting (11-38) through (11-43) into (11-45) and (11-46),

$$U_1 - U_2 = \frac{P(\omega_1)P(\omega_2)(b_1 - b_2)(D_1 - D_2) + \{P(\omega_1)(a_1/s_1)K_1 + P(\omega_2)(a_2/s_2)K_2\}V}{\{P(\omega_1)b_1 + P(\omega_2)b_2\}[1 - \{P(\omega_1)b_1 + P(\omega_2)b_2\}]} \tag{11-47}$$

For the equal covariance case,

$$K_1 = K_2 = K \quad \text{and} \quad s_1 = s_2 = s \tag{11-48}$$

Furthermore, under the mixture normalization conditions (11-23) and (11-24) [or (4-62) and (4-63)], K and D_2 can be expressed as functions of D_1, so that (11-47) becomes

$$U_1 - U_2 = c_1 D_1 + c_2 V \tag{11-49}$$

where

$$c_1 = \frac{P(\omega_1)(b_1 - b_2) - (1/s)\{P(\omega_1)/P(\omega_2)\}\{P(\omega_1)a_1 + P(\omega_2)a_2\}D_1{}^T V}{\{P(\omega_1)b_1 + P(\omega_2)b_2\}[1 - \{P(\omega_1)b_1 + P(\omega_2)b_2\}]} \tag{11-50}$$

$$c_2 = \frac{(1/s)\{P(\omega_1)a_1 + p(\omega_2)a_2\}}{\{P(\omega_1)b_1 + P(\omega_2)b_2\}[1 - \{P(\omega_1)b_1 + P(\omega_2)b_2\}]} \tag{11-51}$$

The normal of the new hyperplane has a component in the direction of V and another in the direction of D_1. If the coefficient of D_1 has the same sign as $D_1{}^T V$, then the successive hyperplanes become more nearly parallel to D_1. To prove this result we must show that the numerator of c_1 of (11-50) has the same sign as $D_1{}^T V$, because c_2 and the denominator of c_1 are always positive. We need only examine in detail the case where $D_1{}^T V > 0$. The discussion for $D_1{}^T V < 0$ is similar to the one for $D_1{}^T V > 0$. For $D_1{}^T V > 0$, we see from Fig. 11-2 that

$$l_1 + l_2 = (D_1 - D_2)^T V = [1/P(\omega_2)]D_1{}^T V \tag{11-52}$$

and the condition for convergence becomes

$$b_1 - b_2 - [(l_1 + l_2)/s]\{P(\omega_1)a_1 + P(\omega_2)a_2\} > 0 \tag{11-53}$$

It is easily seen that the inequality of (11-53) is not satisfied for certain combinations of parameters. However, the region of parameters where (11-53) is satisfied can be calculated numerically. The result is shown in Fig. 11-3. Equations (11-42), (11-43), and (11-48) with (11-53) show that we have three parameters in (11-53), l_1/s, l_2/s, and $P(\omega_1)$ $[P(\omega_2)=1-P(\omega_1)]$, or,

$$k = (l_1 + l_2)/s, \qquad \alpha = l_1/(l_1 + l_2) \qquad \text{and} \quad P(\omega_1). \tag{11-54}$$

In Fig. 11-3, the convergence regions of α and $P(\omega_1)$ are plotted for various k. The figure shows that convergence is quite likely in practice, except for either extreme $P(\omega_1)$'s or α's.

Convergence for the Unequal Covariance Case

As we discussed in Fig. 4-10 and (4-68), the hyperplane perpendicular to the mean-difference vector gives reasonable separation of two normal distributions after the mixture normalization, even though two covariance matrices are different.

However, when $K_1 \neq K_2$, it is difficult to find the convergence region as we did previously. The convergence can be proved when the hyperplane passes a certain point. Therefore, it can be said that some convergence region around the point should exist.

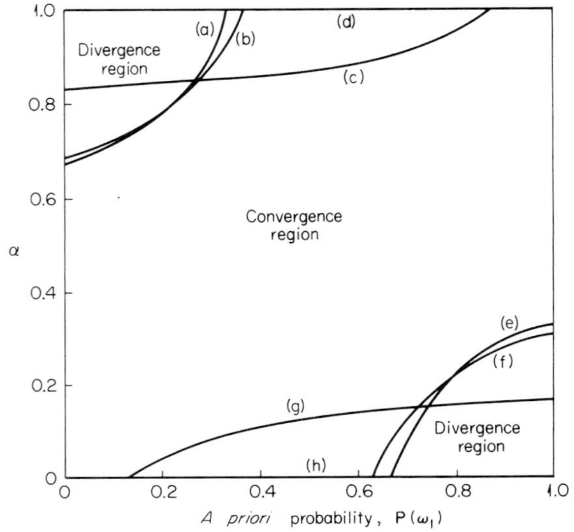

Fig. 11-3 Regions of convergence: where (a) $k < 0.1$; (b) $k = 1$; (c) $k = 10$; (d) $k = 100$; (e) $k < 0.1$; (f) $k = 1$; (g) $k = 10$; (h) $k = 100$ [Fukunaga, 1970d].

Let us suppose that the hyperplane passes the point where

$$a_1/s_1 = a_2/s_2 = \gamma \tag{11-55}$$

Then, substituting (11-23) and (11-24) into (11-47), we have

$$U_1 - U_2 = \frac{[P(\omega_1)(b_1 - b_2) - \gamma\{P(\omega_1)/P(\omega_2)\}D_1{}^T V]D_1 + \gamma V}{\{P(\omega_1)b_1 + P(\omega_2)b_2\}[1 - \{P(\omega_1)b_1 + P(\omega_2)b_2\}]} \tag{11-56}$$

Using the same reasoning as before, we obtain the following convergence condition:

$$b_1 - b_2 - \gamma(D_1{}^T V)/P(\omega_2) > 0 \tag{11-57}$$

this condition can be expressed, using (11-52) and (11-55), as

$$b_1 - (a_1/s_1)l_1 - b_2 - (a_2/s_2)l_2 > 0 \tag{11-58}$$

or

$$
\begin{aligned}
&(2\pi)^{-1/2}\left[\int_{-l_1/s_1}^{\infty} \exp(-\tfrac{1}{2}u^2)\,du - (l_1/s_1)\exp(-\tfrac{1}{2}l_1^2/s_1^2)\right.\\
&\qquad \left. - \int_{l_2/s_2}^{\infty} \exp(-\tfrac{1}{2}u^2)\,du - (l_2/s_2)\exp(-\tfrac{1}{2}l_2^2/s_2^2)\right]\\
&= (2\pi)^{-1/2}\left[\int_0^{l_1/s_1} [\exp(-\tfrac{1}{2}u^2) - \exp(-\tfrac{1}{2}l_1^2/s_1^2)]\,du\right.\\
&\qquad \left. + \int_0^{l_2/s_2} [\exp(-\tfrac{1}{2}u^2) - \exp(-\tfrac{1}{2}l_2^2/s_2^2)]\,du\right] > 0 \qquad (11\text{-}59)
\end{aligned}
$$

This inequality holds for all l_1/s_1's and l_2/s_2's.

Thus, when the hyperplane passes the point where (11-55) is satisfied, the new difference-in-mean vector $U_1 - U_2$ is more parallel to $D_1 - D_2$ than V is. Although no theoretical justification is offered, there should be a region of convergence around the point.

EXAMPLE 11-1 In addition to our analytical study, we can perform numerical experiments. Samples are obtained by generating normal random vectors according to a prescribed expected vector and covariance matrix. The expected vectors and covariances are taken from Standard Data.

Two-classes

For the first experiment, we generate 100 samples, each corresponding to Standard Data $i = 1, 2$. We first classify the samples in the original coordinate system according to the nearest-mean classification rule. Then we "mixture-normalize" the samples and classify them once again. Table 11-1 shows the confusion arrays that result in each case. Fewer misclassified samples result when the samples are mixture-normalized.

TABLE 11-1

CONFUSION ARRAYS FOR STANDARD DATA $i = 1, 2$[a]

Original coordinates		Assigned class 1	Assigned class 2	Normalized coordinates		Assigned class 1	Assigned class 2
Actual class	1	86	14	Actual class	1	100	0
Actual class	2	30	70	Actual class	2	19	81

[a] [Fukunaga, 1970d].

TABLE 11-2

CONFUSION ARRAYS FOR STANDARD DATA $i = 1, 2, 3$[a]

Original coordinates

		Assigned class 1	Assigned class 2	Assigned class 3
Actual class	1	84	16	0
	2	26	73	1
	3	14	11	75

Normalized coordinates

		Assigned class 1	Assigned class 2	Assigned class 3
Actual class	1	100	2	0
	2	27	73	0
	3	18	0	82

[a] [Fukunaga, 1970d].

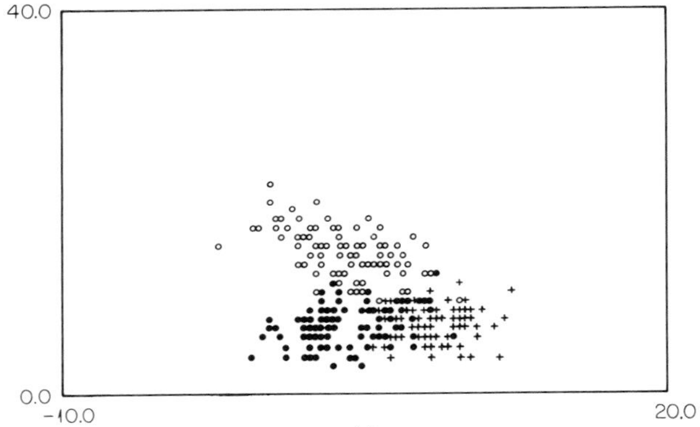

(a)

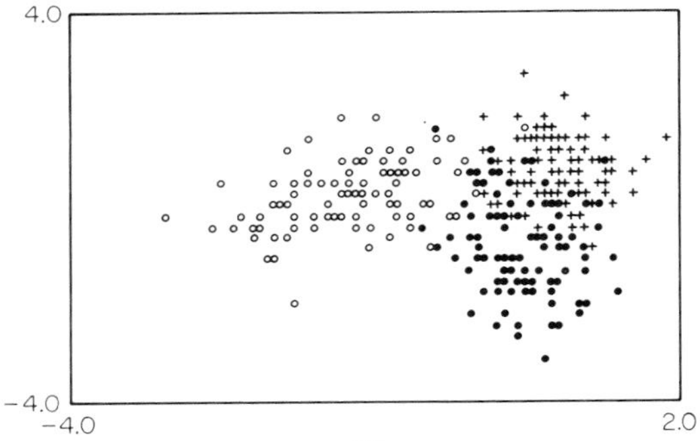

(b)

Fig. 11-4 Scatter plot of the experimental samples: (a) original distributions; (b) after the mixture normalization [Fukunaga, 1970d].

Three classes

In this experiment we have 100 samples for each of Standard Data $i = 1, 2, 3$. The same procedure is applied. The resulting confusion arrays are shown in Table 11-2 for samples both before and after the mixture normalization.

Figure 11-4 is a plot of two coordinates of the data in the original and in the normalized coordinate system.

11.3 Nonparametric Clustering Criteria

In this section, we will derive another family of criteria using a somewhat different point of view. The results will not, in general, depend on familiar parameters, such as scatter matrices. Thus, we refer to them as nonparametric criteria [Koontz, 1972b].

Criteria Based on Goodness of Fit

For each pair of vectors X_r, X_s we can determine the distance $d_X(X_r, X_s)$ separating them. For example

$$d_X(X_r, X_s) = \| X_r - X_s \| \tag{11-60}$$

Suppose we also define an interclass metric $d_\omega(\omega_{k_r}, \omega_{k_s})$ on Ω, that is,

$$d_\omega(\omega_{k_r}, \omega_{k_s}) = d_X(M_{k_r}, M_{k_s}) \tag{11-61}$$

or

$$d_\omega(\omega_{k_r}, \omega_{k_s}) = \begin{cases} c > 0, & \omega_{k_r} \neq \omega_{k_s} \\ 0, & \omega_{k_r} = \omega_{k_s} \end{cases} \tag{11-62}$$

Following the ideas discussed under nonlinear mapping, we can define the *goodness of fit* between the classification Ω and the configuration X^* as

$$J(\Omega: X^*) = (1/N) \sum_{r=2}^{N} \sum_{s=1}^{r} f(X_r, X_s)[d_\omega(\omega_{k_r}, \omega_{k_s}) - d_X(X_r, X_s)]^2 \tag{11-63}$$

Equation (11-63) is the general expression for a nonparametric clustering criterion.

The nonparametric criterion may be far from practical in its general form. The sum contains $N(N - 1)/2$ terms and becomes huge as N increases.

Thus, it is desirable, from a practical point of view, to set a large number of weights $f(X_r, X_s)$ equal to zero. Perhaps the simplest meaningful weighting function is

$$f_R(X_r, X_s) = \begin{cases} 1, & d_X(X_r, X_s) \leq R \\ 0, & d_X(X_r, X_s) > R \end{cases} \tag{11-64}$$

For small R, $J(\Omega; X^*)$ can be approximated as follows:

$$J(\Omega; X^*) \cong (1/N) \sum_{r=2}^{N} \sum_{s=1}^{r} f_R(x_r, X_s)\, d_\omega^2(\omega_{k_r}, \omega_{k_s}) \triangleq J_R(\Omega: X^*) \tag{11-65}$$

Further simplification results if we adopt (11-62) as the definition of $d_\omega(\omega_{k_r}, \omega_{k_s})$. We have

$$\begin{aligned} J_R(\Omega; X^*) &= c^2(1/N) \sum_{r=2}^{N} \sum_{s=1}^{r} f_R(X_r, X_s)[1 - \delta(\omega_{k_r}, \omega_{k_s})]^2 \\ &\triangleq c^2 J_{R0}(\Omega; X^*) \end{aligned} \tag{11-66}$$

where $\delta(\omega_{k_r}, \omega_{k_s})$ is defined as

$$\delta(\omega_{k_r}, \omega_{k_s}) = \begin{cases} 1, & \omega_{k_r} = \omega_{k_s} \\ 0, & \omega_{k_r} \neq \omega_{k_s} \end{cases} \tag{11-67}$$

The term $J_{R0}(\Omega; X^*)$ is simply the number of distinct pairs of vectors whose members are assigned to different classes. It is an extremely efficient criterion to implement because it requires only a counting operation for its evaluation. Also, the criterion is related to the upper bound of the Bayes error through the Bhattacharyya distance and Jensen's inequality as was shown in (9-104) and the subsequent discussion. We will call $J_{R0}(\Omega; X^*)$ the *fixed neighborhood penality rule.*

A Nonparametric Clustering Algorithm

Returning to the general case, we can specify the algorithm in terms of variations in $J(\Omega; X^*)$ with Ω. We have

$$\begin{aligned} \Delta J(i, j, l) = (1/N) \sum_{\substack{r=1 \\ r \neq i}}^{N} f(X_i, X_r)\{&[d_\omega(\omega_j, \omega_{k_r}(l)) - d_X(X_i, X_r)]^2 \\ &- [d_\omega(\omega_{k_i}(l), \omega_{k_r}(l)) - d_X(X_i, X_r)]^2\} \end{aligned} \tag{11-68}$$

Simpler forms result when $J_R(\Omega; X^*)$ and $J_{R0}(\Omega; X^*)$ are used.

$$\Delta J_R(i, j, l) = (1/N) \sum_{\substack{r=1 \\ r \neq i}}^{N} f_R(X_i, X_r)[d_\omega^2(\omega_j, \omega_{k_r}(l)) - d_\omega^2(\omega_{k_i}(l), \omega_{k_r}(l))] \tag{11-69}$$

$$\Delta J_{R0}(i, j, l) = (1/N) \sum_{\substack{r=1 \\ r \neq i}}^{N} f_R(X_i, X_r)[\delta(\omega_{k_i}(l), \omega_{k_r}(l)) - \delta(\omega_j, \omega_{k_r}(l))] \tag{11-70}$$

Both ΔJ_R and ΔJ_{R0} contain two terms, one of which is independent of j. Thus, we can write them as decision functions for the lth iteration. Corresponding to ΔJ_{R0}, we have a decision function D_{R0}, given by

$$D_{R0}(i, j, l) = (1/N) \sum_{\substack{r=1 \\ r \neq i}}^{N} f_R(X_i, X_r)\, \delta(\omega_j, \omega_{k_r}(l)) \tag{11-71}$$

The term $D_{R0}(i, j, l)$ is the number of vectors classified in class j at the lth iteration and separated from X_i by a distance less than R. The classification rule at the lth iteration is then

$$D_{R0}(i, k_i(l+1), l) = \max_j D_{R0}(i, j, l) \tag{11-72}$$

That is, reclassify X_i to the class which presently has the largest number of members within a distance R of X_i. We will call this realization of the basic algorithm the *fixed neighborhood classification rule.*

Both J_{R0} and the associated algorithm have a very reasonable physical interpretation. The nonzero contributions to J_{R0} come from vectors near the boundaries, separating classes. Thus, J_{R0} is smaller when these boundaries pass through regions of low vector density. Consider the boundary separating classes j_1 and j_2 at the lth iteration. Suppose that the density is higher on the j_2 side of the boundary. Then vectors near the boundary will be reclassified to class j_2, and the boundary will move toward the lower density. Thus, the fixed neighborhood clustering procedure is a *valley-seeking technique*. This is a reasonable way to classify vectors when no *a priori* knowledge is available.

The above procedure can be easily coded for digital computer processing of finite collections of samples. The results of two computer experiments are presented in Figs. 11-5 and 11-6 and Table 11-3. The table lists, for each experiment, the number of samples N, the assumed number of classes M, the region size R, the number of distinct pairs of points closer together than R, NNR, the number of iterations required $ITER$, and the initial and final

TABLE 11-3

PERFORMANCE DATA FOR THE FIXED NEIGHBORHOOD CLUSTERING PROCEDURE

Example	N	M	R	NNR	$ITER$	$J_{RO}(I)$	$J_{RO}(F)$
11-2	150	2	1.0	1369	8	115	42
11-3	150	3	0.75	3072	10	729	182

penalties, $J_{R0}(I)$ and $J_{R0}(F)$. The data used for each experiment is defined as follows:

EXAMPLE 11-2 Two-class, two-dimensional data, 75 samples per class:

$$\mathbf{x}_1 = a \cos \boldsymbol{\theta} + m_1 + \mathbf{n}_1 \tag{11-73}$$

$$\mathbf{x}_2 = a \sin \boldsymbol{\theta} + m_2 + \mathbf{n}_2 \tag{11-74}$$

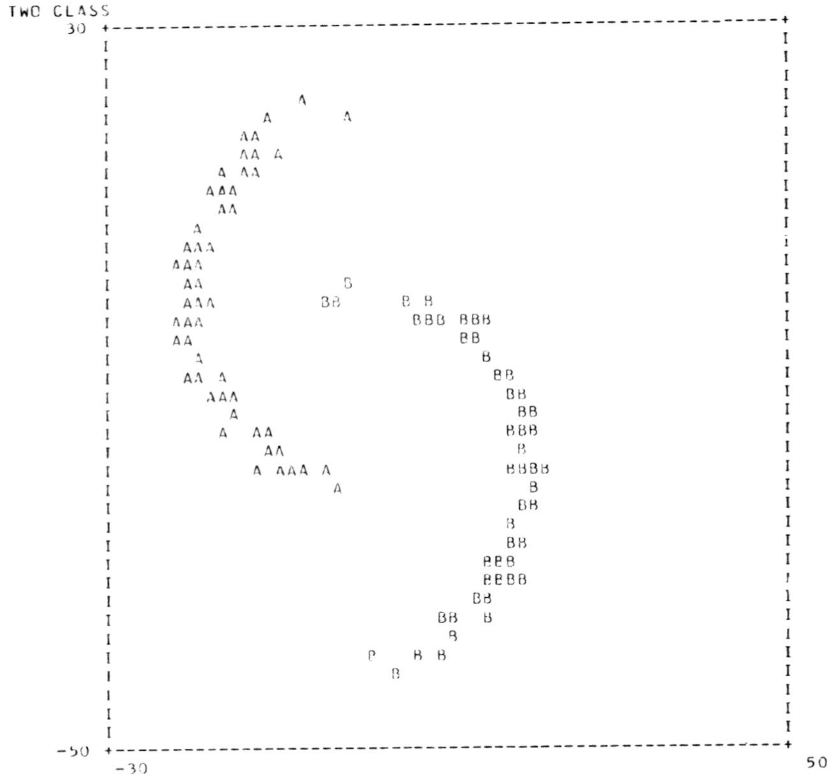

Fig. 11-5 Classification of two-class samples.

where:

(1) The terms $\mathbf{n}_1$ and $\mathbf{n}_2$ are independent, identically distributed normal random variables with zero mean and unit variance.

(2) The terms m_1 and m_2 are fixed for each class:

$$m_1 = 0 \quad \text{and} \quad m_2 = 0 \qquad \text{for class 1}$$

$$m_1 = 0 \quad \text{and} \quad m_2 = -20 \qquad \text{for class 2}$$

(3) The term $\boldsymbol{\theta}$ is normal with mean θ_m and a standard deviation of $\pi/4$ where:

$$\theta_m = \pi \qquad \text{for class 1}$$

$$\theta_m = 0 \qquad \text{for class 2}$$

(4) The term a is fixed for both classes at $a = 20$.

EXAMPLE 11-3 Three-class, two-dimensional data, 50 samples per class: Classes 1 and 2 are as in Example 11-2 with

$$m_1 = 0, \quad m_2 = 0, \quad \text{and} \quad \theta_m = \pi \qquad \text{for class 1}$$

$$m_1 = 20, \quad m_2 = 0, \quad \text{and} \quad \theta_m = 0 \qquad \text{for class 2}$$

Class 3 is bivariate normal with mean vector M and covariance matrix Σ given by

$$M = \begin{bmatrix} 10 \\ 0 \end{bmatrix} \quad \text{and} \quad \Sigma = \begin{bmatrix} 16 & 0 \\ 0 & 1 \end{bmatrix} \tag{11-75}$$

Mixture normalization is applied to all data. Figures 11-5 and 11-6 show that the resulting classifications are reasonable.

The procedure is fairly sensitive to the control parameter R. If R is too large, the vectors tend to all be placed in one class. On the other hand, if R is too small, there are many stable boundaries due to gaps in the distributions. For a given R, there will be N_R $[< N(N-1)/2]$ pairs of points closer together than R. An empirical rule is to select R such that $N_R \cong 10N$. This rule ensures that the storage required to implement this procedure is not excessive and grows only linearly with N.

Asymptotic Properties of the Procedure

We can formalize the above arguments when N is very large. Let Γ_j be the region of the vector space containing the X_i's, which are classified

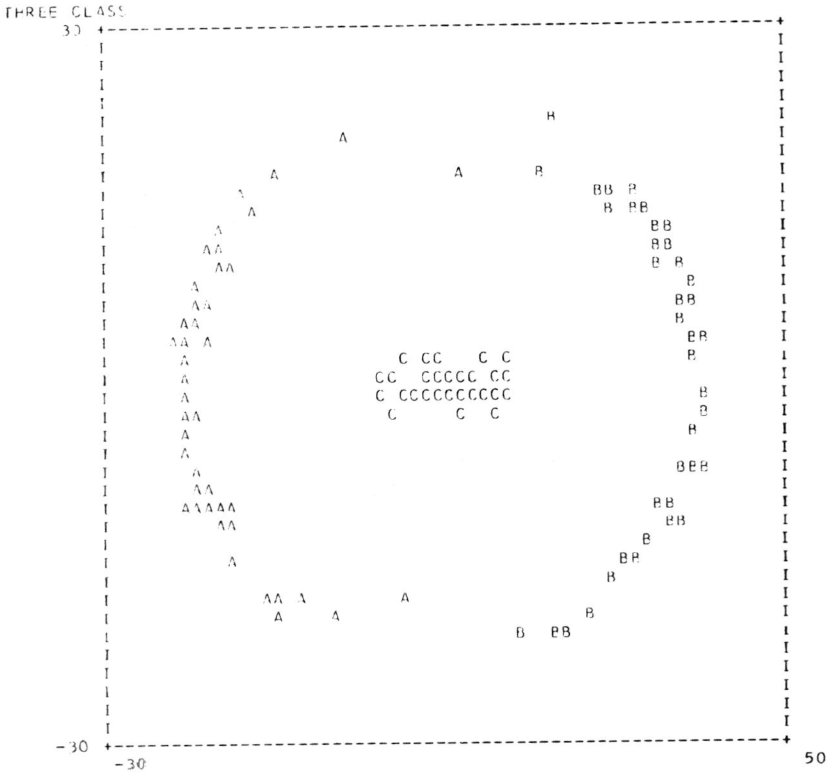

Fig. 11-6 Classification of three-class samples.

into class j. Let $K_{\Gamma_j}(X)$ be the characteristic set function of Γ_j, that is,

$$K_{\Gamma_j}(X) = \begin{cases} 1 & \text{if} \quad X \in \Gamma_j \\ 0 & \text{if} \quad X \notin \Gamma_j \end{cases} \tag{11-76}$$

Then (11-71) can be rewritten

$$D_{R0}(i, j) = (1/N) \sum_{\substack{r=1 \\ r \neq i}}^{N} f_R(X_i, X_r) K_{\Gamma_j}(X_r) \tag{11-77}$$

where the iteration index l is dropped for simplicity's sake. As N becomes large, the right-hand side of (11-77) becomes an integral.

$$D_{R0}(i, j) \to \int_{\Gamma_j} f_R(X_i, X) p(X) \, dX \overset{\Delta}{=} D_{R0}^{\infty}(X_i/j) \tag{11-78}$$

where $p(X)$ is the underlying mixture density of the X_i's. If for any vector Y we define $S_R(Y)$ as the set of all vectors within a distance R of Y, we can write

$$D_{R0}^{\infty}(Y) = \int_{\Gamma_j \cap S_R(Y)} p(X)\, dX \tag{11-79}$$

Consider a vector Y on the boundary currently separating classes j_1 and j_2 and suppose $S_R(Y)$ contains only vectors assigned to either class j_1 or class j_2. Then Y is reclassified according to

$$\int_{\Gamma_{j_1} \cap S_R(Y)} p(X)\, dX \gtrless \int_{\Gamma_{j_2} \cap S_R(Y)} p(X)\, dX \rightarrow \begin{cases} Y \rightarrow \text{class } j_2 \\ Y \rightarrow \text{class } j_1 \end{cases} \tag{11-80}$$

If the top inequality holds, then, because of continuity, all vectors within a small region around the boundary go to class j_2, and the boundary moves into the region formerly occupied by j_1. A similar argument applies to the bottom inequality. If equality holds, the boundary is stationary. When a stationary boundary is unstable, it tends to move farther away from the stationary points under small perturbations.

If R is sufficiently small, we can represent $p(X)$ in $S_R(Y)$ with a truncated Taylor series:

$$p(X) \cong p(Y) + [\nabla p(Y)]^T (X - Y) \tag{11-81}$$

where

$$\nabla p(Y) = [\partial p/\partial x_1 |_{X=Y} \cdots \partial p/\partial x_n |_{X=Y}]^T \tag{11-82}$$

We can also claim that the boundary is a hyperplane which separates $S_R(Y)$ into two hemispherical regions with equal volume. Thus we have

$$\begin{aligned} \int_{\Gamma_{j_k} \cap S_R(Y)} p(X)\, dX &\cong \int_{\Gamma_{j_k} \cap S_R(Y)} p(Y)\, dX + [\nabla p(Y)]^T \int_{\Gamma_{j_k} \cap S_R(Y)} (X - Y)\, dX \\ &= \frac{v}{2} \pm \frac{R^{n+1}}{n+1} \frac{\pi^{n/2}}{\Gamma[\frac{1}{2}n + 1]} [\nabla p(Y)]^T V \qquad (l = 1, 2) \end{aligned} \tag{11-83}$$

where v is the volume of $S_R(Y)$, and V is a unit vector normal to the boundary at Y and pointing toward class j_1. The plus sign is used for $k = 1$ and the minus sign for $k = 2$. Thus, (11-80) becomes

$$[\nabla p(Y)]^T V \gtrless 0 \rightarrow \begin{cases} Y \rightarrow \text{class } j_2 \\ Y \rightarrow \text{class } j_1 \end{cases} \tag{11-84}$$

and a stationary boundary is characterized by having no normal component of $\nabla p(Y)$.

developed based on cohesion [Watanabe, 1969]. Instead of clustering independent observed samples $\mathbf{X}_1, \ldots, \mathbf{X}_N$ as in conventional clustering problems, the cohesion of a set of variables $\mathbf{x}_1, \ldots, \mathbf{x}_n$ is calculated and used to classify these $\mathbf{x}$'s into different groups. Classification is based on the degree of statistical dependence among subsets of the $\mathbf{x}_i$'s. Thus, it is natural to employ the well-known entropy function. Consider all subsets of the $\mathbf{x}_i$'s of the form

$$S_k = \{\mathbf{x}_{k_1}, \mathbf{x}_{k_2}, \ldots, \mathbf{x}_{k_l}\} \tag{11-89}$$

The index of the subset k ranges over all possible subsets, and l is the number of random variables in the kth subset. Let us assume that each $\mathbf{x}_i$ is a discrete random variable. Then, the entropy of S_k is defined as

$$H(S_k) = \sum_{x_{k_1}} \cdots \sum_{x_{k_l}} p(x_{k_1}, \ldots, x_{k_l}) \ln p(x_{k_1}, \ldots, x_{k_l}) \tag{11-90}$$

where the density function of the discrete variables is

$$p(x_{k_1}, \ldots, x_{k_l}) = \Pr\{\mathbf{x}_{k_1} = x_{k_1}, \ldots, \mathbf{x}_{k_l} = x_{k_l}\} \tag{11-91}$$

The entropy is maximized when the $\mathbf{x}_i$'s are statistically independent. It can also be shown that

$$H(S_k) \leq \sum_{i=1}^{l} H(\{\mathbf{x}_{k_i}\}) \tag{11-92}$$

for any subset S_k. The cohesion of S_k is defined as

$$C(S_k) = \sum_{i=1}^{l} H(\{\mathbf{x}_{k_i}\}) - H(S_k) \tag{11-93}$$

Thus, $C(S_k)$ is a non-negative quantity and increases as the elements of S_k become more and more dependent. The cohesion of a subset of statistically independent random variables is zero.

Suppose we divide the set S of all n $\mathbf{x}_i$'s into two disjoint subsets S_1 and S_2. Then the subsets together have no more cohesion than the original set S since

$$C(S) - [C(S_1) + C(S_2)] = H(S_1) + H(S_2) - H(S) \geq 0 \tag{11-94}$$

by the general properties of the entropy function. We would like to divide the random variables into M subsets $S_1, \ldots, S_M$ with a minimum loss of cohesion. Thus, the criterion to be minimized is

$$J(\Omega; S) = C(S) - \sum_{j=1}^{M} C(S_j) = \sum_{j=1}^{M} H(S_j) - H(S) \tag{11-95}$$

The criterion is completely specified when the joint probabilities $p(x_1, \ldots, x_n)$ are known. In practice, however, we have only a set of N observations of the $\mathbf{x}_i$'s. Hence, in order to implement this criterion, we must use the observations to estimate $p(x_1, \ldots, x_n)$ from a relative frequency approach.

It is worth repeating here that the structure of the clustering problem based on cohesion is unlike our earlier formulation. However, this procedure is unique and is capable of solving problems for which other known methods fail.

Hierarchical Clustering

A large number of the existing clustering procedures are designed to generate a classification tree. The initial node of the tree represents a collection of samples, and each terminal node represents an individual sample. With the exception of the terminal nodes, each node denotes a branching operation which divides the set of samples represented by that node into disjoint subsets which form new nodes. Alternately, each node is associated with a "parent node" to which its samples also belong. Finally, each node can be assigned a numerical value, or level.

Once again, we view clustering as finding a representation for some aspect of a collection of samples. In particular, we are concerned with representing pairwise similarities among the samples using a classification tree. To do this, we must define distances between samples in terms of the classification tree alone.

Consider a classification tree for N samples. It consists of a trunk node, N terminal nodes, and intermediate nodes. Every node, except the trunk, has one and only one parent node. Each node has a numerical level assigned to it. From any terminal node, we can construct a unique "path of descent" to its parent node, its parent's parent, and so on, to the trunk. The distance between any two terminal nodes is the level of the node at the intersection of their respective paths of descent.

A typical classification tree is shown in Fig. 11-9. The levels of the terminal and intermediate nodes are indicated. The paths of descent for the terminal nodes labeled X_1 and X_3 are shown, and the distance between these two nodes $d_\tau(X_1, X_3)$ is 3.7.

There are, of course, many ways to assign node levels. If the levels satisfy the following conditions, then the distance defined above has the properties of a metric.

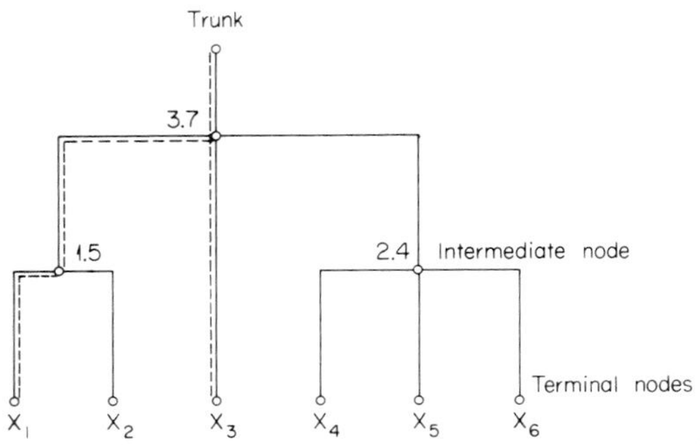

Fig. 11-9 A classification tree.

(1) All terminal nodes have level zero.
(2) All nonterminal nodes have level greater than zero.
(3) The level of a node is always less than that of its parent node.

In particular, if (1), (2), and (3) hold, we have

$$d_\tau(X_j, X_i) = d_\tau(X_i, X_j) \geq 0 \qquad \text{(positiveness and symmetry)} \qquad (11\text{-}96)$$

$$d_\tau(X_i, X_j) = 0 \quad \text{if and only if} \quad i = j \qquad \text{(definiteness)} \qquad (11\text{-}97)$$

and

$$d_\tau(X_i, X_j) \leq \max_k [d_\tau(X_i, X_k), d_\tau(X_k, X_j)] \qquad \text{(ultrametric inequality)} \qquad (11\text{-}98)$$

The reader may verify that the triangle inequality is a direct consequence of the stronger, ultrametric inequality.

Let the samples again be characterized by a set of vectors $X_1, \ldots, X_N$ in a metric space. Denote intersample distances as $d_\tau(X_i, X_j)$. A measure of the goodness of fit between the tree distances and the intersample distances serves as the clustering criterion. Such a measure is given by

$$J(\tau : X^*) = \sum_{i=2}^{N} \sum_{j=1}^{i} f_{ij}[d_X(X_i, X_j) - d_\tau(X_i, X_j)]^2 \qquad (11\text{-}99)$$

where the f_{ij}'s are weighting coefficients. This criterion is nearly identical to (11-63). The variable τ, which denotes the tree, plays the same role as Ω. Note that each tree τ is characterized not only by its structure, but by the node levels as well.

Unfortunately, we cannot apply the basic algorithm of this chapter.

This is because it is difficult to characterize "adjacent trees." Even if we could describe a "tree perturbation", it would be very awkward to compute the resulting change in $J(\tau; X^*)$.

Variations of the following algorithm are often used to find the optimum tree in the sense of $J(\tau; X^*)$ [Johnson, 1967; Rohlf, 1970]. First of all, we must adopt a convention for specifying the distance between two sets of vectors. For example, the distance between the two mean vectors may be used. Having done this, we may apply the following iterative procedure.

Step 1: Assign each sample to a terminal node of level 0 and calculate the distance between every pair of samples.

Step 2: Add a new node as the parent node of the two nodes corresponding to the closest pair of samples (clusters). The level of this node is the distance between the corresponding samples (clusters).

Step 3: Calculate the distance between the cluster represented by the new node and the samples (clusters) corresponding to the remaining terminal nodes.

Step 4: Consider the new node to be a terminal node and delete the two nodes which were merged to form it. If there are two or more terminal nodes left, return to step 2 and repeat. Otherwise, the algorithm is complete.

Step 3 is the most troublesome part of the above procedure. The resulting tree can depend heavily upon the way distances between clusters is defined. This problem is an object of current research in hierarchical clustering.

Interactive Clustering

It has been noted that human beings are fairly adept at clustering. We can apparently perceive class structure in a noniterative *gestalt*. Unfortunately, our power to observe samples is severely restricted because of our confinement to a three-dimensional universe. But we have developed dimensionality-reducing mapping algorithms in Chapter 10, particularly in Section 10-3, for display purposes. It is therefore possible to display high-dimensional data in two or three dimensions. A human observer can easily perform clustering on the basis of the display. This is the principle of interactive clustering.

Distance Preservation

In Section 10.3, we discussed a nonlinear mapping from an n-dimensional space to a two-dimensional space, which minimizes the average error between the corresponding intersample distances in both space. This mapping preserves the structure of distributions relatively faithfully, and can project it on a CRT display. Figure 10-13 shows an example for three Iris species. Thus, observing this display, an operator can draw the natural boundaries of these distributions without any knowledge of class assignment of samples.

Distances from Two Points

For two-class problems, the display, which was discussed in Section 10.3 as "distance from two points", could be used for clustering. The procedure is as follows:

Step 1: Apply the mixture normalization of (11-23) and (11-24).
Step 2: Select two points $D_1(0)$ and $D_2(0)$ arbitrarily.

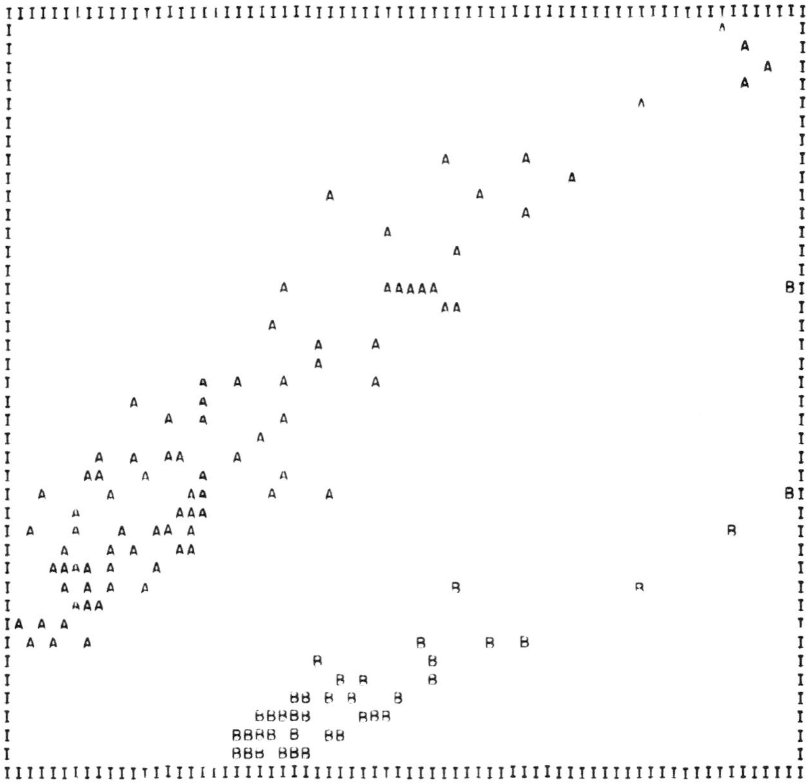

Fig. 11-10 Clustering display of Iris three species [Fukunaga, 1971b].

Step 3: Having $D_1(l)$ and $D_2(l)$ at the lth iteration, display all samples according to $\| Y_i - D_1(l) \|^2$ and $\| Y_i - D_2(l) \|^2$.

Step 4: Draw a boundary using the operator's intuition. If, in early iterations, two distributions are not clearly distinguishable, the operator may select a 45° line, crossing the origin.

Step 5: According to the boundary, samples are reassigned to one of two classes.

Step 6: If the classification of any Y_i is changed, calculate the new sample mean vectors $D_1(l + 1)$ and $D_2(l + 1)$, and repeat from step 3. Otherwise, the algorithm is complete.

The above process is exactly the same as the one in Section 11.2, which maximizes J_1, if we always use a 45° line crossing the origin. The difference

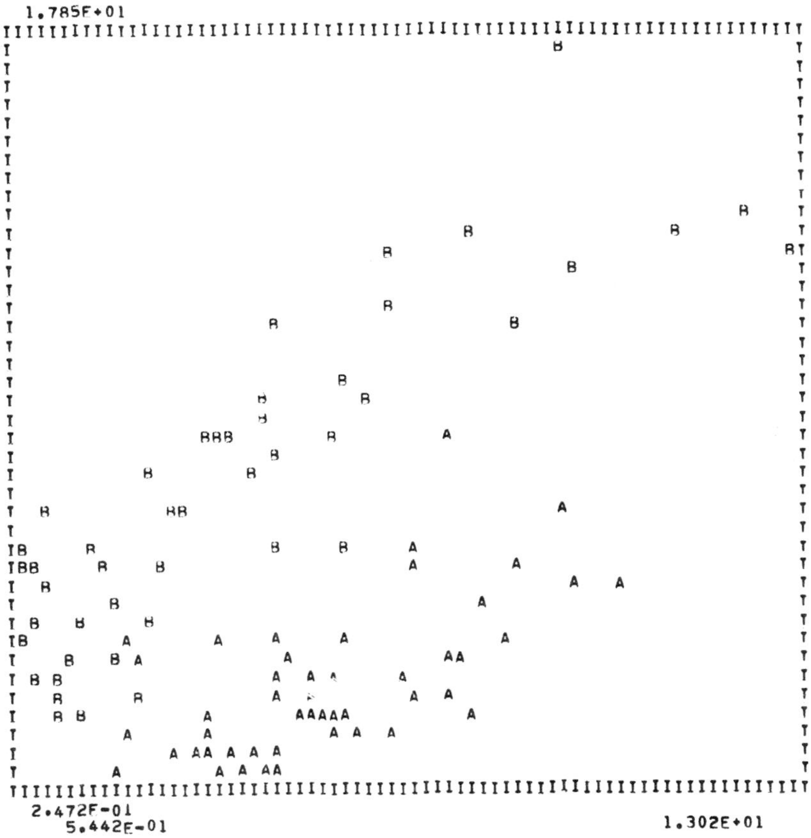

Fig. 11-11 Clustering display of Iris two species [Fukunaga, 1971b].

between the above procedure and the previous one is that we have freedom to choose the boundary by the operator's intuition.

EXAMPLE 11-4 The three species of Iris data are clustered without supervision as follows. First, the mixture of all three species are normalized according to (11-23) and (11-24). The above clustering procedure is applied and the result is shown in Fig. 11-10. *Iris sesota* (B in Fig. 11-10) is clearly separated without any errors from two other species (A in Fig. 11-10) after three iterations.

Then, as the second step, all A's (*Iris versicolor* and *virginica*) are mixture-normalized, and the procedure of this section is applied again. After five iterations the algorithm converges giving the display of Fig. 11-11. Two samples from one class and three samples from the other are misclassified out of 50 samples from each class. Since *Iris versicolor* and *Iris virginica* are known to overlap slightly, this is a reasonable result, and the performance is similar to that of supervised classification.

Computer Projects

Write the following programs:

11-1 Find clusters in a given data set by minimizing J_1 of (11-15) or (11-25).

Data: 50 generated samples for each class according to Standard Data (a) $i = 1, 2$ and (b) $i = 1, 2, 3, 4$.

11-2 Using the generated data of 11-1 (a) and (b), find clusters by maximizing J_2 of (11-17) or (11-27).

11-3 Using the generated data of 11-1 (a) and (b), find clusters by the fixed neighborhood clustering procedure [J_{R0} of (11-16)].

11-4 Using the generated data of Example 11-2, construct a tree and classify the data into two classes.

11-5 Cluster the generated data of 11-1 (a) into two groups, using the display of the distances from two points to each sample.

REFERENCES[†]

Abramson, N., and Braverman, D. [1962]. Learning to recognize patterns in a random environment. *IRE Trans. Information Theory* **IT-8**, 58–63 (Chapter 7).

Agmon, S. [1956]. The relaxation method for linear inequalities. *Canad. J. Math.* **6**, 382–392 (Chapter 4).

Aizerman, M. A., Braverman, E. M., and Rozonoer, L. I. [1964]. Method of potential functions in the problem of restoration of functional converter characteristic by means of points observed randomly. *Autom. and Remote Contr.* [USSR] **25**, 1705–1714 (Chapter 7).

Allais, D. C. [1964]. Selection of measurement for prediction. *Stanford Univ. Tech. Rep.* 6103–9 (Chapters 5, 8).

Anderson, T. W. [1962]. "An Introduction to Multivariate Statistical Analysis." Wiley, New York (G).

Anderson, T. W., and Bahadur, R. R. [1962]. Classification into two multivariate normal distributions with different covariance matrices. *Ann. Math. Stat.* **33**, 422–431 (Chapter 4).

Bahadur, R. R. [1967]. On classification based on responses to *n* dichotomous items. *In* "Studies in Item Analysis and Prediction." (H. Solomon, ed.). Standford Univ. Press, Stanford, California (Chapter 6).

Ball, G. H. [1965a]. Data analysis in the social sciences: what about the details. *AFIPS Proc. Conf. Fall Joint Comp.* 1965, **27**, Pt. 1. 533–559 (Chapter 11).

Ball, G. H. and Hall D. J. [1965b]. ISODATA, a novel method of data analysis and pattern classification. *Stanford Research Inst. Tech. Rep.* (Chapter 11).

[†] G indicates general references.

Bennett, R. S. [1969]. The intrinsic dimensionality of signal collections. *IEEE Trans. Information Theory* **IT-15**, 517–525 (Chapter 10).

Bhattacharyya, A. [1943]. On a measure of divergence between two statistical populations defined by their probability distributions. *Bull. Calcutta Math. Soc.* **35**, 99–110 (Chapters 3, 9).

Blackwell, D., and Girshick, M. A. [1954]. "Theory of Games and Statistical Decisions." Chapters 9 and 10. Wiley, New York (Chapter 3).

Blaydon, C. C. [1966]. On a pattern classification result of Aizerman, Braverman, and Rozonoer. *IEEE Trans. Information Theory* **IT-12**, 82–83 (Chapter 7).

Braverman, E. M. [1966]. The method of potential functions in the problem of training machines to recognize patterns without a teacher. *Autom. and Remote Contr.* [USSR] **27**, 1748–1771 (Chapter 11).

Brick, D. B. [1965]. Wiener's nonlinear expansion procedure applied to cybernetics problems. *IEEE Trans. Systems Science Cybernetics* **SSC-1**, 67–74 (Chapter 6).

Cacoullos, T. [1966]. Estimation of a multivariate density. *Ann. Inst. Stat. Math.* **18**, 179–189 (Chapter 6).

Calvert, T. W. [1968]. Projections of multidimensional data for use in man-computer graphics. *AFIPS Proc. Conf. Fall Joint Comp.* **23**, 227–231 (Chapter 10).

Calvert, T. W. [1970]. Nonorthogonal projections for feature extraction in pattern recognition. *IEEE Trans. Computers* **C-19**, 447–452 (Chapter 10).

Calvert, T. W., and Young, T. Y. [1969]. Randomly generated nonlinear transformations for pattern recognition. *IEEE Trans. Systems Science Cybernetics* **SSC-5**, 266–273 (Chapter 10).

Casey, R. G., and Nagy, G. [1968]. An autonomous reading machine. *IEEE Trans. Computers* **C-17**, 492–503 (Chapter 11).

Chernoff, H. [1962]. A measure of asymptotic efficiency for tests of a hypothesis based on the sum of observations. *Ann. Math. Stat.* **23**, 493–507 (Chapters 3, 9).

Chow, C. K. [1957]. An optimum character recognition system using decision functions. *IRE Trans. Electronic Computers* **EC-6**, 247–254 (Chapter 3).

Chow, C. K. [1970]. On optimum recognition error and reject tradeoff. *IEEE Trans. Information Theory* **IT-16**, 41–46 (Chapter 5).

Cooper, P. W. [1964a]. Hyperplanes, hyperspheres and hyperspadrices as decision boundaries. *In* "Computer and Information Science." 111–139. Spartan Books, Washington, D. C. (Chapter 4).

Cooper, D. B., and Cooper, P. W. [1964b]. Nonsupervised adaptive signal detection and pattern recognition. *Information and Control* **7**, 416–444 (Chapter 11).

Cover, T. M. [1965]. Geometrical and statistical properties of systems of linear inequalities with applications in pattern recognition. *IEEE Trans. Electronic Computers* **EC-14**, 326–334 (Chapter 4).

Cover, T. M. [1968a]. Estimation by the nearest neighbor rule. *IEEE Trans. Information Theory* **IT-14**, 50–55 (Chapter 6).

Cover, T. M. [1968b]. Rates of convergence of nearest neighbor decision procedures. *Hawaii Int. Conf. on Systems Theory* (Chapter 6).

Cover, T. M., and Hart, P. E. [1967]. Nearest neighbor pattern classification. *IEEE Trans. Information Theory* **IT-13**, 21–27 (Chapter 6).

Daly, R. F. [1962]. The adaptive binary-detection problem on the real line. *Stanford Univ. Tech. Rep.* 2003–3 (Chapter 7).

Deutsch, R. [1965]. "Estimation Theory." Prentice-Hall, Englewood Cliffs, N. J. (Chapter 5).

Deutsch, R. [1969]. "System Analysis Techniques." Prentice-Hall, Englewood Cliffs, N. J. (Chapter 6).

Dorofeyuk, A. A. [1966]. Teaching algorithm for a pattern recognition machine without a teacher, based on the method of potential functions. *Autom. and Remote Contr. [USSR]* **27**, 1728–1737 (Chapter 11).

Duda, R. O., and Fossum, H. [1966]. Pattern classification by iteratively determined linear and piecewise linear discriminant functions. *IEEE Trans. Electronic Computers* **EC-15**, 220–232 (Chapter 7).

Fix, E., and Hodges, J. L. [1951]. Discriminatory analysis, nonparametric discrimination. USAF School of Aviation Medicine, Randolph Field, Tex., Project 21–49–004, Rept. 4. Contract AF-41-(128)-31 (Chapter 6).

Fix, E., and Hodges, J. L. [1952]. Discriminatory analysis, small sample performance. USAF School of Aviation Medicine, Randolph Field, Tex., Project 21-49-004, Rept. 11, Contract AF-41-(128)-31 (Chapter 6).

Fisher, A. [1923]. "The Mathematical Theory of Probabilities." Vol. 1. Macmillan, New York (Chapters 3, 4).

Fralick, S. C. [1964]. The synthesis of machines which learn without a teacher. *Stanford Univ. Tech. Rep.* 6103–8, (Chapter 7).

Fralick, S. C. [1967]. Learning to recognize patterns without a teacher. *IEEE Trans. Information Theory* **IT-13**, 57–65 (Chapter 7).

Friedman, H. P., and Rubin, J. [1967]. On some invariant criteria for grouping data. *Amer. Stat. Assoc. J.* **62**, 1159–1178 (Chapter 11).

Fu, K. S. [1968]. "Sequential Methods in Pattern Recognition and Machine Learning." Academic Press, New York (G, Chapters 3, 7).

Fukunaga, K., and Ito, T. [1965]. Design theory of recognition functions in self-organizing systems. *IEEE Trans. Electronic Computers* **EC-14**, 44–52 (Chapter 4).

Fukunaga, K., and Krile, T. F. [1969]. Calculation of Bayes recognition error for two multivariate Gaussian distributions. *IEEE Trans. Computers* **C-18**, 220–229 (Chapter 3).

Fukunaga, K., and Olsen, D. R. [1970a]. Piecewise linear discriminant functions and classification errors for multiclass problems. *IEEE Trans. Information Theory* **IT-16**, 99–100 (Chapter 4).

Fukunaga, K., and Koontz, W. L. G. [1970b]. Representation of random processes using the finite Karhunen–Loève expansion. *Information and Control* **16**, 85–101 (Chapter 8).

Fukunaga, K., and Koontz, W. L. G. [1970c]. Application of the Karhunen–Loève expansion to feature selection and ordering. *IEEE Trans. Computers* **C-19**, 311–318 (Chapters, 4, 11).

Fukunaga, K., and Koontz, W. L. G. [1970d]. A criterion and algorithm for grouping data. *IEEE Trans. Computers* **C-19**, 917–923 (Chapters 4, 11).

Fukunaga, K., and Olsen, D. R. [1971a]. An algorithm for finding the intrinsic dimensionality of data. *IEEE Trans. Computers* **C-20**, 176–183 (Chapter 10).

Fukunaga, K., and Olsen, D. R. [1971b]. Two dimensional display for the classification of multivariate data. *IEEE Trans. Computers* **C-20**, 917–923 (Chapters 10, 11).

Fukunaga, K., and Kessel, D. L. [1971c]. Estimation of classification errors. *IEEE Trans. Computers* **C-20**, 1521–1527 (Chapter 5).

Girshick, M. A. [1939]. On the sampling theory of roots of determinantal equations. *Ann. Math. Stat.* **10**, 203–224 (Chapter 8).

Gnanadesikan, R., and Wilk, M. B. [1969]. Data analytic methods in multivariate statistical analysis. *In* "Multivariate Analysis." (P. R. Krishniaih, ed.), Vol. II. Academic Press, New York (Chapter 11).

Greenstadt, J. [1962]. The determination of the characteristic roots of a matrix by the Jacobi method. *In* "Mathematical Methods for Digital Computers." (A. Ralston and H. S. Wilf, eds.). 84–91. Wiley, New York (Chapter 8).

Guttman, L. [1968]. A general nonmetric technique for finding the smallest coordinate space for a configuration of points. *Psychometrika* **33**, 469–506 (Chapter 10).

Hammersley, J. M. [1950]. The distribution of distances in a hypersphere. *Ann. Math. Stat.* **21**, 447–452 (Chapter 10).

Hart, P. E. [1968]. The condensed nearest neighbor rule. *IEEE Trans. Information Theory* **IT-14**, 515–516 (Chapter 6).

Hartigan, J. A. [1967]. Representation of similarity matrices by trees. *Amer. Stat. Assoc. J.* **62**, 1140–1158 (Chapter 11).

Hellman, M. E., and Raviv, J. [1970]. Probability of error, equivocation, and the Chernoff bound. *IEEE Trans. Information Theory* **IT-16**, 368–372 (Chapter 9).

Helstrom, C. W. [1968]. Sequential detection. *In* "Communication Theory." (A. V. Balakrishnan, ed.). McGraw-Hill, New York (Chapter 3).

Henderson, T. L., and Lainiotis, D. G. [1969]. Comments on linear feature selection. *IEEE Trans. Information Theory* **IT-15**, 729–730 (Chapter 9).

Heydorn, R. P. [1968]. An upper bound estimate on classification error. *IEEE Trans. Information Theory* **IT-14**, 783–784 (Chapter 9).

Highleyman, W. H. [1962]. The design and analysis of pattern recognition experiments. *Bell System Tech. J.* **41**, 723–744 (Chapter 5).

Hills, M. [1966]. Allocation rules and their error rates. *J. Royal Stat. Soc. Ser. B* **28**, 1–31 (Chapter 5).

Ho, Y. C., and Agrawala, A. K. [1968]. On pattern classification algorithms, information and surveys. *Proc. IEEE* **56**, 2101–2114 (G).

Ho, Y. C., and Kashyap, R. L. [1965]. An algorithm for linear inequalities and its applications. *IEEE Trans. Electronic Computers* **EC-14**, 683–688 (Chapter 4).

Ho, Y. C., and Kashyap, R. L. [1966]. A class of iterative procedures for linear inequalities. *J. SIAM Contr.* **4**, 112–115 (Chapter 4).

Ito, T. [1968]. A note on a general expansion of functions of binary variables. *Information and Control* **12**, 206–211 (Chapter 6).

Johnson S. C. [1967]. Hierarchical clustering schemes. *Psychometrika* **32**, 241–254 (Chapter 11).

Kadota, T. T., and Shepp, L. A. [1967]. On the best set of linear observables for discriminating two Gaussian signals. *IEEE Trans. Information Theory* **IT-13**, 278–284 (Chapter 9).

Kailath, T. [1967]. The divergence and Bhattacharyya distance measures in signal selection. *IEEE Trans. Commun. Technol.* **COM-15**, 52–60 (Chapters 3, 9).

Kanal, L. [1962]. Evaluation of a class of pattern recognition networks. *In* "Biological Prototypes and Synthetic System" (E. E. Bernard and M. R. Kare, eds.). 261–270. Plenum, New York (Chapter 3).

Kanal, L., and Chandrasekaran, B. [1968]. On dimensionality and sample size in statistical pattern classification. *NEC*, 2–7 (Chapter 5).

Kashyap, R. L., and Blaydon, C. C. [1966]. Recovery of functions from noisy measurements taken at randomly selected points and its application to pattern classification. *Proc. IEEE* (*Letters*) **54**, 1127–1128 (Chapter 7).

Keehn, D. G. [1965]. A note on learning for Gaussian properties. *IEEE Trans. Information Theory* **IT-11**, 126–132 (Chapter 7).

Koontz, W. L. G., and Fukunaga, K. [1972a]. A nonlinear feature extraction algorithm using distance transformation. *IEEE Trans. Computers* **C-21**, No. 1 (Chapter 10).

Koontz, W. L. G., and Fukunaga, K. [1972b]. A nonparametric valley-seeking technique for cluster analysis. *IEEE Trans. Computers* **C-21**, No. 2 (Chapter 11).

Kruskal, J. B. [1964a]. Multidimensional scaling by optimizing goodness of fit to a nonmetric hypothesis. *Psychometrika* **29**, 1–28 (Chapter 10).

Kruskal, J. B. [1964b]. Nonlinear multidimensional scaling: a numerical method. *Psychometrika* **29**, 115–130 (Chapter 10).

Kullback, S. [1959]. "Information Theory and Statistics." 197–200. Wiley, New York (Chapter 2).

Lachenbruch, P. A. [1965]. Estimation of error rates in discriminant analysis. Ph.D. dissertation, Univ. of California, Los Angeles (Chapter 5).

Lachenbruch, P. A., and Mickey, R. M. [1968]. Estimation of error rates in discriminant analysis. *Technometrics* **10**, 1–11 (Chapter 5).

Lainiotis, D. G. [1969]. A class of upper bounds on probability of error for multihypotheses pattern recognition. *IEEE Trans. Information Theory* **IT-15**, 730–731 (Chapter 9).

Loftsgaarden, D. O., and Quesenberry, C. P. [1965]. A nonparametric density function. *Ann. Math. Stat.* **36**, 1049–1051 (Chapter 6).

McLaughlin, J. A., and Raviv, J. [1968]. Nth order autocorrelations in pattern recognition. *Information and Control* **12**, 121–142 (Chapter 2).

MacQueen, J. [1967]. Some methods for classification and analysis of multivariate observations. *Proc. Berkeley Symp. on Probability and Statistics 5th*, 281–297 (Chapter 11).

Marill, T., and Green, D. M. [1963]. On the effectiveness of receptors in recognition systems. *IEEE Trans. Information Theory* **IT-9**, 11–27 (Chapters 2, 9).

Mendel, J. M., and Fu, K. S. [1970]. "Adaptive Learning, and Pattern Recognition Systems; Theory and Applications." Academic Press, New York (G, Chapters 4, 7).

Morrill, W. K. [1951]. "Analytic Geometry." 104–108. International Textbook, Scranton, N. J. (Chapter 10).

Murthy, V. K. [1966]. Nonparametric estimation of multivariate densities with applications. *In* "Multivariate Analysis." (P. R. Krishnaiah, ed.). Academic Press, New York (Chapter 6).

Nagy, G. [1968]. State of the art in pattern recognition. *Proc. IEEE* **56**, 836–862 (G).

Nilsson, N. J. "Learning Machines." McGraw-Hill, New York (G, Chapters 4, 7).

Novikoff, A. [1962]. On convergence proofs for perceptrons. *Proc. Symp. on Mathematical Theory of Automata, Brooklyn, N. Y.*, 615–622 (Chapter 7).

Okamoto, M. [1963]. An asymptotic expansion for the distribution of the linear discriminant function. *Ann. Math. Stat.* **34**, 1286–1301 (Chapter 5).

Okamoto, M. [1968]. Correction to an asymptotic expansion for the linear discriminant function. *Ann. Math. Stat.* **39**, 135 (Chapter 5).

Papoulis, A. [1965]. "Probability, Random Variables, and Stochastic Processes." McGraw-Hill, New York (Chapters 2, 3).

Parzen, E. [1962]. An estimation of a probability density function and mode. *Ann. Math. Stat.* **33**, 1065–1076 (Chapter 6).

Patrick, E. A., and Hancock, J. C. [1966]. Nonsupervised sequential classification and recognition of patterns. *IEEE Trans. Information Theory* **IT-12**, 362–372 (Chapter 7).

Patrick, E. A., and Fischer, F. P., II. [1969]. Nonparametric feature selection. *IEEE Trans. Information Theory* **IT-15**, 577–584 (Chapter 10).

Penrose, R. [1955]. On the generalized inverse of a matrix. *Proc. Cambridge Philos. Soc.* **51**, 406–413 (Chapter 2).

Peterson, D. W. [1970]. Some convergence properties of a nearest neighbor decision rule. *IEEE Trans. Information Theory* **IT-16**, 26–31 (Chapter 6).

Peterson, D. W., and Mattson, R. L. [1966]. A method of finding linear discriminant functions for a class of performance criteria. *IEEE Trans. Information Theory* **IT-12**, 380–387 (Chapter 4).

Raiffa, H., and Schlaifer, R. [1961]. "Applied Statistical Decision Theory." Harvard Business School, Boston, Mass. (Chapter 7).

Raviv, J., and Streeter, D. N. [1965]. Linear methods for biological data processing. IBM Corp., Yorktown Heights, N. Y. *Res. Rep. RC*-1577 (Chapter 2).

Rohlf, F. J. [1970]. Adaptive hierarchical clustering schemes. *Syst. Zool.* **19**, 58–82 (Chapter 11).

Ruspini, E. H. [1969]. A new approach to clustering. *Information and Control* **15**, 22–32 (Chapter 11).

Sammon, J. W., Jr. [1969]. A nonlinear mapping algorithm for data structure analysis. *IEEE Trans. Computers* **C-18**, 401–409 (Chapter 10).

Sammon, J. W. Jr. [1970]. Interactive pattern analysis and classification. *IEEE Trans. Computers* **C-19**, 594–616 (Chapter 10).

Sebestyen, G. S. [1962]. "Decision-making Process in Pattern Recognition." Macmillan, New York (G, Chapter 9).

Sebestyen, G. S., and Edie, J. [1966]. An algorithm for nonparametric pattern recognition. *IEEE Trans. Electronic Computers* **EC-15**, 908–915 (Chapter 6).

Selin, I. [1965]. "Detection Theory." Princeton University Press, Princeton N. J. (G, Chapters 3, 8).

Shepard, R. N. [1962a]. The analysis of proximities: multidimensional scaling with an unknown distance function I. *Psychometrika* **27**, 125–140 (Chapter 10).

Shepard, R. N. [1962b]. The analysis of proximities: multidimensional scaling with an unknown distance function II. *Psychometrika* **27**, 219–245 (Chapter 10).

Shepard, R. N., and Carroll, J. D. [1966]. Parametric representation of nonlinear data structure. *In* "Multivariate Analysis." (P. R. Krishnaiah, ed.). Academic Press, New York (Chapter 10).

Sitgreaves, R. [1967]. Some results on the distribution of the W-classification statistic. *In* "Studies in Item Analysis and Prediction." (H. Solomon, ed.). Stanford Univ. Press. Stanford, California (Chapter 5).

Sokal, R. R., and Sneath, P. H. A. [1963]. "Principles of Numerical Taxonomy." E. H. Freeman, San Francisco, Calif. (Chapters 8, 9, 11).

Specht, D. F. [1966]. Generation of polynomial discriminant functions for pattern recognition. Stanford Electronics Laboratory, Tech. Rep. 6764–5 (Chapter 6).

Spragins, J. [1963]. Reproducing distributions for machine learning. Stanford Univ. *Tech. Rep.* 6103–7 (Chapter 7).

Spragins, J. [1965]. A note on the iterative application of Bayes' rule. *IEEE Trans. Information Theory* **IT-11**, 544–549 (Chapter 7).

Spragins, J. [1966]. Learning without a teacher. *IEEE Trans. Information Theory* **IT-12**, 223–229 (Chapter 7).

Tou, J. T., and Heyden, R. P. [1967]. Some approaches to optimum feature selection. *In* "Computer and Information Sciences." (J. T. Tou, ed.), Vol. II, 57–89. Academic Press, New York (Chapters 8, 9).

Trunk, G. V. [1968]. Representation and analysis of signals: statistical estimation of intrinsic dimensionality and parameter identification. *General System* **13**, 49–76 (Chapter 10).

Tsypkin, Y. Z. [1966]. Adaptation, training and self-organization in automatic systems. *Autom. and Remote Contr.* [USSR] **27**, 16–52 (Chapter 7).

VanTrees, H. L. [1968]. "Detection, Estimation and Modulation Theory." Wiley, New York (G, Chapters 3, 5).

Wald, A. [1947]. "Sequential Analysis." Wiley, New York (Chapter 3).

Wald, A., and Wolfowitz, J. [1948]. Optimum character of the sequential probability ratio test. *Ann. Math. Stat.* **19**, 326–339 (Chapter 3).

Watanabe, S. [1965]. Karhunen–Loève expansion and factor analysis. *Trans. 4th Prague Conf. on Information Theory* (Chapter 8).

Watanabe, S. [1969]. "Knowing and Guessing." Wiley, New York (G, Chapters 8, 11).

White, P. A. [1958]. The computation of eigenvalues and eigenvectors of a matrix. *J. Soc. Indust. Appl. Math.* **6**, 393–437 (Chapter 8).

Widrow, B., and Hoff, M. E. [1960]. Adaptive switching circuits. *Stanford Electronic Laboratory*, *Tech. Rep.* 1553–1 (Chapter 4).

Wilde, D. J. [1964]. "Optimum Seeking Methods." Chapter 6. Prentice-Hall, Englewood Cliffs, N. J. (Chapter 7).

Wilkinson, J. H. [1965]. "Algebraic Eigenvalue Problem." Oxford, Univ. Press, London and New York (Chapters 2, 8).

Wilks, S. S. [1960]. Multidimensional statistical scatter. *In* "Contributions to Probability and Statistics." (I. Olkin, ed.), Vol. I. Stanford Publ. Stanford, Calif. (Chapter 8).

Wilks, S. [1963]. "Mathematical Statistics." Wiley, New York (G).

INDEX

ELECTRICAL SCIENCE

A Series of Monographs and Texts

Editors

Henry G. Booker
UNIVERSITY OF CALIFORNIA AT SAN DIEGO
LA JOLLA, CALIFORNIA

Nicholas DeClaris
UNIVERSITY OF MARYLAND
COLLEGE PARK, MARYLAND

Joseph E. Rowe. Nonlinear Electron-Wave Interaction Phenomena. 1965

Max J. O. Strutt. Semiconductor Devices: Volume I. Semiconductors and Semiconductor Diodes. 1966

Austin Blaquiere. Nonlinear System Analysis. 1966

Victor Rumsey. Frequency Independent Antennas. 1966

Charles K. Birdsall and William B. Bridges. Electron Dynamics of Diode Regions. 1966

A. D. Kuz'min and A. E. Salomonovich. Radioastronomical Methods of Antenna Measurements. 1966

Charles Cook and Marvin Bernfeld. Radar Signals: An Introduction to Theory and Application. 1967

J. W. Crispin, Jr., and K. M. Siegel (eds.). Methods of Radar Cross Section Analysis. 1968

Giuseppe Biorci (ed.). Network and Switching Theory. 1968

Ernest C. Okress (ed.). Microwave Power Engineering:
Volume 1. Generation, Transmission, Rectification. 1968
Volume 2. Applications. 1968

T. R. Bashkow (ed.). Engineering Applications of Digital Computers. 1968

Julius T. Tou (ed.). Applied Automata Theory. 1968

Robert Lyon-Caen. Diodes, Transistors, and Integrated Circuits for Switching Systems. 1969

M. Ronald Wohlers. Lumped and Distributed Passive Networks. 1969

Michel Cuenod and Allen E. Durling. A Discrete-Time Approach for System Analysis. 1969

K. Kurokawa. An Introduction to the Theory of Microwave Circuits. 1969

H. K. Messerle. Energy Conversion Statics. 1969

George Tyras. Radiation and Propagation of Electromagnetic Waves. 1969

Georges Metzger and Jean-Paul Vabre. Transmission Lines with Pulse Excitation. 1969

C. L. Sheng. Threshold Logic. 1969

Dale M. Grimes. Electromagnetism and Quantum Theory. 1969

Robert O. Harger. Synthetic Aperture Radar Systems: Theory and Design. 1970

M. A. Lampert and P. Mark. Current Injection in Solids. 1970

W. V. T. Rusch and P. D. Potter. Analysis of Reflector Antennas. 1970

Amar Mukhopadhyay. Recent Developments in Switching Theory. 1971

A. D. Whalen. Detection of Signals in Noise. 1971

J. E. Rubio. The Theory of Linear Systems. 1971

Keinosuke Fukunaga. Introduction To Statistical Pattern Recognition. 1972

Jacob Klapper and John T. Frankle. Phase-Locked and Frequency-Feedback Systems: Principles and Techniques. 1972